Simon Dunning

November 1995

BOSS & Co.
BUILDERS OF BEST GUNS ONLY

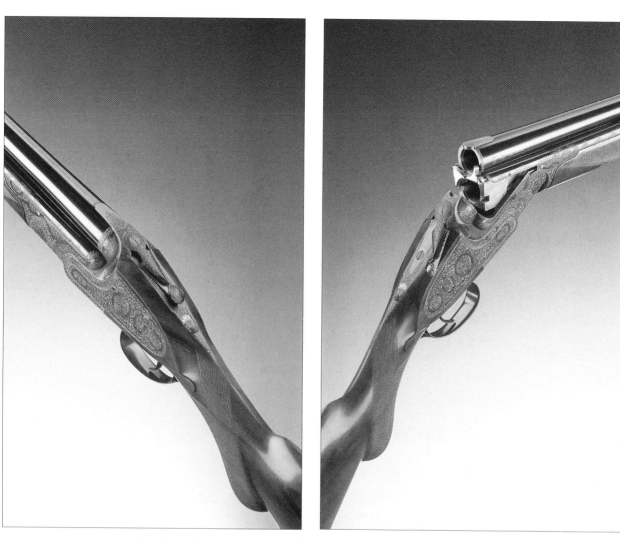

New Boss 12-bore over-and-unders. Above: a single; Below: a pair.

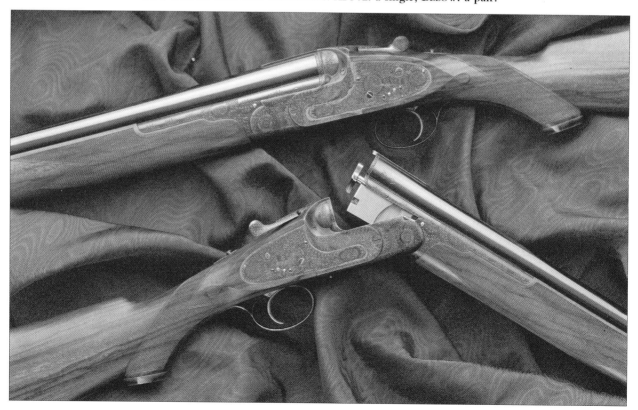

BOSS & Co.

BUILDERS OF BEST GUNS ONLY

THE DEFINITIVE HISTORY,
AUTHORISED BY BOSS & CO

DONALD DALLAS

Quiller Press
London

First published 1995 by Quiller Press Limited
46 Lillie Road London SW6 1TN
ISBN 1 899163 05 0

Designed by Tim McPhee
Produced at Book Production Consultants plc, Cambridge,
for Quiller Press
Printed in Milan, Italy by Rotolito Lombarda

"In presenting this booklet, we would say at the outset that we make only one grade of gun, and have never placed a second quality make upon the market. This policy has enabled us to retain the services of the finest workmen in London and to give them continuous employment. The advantages attending the production of best work only are manifold. There is no opportunity for the work of inferior men to be utilised in the economy of the workshop, which is frequently the case when more than one class of weapon is produced.

The owner of a Boss gun has the satisfaction of knowing that he has the best gun that money can buy, and that no-one has a better. The Boss gun has, therefore, always a standard value, whether new or second hand. Our output is limited strictly according to the amount of first-class labour available."

From the frontispiece of a booklet produced by
Boss & Co., describing their guns *circa* 1920.

To my wonderful son, Donald,
aged seven, and my lovely daughter,
Kate, aged four.

CONTENTS

ACKNOWLEDGEMENTS

I would like to thank Tim Robertson, Manager of Boss & Co. and a direct descendant of John Robertson, for the considerable help he has given to me in researching and writing this book. He searched the cellars in Dover Street and found an amazing array of historical material that he put at my disposal. In particular, his enthusiasm for the project was contagious – at times a very necessary enthusiasm in the dark alleys of research.

Dave Cox, a gunmaker at Boss & Co. in the 1950s and 1960s must receive a special mention since he helped me with much of the information on the present century and provided detailed information on the construction of guns. In addition Andy Gouldsbury, a practical gunmaker with Boss & Co., gave me valuable insight into the guns and the company over the years. The gunmakers at the Boss factory assisted me greatly by explaining the technical aspects of Boss gun construction. Peter Sanderson provided several photographs and sketched the history of his father Arthur Sanderson.

I would also like to thank Mike Clarkson, Gunmaker, St Boswells, Scotland, for his invaluable assistance, advice and comments. As a working gunmaker, his remarks were particularly helpful in ratifying some of the more difficult technical aspects. Mike went to considerable effort to locate and make available many Boss guns for examination and photography. In addition, thanks to his wife Jean for her artistic direction regarding the front cover. John Wilkes, Gunmaker, 79 Beak Street, London, supplied many interesting anecdotes.

John Robertson's granddaughter, Kitty Hancock, who remembered John Robertson well and her nephew Col. Brian Awford, brought John Robertson to life. Many interesting anecdotes were discussed over a very lively lunch.

The following sources of information were used – I am grateful to all the staff concerned for their time and help:

1. The books and ledgers of Boss & Co.
2. The General Register Office, St Catherine's House, London.
3. The Public Record Office, Portugal Street, London.
4. The Public Record Office, Chancery Lane, London.
5. The Public Record Office, Kew, London.
6. The Victoria Public Library, Buckingham Palace Road, London.
7. The Guildhall Library, Aldermanbury, London.
8. The Marylebone Public Library, Marylebone Road, London.
9. The Brighton Central Reference Library, Brighton.
10. The National Library of Scotland, George IV Bridge, Edinburgh.
11. The Newspaper Library, Colindale Avenue, London.
12. The Department of the Environment, Marsham Street, London.
13. The Society of Genealogists, Goswell Road, London.
14. The Scottish Record Office, Register House, Edinburgh.
15. The Registrar of Births, Deaths and Marriages, Haddington.
16. The Greater London Record Office, Northampton Road, London.
17. Lambeth Archives Department, Knatchbull Street, London.
18. Westminster Abbey Muniments and Library, London.
19. The Patent Office, Southampton Buildings, London.
20. Companies' Registration Office, Companies' House, Cardiff.
21. Photographs lent by the Robertson family.

PREFACE

The firm of Boss & Co. have been in continuous existence for around two hundred years, and are world renowned as top makers of best London guns. They are unusual in that they have always built best guns, concentrating on high quality rather than the volume production of various grades of gun that several of their rivals have undertaken from time to time. Their motto "Builders of Best Guns Only" is justly apt. They are also unusual in that they have remained a family firm over this period, firstly under the Boss/Paddison families to 1891 and subsequently under the Robertson family to the present day.

Yet what is remarkable about the firm is that virtually nothing is known of their early history. In 1891 a watershed occurred in the firm when a new proprietor, John Robertson who had no connection with the original business, bought the firm. Today the company is still owned by his descendants and therefore the company history is roughly known from 1891 to the present. Of the preceding period, only a few sparse details are known.

Most recent published work on Boss relies upon a single source – the book, *Experts on Guns and Shooting* by G T Teasdale-Buckell, published in 1900. This book contains a chapter on Boss history. It is deficient and inaccurate in many respects. Teasdale-Buckell himself used an article published in *Land and Water* in 11th August, 1888 as the basis of his history.

To be absolutely fair to Teasdale-Buckell, when he wrote the book in 1900 some 100 years of Boss history had taken place, memories were poor, and no original member of the Boss family worked in the firm. It is hardly surprising that facts were wrong.

This book is the result of considerable research and hopefully it will provide an accurate history of the firm.

DONALD DALLAS
BSc (ECON) LONDON

CHAPTER ONE

FAMILY ORIGINS

The old established firm of Boss & Co. "Builders of Best Guns Only" does not have very auspicious beginnings. The surname "Boss", "Bossey", "Bossy" was a relatively common surname in the 12th and 13th centuries. The name has several possible origins. It could mean "wicked" from the old French "bos" or "boson" – possibly "hunchbacked", "protuberance" a nickname from the old French "boce", or Middle English "boce" or "bos" – or finally a vessel called a "bos" that was used for carrying mortar, an early type of plasterer's hod.

These spurious explanations of the Boss surname were of no relevance to Thomas Boss who was baptised on the 13th June 1790 in the Parish of St Ann's, Blackfriars, London, the third son of William and Catherine Boss. Thomas Boss would found the gunmaking firm that would bear his own name, firstly as Thomas Boss, then Thomas Boss & Co., then E. F. P. Boss & Co., and lastly as Boss & Co.

The Boss family came from Leicestershire. The earliest records that can be found come from the Bishop's Transcripts (a form of Births, Marriages and Deaths) of Seagrave, near Loughborough. A William Boss born at Woodthorpe in 1722 (occupation unknown) married a Parnell Newberry at Seagrave in October 1752. A son was born to them at Narborough, around 1757, also named William, the future father of Thomas Boss. Although there is no record of his birth in the Parish Records, it is almost certain that he was born to this family, since the unusual Christian name of Parnell was given to one of his daughters, a sister of Thomas Boss. Non recordance of a birth was not unusual in this era.

WILLIAM BOSS – GUNMAKER
1758?–1809

William Boss was a gunmaker. In 1773, around the age of fifteen, he began his apprenticeship with the Birmingham gunmaker, Thomas Ketland. Ketland was a gun- and pistol-maker producing a wide variety of arms both civil and military.

As an historian, I realise it is very difficult to put precise dates on the establishment of a business, how long firms have been in existence, etc. However, one could argue that the date 1773 marks the beginning of Boss & Co. as gunmakers. As such, they are one of the oldest gunmaking firms to be continually in existence. Although we do not know the occupation of his father, the William Boss born in 1722, it is possible that he was involved in some aspect of gunmaking. Hence the start up date of the firm could be even earlier.

The first entry that the *Trade Directories* (similar to our present day *Yellow Pages*) gives us is that, in 1767, Ketland was at 7 Lichfield Street, Birmingham. It is at this address that William Boss began his apprenticeship. By 1777 he had moved to Catherine Street. Boss would move with him since his Indenture had still some three years to run. After this period, the company underwent various changes of address and changes of partnership. The firm appears to have folded after 1832.

William Boss's apprenticeship is recorded in the Apprenticeship Books at The Public Record Office. In 1710, in the reign of Queen Anne, Stamp Duty was payable on Indentures of Apprenticeship. This tax continued until it was abolished in 1811. Stamp Duty was payable by the master in proportion to the amount of money he received for taking on the apprentice. Consequently, the following information is given from the year 1773.

Master's name	Place	Trade	Apprentice's name
Thomas Ketland	Birmingham Co of Warwick	Gunmaker	William Boss

Date of indenture	Period of indenture	Consideration money	12d Duty
17 August 1773	7 Years	£21.00	£1.1s.0d.

So he began his apprenticeship in 1773 and finished it in 1780, seven years being the normal period for most apprenticeships.

The City of Birmingham has long been synonymous with the manufacture of guns, consistently rivalling

London as a gunmaking centre. At the time William Boss was undergoing his apprenticeship, Birmingham was about to "take off" as a gunmaking centre. During the second half of the 18th century, Birmingham was one of the principal cities leading the Industrial Revolution. Her population had expanded from 15,000 in the year 1700 to 730,000 in the year 1801. From an early period she had been a seat of manufacture in metal and several factors favoured her growth. One factor was the absolute freedom of the town, there being few Guilds or restrictions of any kind. In addition, cheap coal and iron helped development. This great hive of industry and development must have been an exciting place for a fifteen-year-old boy to begin his working days. On the completion of his Indenture in 1780, William Boss decided that his employment opportunities would be greater if he moved to London.

Why did William Boss go to London? By the end of the 18th century, Birmingham tended to specialise in military arms, guns for the slave trade and gun components that were finished in London. Colonel Hawker in his *Instructions to Young Sportsmen* first published in 1814, one of the standard shooting books of the 19th century with enormous influence, makes reference to the Birmingham Gun Trade.

Many wise-cracks abuse all the heads of the trade, and swear that they can always get the best of guns at a quarter the price from Birmingham! This may be provided a person has good judgement, or interest there as to get picked workmen for the whole process of his order; but in general the immense business carried on at this place is for the wholesale line and only requires to be in the rough; from which circumstance the workmen are not so much in the habit of finishing as those employed daily for that purpose. Moreover, if there is a first rate and enterprising workman he hears of high wages and contrives to get off to London.

The last sentence gives us the answer. London-made guns had by this time established themselves as the best guns, highly finished and well constructed. Best guns required the best journeymen and to obtain them, gunmakers had to pay high wages. This was the simple reason William Boss came to London – better wage prospects.

This move to London took place between 1780 and 1784. In 1784 he married Catherine Seymour in the parish of St Matthew's, Bethnal Green in East London. They set up home close by in Cumberland Street, Shoreditch after their marriage. Their first son was born here on 25 February 1787 and was christened after his father and grandfather, William. This William would follow in his father's footsteps and later set himself up in business as a gunmaker. Soon after William's birth, the family again moved, this time to Blackfriars, close by the river Thames. A second son, Fisher, was baptised on 23 November 1788 in the parish of St Ann's, Blackfriars. Fisher Boss would also become a gunmaker. What became of him I do not know – he seems to fade from the picture and further research needs to be done on Fisher Boss. He is certainly not recorded as an independent gunmaker.

There exists in the United States a double flintlock sporting gun by Fisher Boss but I have never seen another gun by him. Although I have not personally examined this gun, the owner has been kind enough to supply me with several photographs.

The gun is a 20-bore, *circa* 1810 with 28½″ twist barrels. There are no markings whatsoever on the barrels although they could have been removed when the barrels were re-browned. The locks are marked "F Boss" and have rainproof pans, roller frizzens and throat-hole cocks. The guns is well made and of very elegant proportions. Whether this gun was a one-off by Fisher or whether he did go into business for a short time is unknown. See Plate 1.

On 13 June 1790, again in the parish of St Ann's, Blackfriars, their third son Thomas – the future founder of Boss & Co. – was christened

After Thomas's birth, the family made their final move across the river Thames to White Hart Place, Kennington Lane, very near to the present-day Oval Cricket Ground. In such days of sparse family planning, Boss babies arrived in rapid succession – Mary (?), Parnell (1796), Catherine (1798), Jane (1801), Henry Edward (1803) and Jane Charlotte (1804).

Their father, William Boss, worked for Joseph Manton, one of the leading London gunmakers in the late 18th/early 19th centuries. Manton worked at Davies Street, Berkeley Square, at this time, only employing top-rate journeymen. To get the best he paid the most and William Boss was regarded as one of Manton's best. He must have been highly skilled indeed not only to work for Manton but to be considered one of the best. His enthusiasm and skill for gunmaking must have been contagious since his three eldest sons all became gunmakers.

Life was not to be kind to William Boss and his family. In 1808, his wife Catherine died and was buried in the local graveyard at Kennington Lane in February. Disaster struck again a year later. Her husband William died in June 1809 around the age of fifty and was buried beside her. Thomas Boss was nineteen years of age, still with three years of his apprenticeship to go, and the youngest daughter five years of age.

In the closing days of his life when he was a very sick

man, William made a Will, his chief preoccupation being the welfare of his young children about to be orphaned.

The Will states the following:

This is the last Will and Testament of me, William Boss, of White Hart Place, Kennington Lane, in the County of Surrey, Gunsmith; I first give a set of tools in my trade as a Gunsmith to my son Fisher Boss to be selected by my son and Executor William Boss from my workshop as soon as my said son Fisher Boss shall have attained his age of twenty-one years; I give my watch to my daughter Mary Boss and as to all the rest and residue of my personal Estate and effects of what nature or kind   which I shall sit possessed of, I give and bequeath the same and to my daughter, Mary Boss and said William Boss and Thomas Boss upon trust that they will apply the same as it will go towards the maintenance and support of my four youngest children until they shall have respectively attained their age of twenty-one years. I nominate, constitute and appoint my said son William Boss and Thomas Boss and my said daughter Mary Boss, Executors and Executrix of this my Will in witness thereof I have hereunto set my

hand and seal this eighth day of June in the year of our Lord

One Thousand Eight Hundred and Nine – William Boss – signed, sealed, published and declared by the said Testator as and for his last Will and Testament in our presence, Jas. Wrentmore, Thomas Simmonds.

This Will was proved at London the twentieth day of December in the year of our Lord One Thousand Eight Hundred and Nine before the Worshipful Charles   and Surrogate of the Right Honourable Sir John   Knight Master Keeper or Commissary in the Prerogative Court of Canterbury, lawfully constituted by the oath of William Boss, the son of the   and one of the Executors named in the Will to whom Administration was granted of all and singular, the goods, chattels and credits of the said deceased having been first sworn only to administer. Power reserved to Thomas Boss, the son and Mary Boss, spinster, the daughter, the other Executors.

Proved at London, twenty-ninth November 1817 before the Worshipful Samuel Pearce Parsons, Doctor

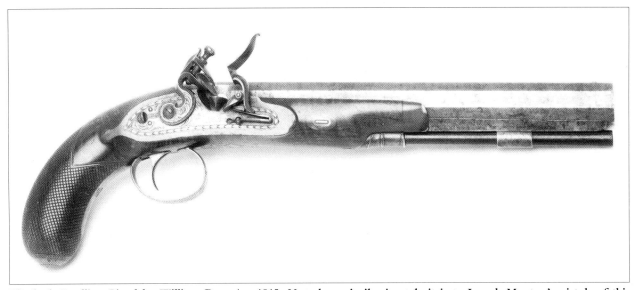

Flintlock Duelling Pistol by William Boss *circa* **1815. Note how similar in style it is to Joseph Manton's pistols of this period.**

of Laws Surrogate by oath of Thomas Boss, the son, the other Executor, to whom Administration was granted being first sworn duly to administer. Power reserved of making the like grant to Mary Boss, the daughter, the other Executor.

NB. Blanks indicate illegible words in the Will.

The Will was proved on 20 December 1809. It is interesting to note that the Will had to be proved again in 1817, the reason for this being that his son and daughter, Thomas and Mary, the other Executors, were under age in 1809. Executors had to be of full age, ie twenty-one years old, for a Will to be legally proved.

Two things are of interest in this Will. Firstly, he left a set of "tools in my trade as a Gunsmith" to his second son Fisher Boss as soon as he reached the age of twenty-one. Fisher would actually be twenty-one in a few months. Why did Fisher get the tools and not Thomas who was aged nineteen and in the last years of his apprenticeship as a gunsmith? Favouritism? Tradition when a son reached twenty-one?

Secondly, William, Thomas and Mary were appointed Executors. Why was Fisher who was older than Thomas not appointed as an Executor?

Times must have been very hard for the nine children with so many being so young. Some four months after her father's death, his daughter Jane died and was buried alongside her parents.

WILLIAM BOSS (JNR.), GUNMAKER, 9 CROWN STREET, WESTMINSTER, LONDON

The eldest son of William Boss, also called William after his father and grandfather, followed the example of

his father and became a gunmaker. Incidentally, all published works on Boss history confuse the two.

William Boss (Jnr.) was apprenticed to his father around 1801. Apprenticeship to a father was a relatively common and convenient arrangement. Since no "Consideration Money" was payable by the apprentice to the Master in a family situation, no tax would have to be paid. The apprentice could remain with his family keeping costs down and pocket money could be given by the father to his son for work done. This means that no official record exists of this apprenticeship. The only problem for a father/son apprenticeship could be personal. They would have to get on well with each other for it to succeed.

This apprenticeship meant William Boss (Jnr.) worked at Joseph Manton's. He would acquire the highest skills and learn the trade of a first-class gunmaker.

In 1814, at the age of twenty-seven, he commenced business for himself at 9 Crown Street, Westminster. Crown Street was very close to the present day Downing Street. It was demolished in the late 19th century to make way for the Foreign Office that stands on its site today.

The Rate Books in the Victoria Public Library give the following details on 9 Crown Street:

	Rack rent	*Poor rate*	*Watch rate*
1814	£25	£1.6s.11d.	4s.8d.
	(Similar to Rateable Value)	(To maintain the Poor)	(To finance the Watchmen – the early Police Force)

His gunmaking business did not last long. He remained at 9 Crown Street until late 1817. Like his younger brother, Fisher, he remains something of an

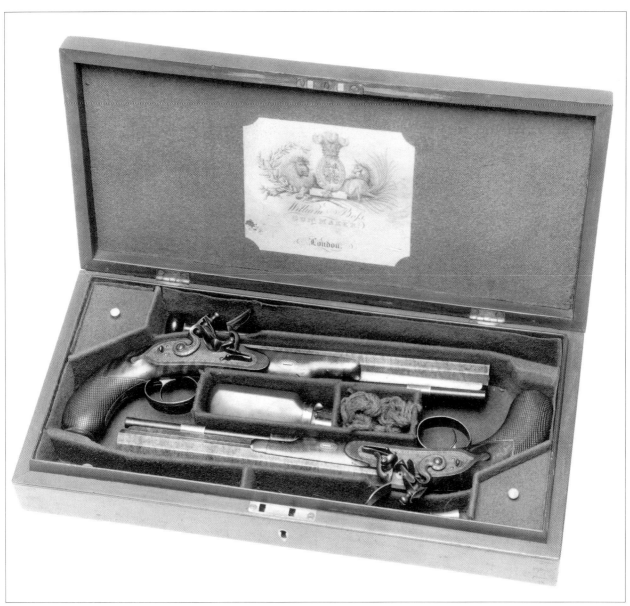

The same pistol with its partner in their original mahogany case.

The engraving on the barrel flat showing absence of the 9 Crown Street address.

enigma – no record of him appears to exist after 1817. Perhaps he went bankrupt, perhaps he went back to "working for the trade". He did not die then since there is a record of William renting a room from his brother Thomas later on in 1819. Further research requires to be conducted on his life after 1817.

There exists, in the Royal Museum of Scotland in Edinburgh, a superb cased pair of flintlock duelling pistols by William Boss. These pistols are of very high quality. The locks with rainproof pans are inscribed, "William Boss, London". They are feather engraved in contemporary style around their edges and safety bolts are fitted. Roller-frizzens are used. The barrels are engraved, "William Boss, London". The touch-holes are lined in gold.

They are contained in their original green-baize-lined mahogany case complete with trade label and accessories. The trade label says simply, "William Boss, Gunmaker, London". It is interesting that the address "9 Crown Street" is not given either on the gun or label. The case contains the following accessories: a copper powder flask, a bullet mould marked "60", a bristle cleaning brush and a cleaning rod. A beautiful pair of top quality pistols.

THOMAS BOSS – GUNMAKER

Around the year 1804, young Thomas Boss aged fourteen was apprenticed to his father William for seven years. William was working for Joseph Manton, the King of the London gunmakers. Seven years was the normal time-span for an apprentice gunmaker to become fully competent at mastering his trade. The arrangement was the same as per his elder brother William – low costs, free training, etc. Once again no official record of this apprenticeship exists.

Young Boss served his apprenticeship when the flintlock era was at its zenith. Joseph Manton was in part responsible for perfecting the flintlock. Manton was born in April 1766 at Grantham in Lincolnshire. He was at first apprenticed to a local Grantham gunsmith, Newton, and then to his eldest brother John Manton, in business at 6 Dover Street, London. By 1789 he had established his own business at 25 Davies Street, Berkeley Square, London.

Joseph Manton was primarily a maker of fine sporting guns and established the form and style of the double-barrel sporting gun that to all intents and purposes is basically the same today. He also developed the flintlock to ignite rapidly and fire just that little bit quicker than contemporary guns. Both these facts give Joe Manton the reputation he undoubtedly deserves.

He experimented with early detonating systems. His pellet lock of 1816 was a failure – although ingenious it was a time-consuming and tricky ignition method. His tube-lock of 1818 on the other hand was an immediate success, ignition was certain. Thomas Boss was impressed by Manton's tube-locks and later on he would construct tube-locks of his own even as late as the 1840s when they were out of fashion. However, business problems dogged Manton and by 1826 he was bankrupt. He died in 1835.

For a flintlock gun to function perfectly, to ignite rapidly, to be relatively impervious to rain, meant top quality work and young Boss would be shown and instructed in the art of making a flintlock so described. In addition, he would learn how to stock a gun, to manufacture "twist" barrels, to make nails and to set a gun up. Setting a gun up means finishing and final assembly – making sure the trigger pulls are correct, etc. He must have impressed Manton since, on the death of his father, his Master in 1809, Manton kept him on in his apprenticeship even though it still had another three years to run. In Neal and Back's book, *The Mantons*, they state that Manton would take no apprentices. Bearing this in mind and although the circumstances were unusual, it speaks volumes for Thomas Boss that Manton would make an exception.

By 1812, he had completed his apprenticeship and was now a journeyman gunmaker aged twenty-one or twenty-two. Some 20th-century labels of Boss & Co. and the headed notepaper of Boss & Co. state, "Established 1812". This is a reference to the completion of Thomas's apprenticeship and that he was now a skilled worker in his own right. Joseph Manton was impressed with the quality of Thomas Boss's work and took him on as a journeyman. One of the most famous journeymen in Joseph Manton's firm of this period that Boss would have known was James Purdey. James Purdey worked for Manton between 1805 and 1808 after having served his apprenticeship under Thomas Hutchison, his brother-in-law. Later Purdey would work for Forsyth, the inventor of the detonating gun, until he set up on his own in 1814 at 4 Princes Street, Leicester Square.

On the completion of his apprenticeship Boss continued to work with Joseph Manton. How long he continued to work with Manton I do not know – no record exists – I am inclined to think it was until 1816 for reasons that will shortly be explained.

EARLY BUSINESS VENTURES, OR BOSS & CO., "BUILDERS OF BEST GUNS AND BEST…"!

Exactly when Thomas Boss set up in business on his own is not known. Incredibly, a ledger book dating from the period April 1820–12 June 1822 survives at Boss & Co. This small leather-bound notebook has entries by Thomas Boss detailing his early business ventures and it gives the researcher very valuable information into Thomas Boss's activities in this early period.

At the front of this book is a heading in Boss's writing:

This Cash Account copied from the Collecting Book, 7th January 1819, Thos. Boss (signed).

The Cash Account covers the period 27 April 1816 to 12 August 1819. It details Boss's Income and Expenditure and shows that he was taking in approximately £3 per week. It proves that Boss had either commenced his business in the spring of 1816 or else his business was underway by that time. I am inclined to believe the former since the opening balance of 27 April 1816 was very low at £2.0.7d.

Exactly where Boss was working from in this period is not clear either. Around 1817 he moved to 3 Bridge Road, Lambeth, very close to his old White Hart Place residence. Unfortunately I cannot be more accurate; the majority of the Ratebooks from this period are missing and only the 1824 Ratebook survives and gives the following information on 3 Bridge Road:

Occupier	Value assessed	Rates paid
Thomas Boss	£45	£1.10.0d

Bridge Road had far bigger houses than his old White Hart Place and was a main thoroughfare with several businesses on it. It was ideal for Boss's early business. A wide variety of businesses practised in Bridge Road – Booksellers, Hatters, Cutlers, Tea Dealers, Japan Makers, Wax Chandlers, Potato Salesmen, etc. Boss would remain for around ten years until *circa* 1827.

A careful study of the few letters and ledgers that survive of Thomas Boss prove that he was a successful businessman and an entrepreneur. Everything he did in business was meticulously recorded in his own hand. He pursued many angles to make money and was so successful that when his wife died in 1872 she left a staggering £25,000.

But what was this early business in the period *circa* 1816 to *circa* 1827? The answer is that he was a Truss-maker! Trusses are a type of medical harness used to relieve ruptures or hernias.

Ruptures and hernias were just as common in the early 19th century as they are today. Today a simple operation cures most of them and truss harnesses are not in much demand but in Boss's time, with anaesthetics very primitive and antiseptics unheard of, only

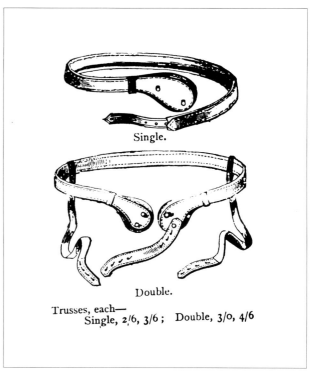

Trusses, each—
Single, 2/6, 3/6 ;   Double, 3/0, 4/6

Trusses of the type made by Thomas Boss in the 1820s at 3, Bridge Road, Lambeth, London.

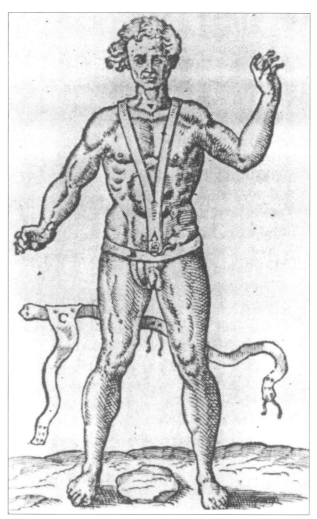

The application of a truss to relieve hernias or ruptures.

1820 Parish Truss.s
Jan 26th Benjn Wilson L.D.Single 0 10 6
in the workhouse
Feby 9th Bilford Byas R.S.Single 0 10 6
14 Ann Giddins Single Truss
Recovered new Buttons and 0 5 0
Cork Cr. Mr Brown Mr Massey
March 9th John Davis Right S. Truss in the house March 9. 1820 0 10 6
Mar 13th J.L.S Richards Double Truss in Ashe Ward No 6 1 1 0
30th Wm Blake L.S.Single Cr. by the Com... 0 10 6
April 3th Henry Thornton L.S.S.T from Norwood 0 10 6
the above Bill Del'd up to Lady Day, Cr March 13th omitting Blake and Thorntons Truss.s Cr April 10th 2 17 6
Bill Del'd and Paid April 10th 1820
Ths Boss

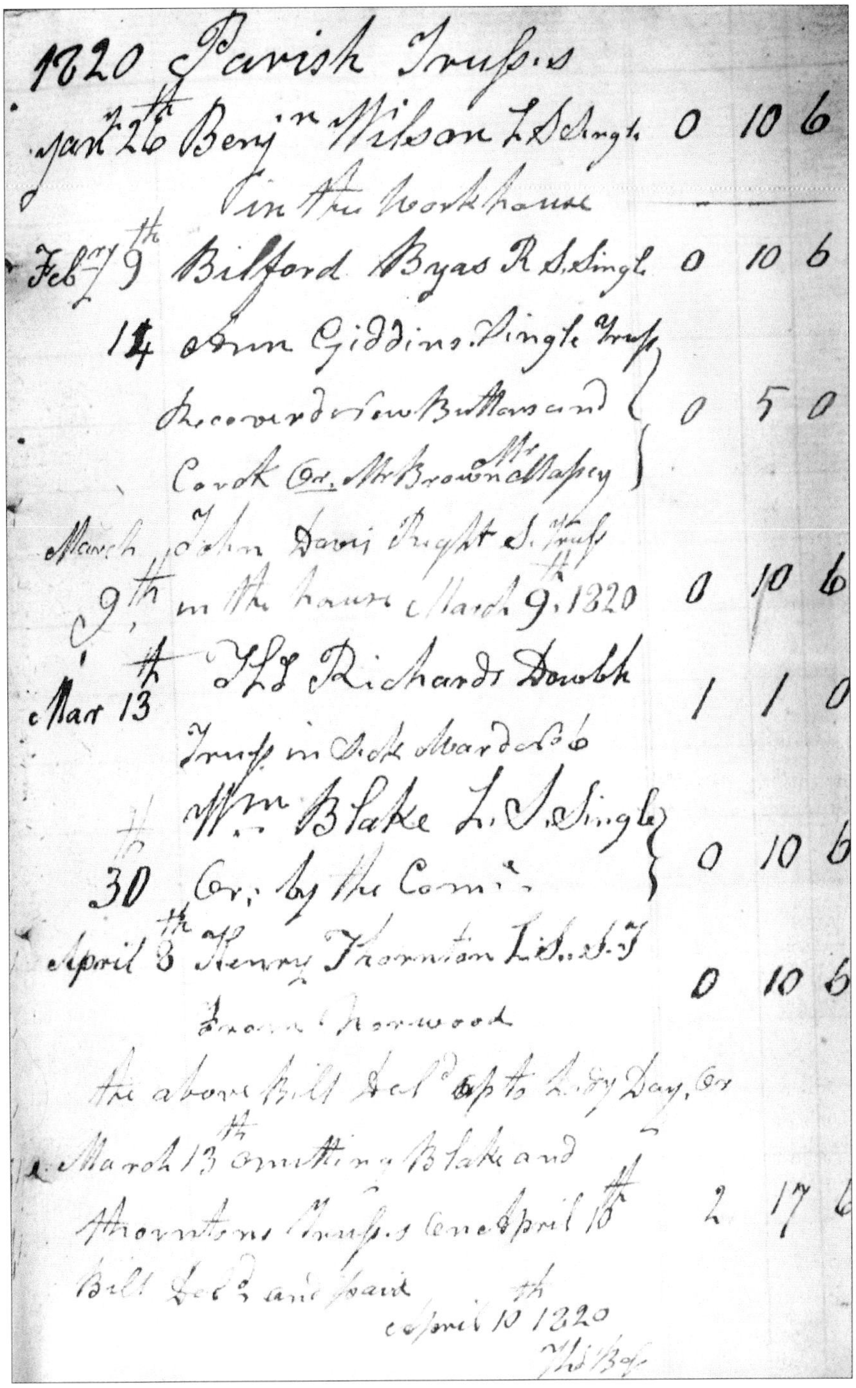

A page from the early ledger book detailing trusses Boss supplied to the parish of Lambeth in 1820.

the very brave or the very distressed would "submit to the knife". A truss was a far better alternative.

How on earth Boss as a fully trained gunmaker (and one of the best at that) got in to trusses, I do not know, but as I said before he was an astute businessman and tried any angle to make money.

The illustration above shows a page dated 1820 from his early ledger book. It shows that he had the contract for the parish trusses for Lambeth.

Parish trusses refers to the system for helping the poor at this time. Each parish was responsible for the maintenance of its own poor and ratepayers paid a proportion of their rates for this purpose. How the poor were helped depended upon the individual parish. Some parishes gave "Outdoor Relief" which was a simple dole payment given weekly. Others used "Indoor Relief" whereby the pauper had to enter the workhouse. Workhouses could often be inhumane, degrading places, feared by the lower classes and were often not dissimilar to prisons, with petty rules and repetitive work. In return for work they received free board and lodging.

There was a workhouse in Boss's Lambeth parish – notice the third line down "in the workhouse". Boss or his assistant would have to go to the workhouse to measure up some unfortunate soul for a truss, the bill

The ledger book from the spring of 1820 detailing Boss's work for Purdey. Note Boss's quote at the bottom for 29 June 1820. "Mr Purdey put the escutcheons himself – Fancy Ones."

being met by the parish. Also note the signature at the bottom. Boss had to employ people to help him make his trusses and there is a record in the ledger book of a wage bill, "paid Mrs ...? on account of wages due to her 25 June 1823 £1.0.0.".

To give the impression that Boss was only a truss maker in this period is incorrect. His main business was his calling as a gunmaker. Most of the Trade Directories list "Thomas Boss, 3 Bridge Road, Lambeth" as a "Truss-maker". One or two however list him as a "Truss and Gun Manufacturer". This gives the conception that his main business was as a truss manufacturer and the reason for the lack of advertising on the gunmaking side

was that he was "working for the trade". Working for the trade means that he was an outworker, finishing guns for established makers. There was no need to advertise himself when he had steady work through gunmakers.

Again the early ledger book gives an interesting insight into his work. The type of work he did for the gunmakers consisted of "filing scroll handles", "screwing together", "touch-holing", "forging triggers", "fitting silver mounts", "stocking", "filing furniture", etc. He worked for a variety of gunmakers, for example Beckwith and Moore. However, ninety-five per cent of his work was with James Purdey. Purdey had worked

The ledger from 22 – 27 August 1820 again detailing his Purdey work and the amounts he charged Purdey.

for Joseph Manton between 1805 and 1808 and hence would have known Boss from an early date. Purdey then went on to work for the Rev. Dr Forsyth, the inventor of the detonating lock. This system created great interest since it was a totally new method of ignition, the old flintlock having been in existence for two centuries. Forsyth's detonating lock required a high degree of workmanship. Forsyth knew of Purdey's prowess and so took him on.

In 1814 he set up on his own at 4 Princes Street off Leicester Square. Thanks to his work with Manton and Forsyth his reputation as an excellent gunmaker was assured. As is oft quoted, Col. Peter Hawker in

Instructions to Young Sportsmen, etc in the seventh edition of 1833 states that, "Mr Purdey has, at this moment, perhaps the first business in London and no man better deserves it. I once asked Joe Manton whom he considered the best gunmaker in town (of course excepting himself) and his answer was, 'Purdey gets up the best work next to mine.' This was when Purdey occupied a small shop in Princes Street."

With his expanding business and reputation Purdey found it difficult to find first-class journeymen. He would be forced to go to outworkers and, knowing of Thomas Boss's skill, realised that he could produce the quality work he needed.

William Boss rented a room from his younger brother Thomas in 1819 – an entry in Boss's early ledger book.

The early ledger book shows that virtually every week Boss was working on Purdey guns. He tended to finish them off for Purdey, his main work being in "screwing them together". Screwing a gun together refers to making all the screws for a gun and then fitting together all the various parts, like trigger guards, trigger plates, tangs, etc. – a tricky job. So, it could be said that some early Purdey guns are really Boss guns.

In the 1830s, Boss would make much of the fact that, not only had he worked for Manton, but he had also worked for Purdey. This was a deliberate attempt to give himself more esteem when he set himself up in business solely as a gunmaker. This fact has led many writers to assume that Boss worked under Purdey for many years but, as we now know, Boss had his own business in this early period and Purdey was one of his clients.

It is unclear if Thomas Boss built any guns bearing his own name at the 3 Bridge Road address in the 1820s. The ledgers certainly do not show any of his own guns being produced and I have never seen a Boss gun with this address on it. I think it likely that he continued "working for the trade" at this time. In the mid to later 1820s he did a lot of outwork for Charles Lancaster. Lancaster, famous for his barrels that he supplied to the trade, started up on his own in 1826 at 151 New Bond

Street. Like Purdey, his reputation and skill meant that he could not cope with orders in his fledgling business and he had to utilise outworkers. Perhaps a gun will surface as a result of this book bearing the early address of 3 Bridge Road.

So, Boss finished guns and built trusses, receiving a steady stream of work for both. Yet Boss, ever the businessman, found another angle to make money. He had taken the lease on 3 Bridge Road because it was a good size deliberately so that he could rent out rooms to generate more income. The ledger book details all his tenants' comings and goings and what rent they paid. For example:

Mr H. Hornblower entered my second floor October 1818. The rent to be paid quarterly at 22 guineas per year.

Mr Barrymore entered on my first floor with the use of back kitchen the 14 January 1819. The rent to be paid quarterly £30 per year.

Mr Henry Holt entered my parlour on the 13 March 1820 at 15s. per week on a Monday.

There is an interesting entry for 31 January 1821: "Mr Chipchase called Jan. 31st 1821 and borrowed a £1 note"! I wonder what that was all about?

In conclusion to sum up this period from *circa* 1816 to 1827, Thomas Boss received constant work in both gun- and truss-making and supplemented his income by renting rooms. He did not want to launch out entirely into gun manufacture bearing his own name as it was too risky a business bearing in mind the problems in getting "gentlemen" to settle their bills promptly. Boss the businessman was careful, intent on building up capital and building up his reputation as a quality gunmaker. Advertising as we know it today hardly existed. Word of mouth reputation was what mattered and this Boss assiduously cultivated.

THOMAS BOSS – GUNMAKER – 33 EDGWARE ROAD, MARYLEBONE

By the late 1820s with Boss in his thirties and with capital and experience behind him, he decided it was time to set up in his own right as a gunmaker. It would not be easy. Taking a typical Trade Directory of the period such as *Pigot's Commercial Directory for Merchant Manufacturers and Traders in London* for 1828, the following London gunmakers and associated trades are listed:

88 gun and pistol makers
4 gun-barrel makers
2 gun-flint manufacturers
5 gun-implement makers
4 gun-lock makers
2 gunpowder-flask makers
9 gunpowder makers
5 gun-stock makers

In Hawker's *Instructions to Young Sportsmen, etc* in the seventh edition of 1833, he lists sixty gunmakers in London. His list tended to be the more established makers. As such, Boss is not mentioned since he would only recently have commenced his business at the time of Hawker's writing the book.

There was severe competition for Boss, yet he felt confident that with his contacts and reputation he could make a go of it. Bridge Road in Lambeth, south of the river Thames, was not the best area to establish a gunmakers business. The quality of gun he intended to produce meant that he had to move to a better location in London. The West End of London with its monied people, its high class, tradesmen's shops and well established best gunmakers was the obvious place to go. Accordingly around 1827 he moved across the river to the Edgware Road in Marylebone.

The Edgware Road housed various gunmakers in

this period. Examples are William Moore at number 78 and Joseph Manton briefly at Burwood Place, Edgware Road. It was not "the proper West End" but it was a good start.

Boss did not take the lease on number 33 but rented it from Mrs Ann Thomson. The Trade Directories do not mention Boss at this address until 1833 when they state, "Thomas Boss, 33 Edgware Road, Marylebone, Gun and Pistol Repository". Joseph Lang used the same term "Repository" to describe his business in the same period in reference to the fact that not only was he making guns, he was buying and selling as well. Boss the businessman on "the make" again.

At 33 Edgware Road, Boss definitely made guns bearing his own name and address. He made primarily double percussion sporting guns and tube-locks. His output was low since he was recently established and so he continued working for the trade. On 3 June 1832 he advertised in the weekly sporting periodical, *Bell's Life in London*. The full title in this newspaper was, "Bell's Life in London (and Sporting Chronicle) combining with the news of the week a rich repository of fashion, wit and humour and the interesting incidents of real life". It was primarily a sporting paper with news of wrestling, boxing, pigeon shooting, cricket, etc. Gunmakers like Reilly, Lang, Joyce, Bissett, and Probin all advertised. Hawker's *Instructions to Young Sportsmen* was heavily advertised. Boss's advert is in typical 19th-century servile tradesman tone (reproduced on the previous page):

Bell's Life being a gentleman's magazine has some other lovely "gentlemanly" adverts, eg "Cures for Gnorrhoea", "Artificial Teeth", "Wheelchairs", titilation "Penny Dreadfuls" such as "The Amours of a Nobleman".

The mention of the safety device is in reference to a trigger guard safety. They were very much in vogue at

the time. Boss's claim to be the inventor is advertising rhetoric. The trigger guard safety had been around in flintlock days.

It was often difficult to tell at a glance if the hammers were at the half-cock position (ie safe and impossible to fire) or whether they were at the full-cock position (ready to fire). Only quarter of an inch or so separated the positions. To the experienced shooter this presented no problems, but to the young and inexperienced mistakes could often happen with fatal consequences.

In 1826, the Minister in the Parish of Currie near Edinburgh, the Rev. John Somerville, invented a safety slide that locked the triggers when drawn back. He published a book on this subject called, *Essay in the Safety Gun by the Inventor*. His book extoled the virtues of his invention by describing over one hundred accidents that occurred due to accidental discharge. He tells of a boy of twelve at Sittingbourne in Kent. The story has been told several times. The boy thought the gun was unloaded, pulled the triggers and promptly killed two of his friends. In those days it was not a question of a quick check by opening the barrels and checking to see if cartridges were in the breech. Muzzle-loaders could only be checked by lowering the ramrod down the barrel or blowing through the barrels – too complicated for the novice or youth. In addition, muzzle-loaders were often deliberately left loaded for the quick shot at the rabbit that appeared in the back garden. Even out shooting, the shooter could stumble and the gun go off.

In the late 1820s most of the good makers began to fit safety guards. Boss had to join contemporary fear and fashion and follow suit. Having shown that he was in the forefront of safety and fashion, he attempted to establish his credentials by name-dropping Manton, Purdey and Lancaster. To state that he had worked for them would imply that his standards and guns were as good as theirs. Gunmakers have done this since time immemorial. A study of trade labels shows how common it is.

FURTHER CHANGES OF ADDRESS

In the middle to late 1830s Thomas Boss moved his business no fewer than five times (see Appendix 2). The exact dates of these moves presents any researcher with real problems. The main difficulty is that with one exception all his properties were rented. The Ratebooks do not mention Boss. The addresses of Boss given in the Trade Directories must be viewed with scepticism as they are frequently out of date and should only be used as a rough guide.

I would put forward the following chronology of Boss's addresses in this period based on a careful study of the Ratebooks bearing in mind when buildings are

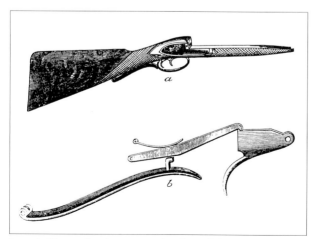

Joseph Manton's trigger guard safety of the same type that Thomas Boss used. It was not a real safety in that it only locked the triggers not the gun locks themselves.

shown as "empty" and when changes of occupiers took place.

He left 33 Edgware Road around 1833 and moved to 1 Lower Grosvenor Street, in the heart of the West End, again renting the property. It was a well situated street for a high-class gunmaking establishment. He shared the building with a pub called the Grosvenor Arms and Madame Merrard "a stay-maker" who also plied her trade from the building. Teasdale-Buckell mentions that he was at 3 Grosvenor Street in this time, but an examination of the Ratebooks reveals that 1 Lower Grosvenor Street and 3 Grosvenor Street are one and the same thing. Most sources actually use the term "Grosvenor Street", so I will use it in preference to the Lower Grosvenor Street referred to in the Trade Directories. Thomas Boss regarded his address as 1 Grosvenor Street. This is the address that will be found engraved on the ribs of guns from this period.

Boss remained at Grosvenor Street for a couple of years and then, around 1835, moved very close-by to 14 Clifford Street. Clifford Street runs off Bond Street, one of the principal thoroughfares in this area. This was rented property once more. He remained another couple of years here and in 1837 (a definite date) he moved to the prestigious address that is synonymous with Boss & Co. – St James's Street.

CHAPTER THREE

73 ST JAMES'S STREET

In 1837 two far-reaching events happened to Thomas Boss. He moved to St James's Street and he got married at the ripe old age of forty-seven.

St James's Street probably came into existence in the 16th century. The first time the name appears is in the Ratebook for 1660. There was much building in the 17th century, although none of this survives today, including a pillory constructed in 1690.

The fame of St James's Street rests mainly upon its association with the coffee or chocolate houses and clubs which for some two-and-a-half centuries had made it and Pall Mall the social rendez-vous of masculine aristrocratic society in London. Examples of such houses are the Cocoa Tree, 1698, the Thatched House Tower, 1705, St James's Coffee House, 1705, all catering for the new clientele created in the neighbourhood of the Court of St James.

St James's Street thus became a centre of fashionable trade rather than a fashionable residence. A commentator in 1815 recorded that "the West side is chiefly composed of stately houses belonging to the nobility and gentry, one or two expensive hotels, etc. The opposite side consists of elegant shops which appear to a stranger rather as lounging places than the resorts of trade and busy pursuits of merchandise". With the emphasis on trade it is therefore not surprising to find, with the exception of the three great club houses, White's, Brooks and Boodles, the 18th-century buildings of St James's Street were by the standards of the time undistinguished.

His first stay was in 76 St James's Street where he would remain until 1839. This was rented accommodation, with the rates paid by Uriah Wright, a carpenter. At this time he is described in the Directories as "a Patent Gunmaker". Later in the early 1840s, number 76 would be demolished to make way for the new Conservative Club.

On 10th September 1837, in the Parish Church of St George, Bloomsbury, Thomas Boss, bachelor of 76 St James's Street, London married Amy Chapman Fields, spinster, of 9 Charing Cross, London. Thomas was 47 and Amy 42 years. The witnesses were Martha Simpson and George Fatt, a cousin of Amy's. They were soon to be married themselves. George Fatt was a gas-fitter and their son also known as George, born in 1841, would become a journeyman gunmaker with Boss.

By coincidence, 9 Charing Cross was the business address of John Prosser the gunmaker. I wonder if that was how Thomas Boss came into contact with Amy Fields?

The Marriage Certificate of Thomas and Emma Boss, 10 September 1837.

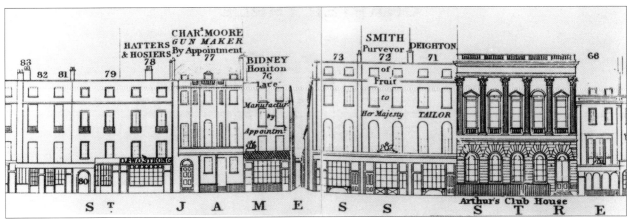

The west side of St James's Street, showing Number 73. From John Tallis's *Street Views of London* **1838–1840**

Amy, always known to her family and friends as Emma, came from Louth, Lincolnshire. She was born in 1795 to Edward Fields, a baker. When Thomas Boss died in 1857, until John Robertson took over in 1891, the Fields and their descendants would figure greatly in the gunmaking firm.

Emma's sister, Susannah Fields, had married William Paddison, a shoemaker in Louth and raised the normal large Victorian family. Two of the boys would eventually take over the firm. Edward Fields Paddison was born in Louth in 1825 and was apprenticed to Thomas Boss on 21st June 1838 and became a journeyman gunmaker with the firm in 1845. For a short time in the 1880s and early 1890s the firm was known as "EFP Boss & Co." in reference to Edward Fields Paddison until John Robertson took over in 1891.

Edward's brother, James Joseph Paddison born on 28th January 1842 at James's Street, Louth, also came down and joined the firm in 1856. Like his brother Edward, he too served his apprenticeship with the firm and became a journeyman gunmaker by 1863.

Due to the fact that Thomas and Emma had married late in life, they bore no children. Hence their desire to attract their nephews into the firm to carry it on. Later, when Mrs Boss died in 1872, the business would be left to the two Paddison brothers.

In March 1839, Thomas Boss moved one block up across Little St James's Street and took the lease on number 73. This lease ran for sixty-nine years until 1908, the date when the building was demolished and the firm moved to Dover Street. Previously, number 73 St James's Street was leased by Simon Halpin and Robert Wainwright, tailors.

The estimated rental was £63, the yearly rateable value £57 and the rate in the pound £4.5s.6d. Boss's early business ventures had prospered to such an extent that he was able to set up business in this exclusive street, assisted by a legacy given to his wife. Emma must have been the apple of her father's eye for, under the terms of her father Edward Field's will

dated 22nd September 1837, out of an estate valued at just under £600, she was to receive £300 on the death of her mother, far more than the rest of her relatives were to receive.

The corner shop of 73 St James's Street was a typical late 18th/early 19th-century shop. We can get a good idea of what it looked like from John Tallis' *Street Views of London*. This view must have been drawn around the time Boss moved from number 76 to 73 St James's Street – his name does not appear on the plan. The building was brick built on four storeys with a cellar.

The entire building was used by the firm with a flat for Mr and Mrs Boss and accommodation for the Paddison boys in their early days. As usual, Boss rented rooms out to tenants in this building. A large window facing the street in the customary style of many small panes of glass displayed the guns. To the left was the door by which you entered into the shop, to the right the door that led upstairs.

St James's Street in the early 1840s was a mixture of clubs and exclusive shops, most with "Royal Appointment" signs. There was the Conservative Club, Arthur's Club House, White's, Brooks and Boodles. At number 8 St James's Street was Osman Giddy, Chemist to the Royal Family, at number 4 Crellin, Tailor to the Royal Family, at number 3 Wiegall, Engraver to the Queen, at number 1 Sams, Book and Print Seller to the Queen, at number 72 Elizabeth Smith, Purveyor of Fruit to Her Majesty, at number 24 Welch and Gwynne, Print Sellers and Publishers to the Royal Family, and so on.

Such an exclusive environment would mean that Boss was in a prime position to attract wealthy patrons. Advertising as we know it today hardly existed during this time – in fact it was often thought vulgar and in bad taste at the top end of trade. Hence the right shop in the right area was important to conduct good business.

Many other gunmakers also sought a site in St James's Street. The more famous are listed as follows:

J D Dougall at number 59 from 1863 to 1883.

73 St James's Street *circa* 1892 shortly after John Robertson bought the business.

An engraving of the west side of St James's Street by Marchant *circa* **1846. Boss's shop extreme right, with Mrs Boss and friend looking out of the window!**

William Eley (Wadding Manufacturer) at number 36 *circa* 1842.

Charles Moore, very close to Boss at number 77 from 1825 to 1842.

John Rigby, next door to Boss at number 72 from 1866.

Gye and Moncrieff at number 60 from 1876 to 1885.

James Woodward at number 64.

Stephen Grant at number 67a from 1866.

THE FAMILY FIRM

During mid-century Thomas Boss employed ten journeymen and two apprentices. Of his known workers during this period and later, the following can be identified:

Edward Paddison, his nephew.

James Paddison, his nephew.

George Fatt, his cousin.

William Mears (gunmaker/finisher), husband of his niece Ann Paddison.

Stephen Grant (Grant was probably the most experienced worker since he eventually entered into partnership with Mrs Boss on the death of Boss in 1857 and subsequently managed the firm for nine years).

William John Mears (stocker), a son of William Mears. On many Boss guns of the 1870s and 1880s, the initials "WJM" are stamped on the stock under the trigger guard – William J Mears mark as a stocker.

Joseph Chapman Mears (gun action finisher), another son of William Mears.

Walter Fields Paddison, a nephew of Edward Paddison.

In the second half of the 19th century Boss & Co. were primarily a family firm employing cousins, nephews, etc. Unfortunately, no wage books exist until the late 19th century and it is most probable that other family members were involved whom I have been unable to trace.

Like most gunmakers who were well established, Boss found that at certain times of the year, notably in the summer before the season started, demand was high, his workforce could not cope and he had to use outworkers. In Boss's order ledgers the names of these outworkers are often recorded so that any faulty work could be traced back to them. The following outworkers all did work for Boss:

Edwin Wilkes – Finisher

Edward Paton – Finisher

Whitehouse – Stocker

Groves – Finisher

McEvoy – Finisher

Holliman – Stocker

E. C. Hodges – Actioner

Byrne – Finisher

Edwin – Actioner

Henry Glazier – Stocker, 3 Russell Street, Chelsea, London.

Atkins – Actioner

Finucane – Finisher

John Sumner – Engraver, 10 Queen Street, Soho, London.

SPECIALIST SUPPLIERS

Like all the gunmakers, Boss found it more convenient to buy ready-made items from specialist suppliers. Locks and barrels were the two components that were bought in completed and ready to be engraved in the Boss style. Boss used the following suppliers:

Joseph Brazier – Barrel- and lock-maker, Wolverhampton.

John Stanton – Lock-maker, 13 Clifton Street, Wolverhampton.

Hutchison – Barrel-maker.

Amos Elvins – Barrel-maker, 58 Poland Street, Oxford Street (from Purdey's) London.

Henry Squires – Barrel-maker, 3 George Yard, Princes Street, Soho, London.

Thomas Parkin – Barrel-maker, 5 Meards Court, Soho, London.

John Portlock – Barrel-maker, 2 Globe Yard, South Molton Street, London.

Christopher Aston – Barrel-maker, 26 Little Windmill Street, Golden Square, London.

THOMAS PARKIN, BARREL-MAKER TO BOSS

The London gunmakers rarely made their own barrels. It involved a lot of heavy machinery, lathes, forges and extremes of heat. Gradually, specialist barrel-makers developed. In the old flintlock days William Fuller of Clerkenwell and Charles Lancaster at Drury Lane supplied much of the trade.

In Boss's era the top barrel-maker was Thomas Parkin, of 5 Meards Court, Soho. On Boss guns of the 1840s and 1850s the initials "TP" will be found stamped underneath the barrels – TP showing that they are Parkin barrels. All the top London makers used him, Purdeys, Manton, etc. Thomas Boss's orders to Parkin have survived in a copy book entitled "Parkin's Orders". This book covers the period 27 January 1849 to 7 January 1850 and contains copies of barrel orders from Thomas Boss to Parkin.

In his order Boss would detail precisely the type of breeching, type of Damascus twist, length, bore, height of rib, weight, ramrod pipes or not, date received and date ordered (usually within the month). In addition Boss would give a general description of what the barrels were to look like. So he would not get confused the name of the future owner of the gun was also included.

In his order to Parkin of 29th August 1850 notice how he instructs Parkin to copy the Westley-Richards barrels supplied as a pattern. The owner of the Westley-Richards, Major Hanner, wanted a similar gun in weight, etc built by Boss. Notice how Boss wanted them "next week" – not bad, he got them in a fortnight. Parkin is warned in the last sentence "be careful not to scratch old Barrels". These barrels were for a 14-bore double gun number 1035 built in 1850 for Major Hanner.

A great many of Boss's orders to Parkin were for barrels to match existing guns. Composite pairs were very common, a single gun being ordered and perhaps a year or two later another gun being built to match.

Not only did he order all his new barrels from Parkin, he also sent his barrels for repair there. Bulges, dents, new breeches, ribs, shortening, etc were com-

The stamp "TP" of the barrel-maker Thomas Parkin, 5 Meards Court, Soho, London under the breeches of gun no. 763.

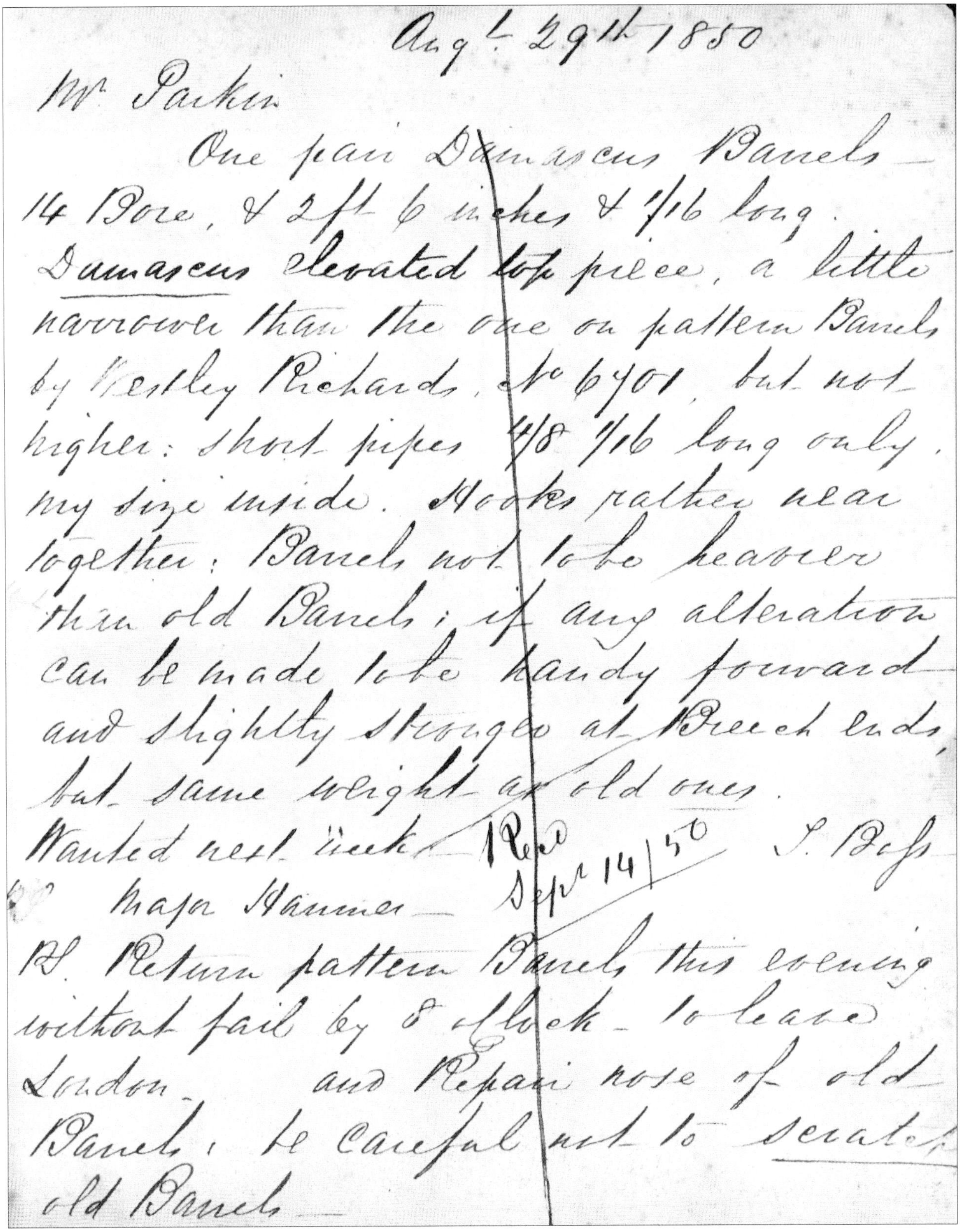

Aug.t 29th 1850

Mr Parkin

One pair Damascus Barrels —
14 Bore, & 2 ft 6 inches & 7/16 long.
Damascus elevated top piece, a little
narrower than the one on pattern Barrels
by Westley Richards, No 6701, but not
higher: short pipes 7/8 7/16 long only.
my size inside. Hooks rather near
together; Barrels not to be heavier
than old Barrels; if any alteration
can be made to be handy forward
and slightly stronger at Breech ends,
but same weight as old ones.
Wanted next week — Rec. Sept 14/50 — S. Boss
Major Hammer —
PS. Return pattern Barrels this evening
without fail by 8 o'clock — to leave
London, and Repair nose of old
Barrels, be careful not to scratch
old Barrels —

Boss's Note to Thomas Parkin, Barrel-maker, 29th August 1850, Ordering Barrels for Future Gun Number 1035. From "Parkin's Orders".

monplace. He is usually quite frank with Parkin "be careful not to injure the brown" is a common remark in his orders.

His Parkin book shows his rate of gun production at this time. In just over a year he sent in 102 orders, roughly two per week. Boss was making approximately seventy to eighty guns per year, the rest would be new barrels or repairs. It is hardly surprising that he said in every second letter to Parkin that the barrels were wanted almost immediately.

In the 1850s, Thomas Parkin ceased his business. Boss went elsewhere and used other barrel-makers in the vicinity. The two barrel-makers most commonly used were Henry Squires, 3 George Yard, Princes Street, Soho, London and John Portlock, 2 Globe Yard, South Molton Street, London. Boss began a long association with Squires. They used his barrels and those of his son, Frank Squires, throughout the 19th century and into the 20th century. By design or coincidence, Squires's workshop at 3 George Yard was where John Robertson first set up business. Squires barrels are either stamped "H S" or "F S" on the underside. Portlock barrels likewise can be recognised by "J P" being stamped on the underside.

E. C. HODGES – ACTIONER

Boss used in the early breech-loading period a leading London outworker actioner, E. C. Hodges. Actioning the early breech-loaders was too difficult a job for the muzzle-loading journeymen and Hodges specialised in actioning for most of the leading London gunmakers in the 1850s and 1860s. It is rumoured that it was Hodges who saw the first publicly unveiled breech-loader, the French Lefaucheux pinfire, at the Great Exhibition in 1851 and produced a copy of it that he later sold to Joseph Lang, who is usually credited with producing the first breech-loaders in Britain. That he commercially exploited the early breech-loaders is undoubtedly true but a question-mark must remain whether it was Hodges who produced the first modern British breech-loader.

THE LETTERS BOOK

Boss & Co. have today in their possession a "Letters Book" containing all the business letters written by Thomas Boss himself dating from the period October 1845 to December 1850. There are literally hundreds of letters written in elegant copperplate handwriting. The spelling is good and the grammar adequate. Since reading and writing were not universal accomplishments in these days, they prove that Boss was an intelligent educated man. Boss must have laboriously burned the midnight oil, writing the letters first and then copying them all out by hand.

It must be remembered that what exists in the letters' book are Boss's copies only. They are abridged and often he has not bothered with proper punctuation. When I have reproduced them I have not attempted to correct them. All together, this letters' book gives us a depth of insight, far more than any official record, into Boss & Co. in the heyday of Thomas Boss in the late 1840s.

An interesting letter dated 27th March 1850 shows a Norfolk gunmaker trying to conduct a deal but with no satisfactory conclusion.

> London, 73 St James's Street,
> 27th March 1850
>
> Sir,
>
> I received your letter and also the two Gun Stocks which being only fist cut and not seasoned with being rather cross grain in the hands and much too high in price will not suit me although the figure is good. I will therefore return them on Monday next per Luggage train unless I can serve you by sending them to anyone in London you may wish to see them. I think they ought to be handsome, dry and fit to work and well grained in the hand at 18s. each. You will never obtain 18s. for wet stocks.
>
> Yours respectfully
> Thos Boss
>
> Mr Bond, Gunmaker
> Thetford

GUN APPARATUS MANUFACTURERS

Most of the paraphernalia that accompanied muzzle-loaders was supplied by outside makers. Muzzle-loaders required powder flasks, shot pouches, nipple keys, etc. In common with all the other manufacturers, Boss used these specialist suppliers. Since his guns were London best he used the best makers, ie Brazier and Hawksley.

G. W. Hawksley of Sheffield were Gun Implement Makers. They made every accessory needed for the muzzle-loader from powder flasks to oil bottles. Boss sent a typical order to Hawksley on 16th April 1849:

> London, 73 St James's Street,
> 16th April 1849
>
> Please send me a few powder flasks, six 8 oz. and two 10 oz.: but not the new way with the springs opening only half way round the top: they do not work so well as those the old way: when the spring opens all round the top from the flask it is more lively. Let me have them in two or three days if possible.
>
> Yours respectfully
> Thos Boss
>
> Messrs Hawksley
> Gun Implement Makers
> Smithfield
> Sheffield

The interior of a percussion lock used in Boss gun no. 827 by Joseph Brazier, Wolverhampton. Note how the lock is engraved "IB".

His orders to Joseph Brazier of Wolverhampton were slightly different. Although Brazier supplied gun implements like Hawksley, his forte was in supplying top quality locks to all the famous makers. Making locks was a very specialised business so all the best manufacturers found it far more convenient to go to a specialist supplier like Brazier. He would supply his lock plates "soft" and in the white to the gunmakers' pattern so that the gunmaker could then engrave them in his own style. Brazier's locks are superb pieces of crafts-manship. The insides are engraved either "IB" or "Brazier".

Several letters to Brazier survive, eg:

London, 73 St James's Street,
July 30th 1850

Mr Brazier,

Send two pairs full-size 12-bore locks, long sear springs and long plates: the tube-locks are wanted this week.

Yours respectfully
Thos Boss

Mr Joseph Brazier,
Wolverhampton

It is interesting to note the request for tube-locks long out of fashion. Pair nos. 990 and 991 and 997 and 998 were built in 1850. These locks could be for either of these pairs.

Another order dated 19th April 1849 is for another of Brazier's specialities, rifle sights.

London, 73 St James's Street,
19th April 1849

Sir,

Please to make a choice leaf Rifle Sight, not cut through, about 1/4″ long, the leaves 3/4″ wide: a thick standard and rather a small pin. Have the goodness to forward it in a letter as early as possible.

I am Sir
Your Obedient Servant
Thos Boss

Mr Joseph Brazier,
Wolverhampton

I rather think that this sight was for number 895, a 100-bore pea rifle, or number 906, a 95-bore pea rifle. Pea rifles were small-bore rifles for shooting rabbits or such like.

He also ordered bullet moulds from Brazier.

London, 73 St James's Street,
17th March 1849

Mr Brazier,

Have the goodness to send me with the two pairs of small-size neck moulds you have in hand, five pairs more the following sizes, 1 pair no 19, 2 pairs no 18, 1 pair no 16, 1 pair also no 34, all to have necks made as those last sent.

Yours respectfully
Thos Boss

Boss would also use gun-case-makers though no record exists of these orders. He would supply his guns and accessories to the case-maker, who would then individually fit each case to the gun.

GUN TESTS, GUN DISPATCH AND THE PERENNIAL PROBLEM

Before rifles were delivered they had to have their sights regulated. In addition customers sometimes wanted to see the shot patterns of their guns. The shooting ground that Boss used for these purposes was the Red House Shooting Grounds, Battersea Fields. The Red House was a gun club where all manner of shooting took place and was one of the main venues for the then fashionable live pigeon shooting.

Battersea was not too far from St James's Street and in those days it was relatively open and ideal for gun use. It was busy mainly in the afternoons and weekends. Boss advised any customers who wanted to try out his guns to go there "the best time being 8 till 12 in the forenoon".

Due to the delay between the order of a gun and its completion date, Boss always wrote to a customer advising him of the imminent arrival of his gun.

A typical such letter, opposite, refers to the dispatch of a double gun no. 911 on 27th June 1849 to John Hamlyn Bovier, Lindfield, Sussex.

One of the big problems faced by all the gunsmiths of the day was cash flow. Barrels from Parkin, locks from Brazier, rates on St James's Street, wage bills, etc were all expensive. Since Boss's guns were not cheap and he made a good profit on them, these expenses should have proved no problem. The problem was that getting payment from clients could sometimes prove difficult. They would often take months, in many cases years to pay. It was this problem that forced Joseph Manton into

bankruptcy and Purdey's letters of the period show that they experienced exactly the same scenario.

The chief difficulty lay in the social system of the period. Boss was regarded as a tradesman and tradesmen had to be deferential to their superiors. Just look at the style of his letter closure. In contemporary fashion Boss had to adopt:

"I remain Sir,
Your very humble servant,
Thos Boss"

Guns and gun repairs went out the door unpaid for. He simply could not insist on the money first to the aristocratic type of person he dealt with. They would regard it as presumptuous and go elsewhere.

Although most people paid up on time, a minority did not. When pairs of guns cost around £70, this was a great deal of money to have owing. On 18 March 1850, Boss had to write the following letter:

London, 73 St James's Street,
18th March 1850

Dear Sir,

I received your note yesterday and regret to say that I cannot meet your bills as Gentlemen delay the payment so very long. I cannot with safety name shorter dates or I would with pleasure. Mrs Boss sends Kind Regards to Mrs James. Hoping yourself with her are quite well.

Remain most respectfully
Your humble servant
Thomas Boss

To Mr James

Unfortunately I have no idea who Mr James was or what the bill was about.

Of all the surviving letters in the Letters Book, most are letters to "Gentlemen" regarding the non-payment of their bills. Boss had to adopt a patronising tone and appeal to the better nature of his clients. Very, very rarely is there any hint of assertiveness. He could not do much more. The ball was completely in the client's court. They had all the money, power and influence and he could not really take them to court for default. In any case if word got round that Boss was pursuing strong action, his clients might desert him.

The letter opposite dated 27th October 1845 refers to a double tube-lock gun no. 640 built in early 1845:

Copy London – 73 St James's Street
June 27th/49
Sir
I beg leave to inform you that
I have sent your new Gun by this
evenings Train, directed as under –
John Hamlyn Borrer Esqre Junr –
Lindfield,
Nr Cuckfield,
Sussex,
pr Passenger's Train.
The Gun was enclosed in a large
Packing Box, with Caps – Wadding
&c
I remain, Sir
Your very humble Se
To
J H Borrer Esqre Junr Thomas Boss –
Lindfield
Nr Cuckfield
Sussex.

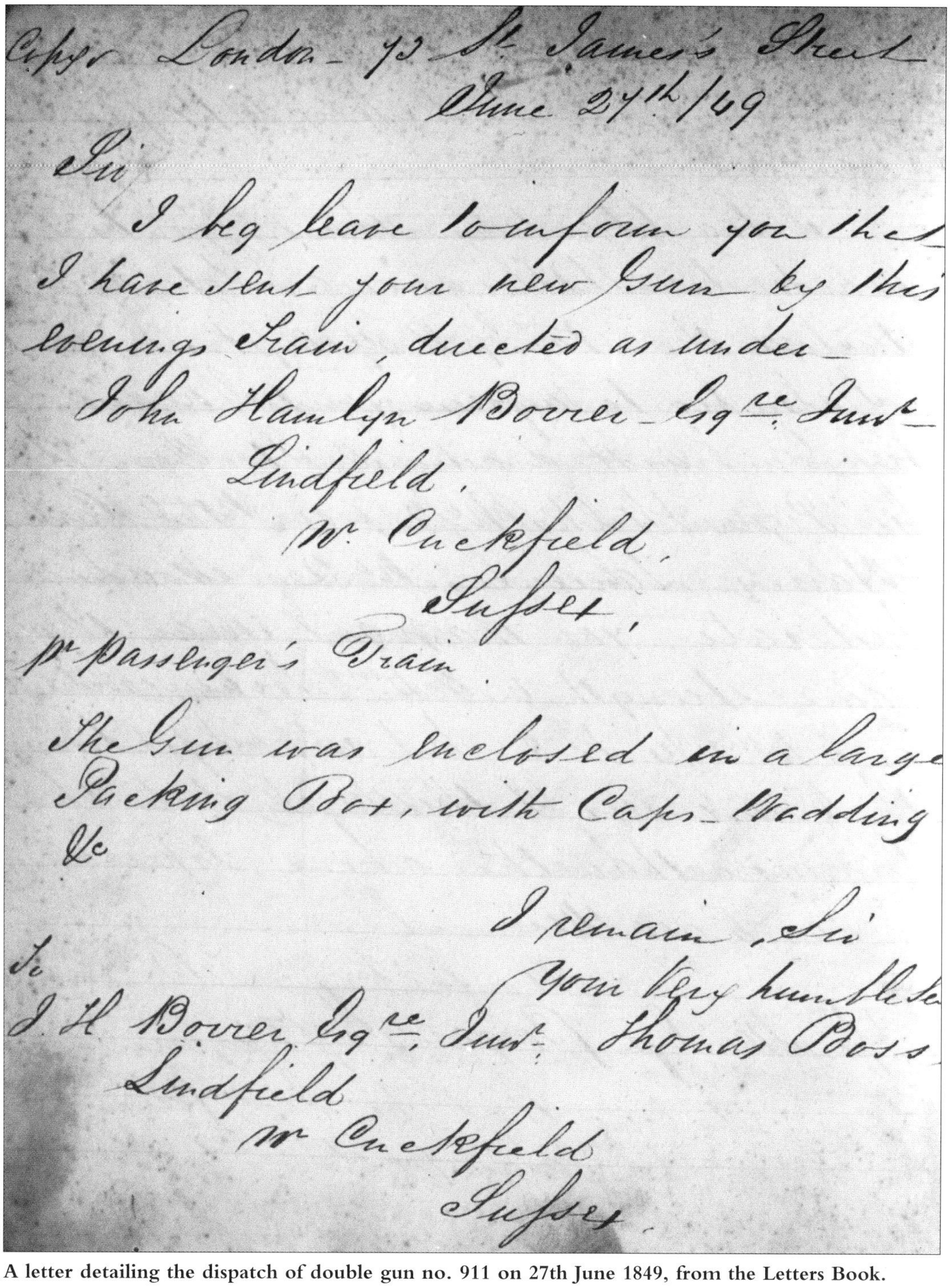

A letter detailing the dispatch of double gun no. 911 on 27th June 1849, from the Letters Book.

London, 73 St James's Street,
27th October 1845

Sir,

I ask pardon troubling You for the favour of my account £42. Through great want of Money to complete Orders which I do for cash only, the price not being high and my Guns inferior to none. Some Gentlemen think it not safe to send a cheque by post – but they cut it across and send me one half which I acknowledge with a Stamp Receipt for the whole by return of post when the other part is forwarded.

Your very Humble
and Obedient Servant
Thos Boss

To A L Goddard,
The Lawn
Swindon

This cutting of the cheque and sending the two halves separately was common practice at this time. Sending anything through the mail was risky since

Copy London – 73 St James's St –
May 17th 1849

Sir

I am greatly disappointed at not receiving the amount of my account £ , according to your promise: having fully depended on it, as I am greatly inconvenienced for money to complete orders. I trust you will help me with it, this week, without fail: as I entirely depend on your assistance

I remain Sir &c
&c

Edward Bray Esqre S. B –
Shere
Guildford –

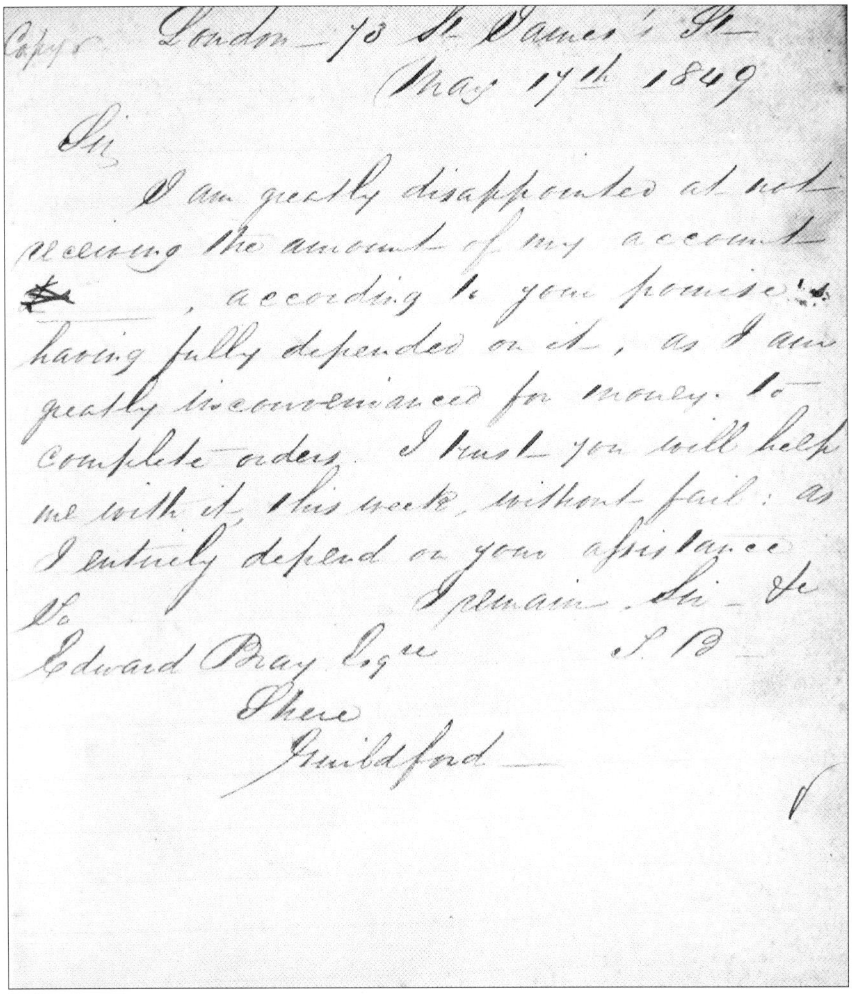

The problem faced by all gunmakers in this period – tardy payment. From the Letters Book.

security was in its infancy and compensation difficult. Boss used exactly the same technique in his cash deals. He instructed his clients to cut their £10 notes in half – a simple but foolproof security system, somewhat disapproved of by banks!

The following letter was the standard one he sent to clergymen. Evidently some clergymen had means and enjoyed shooting, since a fair number ordered Boss guns. He appealed to the clergyman's moral value:

London, 73 St James's Street,
18th November 1847

Sir,

I am sorry to be troublesome but I am very poor and the favour of my account would, Sir, very greatly oblige £34.5s.

I remain Sir
your obedient servant
Thos Boss

The Rev. R Worsley
Little Panton,
Grantham
Lincs

This letter refers to double gun no. 755.

He took a slightly stronger tone with the letter illustrated above. This was for gun no. 856, a double 16-bore gun supplied in 1849.

However, many of his letters were far more pleasurable to write. A great many clients wrote to Boss asking his advice on various aspects of his guns. With a muzzle-loader, it was simple to change powder charge, shot loads, etc. Many shooters asked his advice on this and Boss was always ready to help.

One customer was not very sure about how hot the water should be for cleaning. Black powder leaves a sulphurous residue that must be washed out immediately after shooting to prevent corrosion. Boss's advice of 30th June 1848 was:

> in cleaning barrels, water not warmer than milk is best – if very hot water is put into them, it extracts all the oil from Patent Breeching and Nipples and makes it very difficult to screw them out again. The Servant should be careful to oil the inside well after cleaning.

As regards the maintenance of stocks he recommends raw linseed oil:

Servants on cleaning the gun apply a little raw linseed oil and rub it in with a wad of cloth.

There were several makes of black powder on the market. Often he was asked what was best. He was always unequivocal in his answers:

Never try Diamond Powder. I prefer Curtis and Harvey's no. 2 (Diamond Powder dirties the gun especially in damp weather).

On 3rd January 1850 he gave advice to the Rt. Hon. Lord Huntingfield on charges:

My Lord,

I have this morning returned 8 lbs 13-bore Wadding with 2 lbs of no. 2 Powder by Passenger Train and hope it will arrive before this letter. As it regards the charge to kill at long distances, 14-bore, I think $2\frac{2}{3}$ drams to $1\frac{1}{8}$ oz of shot with felt wadding full $1\frac{1}{4}$ of an inch in thickness over the powder, I think the best charge.

I believe $1\frac{1}{4}$ oz of shot will shoot closer to the above charge of powder, but not with equal strength to kill at long distances.

OTHER ASPECTS OF BOSS'S BUSINESS

In addition to manufacturing guns and rifles he had a large stock of second-hand guns by himself and other makers for sale, eg on 24th August 1845 he had a single gun by Lancaster in a mahogany case for sale at £15.

He also acted as a middleman to Gentlemen in selling or arranging any shooting associated items. He regularly bought and sold pheasants on a commission basis. I do not think the pheasants actually hung in the basement of no. 73, rather he arranged the buying and selling by finding potential customers! He also bought and sold gun dogs. He had a spaniel called Flint for sale at 3 gns. Sometimes in *Bell's Life in London* he would advertise for gun dogs. This would be another middle-man deal or a service to a valued client.

In *Bell's Life* of 1849, he advertised for a gamekeeper for a customer. He received thirty-nine replies from all around the country. Boss copied every single one of these replies into his Letters' Book making comments about some of them.

He continued in his previous ways by renting out rooms at 73 St James's Street and in another property he had at Great Titchfield Street, London, close to Oxford Street. He gave up this particular apartment on 3 April 1849.

73 St James's Street was a large building on four floors. Although the gunmaking business took up most of it and the Bosses had their own flat along with their nephew Edward Paddison, there was ample space to let out the occasional room to bring in extra income.

A John Cameron had been renting a room from Boss. When Boss tried to increase his rent, it backfired and he was forced to evict Cameron. Three letters tell the story

September, 29th 1849

To Mr John Cameron
    Sir,
        I hereby give you notice to quit and deliver up possession of the apartments you occupy in my house no. 73 St James's Street on or before Christmas Day next the 23rd December 1849.

Witness my hand this
29th day of September 1849
Thomas Boss

25th December 1849

We hereby agree to rescind our former agreement respecting the tenancy of the first floor on no. 73 St James's Street and from that date, I, Thomas Boss agree to let the same to J Cameron by the week at the weekly rent of 24s.6d. and I John Cameron agree to take the same on these terms and to be paid weekly, one week's notice to be given on either side.

Witness my hand this 25th day of December 1849
Thomas Boss
John Cameron

1st January 1850

To Mr John Cameron,
    Sir,
        I hereby give you notice to quit and deliver up possession of the Aparments you occupy in my house no. 73 St James's Street on or before the 8th day of January 1850.

Witness my hand this 1st day of January 1851
Emma Boss for Thomas Boss

Note the signature at the bottom of the last letter. In all the hundreds of letters in the Letters Book this is the only one signed by Boss's wife Emma. I rather

Boss's letter telling of his narrow escape from cholera and his concern over poor sanitation in his area. From the Letters Book.

suspect she wrote other letters since some of the writing is obviously different from Thomas's! On the other hand the different writing could be that of his nephew Edward Paddison. All letters with the above exception are signed Thomas Boss.

BEST GUNS AND BAD DRAINS

In late July 1849 an event occured of momentous trepidation to Thomas Boss that so easily could have had fatal consequences for him and possibly ended Boss & Co. as a gunmaking firm. Thomas Boss contracted one of the dreaded diseases that were very prevalent in the 19th century – cholera.

On 8th August 1849, Boss wrote a letter complaining about a bad drain near 73 St James's Street, above. In it he mentions how he had recently been affected by "the cholera".

At first glance it looks like Boss's mention of cholera is mere hyperbole to ensure that something is done quickly about the drain. However a study of Boss's

letters before 8 August shows that, although all letters are signed "Thomas Boss", they are in a different handwriting. Boss did not write them. The last letter written by Boss himself was on 26 July. It is obvious that Boss was very ill in the period between 26 July and 8 August. One thing that is apparent from Thomas Boss's correspondence is that he was a workaholic and a conscientious businessman. Even when ill with 'flu or such like, he would still administer his business and write letters. There are no gaps in his letters in the Letters Book from 1845 to 1850 with this exception. So for Boss to have been out of action for around eleven days means he was very ill.

Cholera came from India, travelled overland and first hit Britain in September 1831 at Sunderland. It spread like wildfire and by February 1832 had reached London. By coincidence the first town to be affected in Scotland was Haddington near Edinburgh, the birthplace of John Robertson.

Cholera was a bacteria infection caused by poor sanitation coupled with overcrowding. In London

An illustration from Teale's *Dangers To Health*, 1881 showing the type of problem that affected the drinking water in St James's Street that eventually resulted in Thomas Boss contracting cholera in the great cholera epidemic of 1849.

excrement was deposited directly into rivers or the ground. Water filtered through this contaminated ground into the wells while these wells continued to provide a main source of urban water supplies. Refuse was dumped everywhere and anywhere and noxious trades like slaughterhouses or glue makers had little or no regulation about the dumping of their waste products.

The cholera attacks revealed not only the shortcomings of medical science, but more especially the governmental and bureaucratic shortcomings in the management of towns. Cholera was of paramount importance in helping to convince an enlightened few in London of the imperative need for a systematic public health system. The Public Health Act of 1848 was an attempt to tackle the problem by setting up local Boards of Health with statutory power to enforce regulations.

In 1849 there was a massive epidemic all over the country – the epidemic Boss had the misfortune to encounter. Dr John Snow made a specialised study of the disease producing in 1854 a book entitled *On the Mode of Communication of Cholera*. He summarised his findings by recommending the following:

1. Good drainage.
2. Good water supply, free from the contents of sewers.
3. Sufficient house room for the poor.
4. To inculcate habits of personal and domestic cleanliness among the people everywhere.

No wonder Boss was concerned about the drains near no. 73. Having just recovered from cholera, he would take more than a passing interest in the problem and knew that his letter of complaint would receive cogni-

sance. It would be several decades after Boss's illness before towns properly came to grips with cholera, primarily due to the expense of water and sewage systems.

The passage of the disease fits in with Boss's eleven day absence from work. It is characterised by massive diarrhorea with rapid depletion of body fluids and salts leading to dehydration. The disease usually ran its course in two to seven days and Boss was very, very lucky to survive since the mortality rate was extremely high.

Boss kept a dog of his own and regularly walked it in nearby Green Park. A letter of 5th October 1848 survives detailing an unpleasant experience he had whilst out one day.

London, 73 St James's Street,
5th October 1848

Gentlemen,

It is my duty to complain of the violent conduct of one of the Green Park Keepers, the name of Millar, for injury done by him to a harmless dog. I keep and pay tax for a House Dog; by throwing a large stone at it and so severely injuring the dog that it has not yet recovered from the effects of the blow; he also threatened to send it home on two legs or shoot it without the slightest provocation; the dog is therefore excluded the use of the park through his violent conduct.

Yours respectfully
Thomas Boss

I wonder what the background to this incident was! Emma Boss had come a long way to London from Louth in Lincolnshire. Evidently she had an affection for the area and its produce. Certain aspects of London life did not appeal to her. One of these aspects was the taste of London bread! Her father had been a baker in Louth and her childhood memories of the local bread must have remained strong. Her husband wrote to a baker in Louth to obtain flour for Emma to bake with.

London, 73 St James's Street,
16th April 1849

Mr Hackford,

Sir, please to let me know by return of post the price of your best flour; the last I had was good; also tell me the best way for its conveyance to London.

Yours respectfully
Thomas Boss

Mr Edward Hackford,
Baker
East Gate
Louth

A calotype view of the north west corner of the Great Exhibition, Hyde Park, London, 1851. Exhibitor No. 219 in the Small Arms Section was T. Boss who exhibited "a central fire double and other guns". The most important exhibit was no. 1308, a pinfire gun and cartridge by Lefaucheux, the first public appearance in Britain of the breech-loader.

1851 was the year of the Great Exhibition – a "Great Exhibition of the Works of Industry of All Nations" as originated in the mind of Prince Albert. This temporary exhibition built in revolutionary style in glass and iron, designed by Joseph Paxton, was erected in Hyde Park and proved to be extremely popular. If anything it was designed to show off Britain's industrial leadership and prestige. No better is this leadership displayed than in the number of small arms exhibits at the Exhibition. Sixty-five British gunmakers exhibited compared to fourteen from Belgium, twenty-two from France and eighteen from Germany.

Of the British exhibitors, exhibitor no. 219 was Thomas Boss. The catalogue states "T Boss, 73 St James's Street, A Central Fire Double and Other Guns." "Central fire" in this context has nothing to do with breech-loading. It refers to the comparatively new way of screwing the nipples into the centre of the breech to obtain an even rate of detonation. An unnumbered pair of exhibition quality pistols are illustrated in Chapter 4. I think it highly probable that these pistols were built especially for this Great Exhibition.

Exhibitor no. 218 was W & J Needham, 26 Piccadilly, London, who exhibited "A Patent Self-Priming Gun, Double and Single Guns to Load at the Breech, Etc". The Needham breech-loader is an enigma today. It might have been a needle gun or a capping breech-loader.

Exhibitor no. 220 was H Beckwith, 58 Skinner Street, London, who exhibited "Fowling Pieces and Blunderbusses".

THE DEATH OF THOMAS BOSS, 17TH AUGUST 1857

On 17th August 1857 Thomas Boss died. His death certificate gives the cause of death as "Disease of the Liver". His death certificate and tombstone record inaccurately that his age was sixty-six years when in fact it should have been sixty-seven. This discrepancy is by no means unusual. In an era of high birth rate, high infant mortality and no strict compulsion over recording births, a degree of laxity was commonplace. Sixty-seven was an above average age to live to in the mid 19th century. Housing was poor, sanitation bad and medical knowledge primitive. He died at 3 St George's Road, Kemp Town, Brighton. Why he should die at this address is difficult to answer. It was the home of a Mrs Emily French, a widow and laundress.

The most probable explanation is that he was taking the sea air in Brighton to recuperate from illness. People were obsessed by bad air in cities during this period, blaming it as a cause of cholera, etc. "Disease of the liver" would mean that Boss had been seriously ill for a fair length of time and this sojourn to Brighton might have been an ignorant attempt to ameliorate his condition. There was a Maria Kenna of 12 Brewers Green, Westminster, present at his death. She would have been a servant or a nurse and this tends to support the idea that Boss was in Brighton for health reasons. The fact that his wife did not accompany him suggests that Boss was not on holiday in Brighton and that she remained in London to run the business.

"Disease of the liver" is suspect since gunmakers have

a reputation for replacing lost fluid whilst sweating at the bench. Some of Boss's letters are not in his usual copperplate, they are distinctly shaky!

The body of Thomas Boss was brought home to London by train and he was buried on 24th August 1857. He is interred in private grave compartment, no. A.D., 77.6 x 127.0 in the Brompton Cemetery, London. The funeral ceremony was performed by the Rev A. Badger.

The Brompton Cemetery, founded in 1831, was originally named the West of London and Westminster Cemetery. It covers thirty-eight acres, and was one of the earliest large cemeteries opened to relieve the over-crowded churchyards of London. Several prominent Victorians are buried there. Of note are Emmeline Pankhurst, the Suffragette, and Sir James K. Shuttleworth, the founder of popular education.

On the tombstone, the following epitaph, is inscribed:

Sacred to the memory of Thomas Boss, gunmaker of St James's Street, who died 17th August 1857, aged 66 years. Blessed are the dead which die in the Lord. Also of Emma, wife of the above, who died 29th July 1872, aged 77 years. Looking unto Jesus.

Also interred in the grave is Annie Mears, age 6, the daughter of Boss's niece and nephew Ann and William Mears who died in December 1862.

Unfortunately today the cemetery is very overgrown and delapidated. Boss's grave is difficult to find being covered in undergrowth and vegetation and is in a very poor state of repair.

In his Will, proved in London on 15th October 1857, he left virtually everything to his wife.

The Will states the following:

THIS IS THE LAST WILL AND TESTAMENT OF ME THOMAS BOSS of No. 73 Saint James's Street, Westminster, Gunsmith. I give unto my dear wife Amy Chapman Boss the leasehold house and premises wherein I now reside situated No. 73 Saint James's Street, aforesaid absolutely subject to the payment of the rent and performance of the covenants contained in the lease under which I hold the same. I give unto my two sisters Parnell Boss and Caroline (Catherine) Boss, one hundred pounds each to be paid to them respectively free from legacy duty. I give unto my nephew Edward Paterson (Paddison), now residing with us, fifty pounds free from legacy duty. I give unto Richard Waite of Pelham Square, Louth, in Lincolnshire, Gentleman, one of my trustees here-inafter named, twenty pounds free from legacy duty. I give devise and bequeath unto my dear wife Amy Chapman Boss all the REST, RESIDUE AND REMAINDER of my personal estate absolutely, for her sole and separate use and benefit and I empower my trustees hereinafter named to compound or allow time or attempt security for the payment of debts

The grave of Thomas and Emma Boss in the Brompton Cemetery, London.

Thomas Boss's will proved in London, 15th October 1857.

owing to my estate and to adjust by arbitration or otherwise disputes in relation thereto   I declare that my said trustees shall pay and allow to each other all reasonable expenses they may incur in the execution of the trusts of this my will and also that they shall not be responsible for any involuntary loss, I appoint my dear wife Amy Chapman Boss, EXECUTRIX and James James, of Shotts Croft Edenbridge, Kent, Gentleman, and the said Richard Waite, EXECUTORS and trustees of this my will. Lastly, I revoke all other wills and declare this to be my last will and testament in witness whereof I have hereunto set my hand this twenty-first day of July, the year of our Lord, one thousand, eight hundred and fifty seven.

Thomas

His   X   Mark

Boss

The "blank" indicates an illegible word in the original will.

He was a very sick man at the time of writing this will. Notice how he could not manage to sign his name at the bottom, putting an "X" instead. Only three weeks after writing this Will, Thomas Boss died.

Unfortunately, no obituary exists for Thomas Boss. What type of person was he? From the correspondence that survives, he comes over as an energetic business-man, very astute and keen to do well. He had a great interest and enthusiasm for guns. In particular he was

proud of the reputation that he had established for his company building guns of the highest quality only. That he was a gunmaker of extraordinary skill there is no doubt. By looking at the very early records of his work in the 1820s, he was proficient at every aspect of gunmaking from stocking, to making furniture, to fin-ishing, to barrel-making, etc. This type of consummate skill is very unusual as most gunmakers had the exper-tise to specialise in one particular area only. He had done extremely well for himself. His origins were hum-ble – another journeyman gunmaker. Yet he ended up as a result of his own expertise and diligence as the owner of a highly profitable business at the top end of the trade in St James's at no. 73 St James's Street.

An interesting advertisement appeared in *The Field* from 22 August 1857 onwards for some months. It read:

George Fuller, Gunmaker, 280 Strand (having heard of the decease of Thos Boss, the celebrated gunmaker of St James's Street) begs to inform noblemen and gentlemen, that he, having learnt the business of a gunmaker from the school of Joseph Manton, will be found equally competent to carry out every part of mechanical power as well as shape, weight, etc to the precise model of T. Boss's guns.

Just as Boss had used his old employer, Joseph Manton, for advertising, George Fuller attempted to cash in on the death of Boss.

THOMAS BOSS & CO. 1857–66

When Thomas died, the firm of Thomas Boss was deprived of its gunmaking leadership. Thomas Boss would make, understand and oversee the manufacture of all his guns, since it was a modest sized gunmaking firm. Although Mrs Boss participated in the running of the firm, she would not have the practical knowledge of gunmaking technique that would be required. Boss's death had occurred at a tricky time in gunmaking. The change-over to pinfire and central fire breech-loading guns, was in its infancy. New gunmaking techniques would be required that would be outside the ken of Mrs Boss. In addition, she was now sixty-two years of age and probably felt that she could not manage the business on her own.

She would have to look for a new head well versed in best gun manufacture. Her nephews, Edward and James Paddison, were being groomed to take over the firm. She intended that they should form a partnership and run the business later on. Mrs Boss thought that James was too young and inexperienced for such a venture at present. Edward was thirty-two years of age and his younger brother James, fifteen years of age, still in his apprenticeship.

The gunmaker Mrs Boss chose to head the firm was Stephen Grant. He had served his apprenticeship under the Dublin gunmaker William Kavanagh who, during Grant's apprenticeship, did business at 4 Upper Ormand Quay. After completing his apprenticeship, Stephen Grant moved to the firm of Charles Lancaster, well known for his top quality barrels, beautifully bored and finished, that he supplied to the Trade. His barrels are stamped "C.L.". Colonel Hawker in *Instructions to Young Sportsmen* had high regard for these barrels. He stated, "Lancaster, who has raised many gunmakers to the head of the trade, by allowing them to put their names to what was his work in all the essential part of barrels, has some time started for himself. This I advised him to do if ever Joe retired – and I anticipate that he will sooner or later be entitled to the name of leader, vice Joseph Manton."

Charles Lancaster at 151 New Bond Street was a best gunmaking firm, building guns and rifles of the highest quality. In 1843 he received his first Royal Appointment to the Prince Consort. Stephen Grant would therefore be well versed in the construction of best quality guns and he left Lancaster for Thomas Boss around 1850. Here his work and skills must have been duly noted since Mrs Boss asked Stephen Grant to become managing partner of the firm on the death of Thomas Boss.

Thus in 1857, the firm became a private partnership called Thomas Boss & Co. and the guns of this period are engraved, "Thomas Boss & Co.". Sometimes it is

Stephen Grant 1821–98. Managing Partner of Thomas Boss & Co. 1857–66.

shortened to, "T. Boss & Co.", the style used on some of the firm's headed notepaper. At Boss today, they still use a mahogany gun cabinet built during this period, with the lettering, "T. Boss & Co., 73 St James' Street".

Even at this time, companies had to keep proper records of partnerships by law. The company record file of Thomas Boss & Co. and Boss & Co. 1857–1930 remained intact until 1st July 1963. It was then destroyed by the Public Record Office as being of no historical interest. Very annoying to say the least, since it would have provided a wealth of information during this period.

It would be Stephen Grant that would preside over Boss when the biggest change to gunmaking techniques took place, the changeover to breech-loaders in the 1860s.

Breech-loaders were of continental origin, at first largely ignored by the British gun trade. They first appeared publicly in Britain at the 1851 Great Exhibition. Probably the most important exhibit was no. 1308, a pinfire gun and cartridge by Lefaucheux that would provide the example for the future. Many people assume that sportsmen and gunmakers instantly saw the benefits of the breech-loader and innundated firms with orders. This is certainly not the case. Even two years later in 1853, when *The Field* ran a series of articles entitled "Hints to Young Shooters on Guns", breech-loaders are not mentioned. It was not until the very late 1850s that British gunmakers began to produce pinfire breech-loaders in any quantity.

The Lefaucheux breech-loader and pinfire cartridge as exhibited at The Great Exhibition 1851. Notice the forward underlever, lack of extractors and the single-bite locking mechanism.

Controversy raged over the respective merits of the muzzle-loading and breech-loading systems. Nowhere is this more evident than in *The Field* first published on 1st January 1853 intending to be a weekly newspaper for the country gentleman. By 1858 its editor was John Henry Walsh ("Stonehenge") who organised a series of trials to be held on 9th and 10th April 1858 under his superintendance. He hoped it would settle the rivalry over the two systems. The tests would include driving power of shot, regularity of delivery of shot and the amount of recoil.

The official results were published in *The Field* of 17 April. The trials proved inconclusive, both protaganists finding statistics to suit their own bias. Another trial was held on 4th and 5th July 1859; the breech-loader emerged as the equal of the average muzzle-loader. Even within one year great strides had been made in the understanding and construction of breech-loaders.

It is from this point forward that breech-loaders began to prove their superiority and to be built in increasing numbers.

In both the trials the London gunmakers were notably absent, including Boss. The answer to this is simple. Breech-loaders were in their infancy. Why publicly destroy a hard earned reputation with an un-reliable or inferior breech-loader?

The first breech-loader to be built by Boss was a double-barrel 14-bore pinfire shotgun no. 1600. This gun was ordered on 9th June 1858 by G. B. Bruce, First Regiment Lifeguards and completed shortly afterwards. There is a record of an earlier breech-loader being ordered on 9th April 1858 but for some reason the order ledger states "not to be put in hand at present". No. 1620 was the second example built for H. W. Lindow, 54 Wigmore Street, London. This was another double-barrel 14-bore pinfire gun ordered on 5th July 1858. From then on, Boss built breech-loaders with increasing frequence – by 1863 the breech-loaders accounted for ninety per cent of production. The

production figures in this period show the immensely rapid change. The watershed was the year 1860 when a quite decisive change from muzzle-loaders to breech-loaders occured.

Date	No. muzzle-loders produced	No. breech-loaders produced
1859	75	15
1860	36	74
1861	16	83
1862	10	72

The last muzzle-loader built was no. 3078 a double-barrel 12-bore percussion gun with case and apparatus ordered in 1872 by Sir John Blois.

Stephen Grant became involved in the development of the breech-loader. It was during his period as the Managing Partner of Boss, that Grant brought out patent no. 1538 on 15th June 1861. The address on his patent was T. Boss & Co. 73 St James's Street. This was a patent for an early breech-loading action. The barrels pivoted at the extreme end of a rigid forend and were closed by an under lever. He does not make it clear in his patent exactly what the merit of this improvement is (see Appendix 8). Very few guns to this patent were built by Boss. Known examples are no. 1936, nos. 1967/8, no. 2252, no. 2439.

For some nine years Grant was the Managing Partner of Thomas Boss & Co. He then decided it was propitious for him to set up on his own. This he did in 1866, very close-by at 67a St James's Street. His business did very well receiving orders from the Royal Houses of Europe. He died on 21 January 1898. His obituary in *The Field* of 29th January 1898 makes reference to his time with Boss:

DEATH OF A WELL-KNOWN GUNMAKER

There has just passed away at the ripe age of 77, one who will probably be remembered as being amongst the first gunmakers of the century. We refer to Mr Stephen Grant of St James's Street, London, who died last week at his residence at Twickenham. The late Stephen Grant served his time to a gunmaker in Dublin, a very clever and inventive man named Kavanagh. On leaving Dublin, Mr Grant came to London and worked for Charles Lancaster and after-wards for Thomas Boss, subsequently entering into partnership with the latter. This partnership was dis-solved at the expiration of ten years and then Mr Grant commenced business for himself at 67a St James' Street. Mr Grant was a first class mechanic and was thoroughly acquainted with every department of gunmaking. He has undoubtedly turned out in his time some of the finest guns that have ever been produced for pigeon and game shooting, acquiring in the course of years a great reputation for the excellent workmanship, soundness of construction and good shooting and wearing properties of his guns. Mr Grant was ever content to be known by the quality of his work and thus was perhaps heard of less outside the circle of his clients than were others of his contemporaries.

Land and Water ran a series of articles in the 1880s on well known gunmakers, Stephen Grant being one of them. Teasdale-Buckell abridged this article for his book *Experts on Guns and Shooting* and it is this version that I have quoted below:

The firm of Grant is unquestionably one of the very oldest at present existing of the original London gun trade, Mr Grant having been in partnership with Mrs Boss, after the death of her husband, Thos. Boss. At the expiration of his partnership with Mrs Boss, Mr S. Grant started in business on his own account, and is to be found at 67a St. James's Street. To lovers of the trigger, and to those who are desirous to see what London can produce in the way of the highest class gun manufacture, a visit to the above address will be of great interest; and if Mr Grant should have time to "personally conduct" the visitor over his establishment, the pleasure will be doubly enhanced by the bonhomie of his jolly presence, and his hearty love of a good all-round sportsman and for sport in its various phases; and if the pleasant chat on guns and shooting should be interrupted by individuals dropping in now and again with a word for Mr Grant's private ear, in reference to 'the odds,' why, 'what's the odds,' and we mean to gratify no curiosity except in relation to guns and their equipments at 67a St. James's Street. The world has used Mr Grant well, and he appreciates her kind attentions as is evidenced by the comfortable appearance of his portly figure and the merry twinkle in his eye; nevertheless, he will come forward simply in his shirt-sleeves and working apron to greet any who should chance to call.

After Grant set up on his own there was either some healthy business rivalry or some animosity between Mrs Boss and Grant, for the following announcements appeared several times in *The Field*. For example in *The Field* of 7 January 1871:

Stephen Grant, 67a St James's Street, S.W. (corner of St James's Place) late Managing Partner in the firm of Boss & Co. Breech- and Muzzle-loading Gun and Rifle Manufacturers, begs to inform the nobility and gentry that the partnership is dissolved and his business is now carried on as above.

Later a rival announcement followed. For example in *The Field* of 6th July 1872:

BOSS & CO. GUN AND RIFLE MANUFACTURERS

Boss & Co. beg respectfully to inform their numerous patrons and the nobility and gentry generally, that their business is carried on at their old established shop, 73 St James's Street (next door to the Conservative Club) and that they have no connection whatever with any other house. N.B. Several good second-hand guns and rifles for sale by celebrated makers.

CHAPTER FOUR

THE GUNS AND RIFLES OF THE MUZZLE-LOADING ERA

To read through Boss's ledgers of this period is like thumbing through a copy of *Who's Who*. The aristocracy of all ranks feature primarily as his customers. There is a large contingent of army officers and a surprisingly large number of churchmen.

The letter illustrated opposite refers to a double-barrel 14-bore percussion gun no. 900 built for the Duke of Parma, Italy in 1849.

During 1848, there were revolutions in many European countries, caused mainly by economic recession and a sense of political frustration. In Italy this took the form of a patriotism to eject Austrian influence. Many of the rulers were forced to grant constitutional reform. The Austrians fought back, invaded Parma on their way southwards and, with the aid of the French, the revolutions were crushed by the summer of 1849. However, when the Duke of Parma's gun was nearly finished in May 1849, the country was still in a state of flux, hence Boss's letter. The Duke of Parma eventually did get the gun and later went on to order a pair of guns and a rifle.

A shooter and a loader using a pair of guns on an organised shoot in the 19th century.

By the time Thomas Boss had thoroughly established himself as a gunmaker, the style of shooting had changed considerably from the previous century. In the 18th century, most shooters would walk up game with dogs. Organised shoots were not common since flintlock guns could not be loaded quickly enough. This meant that pairs of guns were rarely built.

By the mid 19th century the effects of the industrial revolution had made an impact on the existing class structure. The nouveau riche had made vast sums of money from industry and wanted to find acceptance into the ranks of the landed aristocracy by buying estates. A good example of this is Mr Brassey, one of the main railway contractors in the "railway mania" period in the 1840s. He bought up estates for himself and family, developed an interest in shooting and was one of Boss's best customers.

The upshot of this was that shooting gained in popularity and a new style of shooting evolved. By new style of shooting, I mean organised shoots with keepered game and beaters. The percussion system had a lot to do with the new style since a percussion gun could be loaded far more quickly than a flintlock. This called for a different approach to guns. Pairs of guns were now made in increasing quantities and a loader was employed to cope with the additional barrage. Thomas Boss built nearly as many pairs of guns as he did single guns in the percussion period. A great many of the guns were built with no ramrod, to make them lighter. Substantial loading rods were always provided in the cases for the loader. Many people assume that these guns, bereft of ramrod, were live pigeon guns. Although some of them are, for the greater part this is an erroneous assumption. If they are engraved with a "No. 1" or "No. 2", showing that they are of a pair, then they are game guns.

By far the majority of guns built in this period are double shotguns. A few rifles were built but very, very few pistols. (See Appendix 5A for the breakdown of gun

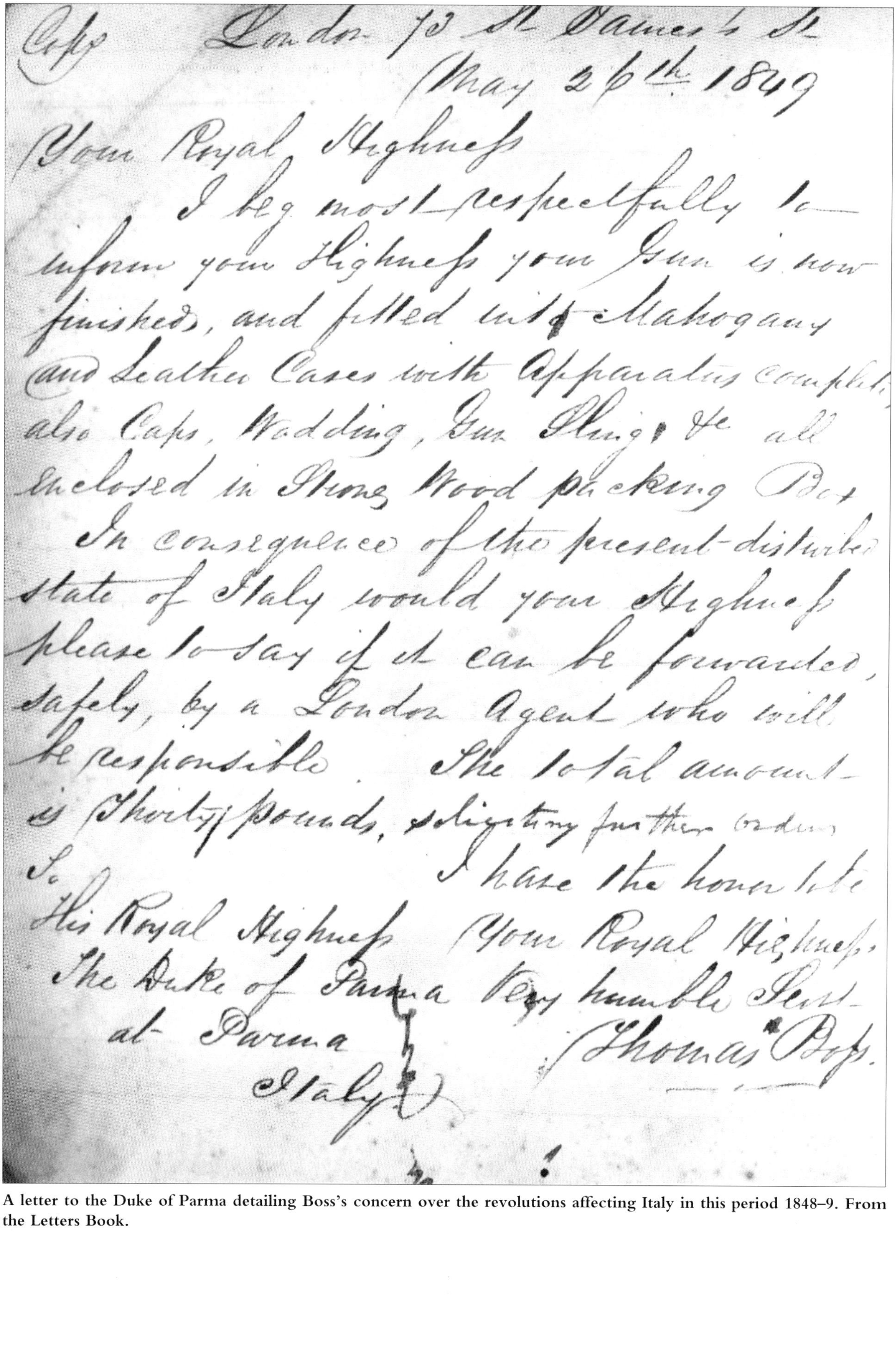

Copy

London 73 St. James's St
May 26th 1849

Your Royal Highness

I beg most respectfully to inform your Highness your Gun is now finished, and fitted into Mahogany and Leather Cases with Apparatus complete, also Caps, Wadding, Gun Slings &c all enclosed in Strong Wood packing Box.

In consequence of the present disturbed state of Italy would your Highness please to say if it can be forwarded safely, by a London Agent who will be responsible. The total amount is Thirty pounds, soliciting further orders

So I have the honor to

His Royal Highness   Your Royal Highness
The Duke of Parma   Very humble Serv.
    at Parma   Thomas Boss.
        Italy

A letter to the Duke of Parma detailing Boss's concern over the revolutions affecting Italy in this period 1848–9. From the Letters Book.

production at this time.) The double shotgun was Boss's bread and butter. It was what his customers wanted and he produced around seventy double guns per year in the 1840s and 1850s.

Boss's guns were not cheap even in their day. Due to the tardy payment problem, he always offered a discount for cash. The prices below are average prices for his guns.

Double Gun, Case and Apparatus	35 gns.
Pair of Guns, Case and Apparatus	72 gns.
Double Rifle, Case and Apparatus	£52.10s.0d.
Single Rifle, Case and Apparatus	£31.10s.0d.
Rifle Barrels	20 gns.
Shotgun Barrels	12 gns.
New Stock and Locks	£14.14s.0d.
Pistol Hand Stock	£4.14s.6d.
Safety Guard Stock	£6.6s.0d.
Cases and Apparatus	£5.0s.0d.
Altering Flintlocks to Percussion	£3 – £6.
Second-hand Pair of Double Guns of his own make	£60.0s.0d.

Usually Boss quoted his terms in guineas and not pounds sterling but there are instances in his correspondence when his customers remitted pounds for guineas. Boss stood out for his price. He had a genial way of reminding his customers of their errors in respect to payments:

My Lord, I have to solicit that your Lordship will remember that when Pounds are taken for Guineas there is a loss, whether the amount be 90 or 100.

Many customers part exchanged their old guns, trading in guns as little as two years old for brand new ones. Guns were built with remarkable rapidity, customers ordering and receiving their guns often within the space of two months. Although the records state that sometimes a stock gun was used for a rushed order, a great many of the guns were made from scratch.

A great many letters survive in the Letters Book detailing prices and quotes for the guns.

London, 73 St James's Street,
24th November 1845,

Sir,

I beg leave most respectfully to inform You I make many Rifles both double and single. I have now new orders for Double Rifles.

The price of a Double Rifle is Fifty Guineas without Cases of Apparatus, the Cases complete with all the Apparatus is Five Guineas extra.

Fitting new Double Rifle Barrels into your flat Gun Stock, cash price is Twenty Guineas.

I remain Sir
Your Very Humble Servant
Thomas Boss

H Cavendish-Taylor Esq
Dalmeny Park
Edinburgh

Making extra rifle barrels later on, to fit a shotgun stock, was not uncommon. When serial nos. of rifle barrels do not match up to a stock, this is what has happened. Cavendish-Taylor in the end did not buy a new rifle from Boss. Later on he would buy a pair of double guns nos. 737 and 738 in 1846.

Another letter dated 30th October 1847 shows other aspects of percussion guns at the time:

London, 73 St James's Street
30th October 1847,

Sir,

I have received the honor of an order for a pair of Guns for you by the recommendation of A. Cator Esq – precisely the same as Mr Cator's new gun; except your guns are not to have Safety Guards, the barrels also are to fit either stock. Permit me to ask you if you wish the Stocks to be varnished? I make most without it; also if you wish the Nipples, Westley Richards' size? – please to inform me if you have shot with Mr Cator's new Gun so as to be certain the stock fits you; the Guns are also to be fitted into separate cases each one complete which may be strapped together for travelling; also please to send an Inscription for the crest if it is to be in each stock.

I have, Sir, no doubt of having the pair ready for trial the beginning of December if not completed in consequence of having barrels made the exact size already; allow me to say it will be Two Guineas extra the Barrel being made to fit either stock; 72 guineas The Pair of Guns Complete.

I have the honor
To be Sir
Your Humble Servant
Thomas Boss

To The Hon. Edward Lawless

Mr Cator's new gun was no. 805 and the pair ordered by Edward Lawless were nos. 801 and 802. This letter illustrates the dating problem of some guns. Boss's building of guns was not strictly numerical. Mr Cator's gun, no. 805, was in existence before Mr Lawless's nos. 801 and 802.

Notice how it costs extra to get the barrels to fit either stock. Matched pairs are often not matched pairs, but rather guns that look identical. Customers often wanted barrels to be interchangeable since it was easy for the owner or servant to damage a gun by fitting the wrong barrels in the wrong stock. Also note how most customers supplied a copy of their crest for engraving on the silver escutcheons fitted to all guns.

Boss offered the guns for trial in 1847. In his letters he makes frequent references to this. Customers could take their guns out for trial before they were fully finished.

Boss could then make adjustments to length of stock bend, etc, rather than alter the final product.

Although Boss could use any gun he wanted he did make a couple of guns for his own use and tests. Guns nos. 667 and 721, both double guns, are listed as being for his own use. Both were later sold. Does anybody have them today?

The gun illustrated above right is a double-barrel 19-bore percussion converted to pinfire sporting gun no.

Pinfire gun no. 196. See plate 2.

196. To date this gun is the earliest extant Boss gun. The address on the barrel is no. 1 Grosvenor Street, so it could be dated fairly precisely to 1833/1835.

The gun has 27¾″ twist barrels originally proved at 19-bore but later reproofed at 18-bore probably at the time of conversion. The number "196" is stamped underneath the forend loop. The raised top rib is engraved, "Thomas Boss, No. 1 Grosvenor St, New Bond St, London". The tang has very fine bold engraving, very similar in style to the later Boss guns of the 1840s. The locks are sparsely scroll engraved in the style

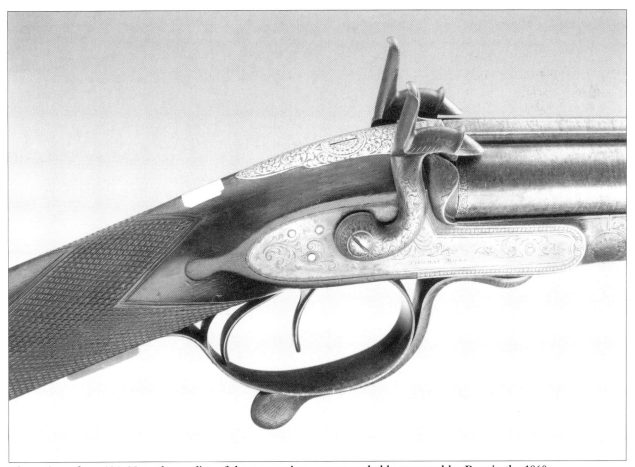

The action of no. 196. Note the quality of the conversion – most probably executed by Boss in the 1860s.

A lock from no. 196. The top of the lock-plate has been cut down to incorporate the conversion.

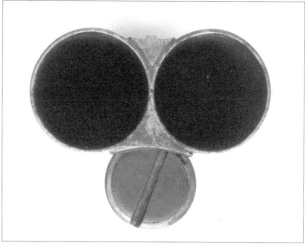

The silver triangular foresight inlet into the end of the barrels on all Boss percussion guns.

of the 1830s and have been cut down at the top to incorporate the conversion. They are engraved, "Thomas Boss". A trigger guard safety is present as befitted contemporary fashion. The stock, although altered, is original with largish checkering and an octagonal silver escutcheon is fitted behind the tang, again in the style of early 19th-century guns. The quality of the entire gun is superb, proving that from the outset Thomas Boss produced only one quality.

Around 1860 the gun was converted to pinfire. I have no doubt that the gun was returned to Boss for this work. Conversion from muzzle-loading to breech-loading was not at all simple and involved considerable rebuilding of the gun. Like the gun itself, the quality of the conversion is first rate, the new breech, hammers and engraving being second to none. Boss's records of the period show them undertaking many such conversions.

The illustration below shows a pair of double-barrel 14-bore tubelock guns nos. 682 and 683 constructed in 1846 for the Marquis of Blandford. John Winston Spencer Churchill, the Marquis of Blandford of Blenheim Palace, was born on 2nd June, 1822. He was Conservative M.P. for Woodstock 1844–1845, 1847–1857 and was an ardent free trade supporter of Sir Robert Peel. On 20th July 1857 he succeeded to become the Duke of Marlborough.

These guns are a late use of the tube-lock. The tube-lock was an early percussion system invented in 1818 by Joseph Manton. A thin copper tube filled with detonating compound was inserted into the vent in the breech. It was held in place by a spring clip. When the hammer struck the tube, the compound exploded and ignited the main charge. Because the tube had a relatively large amount of detonating compound contained within it, detonation was violent and ignition certain; one fact why many shooters preferred tube-locks to the normal copper cap.

The barrels are 30½″ long and have a triangular silver foresight inlet into the *end* of the barrels. This

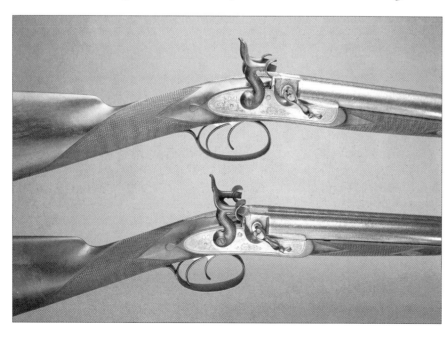

Tube-lock guns nos. 682 and 683. See Plate 3.

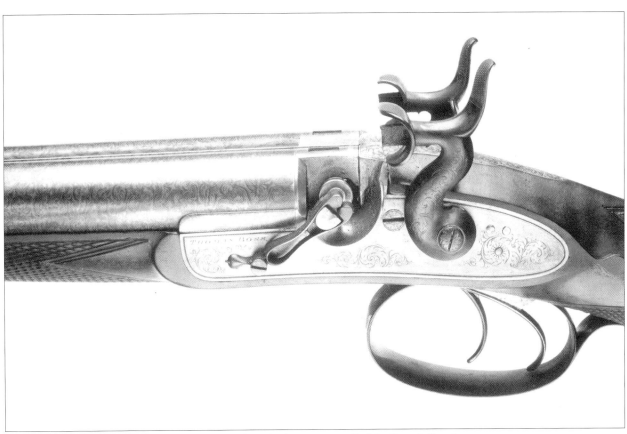

The tube-lock of gun no. 683 built in 1846. These locks were supplied by Joseph Brazier.

triangular foresight will be found on all Boss muzzle-loading sporting guns. If a silver bead foresight is fitted, it is an indication that the barrels have been shortened some time later.

The barrels are stamped, "TP" underneath. This is the mark of the barrel-maker, Thomas Parkin, 5 Meards Court, Soho, London. The top ribs are engraved, "Thomas Boss, 73 St James' Street, London". There are no ramrods fitted to the gun. The breeches have platinum poincons inlet into them. These are stamped, "Thomas

Boss, London". Poincons are usually associated with the flintlock/early percussion era. Like the tubelocks this is a late use for them in the 1840s. The locks are engraved, "I.B." being supplied by Joseph Brazier, Wolverhampton. The stocks are finely figured and chequered at both wrist and forend. These guns are in remarkable original condition, with much original barrel colour and furniture blue. In addition, they show little evidence of use. Unfortnately the original two-tier oak case for the guns is missing.

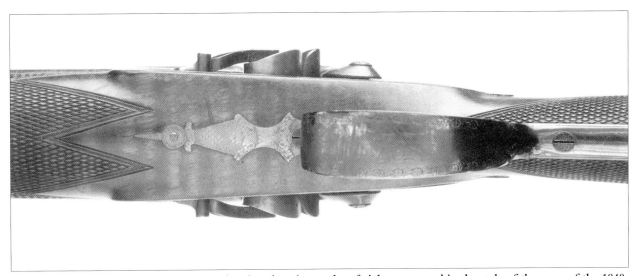

The underside of tube-lock gun no. 683 showing the trigger plate finial as engraved in the style of the guns of the 1840s and early 1850s.

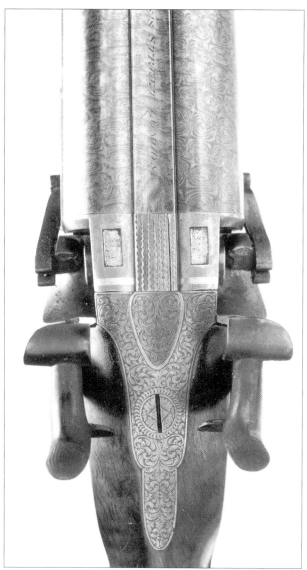

The breech of tube-lock gun no. 682 showing the platinum poincons stamped, "Thomas Boss, London".

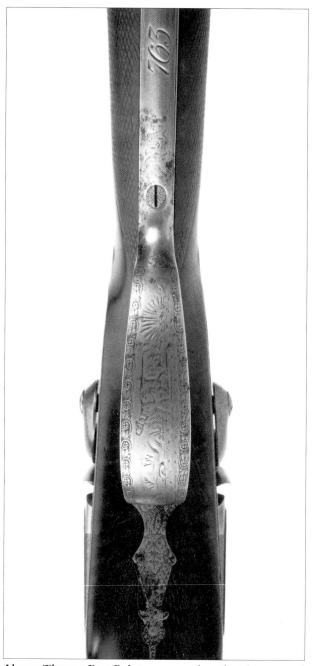

Above: Thomas Boss Pointer engraved on the trigger guard of most sporting guns *circa* 1850.
Below: Percussion guns nos. 763 and 827. See Plates 4 and 5.

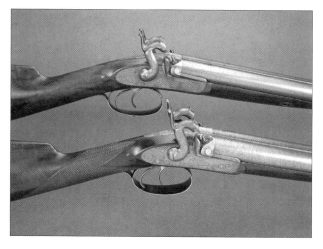

The guns below right are a composite pair of double-barrel 14-bore percussion sporting guns nos 763 and 827 built in 1847/48 for Captain Edward Goulburn, a Captain in the Grenadier Guards from Betchworth House, Surrey. His father was Henry Goulburn, the Chancellor of the Exchequer in Sir Robert Peel's Administration of 1841–1846. Captain Goulburn was born in 1816, retired as a Colonel in 1860 and died in 1887. He was a good customer of Boss, ordering many guns from them during his life.

There is a popular misconception about composite pairs of guns. Many people assume that they are two guns put together to make a pair and enhance the value. Although this does happen on occasions, this does not constitute a true composite pair. In this case, Captain Goulburn ordered no. 763 in 1847 as a single gun. He must have been well pleased with the gun for one year later in 1848 he ordered no. 827 to be built to match no. 763. A double case was then supplied to fit the pair.

The gun numbers 763 and 827 stamped onto the lid of the case.

This type of situation was not uncommon. In the firm's ledgers, there are frequent references to guns being ordered to match guns bought, in some instances several years previously. Double gun cases are always stamped beneath the trade label with the gun numbers and this is a very quick check to find out if the pair of guns in the case are a genuine composite pair.

The pair have an almost late flintlock style about them: they are fairly heavy and there is a considerable drop in the stock. The locks by Joseph Brazier are engraved, "Thomas Boss".

No. 763 has a highly figured stock, no. 827 not quite so spectacular. The stocks, chequered at both wrist and forend, have drop points behind the locks. Apart from stock colour the guns are identical in all other respects.

The Damascus barrels are 30¾″ long, have platinum vents and have the usual triangular silver foresight inlet into the end of the barrels. The barrels are stamped, "T.P." underneath, the mark of the barrel-maker Thomas Parkin. The top ribs are engraved, "Thomas Boss, 73 St James' Street, London". The trigger guards have the gun numbers engraved in bold scroll engraving and pointer dogs are engraved on the bow of the guards.

The tangs have fine scroll engraving.

A pheasant is engraved on the butt plate. Captain Goulburn's family crest is engraved on the escutcheons and also on the lid of the case – a dove with an olive branch – a slightly ironic engraving considering the nature of the article! Each gun has the relevant No. 1 or No. 2 engraved on the top rib, on the trigger guard and on the butt plate.

When dismantled these guns display the qualities that explain why Thomas Boss rose to such prominence as a leading gunmaker. Every single part is finished to the

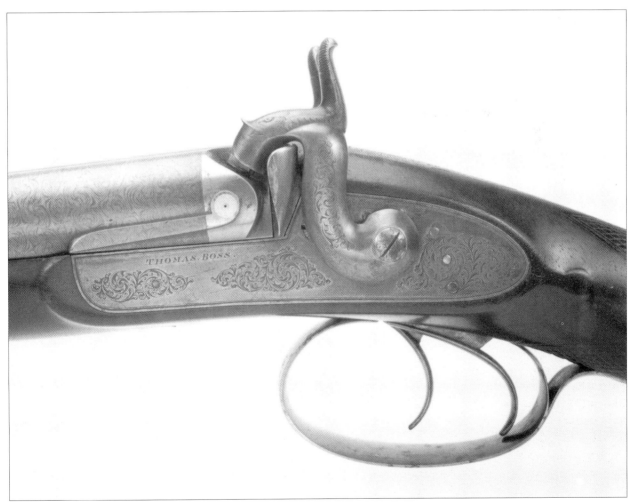

Detail on the lock work of gun no. 827.

The finely engraved tang of gun no. 827, having been engraved by John Sumner, 10 Queen Street, Soho, London.

highest standard both inside and out and most are numbered to the gun. The nipples are engraved L1, L2, R1, R2. (L2 and R2 refer to the spare nipples in the case.) The trigger guards, tangs, barrel bolts, inside of hammers, triggers, inside of locks, side nails and ramrods are all engraved with the relevant number. Even the forends of the stock are so stamped.

The guns are contained in their original oak two-tier case. The top tray contains the barrels, two loading rods, a spare ramrod, two leather shot pouches, one stamped, "Bishop, Bond Street" (this one supplied by Westley Richards), both engraved with the owner's initials, "E.G.", two steel-bodied powder flasks by Brazier again engraved, "E.G." and a linen bag containing cleaning jags.

The lower compartment contains two shot belt slings, a shot belt by Hawksley, a nipple key, a percussion cap

tin, two wad punches, a pigskin nipple and side nail pouch, three turnscrews and a bag of Westley-Richards percussion caps.

A cased double-barrel 13-bore gun no. 778 is illustrated below. This gun was built in 1847 for G. S. Elliot, the Earl of Minto of Minto House, Hawick. The gun, case and accessories are all in original unrestored condition that to my mind makes them of greater interest to the historian in search of authenticity. The locks with their typical 1840s simple scroll engraving are marked, "I B", being Brazier locks. The stock, chequered at wrist and forend and with carved drop points, bears the crest of Elliot on the escutcheon. The gun's number "778" is visibly stamped on the forend wood and engraved upon the trigger guard. As usual the pointer dog is there on the guard. The 30½" Damascus barrels with platinum vents are stamped underneath, "C A", being the mark of the barrel-maker Aston, a barrel-maker little used by Thomas Boss. The silver triangular foresight and address, "Thomas Boss, 73 St James' Street, London" completes the barrels. The ramrod is numbered to the gun.

The gun is contained in its original oak case, being numbered, "778" on the body of the case beneath the label and beneath the compartment lid. The baize lining is of a slightly darker green than usual. What is interesting about the case is that it does not have the correct label for the period – it has the later 19th-century Boss label. Immediately I assumed that the case had been relined and a new label fitted. However on close examination, the new label has been pasted over the original label. What happened was that the gun must have gone back to Boss for service or repair in the late 19th century and they pasted a new label on top of the original one. Labels are, after all, a form of advertising and Boss would have wanted to bring this gun up-to-date.

Most original accessories survive in the case. The steel bodied powder flask by Brazier is graduated 2½–3 drams and is stamped, "G S E", the owners initials. A

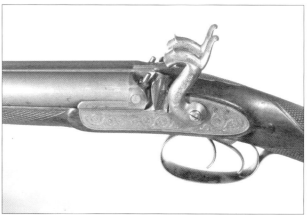

Percussion gun no. 778. See Plates 6 and 7.

Percussion gun no 813. See Plate 8.

silver mouthed shot pouch, again by Brazier, graduated 1⅛ oz – 1¼ oz. is of exceptional quality. There is a wad punch stamped, "No. 13", a turned ivory nipple box and an ivory nipple brush. The pigskin pouch contains a steel nipple key with pricker and detachable ends for storing spare nipples. Contained within this pouch is a spare side-nail engraved, "778". Again this pouch and contents are of very high quality. An ebony handled turnscrew and spare ramrod complete the accessories.

The illustration above is the gun that started my interest in Boss & Co. I purchased it as a teenager from a gamekeeper near Dunoon in Argyll. I was immediately impressed by the quality displayed throughout the gun.

Sir Archibald Islay Campbell, 1825–66, who ordered the pair of Boss percussion guns nos. 812 and 813. A portrait painted around the time that he received the guns in 1847.

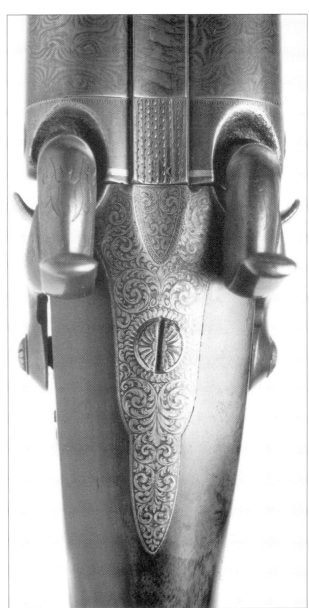

The acanthus engraved tang of double gun no. 813, engraved by John Sumner.

I read up most of the books that published accounts of early Boss history and was disappointed at the paucity of information. Embryonic research eventually resulted in this book.

No. 813 is the No. 2 gun of a pair. It is actually a mixture of the pair. The barrels are from the No. 1 gun, no. 812 and the stock from the No. 2 gun, no. 813. This is not uncommon. When percussion guns went out of fashion, they were often passed to gamekeepers or estate workers and pairs were split up and often muddled up in the process. When bought this gun had not been disturbed for many years and one barrel was still loaded!

Nos. 812 and 813 were built for Sir Archibald Islay Campbell of Garscube near Glasgow. The family had other estates at Cumlodden near Inverary, Argyll (near the present day Crarae Gardens) and it was probably here that the guns were used. Sir Archibald was born in

1825 and was MP for Argyll between 1851 and 1857 before dying at a comparatively young age in 1866.

Although well worn, the gun has a wonderful appearance. It has a highly figured stock and very graceful lines. The locks, by Joseph Brazier, are engraved, "Thomas Boss" and the 31″ Damascus barrels engraved, "Thomas Boss, 73 St James' Street, London". The barrels have "T.P." stamped underneath being made by Thomas Parkin, London. The barrels have the typical Boss triangle silver foresight. The tang has very fine scroll engraving as shown in the illustration previous page, and was once again executed by John Sumner. The trigger guard has the standard Boss pointer dog engraved upon it. The stock is chequered at both wrist and forend and drop points are carved behind the locks.

The rifle illustrated right is a double barrel 16-bore big game rifle no 1037 ordered on 20th May, 1853 by an army officer, C. Williamson, serving with the 60th Rifles in the Cape of Good Hope. Double percussion rifles by Boss are extremely rare, a mere thirty-one being produced overall.

The 30″ barrels are by Thomas Parkin and have ten groove rifling. They are engraved, "Thomas Boss, 73 St James' Street, London". A Brazier made folding flap platinum lined sight is graduated in four flaps from

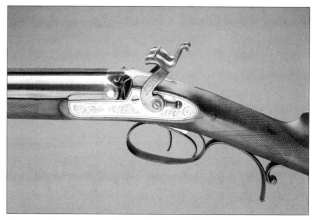

ABOVE: Percussion rifle no. 1037. See Plate 9.

RIGHT: The order for rifle no. 1037 completed on May 20th 1853 for C. Williamson Esq. of the 60th Royal Rifles. It had to be rifled the "same as Purdey and Joseph Manton" and was to be forwarded to "the Frontier" in the Cape of Good Hope. This order is yet another caveat in attempting to date precisely Boss guns from their serial numbers. No. 1037 should be placed in the year 1850, yet for some reason this serial number was not allocated until 1853.

BELOW: Detail on the lock of rifle no. 1037. Notice the flat hammers instead of the usual rounded examples.

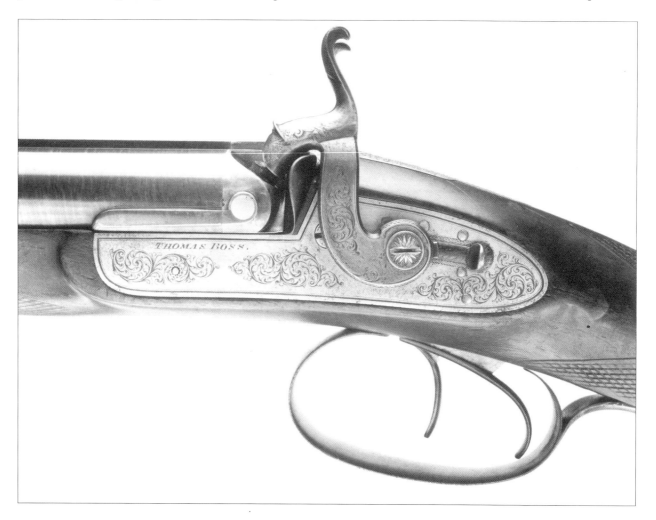

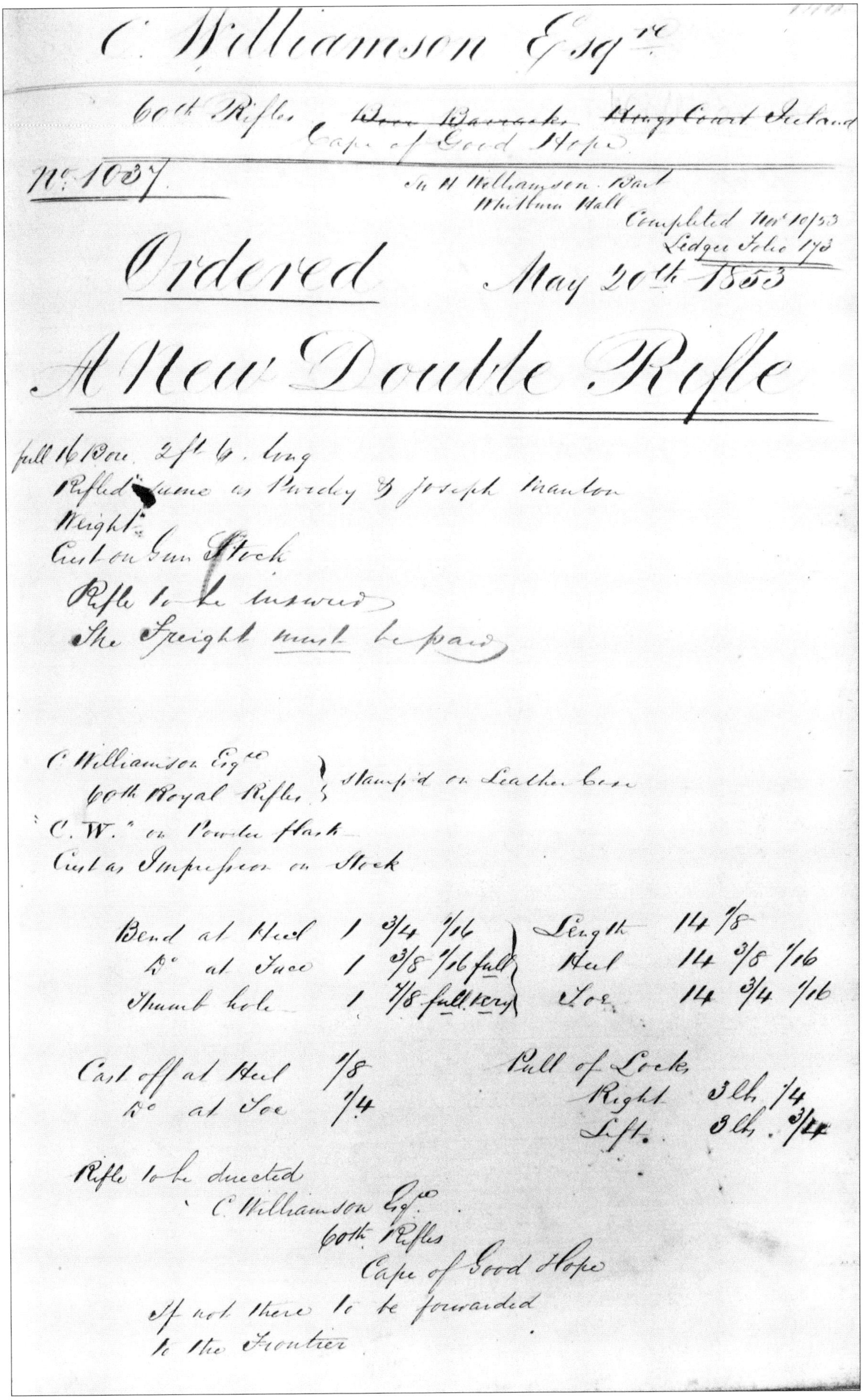

C. Williamson Esq.ᵗ

60th Rifles, Been Barracks Kingstown Ireland
Cape of Good Hope.

Nº 1037.

Sir H. Williamson Bart
Whitburn Hall
Completed Novʳ 10/53
Ledger Folio 173

Ordered May 20ᵗʰ 1853

A New Double Rifle

full 16 Bore. 2 ft 6. long
Rifled same as Purdey & Joseph Manton
Weight -
Crest on Gun Stock
Rifle to be answered
The Freight must be paid

C Williamson Esqʳᵉ
60th Royal Rifles } Stamp'd on Leather case
"C.W." on Powder flask
Crest as Impression on Stock

Bend at Heel	1	3/4 7/16	Length	14 1/8	
Dº at Face	1	3/8 7/16 full	Heel	14 3/8 7/16	
Thumb hole	1	7/8 full very	Toe	14 3/4 7/16	

Cast off at Heel 1/8
Dº at Toe 1/4

Pull of Locks
Right 5 lb. 1/4
Left 5 lb. 3/4

Rifle to be directed
C. Williamson Esqʳᵉ
60th Rifles
Cape of Good Hope
If not there to be forwarded
to the Frontier

The patch box of rifle no. 1037 showing the superb John Sumner engraving of a lion.

50–200 yards. The raised top rib is smooth over its entire length apart from a matted area round the foresight.

The Brazier supplied locks, engraved, "Thomas Boss" have safety bolts fitted to lock the hammers. What is unusual for a Boss percussion gun is that the hammers are flat instead of rounded. A grip tail guard is used and sling swivels are fitted. The figured stock has a cheekpiece. A patch box is fitted to the butt with a superb Sumner engraving of a lion (above). Originally the rifle was supplied in a case complete.

Thomas Boss built primarily sporting guns and rifles; hardly any pistols were built. The records state that sixteen pistols and four duelling pistols were constructed in total by the firm and an absolutely superb pair of pistols of the highest possible quality exist today in mint condition. Apart from their rarity and their incredible quality, what makes the pistols interesting is that no serial numbers are evident anywhere. These pistols were completely stipped down and no numbers or markings were present. In addition, Boss's records have no reference to them.

By examining the style of engraving on the locks, the pistols date from around the period 1850. The style of the pistols is quite flamboyant and coupled with their incredible quality leads one to assume that they were built especially for the Great Exhibition of 1851. The

reason that they do not appear in Boss's records, is that the records were for gun orders only. These pistols were never ordered, hence their lack of serial number and reference record. This further helps to ascertain the assumption that they were a one-off, specifically built by Thomas Boss himself for an auspicious occasion.

Originally the pistols must have been housed in a very special case with accessories, but unfortunately this is missing. Very little of their history is known but it is rumoured that for some time they existed in South America. It is indeed very fortunate that, sans case, they have remained in mint condition. The style is almost French, with their ornate barrels, checkering and chased silver mounts. They are so out with the normal Thomas Boss restrained British style that they must have been built as an example of "art" in combination with the skill of the gunmaker – another factor leading to the conclusion about their exhibition status.

The octagonal barrels have a quite extraordinary Damascus pattern of exceptional quality. The Damascus is in fact a thick veneer over an inner steel barrel tube. Muzzle-locking nuts about ¾″ long are screwed into the Damascus. The inner steel barrel tubes are attached to these muzzle-locking nuts – to make a barrel within a barrel. The barrels are rifled and so sharp is this rifling that if you put your little finger into it, and turn it, it

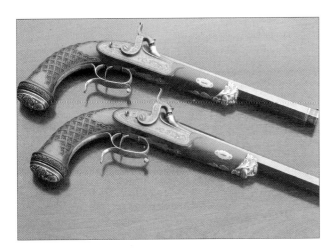

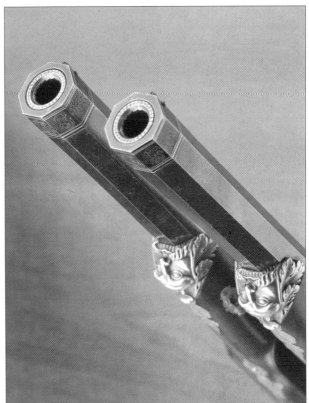

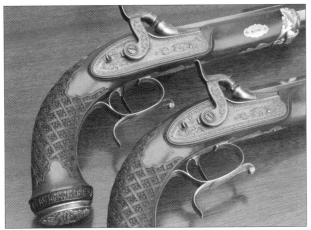

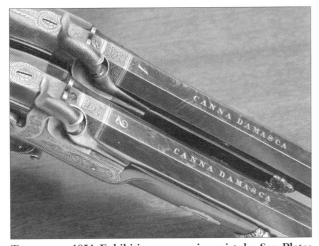

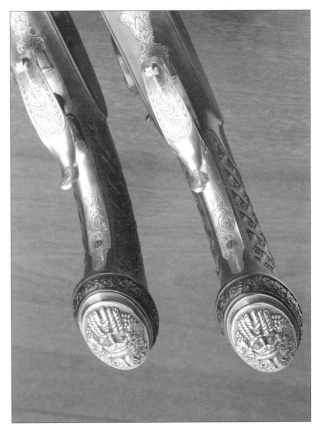

THIS PAGE: **1851 Exhibition percussion pistols. See Plates 11–15.**

will cut your finger! The barrels are inlaid with gold lettering "CANNA DAMASCA". "Canna" is the Latin word for a reed. "Canna Damasca" is in reference to the reed or barrel tube within the Damascus. At the breech end of the barrels a gold "1" or "2" is inlaid and gold lines circumvent the breech plugs and muzzle-locking nuts. Sights are fitted to breech and muzzle ends of the barrels. The breech plugs have platinum vents.

The lock plates and cocks are the only part of the pistols that have not been embellished. They are very typical Boss locks of the mid 19th century and have

been engraved by John Sumner. Safety bolts are fitted. The lock plates are engraved "Thos Boss".

The butts are of figured walnut and are checkered to an incredible standard in the form of a latticework infilled with roses. The forends have no checkering. The

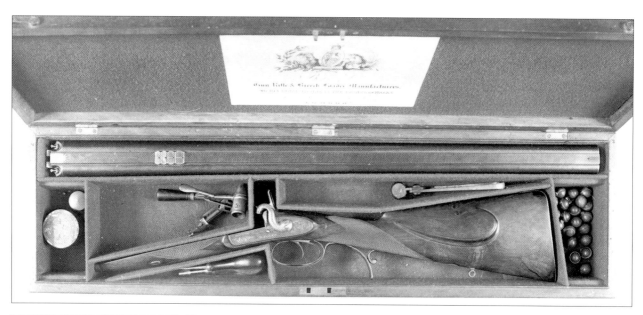

A double-barrel 16-bore belted ball two-groove deer rifle no. 1098 ordered on 6th June 1851 by The Hon. Beilby Lawley (case and label non original). See also plate 10.

The order for rifle no. 1098 dated 6th June 1851 from The Hon. Beilby Lawley. It states categorically, "No Pad on Rifle Stock" and that a, "New Bag Case of Leather" should be supplied. A later order was a, "Black Carriage Case" being in reference to a waterproof sailcloth case for limited carriage. Note the length of time it took to complete. December 17th 1852 was the completion date. From Boss's order ledgers.

stocks are complimented by chiselled and chased silver mounts again of exceptional quality. Silver butt caps in the shape of a grotesque bearded man complete the butts. The trigger guards are made out of silver and have a finger steady and fancy scroll to the bow of the guard. The barrel bolt escutcheons are of silver and the silver forend finials are in the same pattern of the grotesque bearded man. No hallmarks appear externally on these silver mounts. It was felt that, due to the mint condition of these pistols, it would be inadvisable to remove the mounts to check if any markings were apparent internally.

These pistols represent the art and the skill of the gunmaker at its ultimate. To Thomas Boss they must have been the culmination of his gunmaking career. It is interesting to ponder why he chose a pair of pistols instead of his more usual sporting gun or rifle. Perhaps pistols were something different for him; perhaps he wanted to show the French and Belgians in the 1851 Great Exhibition that he could make anything as good if not better than Le Page or Renette.

The Hon. Beilby Lawley of Escrick Park near York, who ordered the rifle no 1098 illustrated on the left, was born on 21st April, 1818 at the family's London home, 29 Berkeley Square. He was Liberal M.P. for Pontefract 1851–1852. In 1852 he succeeded to become Baron Wenlock. This is a 16-bore double-barrel rifle firing a belted ball through two-groove rifling. The barrels are stamped underneath, "T.P.", being Parkin barrels, and engraved on the rib, "Thomas Boss, 73 St James' Street, London". Platinum breech plugs are fitted and on the plain top rib there is a Brazier made platinum lined express leaf sight, sighted to 250 yds. Sights were platinum lined to assist aiming in conditions of poor light. The gold inlaid sunburst at the breech is non-original being applied comparatively recently.

The locks engraved, "I.B." by Joseph Brazier, are signed, "Thomas Boss" and have safety bolts fitted as was common to most rifles. The bow of the grip tail guard is engraved with a running stag, showing that this rifle was probably intended for deer hunting. The stock, chequered at both wrist and forend, has a cheekpiece and a circular patch box is inlet into the butt. The gun is contained in a mahogany case that is not original to the gun. The trade label dates from the 1880s and most of the accessories are associated and non-original. Nevertheless, it is a rare item. Boss only made thirty-one double percussion rifles.

The 12-bore no 1198 illustrated below was ordered by Hedworth Williamson of Whitburn Hall, Durham on August 30th 1852. Born on 25th March 1827, he was a Liberal M.P. for North Durham, 1864–74 and by 1877 had become High Sheriff of that county. The gun is contained in its original oak two-tier case for a pair of guns. The gun number, "1198" and nothing else is stamped in the usual place beneath the trade label. On 13th July 1854, Williamson ordered gun no. 1342 to match this gun – hence the reason for the double case.

The 30¾" Damascus barrels are engraved, "Thomas Boss, 73 St James' Street, London". They are by Smith, a barrel-maker little used by Boss, and have the silver triangular foresight. It is interesting that there is no mark of Smith the barrel-maker on the barrels though the records list Smith as the barrel-maker. The stock is chequered at both wrist and forend with drop points behind the locks. The Brazier locks are engraved, "Thomas Boss". The usual pointer dog is on the trigger guard and since Boss did not receive instructions to alter the engraving, no number "1" is found anywhere on the gun.

The following original accessories survive in the case:
1. A steel-bodied powder flask by Sykes graduated 2¼–3¼ drams.
2. A silver-mouthed shot pouch by Brazier graduated 1½–1¼ ounces.
3. A steel oil bottle by Hawksley.
4. A nipple key in its pigskin leather case.
5. A tin of percussion caps by Eley.

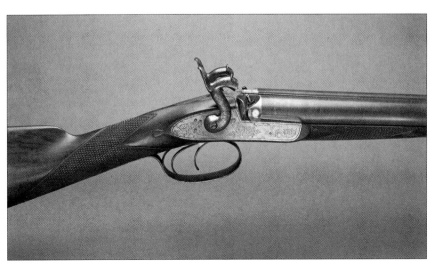

Percussion gun no. 1198. See Plates 17 and 18.

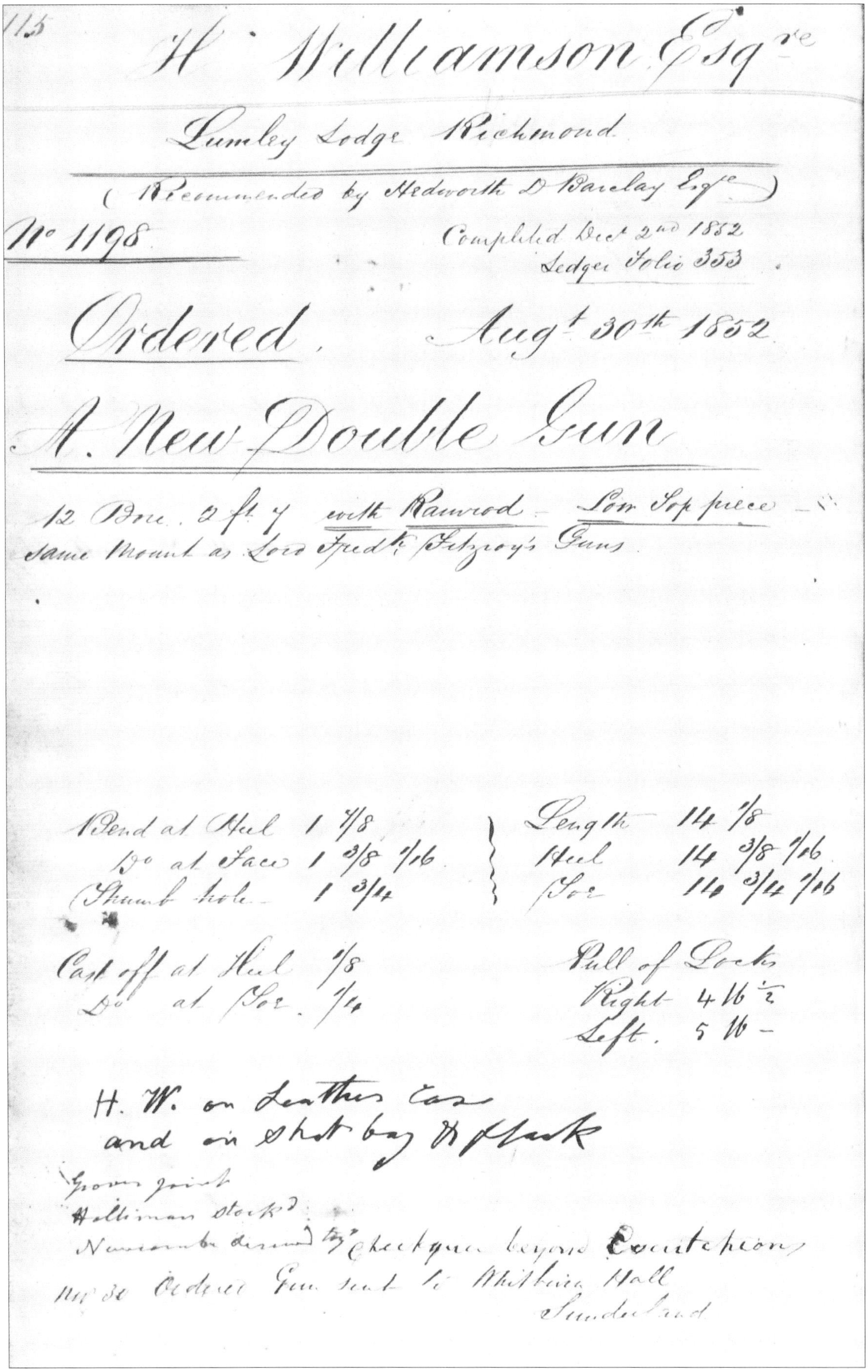

H. Williamson, Esqre

Lumley Lodge Richmond

(Recommended by Hedworth D Barclay Esqre)

N° 1198.   Completed Decr 2nd 1852
                           Ledger Folio 353

Ordered.   Augt 30th 1852.

A New Double Gun

12 Bore. 2 ft 7 with Ramrod — Low Top piece —
Same Mount as Lord Fred^k Fitzroy's Guns

Bend at Heel 1 7/8	Length 14 1/8
D° at Face 1 3/8 7/16	Heel 14 3/8 7/16
Thumb hole 1 3/4	Toe 14 3/4 7/16
Cast off at Heel 1/8	Pull of Locks
D° at Toe 1/4	Right 4 lb 1/2
	Left 5 lb —

H. W. on Leather Case
and on Shot bag & Flask

Brown joint
Williamson stock'd
N... der... by Checkquer beyond Escutcheon
N°... Ordered Gun sent to Whitburn Hall
                      Sunderland

The order for gun no. 1198 dated 30th August 1852 by Hedworth Williamson. Note the recommendation at the top of the order. Recommendation was the usual method for securing orders in this era.

A double-barrel 14-bore percussion gun no. 1359 built in 1853 for Reginald Gipps, to match his previous gun no. 1043.

The 14-bore gun no 1359 illustrated above was ordered by Reginald Gipps, 11 Chester Street, Belgrave Square, London, on 12th October 1853. It was built to match his previous gun no. 1043, thereby creating a composite pair. Reginald Gipps joined the Scots Guards and served in the Crimean War being present at the Battles of Alma and Inkerman. During the course of this conflict he was twice wounded. By 1878 he commanded the Scots Guards and by 1881 had risen to the rank of general. He received gun no. 1359 at the age of twenty-two.

The gun has a wonderful patina consistent with being well used, not abused in some restoration. The present owner bought it around 1950 for 10s. from a retired gamekeeper and it has hung over his mantelpiece ever since.

The Damascus barrels are 30" long and were supplied by Thomas Parkin. They are engraved, "Thomas Boss, 73 St James' Street, London", have platinum vents and the silver triangular foresight. The locks are stamped, "I B" being supplied by Joseph Brazier and are engraved, "Thomas Boss". A no. "2" has been engraved on the barrels, butt and trigger guard. A ramrod is fitted. The stock is of figured walnut, chequered at wrist and forend. The gun was originally fitted in a two-tier oak double tray case built to take the new pair, the old single case being allowed for in the sale.

The gun illustrated overleaf is a double-barrel 14-bore percussion gun no. 1380 ordered by Sir Massey

Lopes on 31st January 1855. Sir Massey Lopes of Maristow, Rodborough, South Devon was born in 1818 and was M.P. for Westbury 1857–1868 and South Devon 1868–1885. He was Lord of the Admiralty between 1874 and 1880. Unfortunately the barrels are missing. Does anyone know their whereabouts? They are 30" long, are by Thomas Parkin and have central fire nipples.

This gun displays all the characteristics of the muzzle-loader in the closing stages of its development. The Brazier made wood bar locks engraved, "Thomas Boss" are slim and elegant. Silver plates are inlet into the stock at the breech end to prevent damage when the barrels are inserted. The usual pointer dog is engraved on the trigger guard. No ramrod is fitted to the gun.

The gun is contained in its original green baize lined oak case bearing the "Thomas Boss, Gun and Rifle Manufacturers, Many Years with the late Joseph Manton" label. What is interesting is that when I examined the case I found the number "1402" stamped in the usual place on the carcass beneath the label. I was immediately suspicious, yet sceptical on account of the snug fit of the gun. The case had certainly never been altered.

An examination of Boss's records provided the answer. In the order the gun was to be built to "Pattern Gun Mr Wright's No. 1268". On looking up the order for gun no. 1402, it stated that it was to be built to "Pattern Gun Mr Wright's No. 1268". Due to the fact that nos. 1380 and 1402 were identical, the cases must have become mixed up in Boss's shop when brand new. So I think it fair to say that case is original to the gun! A chequered history – case mixed up, barrels lost!

The following accessories are in the case and are original to the gun. There is a pig-skin pouch containing a nipple key builders and spare side-nail engraved, "1380". The quality of this item is superb. A wad punch, stamped "14" is supplied as is a stout loading rod. A finely tooled steel mouthed Dixon shot pouch has three graduations, 1⅛ oz, 1¼ oz and 1¾ oz. The Sykes steel-bodied powder flask has three graduations 2¾ drams, 3 drams, and 3¼ drams. There is a pewter G. and J. W. Hawksley oil bottle. For cleaning the top rib an ivory handled brush is supplied. Contained within the lidded compartment is a main spring clamp of superb quality and a brass nipple pricker and primer.

Percussion gun no. 1380. See Plate 19.

LEFT: The order for gun no. 1359 dated 12th October 1853. Note the comment at the bottom, "The gun to be in a state to shoot with on Wednesday, November 9th by 9.00 in the morning at which time Mr Gipps will call for it with 1 cannister of powder, 1 bag wadding and two bags of caps."

The order for gun no. 1380 by Sir Massey Lopes M.P. dated 31st January 1855. From Boss's order ledgers.

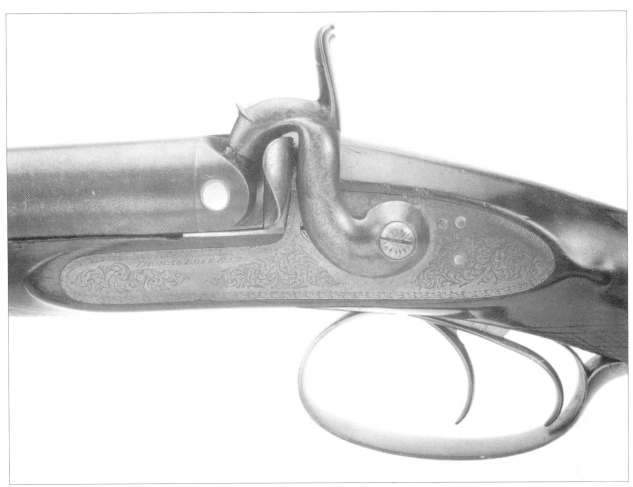

The lock work of no. 1673 showing the new title of the firm adopted in 1857 "Thomas Boss & Co.". Note the wood bar locks. See Plate 20.

Double gun no. 1673 is illustrated in plate no 20. No. 1673 is a double-barrel 13-bore percussion gun constructed in 1859. This gun was built some two years after the death of Thomas Boss and belongs to the era of the Mrs Boss/Stephen Grant partnership. It is the No. 1 gun of a matched pair ordered by Captain Long, 13th Light Infantry, of Hurts Hall, Suffolk. Charles Poore Long was commissioned into the 13th or Prince Albert's Regiment of Light Infantry. He had become a captain on 17th August 1855. Some years afterwards he resigned his commission.

The general style and feel of the gun are very different to the guns of the 1840s. It is light and graceful and in many respects similar to the early pinfire guns. The lock plates are very slim and elegant with the woodwork now coming round over the top of the locks com-

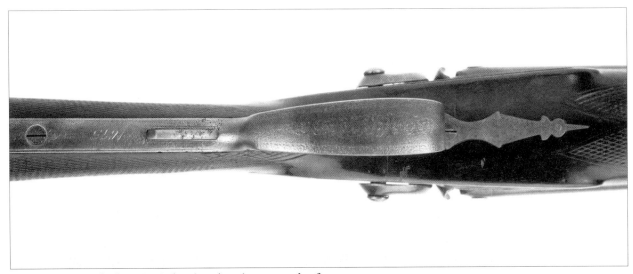

The trigger guard of no. 1673 showing the trigger guard safety.

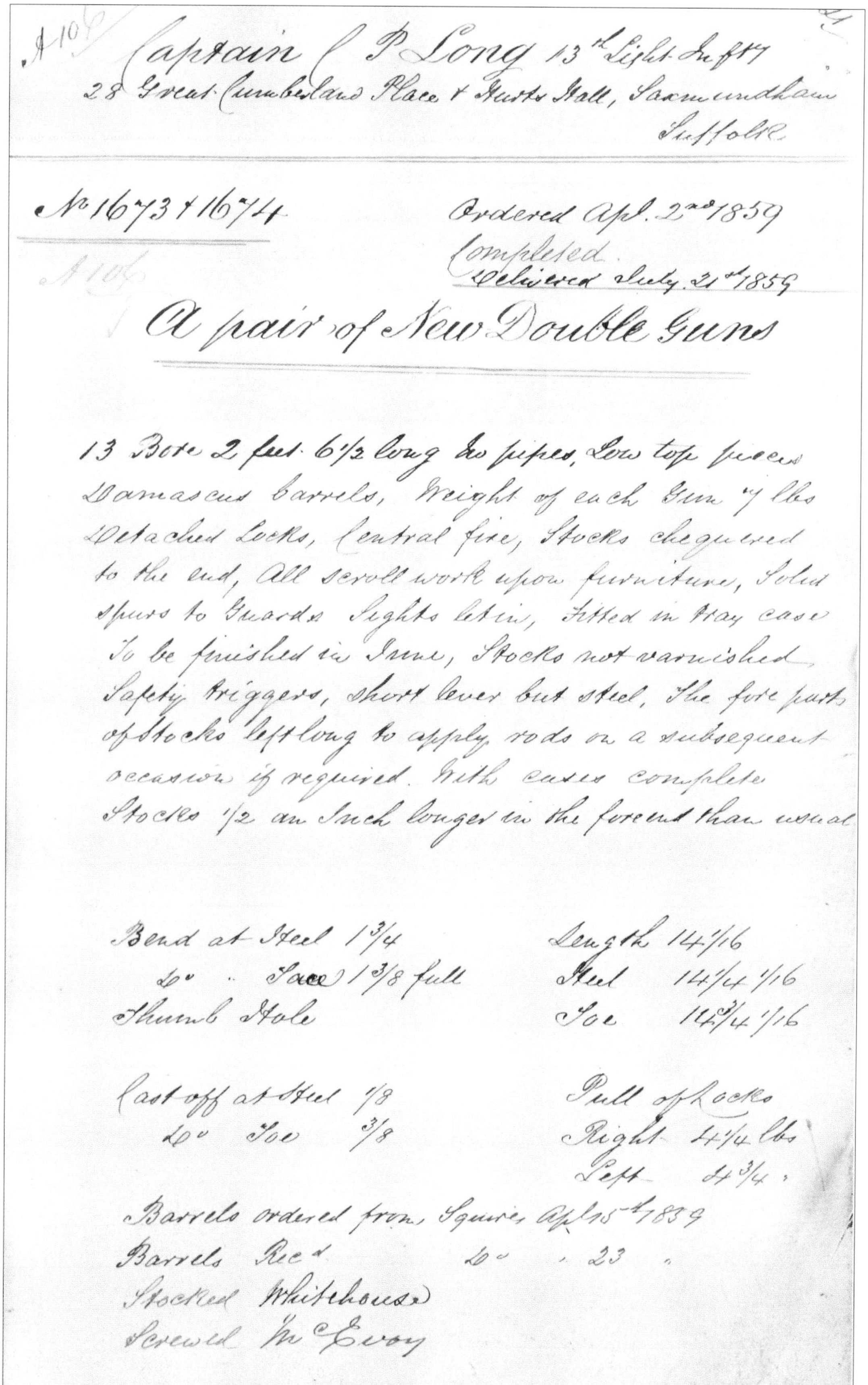

A 10?

Captain C P Long 13th Light Infty
28 Great Cumberland Place & Hurts Hall, Saxmundham
Suffolk

No 1673 & 1674

A 106

Ordered Apl. 2nd 1859
Completed.
Delivered July 21st 1859

A pair of New Double Guns

13 Bore 2 feet 6½ long 2o pipes, Low top pieces
Damascus barrels, Weight of each Gun 7 lbs
Detached Locks, Central fire, Stocks chequered
to the end, All scroll work upon furniture, Solid
spurs to Guards Sights letin, Fitted in Tray case
To be finished in June, Stocks not varnished,
Safety triggers, short lever but steel, The fore parts
of Stocks left long to apply rods on a subsequent
occasion if required. With cases complete
Stocks ½ an Inch longer in the fore end than usual.

Bend at Heel 1¾   Length 14 7/16
   Do Face 1 3/8 full   Heel   14½ 7/16
Thumb Hole   Toe   14½ 7/16

Cast off at Heel 7/8   Pull of Locks
   Do   Toe   3/8   Right 4¾ lbs
                            Left 4¾

Barrels ordered from Squires Apl 15th 1859
Barrels Recd   Do   23   "
Stocked Whitehouse
Screwed McEvoy

The order relating to gun no. 1673. The guns were made rapidly being ordered on 2nd April 1859 and delivered on 21st July 1859. Notice how the owner is considering having ramrods fitted at a later date. The barrel-maker, stocker and screwer of these guns are listed at the bottom of the order, all being out-workers employed by Boss.

monly called wood bar locks. They are Joseph Brazier locks and are now engraved, "Thomas Boss & Co.", the new wording adopted when the firm became a company in 1857.

The 30½″ Damascus barrels have a low rib, usual silver triangular Boss foresight and are engraved, "Thomas Boss & Co., 73 St James' Street, London". They are stamped, "H S" underneath the mark of Henry Squires, barrel-maker, 3 George Yard, Princes Street, Soho, London. The breeches are of the central fire type, with the nipples dead centre. There is no provision for a ramrod. This contributes to its lightness and slender lines. There are silver plates inlet into the stock at the breech end to prevent the stock being damaged as the barrels are put into place. A trigger guard safety is fitted.

This automatically prevents the trigger being squeezed unless the small lever projecting out of the guard is depressed. A late use of this device.

GUN CASES AND ACCESSORIES IN THE MUZZLE-LOADING ERA

Thomas Boss was very conservative in his gun cases and very much followed contemporary fashion. He bought his cases in from outside suppliers who would fit and match them to individual guns. Most of the percussion cases are made from the then fashionable light oak. A few are in the older fashioned mahogany, the style of the late 18th and early 19th centuries. They are reinforced at the corners with brass corner-pieces. A leather outer cover completed the case. Unfortunately, most of these leather outer covers are missing today due to the fact that they were a type of leather slip and inconvenient for easy access to guns. Many owners discarded them or they simply wore out. Some cases were covered in black sailcloth instead. Most cases are lined in light green baize, some were lined in leather.

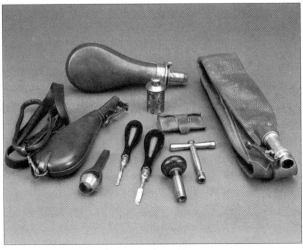

Percussion accessories. See Plate 21.

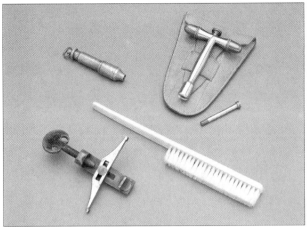

Percussion accessories. See Plate 22.

Trade labels were pasted into the lid. Trade label details often do not match the exact details of the gun, eg a Thomas Boss label might be pasted into a case with a Thomas Boss & Co. gun in it. This is because existing labels would be used up before more relevant labels were applied. The finely engraved trade labels were not mass produced. They were hand cut and hand printed. This is often apparent when labels are studied. The hand cutting can be very evident!

Cases for pairs of guns were usually of the two tier variety. In Boss's records they are referred to as "tray cases". In two-tier cases, the top-tier contained the barrels, loading rods, powder and shot flasks. This was lifted out by ribbons to reveal the bottom tier consisting of the stocks, nipple key, wad punches, turnscrews, oil bottle, etc. All double cases and some single cases have the gun numbers stamped into the carcass of the case just below the trade label. Usually the numbers are also stamped under the compartment lids. This is a useful guide to ascertaining whether a case is original to the gun or not. Beware of any signs of buffing in these areas! Brass escutcheons are fitted in the centre of the lid. Often they have the owner's crest or initials engraved upon them. Since double cases with a full complement of guns and accessories are very heavy; drop down brass carrying handles were fitted to one end of the case to facilitate carriage.

Muzzle-loaders require a plethora of accessories. Since the Victorians loved fussiness and ostentation, every conceivable accessory was fitted to cope with all eventualities. All accessories fitted to Thomas Boss guns are of the highest quality and by the best manufacturers. The pair of double percussion guns no. 763 and 827, already described, are fortunate in having their full set of original accessories. When purchased these guns were "sleepers" and had not been touched for scores of years. Too often original accessories disappear from cases having been purloined for ulterior motives.

The accessories in more detail include the following:

1. Pair of steel bodied powder flasks with fireproof tops by Brazier, both measuring 2½–3 drams black powder.
2. Pair of leather bodied shot flasks graduated 1–1¼ oz one by Bishop, Bond Street, London, the other unmarked. Both powder and shot flasks have the original owner's initials, "E.G." (Edward Goulburn) engraved upon them.
3. Spare ramrods each numbered to their respective No. 1 and No. 2 guns.
4. Two loading rods. They are stouter and not so finely made as the ramrods, but were intended for a loader who would accompany the shooter.
5. Cleaning rod ends.
6. Three ebony handled turnscrews of varying sizes.
7. Two wad punches stamped, "14" indicating the bore size.
8. A nipple key with pricker in the centre for cleaning fouled up nipples.
9. A pigskin leather pouch containing a pair of spare nipples and three spare side nail screws.
10. A leather shot belt with a nickle silver charger by G & J W Hawksley. This has "E Goulburn" written upon it in ink.
11. Two leather slings for suspending shot pouches from a shot belt.
12. Loading rod turned ends to make loading more comfortable.
13. Tins of percussion caps, one manufactured by Fred Joyce, London, and the other by Eleys, London. In addition there is a bag of Westley Richards percussion caps.

Some of the pairs of percussion guns were supplied in separate cases as the owner desired. This means that if a gun bearing a No. 1 or No. 2 is found in a single case, it does not necessarily mean that the case is non original.

A typical Boss two-tier case is illustrated below. This case was for a pair of double guns nos 1054 and 1055 built in 1850 for J. Hutchison, Eggelstone Hall, Durham. The gun nos 1054 and 1055 are stamped on the carcase of the case beneath the trade label and also under the lid compartments.

A letter pertaining to this case and the guns that used to be in it survives in the Letters' Book.

Evidently Mr Hutchison was not satisfied with a previous Boss gun and Boss has agreed to make him a new one.

In the early 1860s, the number of muzzle-loaders built rapidly diminished with the advent of the breech-loader. A sprinkling continued to be made through the later 1860s until double-barrel 12-bore gun no. 3078,

A two-tier oak case for a pair of double guns nos. 1054 and 1055 built in 1850 for J Hutchison.

A letter by Boss to Mr Hutchison detailing Hutchison's dissatisfaction with a gun order. This led to the order of pair nos. 1054/5. From the Letters Book.

the last muzzle-loader built by Boss, was delivered in 1872 to Sir John Blois.

The letter reproduced on plate 23 is one of the few original letters (not a Boss copy) that was sent to a customer to survive. It concerns a double percussion 14-bore gun no. 2108 ordered on 5th November 1863. This gun comes into the category of a late built muzzle-loader, since Boss were now concentrating on breech-loaders. Note the shortening of the signature to "Boss & Co". Around 1862, the signature "Thomas Boss & Co" had given way to the simpler form of "Boss & Co", the style that has been used from that year to the present. The firm used ultramarine blue as a colour on their stamp in the original letter. The account is to Mrs Poole who was buying the gun for her son in Victoria, Australia.

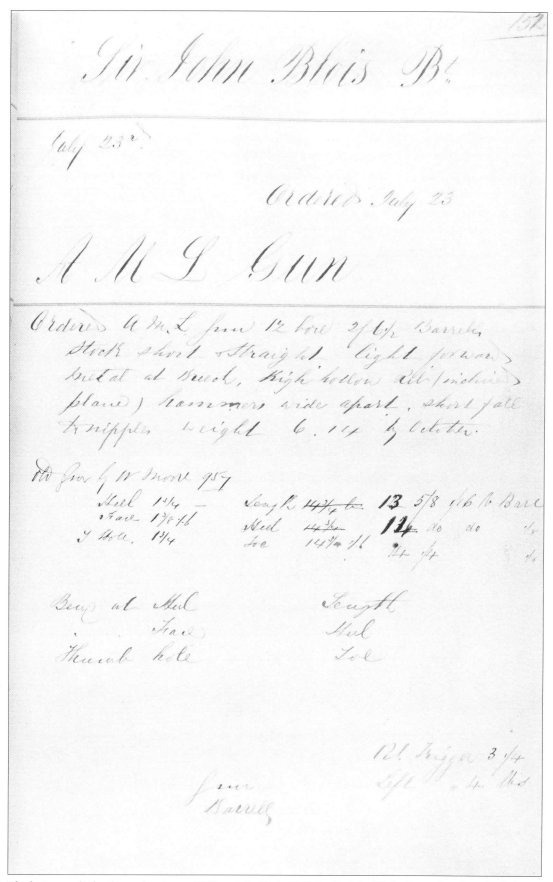

The last muzzle-loader ordered, no. 3078 on July 23rd, 1872 for Sir John Blois. From Boss's order ledgers.

CHAPTER FIVE

E. F. P. – THE ECCENTRIC

When Grant left Boss to set up on his own, Mrs Boss was once more left at the helm. She was now an ageing woman of seventy-one. However, her nephews, the Paddison brothers, were now older and capable of running the establishment: Edward Fields Paddison was forty-one and James Joseph Paddison was twenty-four. Edward had worked for the firm since coming down from Louth in 1838 and his younger brother James had worked for the firm on his departure from Louth in 1856.

The firm continued to prosper since Mrs Boss lived in the style of the affluent Victorian middle class. A servant named Christina Warren lived at no. 73 and attended to her needs. Her income was more than sufficient, for when she died she left considerable cash sums to her various relatives. Apart from the servant she lived alone in the large building of no. 73. The Paddison brothers no longer lived there. Edward Paddison had moved away from his aunt at 73 St James's Street in the late 1850s. By 1870, he was living at South Molton Street, close to New Bond Street.

THE DEATH OF EMMA BOSS 1872

On 29th July 1872, Mrs Boss died from a "decay of nature" at 73 St James's Street. She was seventy-seven years of age and had survived her husband by some fifteen years. She was buried at the Brompton Cemetery beside her husband on 2 August 1872.

She left an estate valued at £25,000, a hefty sum of money in 1872. Due to the value of the estate and the desire to ensure that the business was continued by the Paddison brothers, her Will is long and complicated. It was proved in London, on 12th November 1872. The most important parts of the will are quoted below:

This is the last will and testament of me, Amy Chapman Boss (signed) of 73 St James's Street in the County of Middlesex, widow, made in revocation of all other Wills by me at any time executed. I give and bequeath all my furniture, plate, linen, china, books, utensils and effects and removable stores unto and equally between my nephews Edward Fields Paddison and James Joseph Paddison.

I give and bequeath out of such part of my personal state as is by law applicable to charitable purposes and in priority to the other pecuniary legacies hereby bequeathed the following legacies which I direct to be paid free of duty (such duty being likewise paid out of the last mentioned part of my personal estate and in priority to the aforesaid) to the several institutions hereinafter named the receipts of whose respective treasures for the time being shall be good discharges for the amount so paid that is to say the London Missionary Society, the London City Mission (to be appropriated for the use of the Islington and North London Auxiliary), the Aged Pilgrims Friend Society, the Orphan Working School, the National Benevolent Institution, the Royal Hospital for Incurables, the Asylum for Idiots, Earlswood and the Asylum for Fatherless Children receive the sum of £200 and I bequeath unto Frances Paddison, daughter of my nephew, William Paddison, deceased, the sum of £100 and bequeath unto my nephew the said James Joseph Paddison, a legacy of £600 and to my nephew the said Edward Fields Paddison, the legacy of £400. I bequeath unto each of them, my nieces and nephew, Ann, the wife of William Mears and Emma Chapman, the wife of William Robinson and Jabez Paddison the legacy of £200. I bequeath unto George Fatt now residing with me the legacy of £200. I bequeath unto his brother Joseph Chapman Fields Fatt the legacy of £100.

I bequeath to both of my executors hereinafter named, the legacy of £19.19s. I direct my two dwelling houses situated in Northgate Street, Louth in the county of Lincoln the occupation of Joan

Wilkinson and the other lately in the occupation of William Robinson but now unoccupied unto my nephew Richard Waite of Louth, his heirs and assignees absolutely. I give direct and bequeath all the rest and residue of my real and personal estate . . .

Upon the trusts following that is to say to my leasehold messuage and premises number 73 St James's Street, aforesaid and as to the goodwill of the business not earned on thereupon by me as a gunmaker (but not as to the stock in hand and the book debts due to me in respect of such business).

Upon trust for and equally between my said nephews Edward Fields Paddison and James Joseph Paddison, subject nevertheless to the performance by them of the condition precedent hereinafter imposed and I declare that the condition precedent above referred to is that my nephews shall within the space of three calandar months next after my demise by a proper deed containing all necessary and usual clauses and stipulations appropriate to the circumstances constitute themselves partners in the business of gunmakers in equal shares and upon an equal footing in all respects for the term of twenty-one years if both of them shall so long live . . .

But if my said nephews shall refuse or shall for the space of three calandar months from my demise neglect to enter into such partnership or if by reason of the death of both or either of them whether in my lifetime or within three calandar months next after my demise the abovementioned conditions shall not be performed then I declare that my said trustees shall hold the said leashold premises and goodwill upon trust to sell the same in manner hereinafter directed . . .

I have to this my Will contained as this and the five proceeding sheets of paper set my hand this twentieth day of December one thousand eight hundred and seventy-one.

Amy Chapman Boss Signed by the said testatrix Amy Chapman Boss as and for her last Will and Testament in the presence of us who in her presence at her request and in the presence of each other have hereinafter set our hands as witnesses.

Her benefactions to various charities were an accepted part of Victorian middle-class life. Donating money to charities seemed to be an attempt to absolve responsibility from tackling the real problems of deprivation, education, etc. Mrs Boss was no exception to this in donating her monies to her favoured charitable institutions.

Her family were well looked after. Her benefactions to them were not inconsiderable sums.

The most important part of Mrs Boss's Will are the clauses relating to her gunmaking business. She intended to leave it to the Paddison brothers, but stipulated that they must form a partnership within three months of her demise for a term of twenty-one years.

Thus ended the original Boss business. In addition since the Paddison's had married and left, 73 St James's Street was now used solely as a gunmaking establishment. The only person now living there was a resident housekeeper, Susannah Wheeler.

It would be her job to sweep up the filings and wood shavings and generally tidy up after the gunsmiths had left.

THE PADDISON PARTNERSHIP
1872–73

Whenever Thomas Boss married Emma Fields in 1837 her relations were to feature strongly in the firm in the future. Since Boss and his wife had no children they intended that the business should continue down Mrs Boss's side of the family.

Emma Boss's sister, Susannah Fields, had married William Paddison, a shoemaker in Louth. They raised around ten children. Their first son, born in 1825, they christened after his grandfather, Edward Fields Paddison. At the age of thirteen, it was decided that he would enter the Boss gunmaking business. He duly came down from Louth and took up residence at 73 St James's Street on 21st June 1838. He was apprenticed to Thomas Boss for seven years and became a journeyman gunmaker in 1845. Edward would be directly involved in the firm until his death in 1891.

Another son, James Joseph Paddison, was born on 28th January 1842 at 47 James Street, Louth. Similarly at the age of fourteen in 1856, he travelled to 73 St James's Street, and began his apprenticeship under the ageing Thomas Boss. By 1863 he was a journeyman gunmaker with the firm.

It is not clear after the dissolution of the partnership between Emma Boss and Stephen Grant in 1866, whether the Paddison brothers entered into partnership with her. As explained before, there are no records remaining of the company history in the 19th century.

What is clear is that, when Mrs Boss died in 1872, she left specific instructions in her Will that her two nephews were to form a partnership and inherit the business. It looked as though the future of Boss & Co. in family hands was secure. Unfortunately, this was not to be the case.

James Paddison had married Ellen Grist at Lambeth, London in 1868. Their daughter, called Amy after Mrs Boss, was born soon after. James Paddison however was a sick man – he had been ill for many years with respiratory problems. On 23rd December 1873, he died at 59 Clapham Road, London, aged thirty-two from "phthisis of the lungs". The partnership of the two brothers had lasted approximately one year. Christmas 1873 could not have been a particularly happy time for his wife. Her only son Herbert had died in early January 1874 aged nine months. Ellen herself did not last long – she died in 1893 aged forty-eight.

By this time she had remarried and gone to live in Hastings. Hence this line of the Paddison gunmaking family came to an end.

Both father and son were buried in the Brompton Cemetery, the same cemetery as Thomas and Emma Boss, James being buried on 31st December 1873 and his son Herbert on 14th January 1874.

As a result of his inheritance of the gunmaking business, he left a sizeable amount of money – around £5,000. After leaving £100 to his mother-in-law, he directed that his brother-in-law William Mears, a gunmaker with the firm, should set up a trust fund to provide for the future of his wife and chidren. No mention is made of the business. Since he had been ill for a fair length of time, it was probably decided in advance of the Will that his share of the partnership would transfer to his brother Edward.

EDWARD FIELDS PADDISON –
SOLE PROPRIETOR 1873–91

James's death in 1873 left Edward the sole proprietor of the firm. He had been with the firm since 1838, being apprenticed in that year to his uncle Thomas Boss. He lived at 73 St James's Street with his uncle and aunt until his thirties in the mid 1850s.

On 20th August 1870, Edward married Martha Jane Bowen, a widow, in the Parish Church of St George's, Hanover Square, London. Martha was born in Kensington in London and had her own business as a mantle-maker (mantles were a type of cloak that were very popular during this period). They lived at 177 Hampstead Road and enjoyed a relatively comfortable lifestyle. They had the ubiquitous servant and rented a room to one of Martha's employees. Her business as a mantle-maker was carried on at this address.

Like his uncle Thomas, Edward had married late in life. He was forty-five years of age and Martha was forty-nine. Hence they had no children. Martha was a widow some four years older than Edward and had a grown-up daughter, Angelina Laughton, who was married with four children. The future of her daughter was of paramount importance to her. Prior to her marriage to Edward, they had come to a marriage agreement on 19th August 1870. Martha drove a hard bargain. Essentially this agreement said that Edward had

to support her daughter and in the event of his demise the gunmaking business, or proceeds from the sale of it, would pass to her daughter. This in effect did not happen due to changed circumstances as will be explained later.

Since Mrs Boss was alive at this time, I wonder if she knew about the financial implications of this arrangement. Somehow I doubt it. She and her husband had worked very hard to build up such a successful business – now it could be dissipated very easily. This agreement could be the result of genuine amour, naivety, or perhaps display the eccentricity that is apparent in Paddison's personality.

On 1st August 1884, Martha Paddison died aged sixty-three at their house at 177 Hampstead Road, London. The full extent of her marriage agreement is apparent in her Will proved on 14 November 1884. She gave her share of the gunmaking business "carried on at 73 St James's Street, under the style or name of E.F.P. Boss together with all stock, plant, books, debts and chattels belonging thereto for his own absolute use and benefit during his life free from the control of the Trustees … and that at his decease only the said premises

Edward Fields Paddison 1825–91, a nephew of Thomas Boss. Edward Paddison was apprenticed to Thomas Boss in 1838 and owned the firm between 1872 and 1891.

No. 73 St James's Street, around 1885 with the shop lettering changed to E.F.P. Boss & Co.

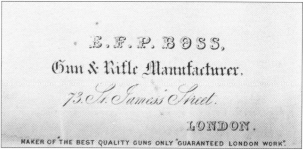

Trade card of E.F.P. Boss & Co. *circa* **1880 to 1891.**

The title seems to have been used on the firm's headed notepaper, adverts and on the shop front.

In the photograph of the shop front circa 1885, the lettering on the wall clearly states, "E.F.P. Boss & Co., Breechloading Gun and Rifle Manufacturers". It was a clumsy title for the firm. It might have been intended to emphasise the fact that Edward Fields Paddison was the sole proprietor, or the fact that he liked to call himself "Mr Boss". He even signed his letters, "E.F.P. Boss". That eccentric personality again.

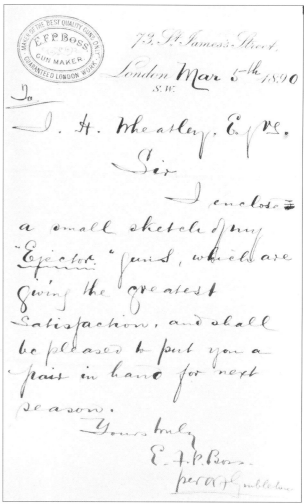

The covering letter and, overleaf, Boss's catalogue from the late 1880s. Notice how there is no variation in the price of hammerless and hammer guns and how Whitworth steel barrels are more expensive. Also notice how Boss continually mention that they produce "best guns only".

shall form part of my residuary estate to be dealt with by my said Trustees".

Since her daughter was divorced with four children, careful provision was made for her in the Will. Her business as a mantle-maker was given equally to her daughter and forewoman, Ann Scott. Her money in the bank and her insurance policies also went to her daughter.

Out of the gunmaking business Edward had to pay an allowance of £5 per week to her daughter Angelina. Since Angelina and her children had moved to 177 Hampstead Road, after the divorce, she expected her to look after Edward. If Edward decided to leave the house, he had to pay Angelina £3 per week and Angelina was to inherit the "furniture and effects and things including musical instruments". On the decease of her husband the residue of her estate was to go to her daughter.

It is interesting to note the change in the name of the firm referred to in Martha's Will. In the early 1880s he renamed the firm, "E.F.P. Boss & Co." – E.F.P. being in reference to Edward Fields Paddison. The firm continued to be known as this until Edward's death in 1891 when it reverted to the simpler "Boss & Co." form under John Robertson's ownership. I have never seen a Boss gun of this period engraved, "E.F.P. Boss & Co.".

E. F. P. BOSS,

GUN AND RIFLE MANUFACTURER,

73, ST. JAMES'S STREET,

LONDON, S.W.

ONE QUALITY ONLY—"THE BEST."

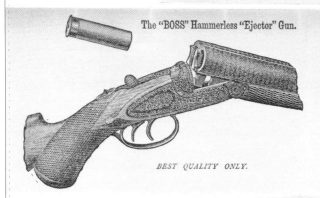

The "BOSS" Hammerless "Ejector" Gun.

BEST QUALITY ONLY.

The "BOSS" Hammerless Ejector Gun is the simplest and most reliable Gun manufactured, combining strength of mechanism, with simplicity and absolute safety.

The "Ejector" work is entirely in the forepart, easily detached, and almost impossible to get out of order, also quite independent of the lock work.

Can be supplied with coiled or flat springs to the Ejector, and built any action.

Hammerless Gun, best Damascus barrels and case complete, £ *57.15.0*

Do.   Whitworth steel   do.   do.   £ *63.0.0*

The "BOSS" C. F. "Ejector" Gun.
REBOUNDING LOCK WITH HAMMERS.

BEST QUALITY ONLY.

The "BOSS" Hammer Ejector Gun, central fire, rebounding locks, for gentlemen who prefer Hammer Guns, making one Gun equivalent to a pair of ordinary Hammer Guns.

Ejector work in forepart, quite independent of lock work, similar to Hammerless Guns.

Can be supplied with coiled or flat springs, to the Ejector, and built any action.

Central Fire, best Damascus barrels and case complete, £ *57.15.0*

Do.   "Whitworth steel barrels"   do.   £ *63.0.0*

EXPRESS RIFLES.

360, 450, 500, or 577 Bore.
BEST QUALITY ONLY.

EXPRESS RIFLES.

360, 450, 500 or 577.

Express Rifles, double barrel, central fire, with safety bolts to hammers.

Lever over guard, double grip action, accurately sighted up to 200 yards, with steel barrels.

BEST QUALITY ONLY.

Double Express Rifle, with case and apparatus, £

Hammerless   do.   do.   £

ROOK, RABBIT & ANTELOPE RIFLES.

230, 250, 300, 320 360 and 380 Bore.

CARTRIDGES ALL LOADED ON THE PREMISES
BY EXPERIENCED MEN.

12 = 16 or 20 Bore Cartridges......*11/-*......per 100 (Cash.)

12 Bore Charge, 38 to 45 grains.

1 oz. to 1½ oz. Shot.

16 Bore, 35 to 40 grains, ⅞ to 1¹⁄₁₆

20 Bore, 28 to 35 grains.

A live pigeon match taking place at The Gun Club, Notting Hill, *circa* **1880.**

Edward Paddison's era at Boss & Co. coincided with the most remarkable period of inventive ingenuity that the gunmaking business had ever witnessed. Patents of all descriptions abounded for opening actions, hammerless guns, ejector mechanisms, etc, yet Edward Paddison contributed nothing. Although he described himself as a "Patent Gun Manufacturer" in the Trade Directories, he never took out any patents himself. The wording is actually true – he did manufacture patent guns, but not guns of his own patent. Such a title would undoubtedly be good advertising for business.

Edward Paddison produced a small fold-over booklet in card described by him as a "Sketch" detailing the guns Boss produced in the late 1880s. See Plate 24. He would supply this catalogue to any potential purchasers.

LIVE PIGEON SHOOTING
Live pigeon shooting was at the height of its popularity in the second half of the 19th century. Along with Stephen Grant and James Purdey, Boss & Co. specialised in pigeon guns. Regular pigeon gun club meetings were held that were highly organised. Considerable betting ensued at these meetings. In the London area examples of such clubs were the Gun Club, Notting Hill, the Red House, Battersea Fields, and the Hurlington Gun Club.

The unfortunate pigeon, or in many cases starling, was placed under a box which was then pulled open by a cord on the command of the shooter. Rules regard-

ing pigeon shooting at these clubs were very lax until the 1860s when some concensus was established and the 12-bore gun became the norm.

The shooters were highly professional and the gun-

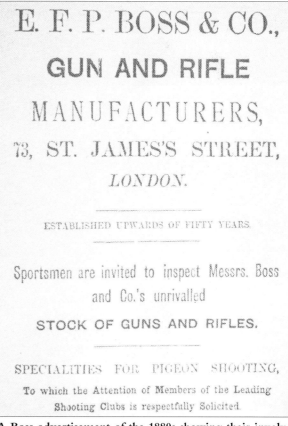

A Boss advertisement of the 1880s showing their involvement in live pigeon shooting.

Inside the advertisement:

E. F. P. BOSS & CO.,

GUN AND RIFLE

MANUFACTURERS,

73, ST. JAMES'S STREET,

LONDON.

ESTABLISHED UPWARDS OF FIFTY YEARS.

Sportsmen are invited to inspect Messrs. Boss and Co.'s unrivalled

STOCK OF GUNS AND RIFLES.

SPECIALITIES FOR PIGEON SHOOTING,

To which the Attention of Members of the Leading Shooting Clubs is respectfully Solicited.

> ── yards.
>
> ### SOUTH LONDON GROUNDS, NUNHEAD.
>
> The Great All-England £25 Starling Handicap, commenced on Thursday last at these grounds, was brought to a successful issue yesterday (Monday) in the presence of a very large company. The conditions of the contest were—eleven birds each, handicap distances, entrance 10s. (to the fund). The entries numbered fifty-four, and, as will be gathered from the annexed details, Mr. Charles (27 yards rise), who shot in splendid form throughout with his favourite gun by Boss, of St. James's-street, grassed all his eleven birds in two chances and secured the first and second prizes, amounting together to £20. The third prize (£5) was well contested for, and ultimately divided between Messrs. Wye (28) and Hearne (24), after killing fourteen out of fifteen. After a short interval a 10s. sweepstakes, with £5 added by Mr. Charles, at seven pigeons each, was next decided, and this resulted in a division between Mr. Bean (26) and Mr. Lewis (29), each killing all seven and sharing £13. The remainder of the afternoon was devoted to sweepstakes, at 35 yards rise, the winners being Messrs. Wye, Johnson, and Clyde. Mr. H. Gardiner acted as handicapper and referee, and a carefully selected lot of birds were provided by Mr. T. Brown, which gave every satisfaction. Appended are the details:—
>
> £25 STARLING HANDICAP: eleven birds each; first prize, £12; second, £8; third, £5.
>
> Yds. rise.
> 27 ... Mr. Charles (second chance). 1 1 1 1 1 1 1 1 1 1 1
> 27 ... Mr. Charles (third chance)... 1 1 1 1 1 1 1 1 1 1 1
> (First and second prize, £20.)
> 28 ... Mr. Wye (second chance) ... 1 1 1 1 1 0 1 1 1 1—1 1 1 1
> 28 ... Mr. Wye (third chance) ...... 1 1 1 1 1 1 0 1 1 1—1 1 1 1
> 24 ... Mr. T. Hearne .... 1 1 0 1 1 1 1 1 1 1—1 1 1 1
> (Divided third prize, £5.)
> 25 ... Bracknell .... 1 1 1 1 0 1 1 1 1 1—1 1 1 0
> Mr. Johnson (25 yards rise) killed 8 birds and (second chance) (26) 7; Mr. Clare (26), 6; Mr. Cuthbert (28), Mr. Lewis (second chance) (28), Mr. Tanner (25), Mr. Davis (25), and Mr. Peard (26), 5 each; Mr. Briggs (25) Mr. Monk (24), Mr. Jones (third chance) (25) (retired), Mr. Baker (24), and Mr. Charles (27), 4 each; Mr. Leach (26) (retired) and (second chance) (26) and Mr. Idle (25) (retired) and (second chance) (25), 3 each. Of the remainder, eighteen killed 2 birds each, seven killed 1 each, and six failed to score.
> £5 ADDED TO A 10s. SWEEPSTAKES; seven pigeons each.—Mr. Bean (26 yards rise), 1 1 1 1 1 1, and Mr. Lewis (29), divided £13; Mr. Dowling (25), 1 1 1 1 1 0; Mr. Bracknell (26), 1 1 1 1 1 0; Mr. Johnson (28), 1 1 1 1 0; Mr. Davis (26), 1 1 1 1 0; Mr. Wye (29), 1 1 1 0; Mr. W. Cuthbert (28), 1 1 0; Mr. T. Hearn (25), 1 1 0; Mr. Vassilla (24), 1 1 0; Mr. Clyde (27), 1 1 0; Mr. Leech (26), 1 0; Mr. Duke (27), 1 0; Mr. Baker (24), 0; Mr. Wynne (25), 0; Mr. Selby (27), 0.

Live bird shooting results from *The Field*, 7th June 1890 – note the reference to "his favourite gun by Boss".

makers, powder and shot makers, etc were in attendance constantly trying out new loads, barrel lengths, bores, etc. The advantage to the gunmakers of this was that when the results went to press in contemporary periodicals like *The Field*, they would receive considerable publicity if their guns had proved to be successful. This would be excellent for business. Boss & Co. feature consistently in the score results at this time.

Boss & Co. occasionally gave prizes of their guns in competitions to popularise and advertise their wares, eg double-barrel 12-bore hammer gun no. 3758 was given on 13th June 1885 as a prize in the "Ascot Optional Handicap".

Most of the pigeon guns made in the 1880s and 1890s were hammer guns with underlevers. In a sport involving betting, complete reliability was necessary hence the reason for the proven underlever hammer gun in preference to the comparatively untried hammerless gun and potentially faulty snap actions.

Towards the end of the century live pigeon shooting declined in popularity as people began to realise the inhumanity of it. In 1910 it was abolished. The Princess of Wales was in part responsible for its fall from high fashion – she disliked the sport and openly condemned

it. Coupled with the fact that the live pigeon gun had been perfected and developed as far as it could, Boss & Co. retired from constant attendance. In any case it was expensive.

To get a mention in the sporting papers gunmakers had to pay a fee but it was not worth it due to its decline in popularity. Clay pigeon shooting eventually took over.

THE DEATH OF EDWARD PADDISON, 1891

When Edward Paddison married late in life, he must have developed a taste for marriage. His first wife Martha had died in August 1884. Very shortly after this, in the spring of 1886, he married again, this time secondly to another widow Mrs Emelia Allen. She was considerably younger than him, being aged forty-four to Paddison's sixty years. In early 1884, she had taken the lease on 19 Portland Terrace, Regent's Park for the sum of £105. It was to this house that Edward Paddison moved upon this second marriage. Portland Terrace was a wealthy area of Marylebone, the home of architects, barristers, civil servants, etc and the newly weds lived a

THE GUN CLUB.

SATURDAY, MARCH 1.—The outlook to-day was anything but inviting for shooting, as, shortly before noon, snow commenced to fall heavily, and this no doubt deterred many members from visiting this resort. Sport proved of an uninteresting character, for, contrary to the general rule, the birds flew anything but well. and, as misses were few and far between, the backers had much the best of the betting. The customary £5 Sweepstakes, at 28 yards rise, commenced proceedings, and this was carried off by that popular sportsman Mr F. Leighton, who killed eight birds in succession, and beat three competitors. As an inducement for members to shoot, the management offered £15 to be competed for in connection with a £3 Handicap Sweepstakes, and this brought together seven subscribers. As the returns will show, a long and tedious struggle was witnessed, and it was not until the sixteenth round that the result was arrived at, when, Mr F. Leighton electing to retire from the contest, Mr Digby was returned the winner of the pool, amounting to £36, having stopped sixteen birds consecutively. In the concluding events the best form was shown by Mr Wentworth, Mr Edwardes, and Mr Digby. The £3 Sweepstakes registered no fewer than sixty-eight kills to five misses. Scores :

£5 SWEEPSTAKES, at 9 birds each ; 28 yards rise ; 4 subs.

	Birds shot at.	Killed.
Mr F. Leighton (Purdey), S (prize, £20)	1 1 1 1 1 1 1 1	8
Mr Digby (Boss), S	0 1 1 1 1 1 1 0	6 out of 8
Mr Edwardes (Dougall), SS	1 1 1 1 1 1 0 0	6 out of 8
Hon. J. Ashburnham (Cogswell and Harrison)	1 1 0 0 1 1	4 out of 6

£3 HANDICAP SWEEPSTAKES, with £15 added ; 7 subs.

Yds.		Birds shot at.	Killed.
24½	Mr Digby (Boss), S (prize, £36)...	1111111111111111	16
29	Mr F. Leighton (Purdey), S	111111111111111 retired	15
24½	Mr Tudor (Grant), S	11111111111110	14
24½	Mr Wordman (Leeson), S	111111111o	9
23	Hon. J. Ashburnham (Cogswell and Harrison), SS	111111110	9
30	Mr Edwardes (Dougall), SS	111110	5
30½	Mr Wentworth (Grant), S, Bk	0	

WEDNESDAY, MARCH 5.—There was a decided break in the weather to-day, and those present enjoyed some good sport. The birds tested the competitors' abilities to the utmost, and small scores were the order of the afternoon. In the preliminary sweepstakes, the best form was shown by Mr C. A. Barton (30½yds.), Mr Digby (24½yds.), and Mr Seymour (25½yds.), the latter gentleman securing a couple of pools. The £3 Handicap Sweepstakes was won by Mr Eltham, who, missing his first bird, elected to " star," with the result that at the end of the second round he was credited with the prize of £21. Scores :

£3 HANDICAP SWEEPSTAKES ; 6 subs.

Yds.		Birds shot at.	Killed.
31	Mr Eltham (Lang), S, Bk (prize £21)	0 1 1	2
25½	Mr Seymour (Reilly), S	1 0	1
29	Mr F. Leighton (Purdey), S	1 0	1
24½	Mr Digby (Boss), S	1 0	1
24½	Mr Wordman (Leeson), S	0	
30½	Mr C. A. Barton (Powell), EC.	0	

£2 HANDICAP SWEEPSTAKES ; 6 subs.

Yds.		Birds shot at.	Killed.
26½	Mr Seymour (Reilly), S (divided £12)	1 1 1	3
24½	Mr Digby (Boss), S (ditto)	1 1 1	3
30½	Mr C. A. Barton (Powell), EC.	1 1 0	2
32	Mr Eltham (Lang), S, Bk.	1 1 0	2
24½	Mr Wordman (Lang), S	1 0	1
29	Mr F. Leighton (Purdey), S	0	

This day (Saturday) a £5 sweepstakes, at nine birds, 28 yards rise, will be shot for at one o'clock, to be followed by a £3 Handicap Sweepstakes, with £15 added.

Report from *The Field* 1st March 1890 on a live pigeon match. The "Mr Digby" referred to was Mr Digby Willoughby, a keen pigeon shot of the period, for whom Boss built many guns.

very comfortable life with three servants attending to their every need.

Once again, sadness was to pervade the Paddisons. His wife Emelia had developed cancer of the throat. On 3 April 1891 she was to undergo an operation on this and, since there was every chance it would end fatally, she made an immediate Will. She was staying in the flat at 73 St James's Street at this time, so that her husband could be constantly near her. Her son quickly attended her lawyer and got him to draft a Will leaving every-

thing to him. Edward Paddison must have got wind of this and quickly dispatched the front shop manager of Boss, Mr Embelton, to the lawyer. The lawyer immediately travelled to 73 St James's Street to see Mrs Paddison personally. She informed him that her son was not to interfere and that everything was to be left to her husband. Unfortunately she did not survive the operation and died.

Edward himself would not outlive her by long. He had not been in the best of health for some years and

SHOOTING

THE ENGLISH EIGHT.

This week we present a photograph of the eight riflemen who this year represented England against Scotland and Ireland at Wimbledon and ran the winners so close.

CRACK GUNMAKERS INTRODUCED TO OUR FOREIGN READERS.

No. 2. – Mr. Boss.

NOTICE.–The numerical order in which we give these has no reference whatever to the estimation in which we hold each gunmaker.

THE GOOD, OLD-FASHIONED name of Boss is one of the very few in these days of mushroom growth of so-called London gun manufacturers that possesses a genuine right and title to the distinguishing appellation of London makers. The said mushroom growth are well cognisant that the superiority of the work of the few firms alluded to have made the name of London guns famous throughout the world, and are therefore not willing to share in the reward, whilst having borne nothing of the burden and heat of the day, being aware that to the majority of sportsmen a gun hailing from a London shop is a London gun. Those, therefore, who are not "in the know" may be informed that Boss and Co. are, and have been, for years long past, absolutely, in every sense of the words, London makers.

To sketch roughly in outline the trade history of Boss and Co., it is enough to say that Thomas Boss, the founder of the firm, served his apprenticeship with his father, one of the best of old J. Manton's workmen. After reaching manhood, Thomas Boss worked many years for Mr. J. Purdey, noticeably during 1817 to 1821 and upwards, as shown by one of his old work books. Thomas Boss commenced business for himself as a gunmaker in 1830 at 3, Grosvenor-street, thence removed to Clifford-street, thence to 76, St. James-street, and finally to 73, St James-street, the present address of the firm. The present proprietor, a nephew of the original Thomas Boss, is of Lincolnshire birth, hailing from Louth, and has been, in the firm as much as fifty years on June 21 last. He served his apprenticeship with his uncle, Thomas Boss, the founder of the firm, who died in 1857.

Mrs. Boss succeeded to the business, and took Mr. Stephen Grant into partnership about 1860 as manager. At the expiration of partnership S. Grant started business for himself, the present owner succeeded in 1872, and is now the sole proprietor.

The business is most exclusive, and only one quality of work is turned out, i.e., the highest. The firm have but one quality and one price, thus standing in a very unique position, since Mr. Purdey has recently relaxed his role of also keeping but one quality, and has added a second. The connection of Boss and Co. is most aristocratic. They have no desire or occasion to popularised their work, for the orders from their regular patrons are such as to tax sufficiently the resources of their not very capacious establishment.

Walking into 73, St. James-street, we find ourselves in a small and rather dingy room, crammed from floor to ceiling with gun cases, guns, and parts of guns. Three individuals in shirt sleeves and aprons are hand at work by the window. Addressing these, we inquire if Mr. Boss is a home? To our inquiries, the shortest and most elderly of the three replies, "Yes, sir; yes, sir," "Can we see him?" "Yes, sir; yes, sir," and without raising his eyes from the lock at which he was filing, or making the least sign of going to fetch Mr. Boss. After beholding him for a moment, it struck us that he might possibly be the gentlemen of whom we were in search, and, on putting the guess into words, we learned that it was correct, and were at the same time confirmed in our first impressions of his eccentricity. "Well, sir, what part of the world have you come from?" "Do you know Lincolnshire? Ah! good shooting there, good shooting! Its cold to-day; don't like cold weather; makes my feet cold; yes, makes my feet cold. John care you doing here? Why don't you send off that gun-case? I told you to send it off before 3." "Yes, sir, good shooting in Lincolnshire. Do you know. So-and-So. Tall young fellow; has house in Grosvenor-square?" "What do I think of those very light guns? Don't think anything of 'em; hate 'em, hate 'em; no good at all; too much recoil; do very well for some stockbroker. My customers use ten or twelve thousand cartridges in the season each." "Like short barrels? Not much, don't; what's the good of 'em? Never makes barrels under 30in.; 30in. proper length for 12-bore."

"Went to So-and-So because he was top of the tree, did you; should have come to me. I could make you the best gun in London. Here, John, take this letter to So-and-So." "You must be very fond of guns, sir; I like anyone fond of guns. Here's a gun, sir (rushing to the end of the room and fetching one), see that!" "Bad work, very bad work; oh, yes, dear, dear me, very bad work." "So-andSo has bad work; he fills up, you know, fills up." "Whose carriage is that, John?" (apropos of a smart turn-out just passed the window). "Duke of B—, sir. Which pit the most, did you say, sir, steel barrels or Damascus? Not a bit of difference, my good sir; oh dear me no, not a bit, not a bit of difference; pit just the same; oh dear, yet just the same, just the same." "Which shoots the best, do you say? Ah, the steel; oh yes, the steel." "Shoot well up, well up." "Look through that barrel, sir". "Back-action locks? Yes; ours are all back-action; leaves the action stronger." "There's not a screw in these guns, my good sir, that is not as good as gold – as good as gold. My customers are not like City stock-brokers; they want guns that can work – that can work." "So-and-So's guns shake all to pieces after a while." (Here came in a name of such prodigious dignity that we really have not the courage to produce it.) "You seem to like Whitworth steel very much, Mr. Boss; a large number of your guns seem to have it." (Just here he dashes into the passage, and his voice is loud pitching into some subordinate.) "What was it you said, my good sir? Oh yes, I use Whitworth steel; it shoots well up, and it makes up into a lighter gun. I like Whitworth. Best steel there is." "There, my good sir, you are very fond of guns, look over that one (producing one, and going back to ule his locks.) "Oh, you my look it well over, ever screw is as good as gold. Did you every see such a bit of wood as that in a stock? So-and-So never has nice stocks (the great name again). To this we rather demurred, though the stock we had in our hands was certainly a beautiful bit of wood. "Oh no, my good sir, you don't take up my time; glad to see you; glad to see anyone fond of guns."

This little extract will serve to point our moral and to illustrate an interview which was one of the most amusing we have ever experienced, carried on, as it was, under difficulties, while Mr. Boss filed at his locks, gave directions to workpeople, fetched guns for our inspection, keeping up meanwhile a running fire of question and answer. The style, however, we have honestly reproduced, also the opinions. In short, it is no use to disguise the fact that Mr. Boss is a character (using the term in its very best sense), but no one even of the dullest comprehension could be in his presence half-an-hour without forming the strongest impression of his sterling directness, of his perfect grasp of his profession and of his strong love for it. That impression leads the way with certainty to another, viz., that his work is honest, thorough, and genuine.

To see Mr. Boss in his work apron, and up to his eyes in steel filings, few would guess his position in his profession, and that scarcely more than two or three are his peers. Unlike many who might be named and who have no a quarter of his status, nor of the balance at his bankers, he makes no pretence of any sort, but is to be found all day and every day in his shop at his bench, in his shirt-sleeves and as hard at work as if he had as much leeway to make up as those above alluded to. He is personally and practically as much as every the soul and centre of his business. His heart is in it; and who-ever gives him an order for a gun will depend on obtaining the most honest and thorough work that it is possible to get, because the building of a gun is to Mr. Boss a labour of love, he is fond of the thing for its own sake, and he is the sort of character that works to satisfy itself, and is independent of outside opinions. So attached is he to his life work that it is our belief that if any cause

should arise to compel him to relinquish it, he would be completely lost and miserable. Othello's occupation would be gone. His guns are light, handy, tight-built weapons, carefully finished. They give the idea of being longer and narrower than those of other celebrated makers, and a 12-bore Boss looks, at first sight, like a 16. The reason of this optical delusion no doubt lies in the fact that their locks are all back-action, and thus the action can be narrower than where room has to be left for the insertion of the locks, as is the case in the forward or bar lock. That style of action, combined with back-action locks, allows of the grasp of both right and left hands being made smaller, and gives a light and rakish look to the gun. The favourite fastening for the Boss gun is the side lever over the right-hand lock, and for foreign customers, or those who shoot in distant countries, where repairs might be difficult, Mr. Boss provides no springs to the fastenings. He builds them chiefly with barrels of Whitworth steel, of which he has a high opinion. Mr. Boss considers 30in. the proper length for a gun-barrel, and he is extremely firm on this point. On no consideration could he be induced to build a gun with shorter barrels than 28in. at the very lowest, and then he would not guarantee the shooting as up to that of 30in. We found him much more decided about this than any other maker. We know from private experience that his guns are extremely good shooters, especially on wild game late in the season, and no doubt he has reason for what he says, particularly as he prefers black powders to the nictro-compounds. So far as we have gone, we have found no long-established London maker who would consider anything less than 28in. at all "in it". Some of the guns of Mr. Boss are finished with a chequered rib, which, he contends, is an assistance to the eye. The average weight of his guns of 12-bore is 6lbs. 10oz, and if hammerless a couple of ounces more. Six pounds he considers an extra light gun for 12-bore, and below that weight he would not go. The 6lbs. guns would, of course, have 28in. barrels; the 6lbs. 10oz. guns have barrels of full length. The name of Mr. Boss (and also Mr. Grant) used to appear not so long ago as the crack makers of pigeon guns, but these names have lately come to be superseded by others. It costs money to keep up an appearance in the columns of newspaper reports of matches, no matter how good the guns may be built. It is not unusual for a gunmaker to pay the newspapers for every insertion of the name of his guns in their pigeon-shooting reports, and to send an attendant to the grounds, wet or fine, on the chances of his customers happening to put in an appearance, is an outlay which, if the thing is followed up persistently, is by no means light. Messrs. Boss and Grant have not seen their way to follow up the matter, and have thus dropped out of the race, and allowed other names to come forward prominently for pigeon guns.

by early 1890 he could not cope with the running of the business. He decided to bring in a partner with a view to later selling it and contacted John Robertson.

John Robertson had his own gunmaking business as an outworker making and repairing guns for Boss and other gunmakers at 4 George Yard, off Wardour Street in Soho, London. He was on the look-out for an established business. When he heard that Boss might be on offer he purchased a share of the business from Edward Paddison. Edward Paddison's proceeds from the sale either went to his first wife's daughter or to pay off his debts to Robertson.

On 2nd September 1891 at 19 Portland Terrace, Edward Paddison died. His death certificate records that he died from "septicaemia three years, exhaustion". He was sixty-six years of age.

On 5th September 1891, *The Field* published the following announcement, "Boss, at his residence, 19 Portland Terrace, Regent's Park, 2nd inst., after a long and painful illness borne with the greatest patience, Edward Fields Paddison Boss, 73 St James's Street, Gunmaker, aged 68. Friends please accept this intimation." *The Field* got his age wrong – he was actually sixty-six years of age, virtually the same life span as his uncle Thomas Boss who died aged sixty-seven.

His Will, proved on 6th January 1892, is in total contrast to Thomas and Emma Boss's Wills. He describes himself as a Gunmaker at 73 St James's Street carrying on business under the style of E.F.P. Boss. He left £23.10s.0d., everything having previously passed either to his first wife's daughter or in paying debts to Robertson. This £23.10s.0d. he left to his nephew Walter Fields Paddison, the son of his deceased brother John Paddison of no. 2 Lygon Terrace, Malvern in Worcestershire, a coachbuilder. Walter was employed as a gunmaker at Boss at this time. One of the witnesses to the Will was Mr Embelton the manager and clerk of Boss & Co.

He was buried in the City of Westminster cemetery, East Finchley on 7th September 1891. The grave was for one internment only. He was not buried with either of his wives.

We can get a very good picture of what Edward Paddison was like from an article that was published in *Land and Water* on 11 August 1888. I make no apologies for reproducing it in full since it gives an excellent description of him and his thoughts on certain aspects of gunmaking. He is referred to as "Mr Boss". See article on previous pages.

This article is of great interest. Note that it refers in the second paragraph to Boss working for Purdey "as shown by one of his old work books". This is the early ledger book circa 1820, still in the possession of Boss. It is this statement that was misinterpreted to give rise to the fallacy that Boss worked under Purdey, a fact copied by all subsequent authors.

Paddison preferred back action locks because they "leave the action stronger". Most of the hammer and hammerless guns were built with back action locks. I suppose it is a matter of personal taste, but I find this use of back action locks as bespoiling the lines and harmony of a gun. He also preferred Whitworth steel for barrels. Whitworth steel was very expensive eg the following are comparison prices for pairs of barrels in the 1880s:

Whitworth's fluid compressed steel	90 shillings
English steel Siemens Martin process	24 shillings
English machine forged best	
Damascus in four rods	31 shillings

From the early 1880s Whitworth's steel was increasingly fitted to best guns. It was stronger than ordinary steel and consequently could be made lighter. Because the metal was even in grain, in contrast to the contrasting grain of Damascus, it could be bored more easily in rifle barrels. It got its name since it was compressed in the ingot whilst the metal was still in its molten state.

The use of a side lever for opening is mentioned. A great many Boss guns were built with this side lever in preference to the more normal top lever. Paddison is quite insistent on the traditional 30″ barrel. Nitro powders were becoming more prevalent at this time and, due to their faster burning rate, they did not require such long barrels. Paddison appears adamant that 30″ is the "proper length".

From 1879 onwards there was a noticeable drop in demand for Boss guns. Around 1850, Boss produced seventy to eighty guns per annum and this increased to around ninety-five guns per annum in the 1860s. In 1878, they still produced seventy guns per annum, yet in 1879 only fifty guns were produced and in 1880 only thirty. By the late 1880s production had steadied to around fifty-five guns per annum.

There are several reasons why the rate of gun production dropped in the 1880s. This was the time of the Great Depression in agriculture, when the vast prairies of America were opened up by the "Iron Road" thereby enabling American grain to flood into Britain and depress British grain prices. Many farmers and landowners suffered severely due to this influx of foreign corn and agricultural rent dropped. In addition, pastoral farmers also suffered due to the development of refrigerated ships bringing dairy produce from Australia and New Zealand and meat from the Argentine. Many landowners under these economic constraints postponed ordering new guns until the market adjusted itself by the 1890s.

Feb. 16. 1886

22. Bruton Street.
Berkeley Square. W.

Lord Hastings is very pleased with the pair of 16 bore guns made for him by Mr. Boss

He has found them extremely handy and accurate and hard hitters.

A letter of commendation written by Lord Hastings's secretary on 16th February 1886. It concerns a pair of 16-bore side snap hammer guns nos. 3875 and 3876 recently completed for Lord Hastings.

London
Sept. 30" 1881,

I have been shooting with a shot gun 3529 made by Messrs. Boss & Co. in Scotland, and it gave me much satisfaction. It killed at long distances and I can recommend Messrs. Boss & Co. to all sportsmen.

Bradley Martin

A letter of commendation written by Mr Bradley-Martin on 30 September 1881 referring to gun no. 3529, a double-barrel 12-bore hammer gun.

Edward Paddison must take some of the blame. He was very conservative in attitude to gun technology. He held out long in favour of the underlever when the snap action had proved its greater convenience, he preferred side levers to the more fashionable and easier top lever and he preferred back action locks that were not so pleasing as front action locks. This conservatism must have had an effect on demand when it must be remembered that customers in the 19th century changed their guns regularly and wanted to keep up with the latest technology. In extenuation, Paddison was ageing and ill from the mid 1880s onwards, found difficulty in running his business and this might explain why he was so set in his ways.

Thus ended the original Boss family business. It had lasted some sixty years. In that time the firm under its various partners had built up a superb reputation as a first-class gunmaking establishment producing nothing but best guns. The combination of this reputation and John Robertson's inventive genius would soon ensure Boss & Co's worldwide status and repute that it still enjoys today.

Edward Paddison received a great many letters of commendation from Boss's customers all over the world. He kept many of these and pasted them into a scrap book still in the possession of Boss & Co. Three of these letters are reproduced above and overleaf.

Denver Colorado U.S.A.
June 10th 1890

Mr E. F. P. Boss

     I received the beautiful gun you built for me on the 3rd of this month and to say that I am satisfied does not do justice For elegant workmanship beautiful finish and symetri-cal proportions it has no superiors I will inform you farther on with the success I meet with in shooting it

     Thanking you very kindly for the attention you paid to my order
     I am Respectfully
     W. Y. Sedam

P. S. The gun has attracted a great deal of attention among the local shooting fraternity here
     W. Y. S.

A letter of commendation written by W. Y. Sedan from the U.S.A. on 10th June 1890 regarding his double-barrel 12-bore hammerless ejector gun no. 4078.

CHAPTER SIX

THE GUNS AND RIFLES OF THE BREECH-LOADING ERA

Boss tended to build the same type of guns in the breech-loading period as in the earlier muzzle-loading period. The double shotgun accounted for the majority of production. Hardly any pistols were made, and revolvers such as Adam or Tranter bearing the Boss name will have been retailed by Boss only.

Inflation meant that gun prices rose accordingly in the second half of the 19th century and the list below gives average prices for Boss guns in this period. They had stopped quoting in the older style of guineas yet still offered a discount for cash.

Pinfire Guns in the 1860s

Double-barrel 14-bore gun plus case	£45.0.0d
Double-barrel 12-bore gun plus cartridge loading apparatus	£40.0.0d
Double-barrel 12-bore gun plus case, plus cartridge loading apparatus	£50.0.0d

Gun and Rifle Prices in the 1880s

Hammer gun, side snap	£42.0.0d
Pair of lever overguard hammer guns and case	£120.0.0d
Hammer gun, side snap plus case	£50.0.0d
Hammer gun, Whitworth steel barrels plus case	£55.0.0d
Double leather case	£7.0.0d
500 Hammer Express rifle plus case	£60.0.0d
450 Hammer Express rifle plus case	£70.0.0d
Hammerless gun	£49.0.0d
Hammerless gun, Whitworth steel barrels plus case	£55.0.0d
Pair of hammerless guns, side snaps plus case	£90.0.0d
Pair of hammerless ejectors, Whitworth steel barrels plus case	£120.0.0d

The first breech-loader built by Boss was no. 1600, a double-barrel 14-bore underlever pinfire gun ordered by G. B. Bruce, 1st Regiment Life Guards on 9th June 1858. The muzzle-loader went into decline as breech-loading guns rapidly took over in the early 1860s as shown in Chapter Three.

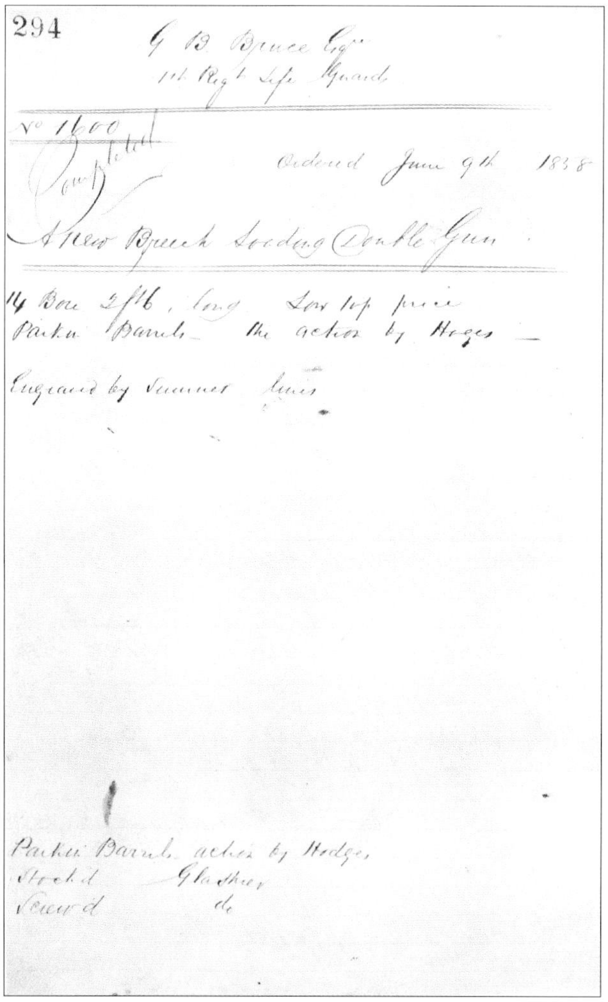

The illustration below shows the first order for a breech-loader dated 9th June 1858 in Boss's order ledger, a 14-bore pinfire gun no. 1600 built for G. B. Bruce of the Life Guards. George Brudenell Bruce had become a sub-lieutenant on the 28th August 1857 in

294
G. B. Bruce Esqr
1st Regt Life Guards
No 1600
Completed
Ordered June 9th 1858
A New Breech Loading Double Gun
14 Bore 2ft 6, long Low top piece
Parker Barrels the action by Hodges
Engraved by Sumner lines
Parker Barrels action by Hodges
Stocked Gladstone
Screwed do

that regiment. He resigned his commission shortly afterwards. Note that the barrels are by Parkin, the engraving by Sumner and that the gun was actioned by the well-known actioner, E. C. Hodges.

Early breech-loaders were primarily of French origin. The early examples were not particularly successful due to the difficulties in obtaining a perfect gas seal at the breech end when the gun was discharged. A Parisian gunmaker, Houllier, patented the first gas-tight cartridge in 1846 and this transformed the breech-loader. Another Parisian gunmaker, Casimir Lefaucheux, developed an efficient locking mechanism in which the barrels were opened and closed by a lever underneath. This gun and cartridge were publicly introduced into Britain at the Great Exhibition of 1851. This gun worked on the pinfire principle: the gun hammer struck a brass pin that projected from the base of the cartridge, the other end of the pin stricking the detonating compound inside the cartridge.

The pinfire was very much an interim development essentially being a muzzle-loader to load at the breech. The protruding cartridge pins were not dissimilar to the percussion nipples and the hammers were set high to strike the top of the primers just as in the percussion

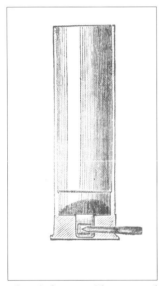

The pinfire cartridge as used in the Lefaucheux gun.

muzzle-loader. Pinfires were by today's standards not only inconvenient, there was always an element of danger associated with them. Cartridges were difficult to store with their protruding pins and finicky to insert into the gun since the pin in the cartridge had to remain upright to slot into a groove cut into the top of the barrels at the breech end. The external pin in the cartridge could receive a knock with possible malevolent result. Finally pinfire cartridges were tricky and expensive to make. The question must be why pinfires lasted so long when the modern centre fire breech-loader developed as early as 1861 was profoundly superior. The answer must lie in the conservatism of the sportsman and the gunmakers. Having recently adopted breech-loaders another major change would take time. To quote the old adage: "Walking takes precedence before running."

Boss built enormous numbers of pinfires, some 766 being produced between 1858 and 1871. The breech-loader by 1860 had proven advantages over the muzzle-loader and most sportsmen ordered new guns on this principle. What is interesting is how few Boss pinfires are extant to this day. A great many were later converted to centre fire in the 1870s and 1880s. These can be spotted due to the fact that the grooves in the top of the barrels at the breech end will have been welded up. A check on the serial number should confirm the gun's origins. If a serial number is from the years 1858 to *circa* 1866 then the gun was originally a pinfire since no centre fire guns were made prior to 1866. When the centre fire gun superceded the pinfire in the 1870s, pinfire guns were regarded as superfluous, discarded and drifted into obsolescence as cartridges fell into short supply. This explains why so few Boss pinfires survive today.

Boss built very few pairs of pinfires. Most sportsmen realised that a metamorphosis was taking place in gun technology and that existing developments were being rapidly superceded by others. Customers bought pinfires mainly to experiment with the new system, there being little point in going to the expense of a pair. Nearly all the pinfires were back action with under-levers, built to the same style and dimensions as muzzle-loaders. The last pinfire produced was no. 2945 a double-barrel 12-bore ordered on 29th September 1871 by the Earl of Jersey.

The next gun illustrated (see plate 25) is a double-barrel 12-bore pinfire gun no 2135 ordered on February 9th 1864 by M. A. Bass. M. A. Bass was born on the 12th November 1837, one of the Bass brewing family. He was a Liberal M.P. for various Staffordshire constituencies 1865–1886 until the latter year when he was elevated to become Baron Burton.

This gun is the No. 1 gun of a matched consecutively numbered pair. Not only is it unusual in that, although Boss built many pinfires, it has survived unaltered, but that it is of a pair. Very few pairs of pinfires were built on account of the fact that breech-loaders were in their infancy and most sportsmen wanted to experiment with them before going to the expense of ordering a pair. The gun is in very original unrestored condition. The back action locks are engraved simply, "Boss & Co.", an early engraved example of the title of the firm as we know it today. There is no maker's mark on the inside of the locks. The gun was actioned by E. C. Hodges and like all pinfires of this period, the breech is very slim due to the fact that breech pressures were not properly understood. An elegant ring underlever opens and closes the action. "No. 1" is engraved on the heel of the iron butt plate, on the trigger guard and on the barrels. The stock is finely figured with "M. A. B." scroll engraved on the escutcheon and the forend is locked by a barrel bolt. The 30" Damascus barrels are stamped, "J P", the mark of barrel-maker John Portlock, and are

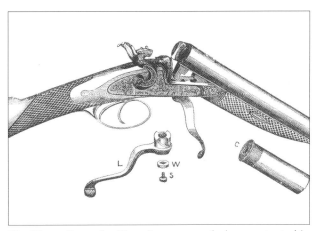

The Henry Jones double-grip screw underlever patented in 1859. During this period Boss always referred to it as "The Lever Over Guard".

engraved, "Boss & Co. 73 St James' Street, London". The muzzle-loading triangular foresight has now been dispensed with and the more common silver bead foresight is fitted. Originally, the gun with its pair was contained within a case complete with apparatus.

The action used on this gun is commonly referred to as the "underlever" – a better terminology is the "inert screw underlever". A lever over the trigger guard is pushed forward a quarter of a turn, releasing the grips on the barrels which then hinge downward of their own accord. After the gun has been loaded the barrels are closed and the lever returned to its original position.

This action is one of the most common types of closing actions to be found on 19th-century breech-loaders. It was patented by a Birmingham gunmaker, Henry Jones, in 1859. He failed to make any money from it because he let his patent lapse in September 1862 due to lack of money to meet the £50 stamp duty necessary to keep it in force. Jones was suffering financial problems at the time and went bankrupt four years later. Underlevers were robust, did not use springs and needed little maintenance. How popular they were and how many were built by Boss is described in Appendix 5B. The 1870s were the heyday of the underlever. Thereafter snap actions that closed automatically, with their greater convenience, took over. Nevertheless there was still a fair demand by customers of Boss for the underlever. Many were built in the 1880s. In Boss's records, this action is always referred to as "L. O. G." – "Lever Over Guard".

Most late use of the lever over guard was confined to larger bore shotguns and double rifles where robustness was of paramount importance. Guns for use in distant lands like India also favoured the system due to its simplicity. Very few pairs of underlevers were made by Boss. Customers who ordered pairs usually specified some type of snap action for speed of loading.

Pasted to the back of Boss's order ledger 1865 to 1870 is a copy of a letter written to a customer who had doubts about the underlever (lever over guard). It

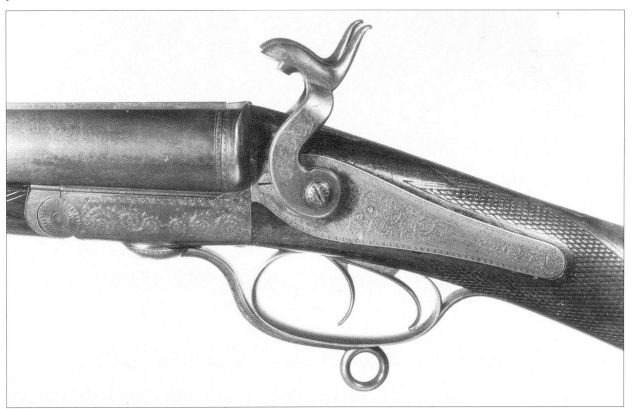

The action of pinfire gun no. 2135 built in 1864 showing the graceful scroll underlever and early style slim breech. The lockplate engraving had been recently changed *circa* 1862 to the simpler form of, "Boss & Co.". See also Plate 25.

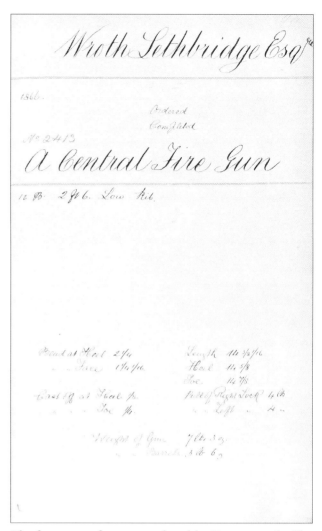

The order for 12-bore pinfire gun no. 2135 showing that it originally was one of a pair ordered on 9th February, 1864 and completed on 17th June, 1864 for M. A. Bass, Esq. Notice the work completed by the outworkers on this gun at the bottom left. From Boss's order ledgers.

The first centre-fire gun produced by Boss was a double-barrel 12-bore gun no. 2413 ordered on 16th June, 1866 by Wroth Lethbridge. This order is illustrated above.

was most probably written by Edward Paddison who makes out a stout defence for this action. Unfortunately, the letter is neither dated nor signed.

Sir,

We beg respectfully to inform you that we use for our Guns the original Horizontal Lever Over the Guard. We have always set our face against springs of any kind, as although many work very well and we have made several kinds, we are sure that no snap or spring to close the Barrels can be so sound or neat like the Double Grip Lever. We have had B.L. Guns and Rifles out in India for seven years and our customers state that no other kind of fastening would have stood half the time.

With regard to the convenience, it is so slight as not to be considered if the levers are neatly filed and brought nicely over the Guard, they are not at all objectionable and a very little practice will leave

scarcely any difference in the opening and closing of the Breech. The beauty of a B. L. Gun is that it shall fit to a nicety at the Breech and that being the case, it is obvious that the lever must be superior to the spring or snap as the latter must work very free and will wear out much faster on all the faces.

The second centre-fire gun was a double-barrel 12-bore gun no. 2461 ordered on 6th July for E. Pryer. From this point onwards the transition from pinfire to centre fire was rapid. By 1869 hardly any pinfires were built, most customers now ordering centre-fires.

Again as in the pinfire, the centre-fire was a French development. Clement Pottet patented a centre-fire cartridge as early as 1829. A Parisian gunmaker, Francois Eugene Schneider of 13 Rue Gaillon, improved upon this cartridge and at the same time invented a snap action of the type that bolts automatically when closed, patenting his invention in 1861. To all intents and purposes this is the modern day centre-fire system.

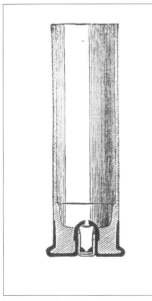

The Pottet centre-fire case.

A London gunmaker, G. H. Daw of 57 Threadneedle Street, recognised the merits of this patent and bought the rights to it. The new system received great acclaim and other makers attempted to copy the system. Daw was forced to take the cartridge-makers, Eley Bros, to court for supposed patent infringement but lost his case. The decision meant that gunmakers now had the freedom to develop and perfect the centre-fire. (above right.)

An early Boss centre-fire gun is illustrated overleaf. This is a double-barrel 12-bore, back action underlever hammer gun, no. 2857 ordered by R. E. Crompton on 22nd October 1870. Rookes Evelyn Bell Crompton of Tanfield House, Bedale, Yorks was born on 31st May 1845. He rose to become a Lt. Col. in the Electrical Engineers and served in the South African campaign of 1900 where he was mentioned in dispatches and won various medals. It displays all the characteristics of an early hammer gun, the underlever action, back action locks and high standing hammers.

The 30″ Damascus barrels are stamped, "J P", being supplied by John Portlock. On the top rib is engraved, "Boss & Co., 73 St James' Street, London". An extended top strap is used and a full steel butt-plate fitted, both betraying the gun's early origins. The forend is fastened by a barrel bolt. Originally the gun was supplied with a case and apparatus.

Internally the locks are stamped, "Stanton". This gun is an early example of Stanton's rebounding locks. The early hammer guns of the 1860s used the same full cock, half cock system with their locks as was used with the muzzle-loaders. With a centre-fire gun this was not only inconvenient, it was dangerous. When the gun was fired, the hammers in the fire position meant that the firing pins were forced into the primer caps of the cartridges. The gun could not be opened. The shooter had to draw back the hammers to half cock to release the spring-loaded firing pins. This was inconvenient.

If a sportsman was in a hurry, or not familiar with handling a hammer gun, he could put cartridges in the chambers, forget to pull back the hammers to half cock and close the gun. The protruding firing pins could strike the primer caps in the cartridges and the gun could go off not properly fastened. This was dangerous.

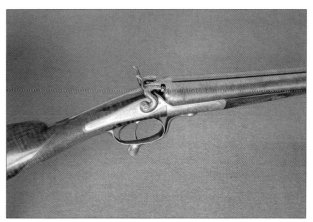

Underlever gun no. 2857. See Plate 26.

John Stanton of Wolverhampton invented the rebounding lock to overcome these problems in 1867. Rebounding locks do not have two positions, half cock and full cock. When the gun is cocked and fired the hammer hits the firing pin. The top limb of the main-spring then comes into operation and "bounces" the hammer back well away from the firing pin. So when the gun is not cocked, the hammer never rests against the firing pin. A great many of the early non-rebound-

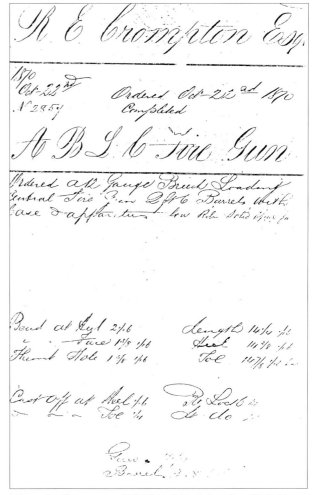

The order for gun no. 2857 dated 22nd October 1870. From Boss's order ledgers.

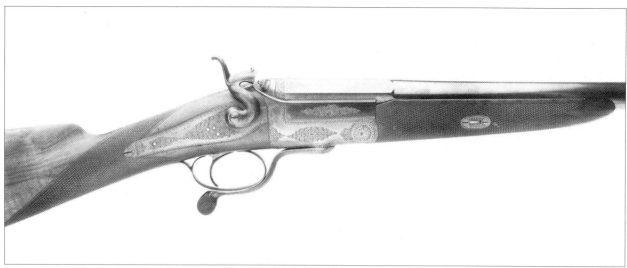

The action of the single-barrel boy's 16-bore. See also Plate 27.

ing type locks were altered by Boss to this system. By the 1870s most hammer guns built had rebounding locks.

A very interesting and very rare Boss hammer gun is illustrated in plate 27. This is a single-barrel 16-bore hammer gun with underlever and back action lock *circa* 1870. Boss built a mere handfull of single-barrel guns on account of the fact that top quality single-barrel guns were rarely demanded. Most single-barrel guns were for boys to learn to shoot with and there was no point in spending a lot of money on an interim gun. This gun was built for a boy, being a 16-bore, very light with a short stock and short barrel. The action is of the inert screw underlever type of typical 1870s style. The back action rebounding lock is stamped, "Stanton" inside and engraved on the exterior, "Boss & Co.". An extended

top strap is used. The 29″ Damascus barrel has no barrel-maker's stamp and is engraved simply, "Boss & Co., London". The stock has a good figure and the forend attached by a barrel bolt has a horn tip.

Apart from its rarity value, what makes the gun interesting is that there is no serial number evident anywhere on the gun. The gun is in excellent original condition, so there is no question of a serial number being removed in a refinish. The only marks on the gun apart from the "Boss & Co." engraving are Stanton's stamp inside the lock and London proof marks on the barrel and action. The most probable reason for the lack of serial number is that the gun was a prototype single-barrel to familiarise the gunmakers with single-barrel breech-loading construction. On account of the fact that the gun was never ordered by a customer it would

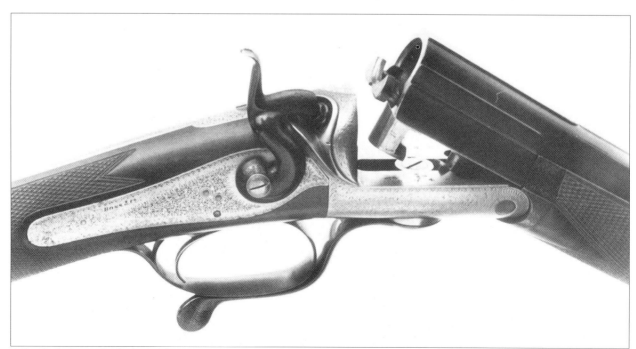

A boy's 16-bore single-barrel hammer gun no. 2746 with rebounding lock built in 1870.

receive no serial number. The gun would remain in the shop and later on be sold to a customer. The owner's initials are engraved on the escutcheon, but due to the fact that there is no record of sales for the 19th century, it is impossible to ascertain who the original owner was.

Another very similar and very rare single-barrel hammer gun is illustrated next. Identical in style to the previous gun, this gun differs in that a serial number is present. No. 2746 is a single-barrel 16-bore underlever hammer gun ordered on 13th January 1870 by John Hick, MP, probably for his son. John Hick of Mytton Hall, Whalley, Lancashire was born in 1815. He was a Liberal/Conservative MP for Bolton between 1868–1880. Again it is a boy's gun. The Damascus barrel engraved, "Boss & Co. London" is 28″ long. The stock is short, being made for a boy. The forend is fastened by a barrel bolt. The lock plate is stamped internally, "Stanton" and externally, "Boss & Co." and is of the rebounding type. The engraving is of the usual Boss standard. Originally the gun was supplied in a leather case with apparatus. Both these single-barrel guns are very handsome and must have given great pride to their novice shooters.

An underlever hammer gun no. 3125 is illustrated below, again typical of the Boss underlever hammer guns of the 1870s. No. 3125 is a double-barrel 12-bore back action underlever hammer gun, built for A. H. Walker in 1873. The action is of the inert screw underlever type. No. 3125 has a finely engraved long top strap to give the gun greater strength, though unfortunately it did not give it enough strength since a very old repair plate has been inlet into the stock to repair a fracture. The forend is attached by the old muzzle-loading

The order for single-barrel gun no. 2746 ordered by John Hick, M.P., on 13th January 1870, most probably for his son.

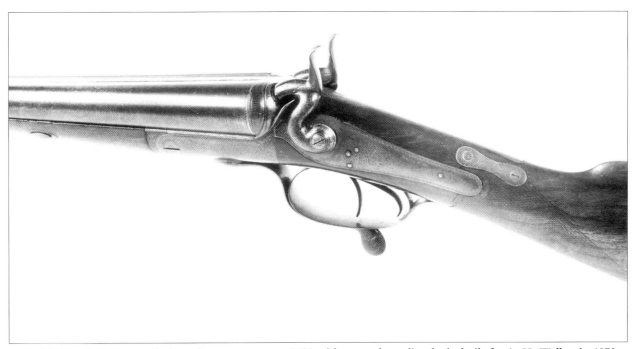

A double-barrel 12-bore underlever hammer gun no. 3125 with non-rebounding locks built for A. H. Walker in 1873.

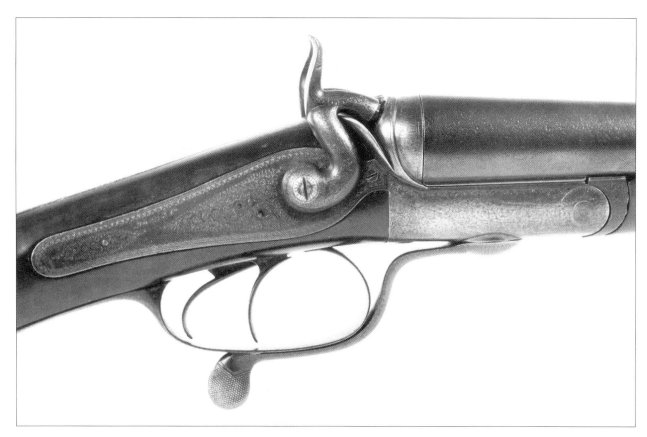

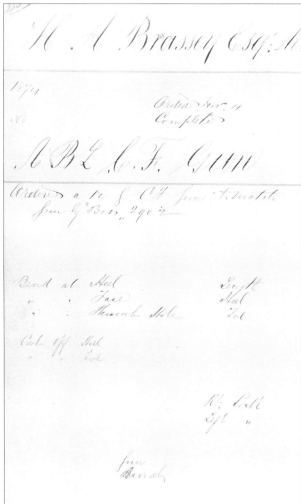

ABOVE: A double-barrel 12-bore underlever hammer gun no. 3208, built in 1874, the no. 2 gun of a pair built to match no. 2902, constructed in 1871 for Henry Brassey, MP.
Left: The order for gun no 3208 dated 4th November 1974 for H.A. Brassey M.P. a double-barrel 12-bore gun built to match a previous Boss gun no. 2902. From Boss's order ledgers.

method of a barrel bolt. The 30″ Damascus barrels are engraved: "Boss & Co., 73 St James' Street, London". They are stamped: "J P", the mark of barrel-maker John Portlock, 2 Globe Yard, South Molton Street, London. A simple silver bead foresight is fitted. Under the trigger guard, stamped in the stock, are initials: "W. J. M." – William Joseph Mears – one of Boss's stockers. The locks are non-rebounding still with the old full/half cock position.

A very similar gun is illustrated above. This is a double-barrel 12-bore back action underlever hammer gun no. 3208 built for Henry Brassey of Preston Hall, Aylesford, Kent. He was M.P. for Sandwich, 1868–85 and High Sheriff for Kent by 1890. His father was Thomas Brassey the famous railway contractor of the mid 19th century.

No. 3208 is the no. 2 gun of a composite pair. Boss's order ledgers state that it was built to match no. 2902 constructed in 1871. The back action locks are engraved: "Boss & Co." and they are of the non-rebounding variety. A screw underlever opens and closes the action and an extended top strap provides extra strength. The 30″ Damascus barrels are engraved, "Boss

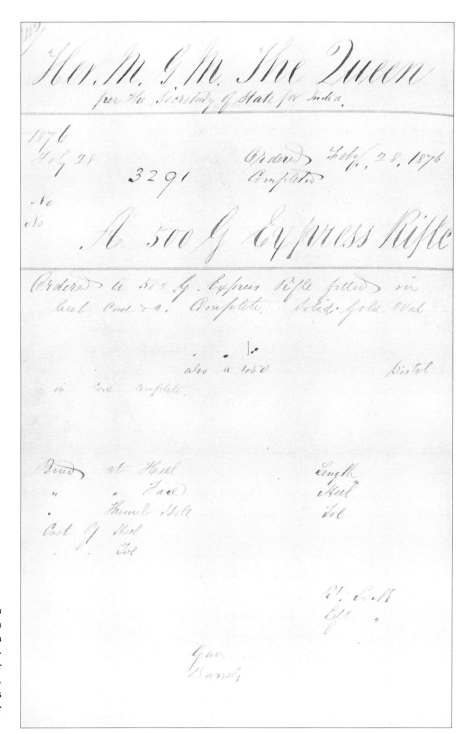

The order from Queen Victoria dated 28th February 1876 for a .500 Express rifle to be given as a gift to Indian royalty or plenipotentiary. Note the other order for a ".450 pistol in case complete". This would not be built by Boss themselves. From Boss order ledgers.

& Co., 73 St James' Street, London". "J P" is stamped under the barrels – John Portlock barrels again. The simple silver bead foresight is fitted. A barrel bolt attaches the forend. Although well worn the stock is nicely figured. The barrels, forend and trigger guard are all engraved with "2" – in reference to it being the no. 2 gun. "W. J. M." is stamped under the trigger guard, the mark of stocker William Mears.

On 28th February 1876, the order ledgers show an order by Her Majesty, Queen Victoria. The relevant page is illustrated above. This order was for a present to some dignitary in India, as it states under the title, "Per

the Secretary of State for India". One year later, in 1877, Queen Victoria would assume the title Empress of India. A great many gifts were made to Indian royalty and plenipotentiaries to smooth the passage of this accolade. This gift might have been used for such a purpose.

The gift was no. 3291, a .500 Express rifle in best case complete. This would be a hammer rifle with an underlever. She also ordered a .450 pistol in case complete. Boss would not make the pistol, they would buy it in and engrave it with their own name and address.

The underlever hammer guns of the early 1870s are, in my opinion, not aesthetically pleasing – there is a

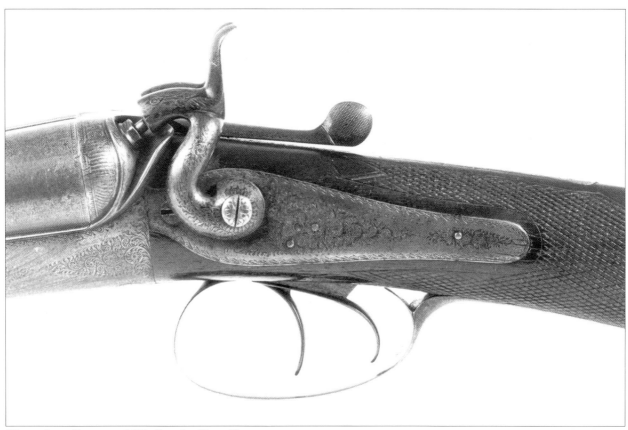

The action of gun no. 3403. See also Plate 28.

clumsiness and heaviness about them. By contrast, the later Boss hammer guns of the late 1870s and 1880s lost this ponderous look. As technical improvements advanced and a better understanding of breech-loading construction ensued, the guns became more graceful.

The use of the snap action was primarily responsible for this. A snap action is an opening and closing system that uses a small lever utilising a spring to snap the action shut. The first snap action was ordered on 18th September, 1867 by Lord Seton, no. 2563 a double-barrel 12-bore gun. Unfortunately the records do not state what type of snap action this was.

Boss used three main types of snap action:

1. The under snap or thumbhole. This was the thumbhole under snap as invented by Purdey.
2. The side snap or side lever.
3. The top snap or top lever.

Appendix 5B shows the breakdown of the various types of action as used by Boss.

Gun no. 3403, illustrated above, is a double-barrel 12-bore back action, top lever hammer gun. This gun was ordered on 15th June 1877 for R. Hutton Squire, Holly Hall, Bedale, Yorkshire. The Purdey top lever is used. The Purdey top lever system of opening would later become by the early 20th century the main method of opening and closing gun actions. Everything

was in its favour, it had handsome lines and it was very convenient to operate. Until this system came along the sportsman had to put his hand under the trigger guard to open the gun. With the Purdey bolt a gun could be opened with one simple movement of the thumb on the top lever without having to release the grip on the wrist of the stock.

"Purdey Top Lever" is a misnomer since it was actually a combination of two patents. Purdey had patented a double bite action in May 1863 which was easy to close and very secure when shut. This double bite is usually found in combination with the familiar top lever patented shortly afterwards by William Scott in 1865. Since only one part of the action is by Purdey, it is technically wrong to call it the Purdey top lever.

An extended top strap is still used. The scroll engraved locks are engraved, "Boss & Co.". They are now of the early rebounding pattern with high rabbit-ear hammers.

The 30″ Damascus barrels are engraved, "Boss & Co., 73 St James' Street, London". The original set of barrels must have been damaged since Boss fitted a new set of barrels in 1887 as the present barrels bear the serial no. 3909. The old lumps were retained still bearing the original no. 3403. The barrels are stamped, "C.L.", being bought in from Charles Lancaster. The old bolted forend has now given way to an Anson forend using a push-button catch.

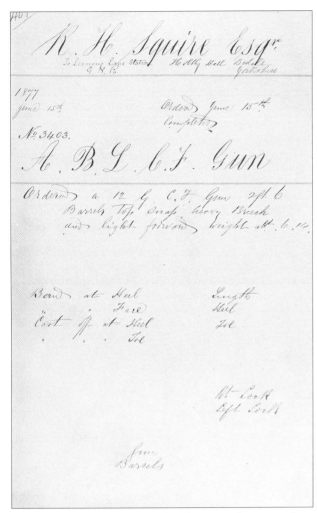

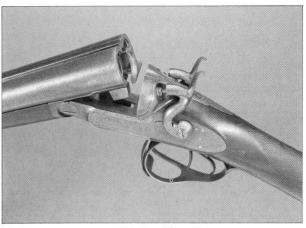

Under-snap gun no. 3455. See Plate 29.

The gun illustrated above is no. 3455, one of the most attractive Boss hammer guns I have seen. It is the No. 1 gun of a pair ordered on 31st October 1877 for Captain V. Montagu. Born in 1841, Captain Montagu served in the Black Sea in the Crimean War and in the Indian Mutiny 1857-8. He rose to the rank of Rear Admiral and retired in 1886. Later he would become the Earl of Sandwich.

No. 3455 is a 12-bore under-snap-action gun with a Purdey "thumbhole lever" and front action locks. The Purdey thumbhole lever was an early method of opening guns before the adoption of the Scott top lever. The trigger guard is bifurcated. A wide short lever at the front of the guard is pushed forward by the thumb to open the gun. The thumbhole gives a gun attractive clean lines. In addition, with the extra width of the trigger guard it makes a gun comfortable to carry over the arm. Perhaps it was this elegance that caused Boss to make many thumbholes well after the introduction

The order for gun no. 3403 dated June 15th, 1877 a double-barrel 12-bore top lever gun ordered by R. H. Squire. From Boss's order ledgers.
BELOW: The breech end of barrels no. 3455 with the stamp, "J.P." showing that they are by John Portlock, 2 Globe Yard, South Molton Street, London.

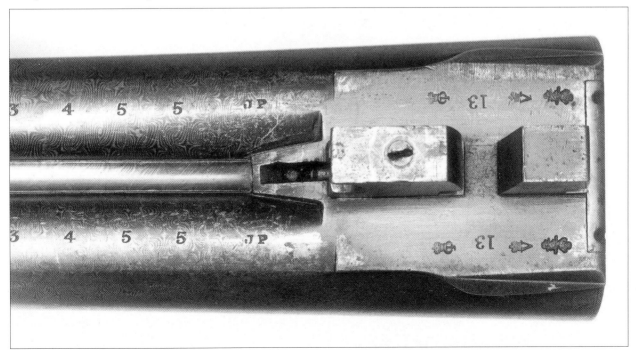

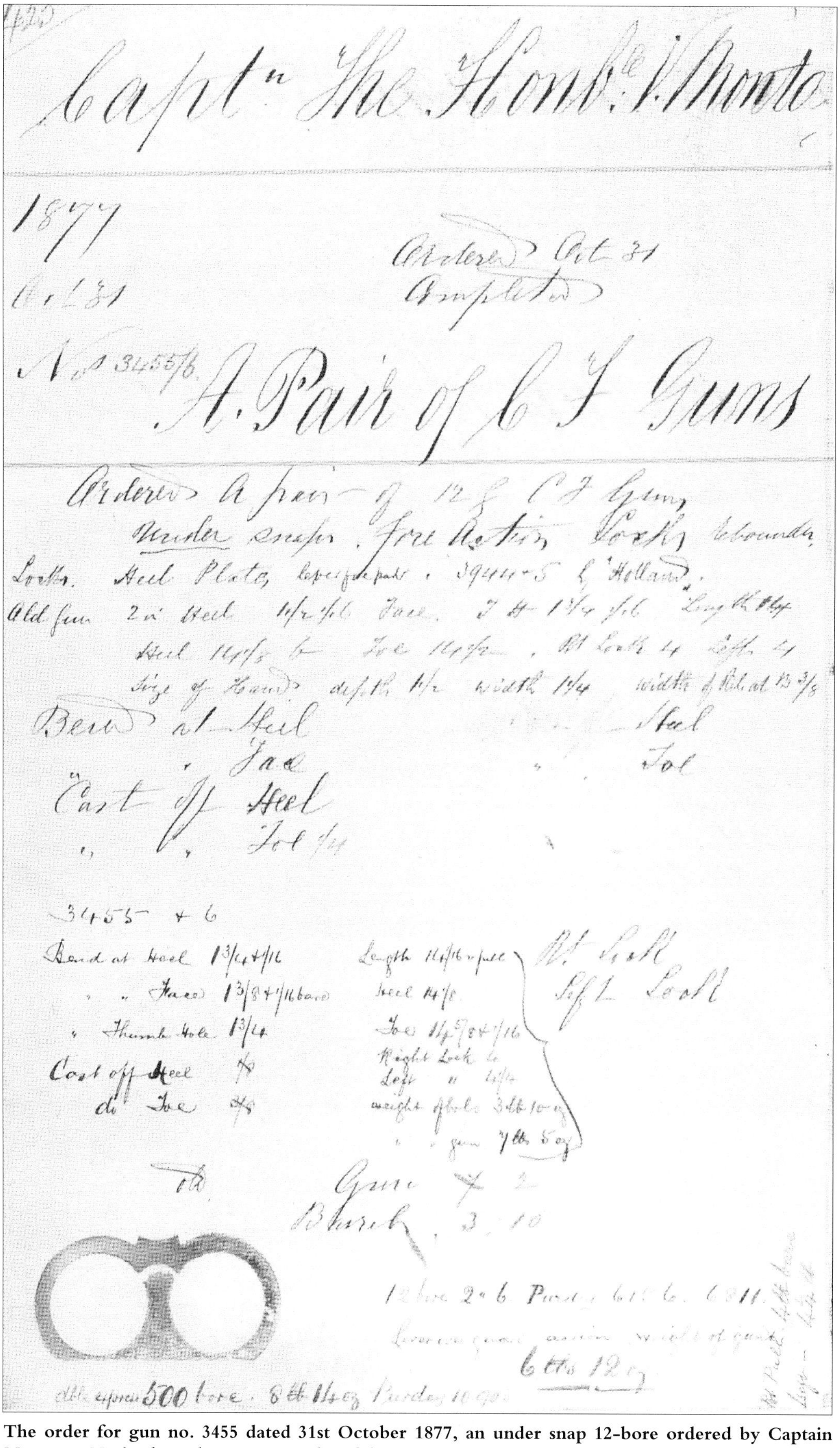

Captn The Honble. V. Montagu

1877

Oct 31

Ordered Oct 31
Completed

No 3455/6. A Pair of C F Guns

Ordered a pair of 12 g C F Guns
Under snap. Free Action Locks Rebounding Locks. Heel Plates, lever for pads. 3944-5 of Hollands.
Old gun 2 in Heel 1 1/2 full Face. T H 1 3/4 full Length 14
Heel 14 1/8 to Toe 14 1/2, Rt Lock 4 Left 4
Size of Hand depth 1/2 width 1/4 width of Rib at 13 3/8
Bend at Heel — Heel
" Face " Toe
Cast off Heel
" " Toe 1/4

3455 + 6
Bend at Heel 1 3/4 + 1/16 — Length 14 1/16 full — Rt Lock
" " Face 1 3/8 + 1/16 bare — Heel 14 1/8 — Left Lock
" Thumb Hole 1 3/4 — Toe 14 5/8 + 1/16
Cast off Heel 1/8 — Right Lock 4
do Toe 3/8 — Left " 4/4
weight of brls 3 lb 10 oz
" " gun 7 lb 5 oz

Old Gun 7 2
Barrel 3 10

12 bore 2" 6 Purdey 61 6. 6811.
weight of gun 6 lbs 12 oz

dble express 500 bore. 8 lb 11 oz Purdey 10 90

The order for gun no. 3455 dated 31st October 1877, an under snap 12-bore ordered by Captain Montagu. Notice how the guns are to be of the same dimensions as his old guns by Hollands. Notice also the print of the breech end of the barrels. This appears frequently in the order ledgers. From Boss's order ledgers.

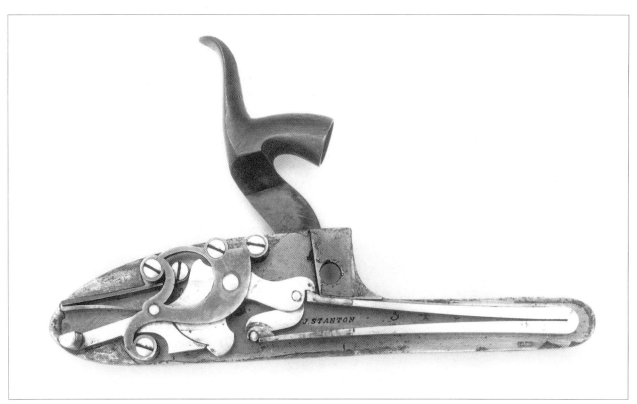

The interior of the left-hand lock from gun no. 3455. This is a rebounding lock by John Stanton, Wolverhampton who supplied large numbers of his quality locks to Boss. The lower part of the main spring provides the power to operate the hammer, he upper part to rebound the hammer backwards after firing.

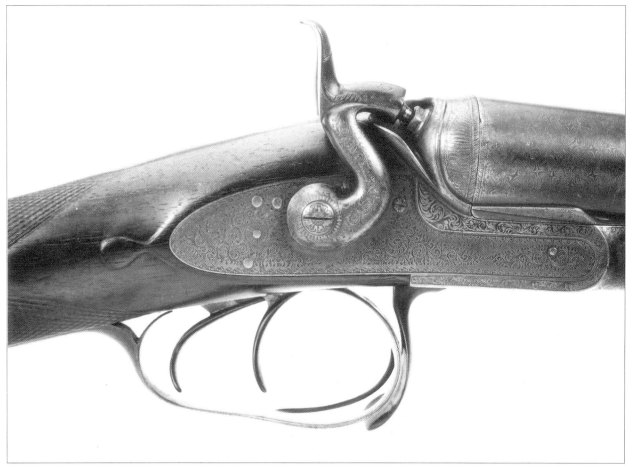

No. 3455 showing the fine scroll engraving popular from the late 1870s.

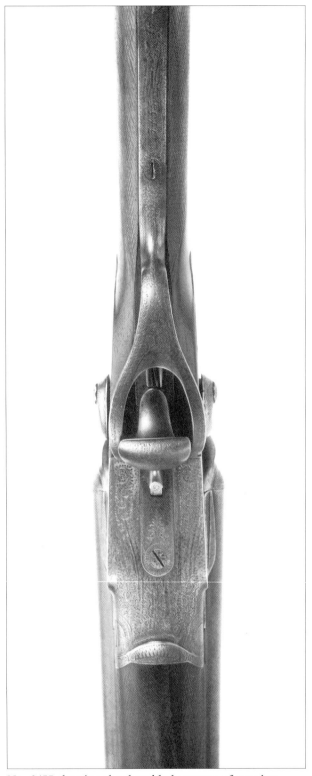

No. 3455 showing the thumbhole system of opening.

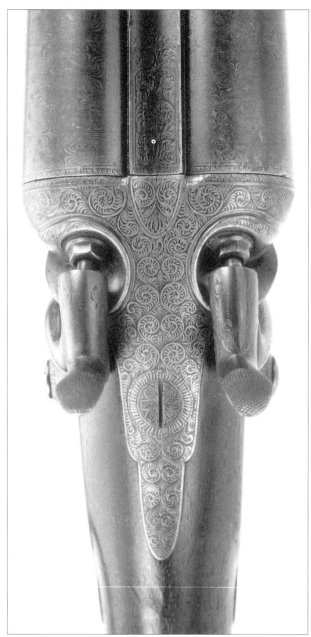

The tang of gun no. 3455, engraved by John Sumner.

of the top lever. Its drawback was that a sportsman had to relax his grip on the wrist of the stock to operate it. Boss made many variants of this under snap depending upon the whim of the customer. Some thumbholes were in the form of a scroll, others were virtually the full width of the guard. These variations are described in the order ledgers as "our own make".

The lines and proportion of this gun are "right" in every detail and the overall effect is of a very elegant gun. The locks and actions are scroll engraved of the very fine close scroll engraving that was popular from the 1880s onwards. They are marked, "Boss & Co.". They are rebounding locks by John Stanton, Wolverhampton, and again as fashion dictated the hammers are getting smaller and lie very nearly out of sight when cocked. The 30″ Damascus barrels are engraved, "Boss & Co., 73 St James' Street, London" and were supplied by Portlocks being stamped, "J.P." A chequered horn heel-plate is fitted to the butt. A Rigby lever forend is used.

So far we have seen two varieties of snap action as fitted to Boss guns, the top snap and under snap. Of all the snap actions built by Boss in this period, the side snap was by far the most common. Edward Paddison

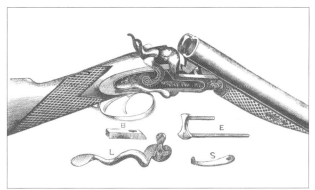

The side snap action as favoured by Edward Paddison and used in most Boss hammer guns.

preferred the side snap having progressed from his adherence to the underlever. Just as he had been dogmatic about the superiority of the underlever, this dogmatism now transferred to the side lever and he persuaded his customers that this system was the best even though in the later period the top lever had become most common. It was not until the late 1880s that Boss began to produce more top levers than side levers.

The gun illustrated below is a double-barrel 16-bore top lever, back action hammer gun no. 3544 ordered by Lord Binning on 31st March 1879. Lord Binning was born on 24th December, 1856. In 1880 he joined the Royal Horseguards and served in the Egyptian Campaign in the 1880s. One of Lord Binning's family homes was Tyninghame House, Preston Kirk, East Lothian – very close to Haddington from where John Robertson came. Later in fact, on the death of his father, Lord Binning would become the Earl of Haddington. It was to be the No. 2 gun of a composite pair being built to match his previous gun by Boss no. 2882. The back action rebounding locks are by Stanton and are finely scroll engraved. The combination of the top lever and being a 16-bore give it the appearance of a slim, elegant gun. A chequered iron heel-plate is fitted to the butt and a "No. 2" is engraved on the trigger guard, barrels and forend. A Rigby lever forend is used. The left barrel of the 29″ barrels is slightly choked and they are engraved, "Boss & Co., 73 St James' Street, London". On account of the fact that the barrels have been refinished, it is impossible to tell who the maker was. Originally a double-tray case housed this gun and its No. 1.

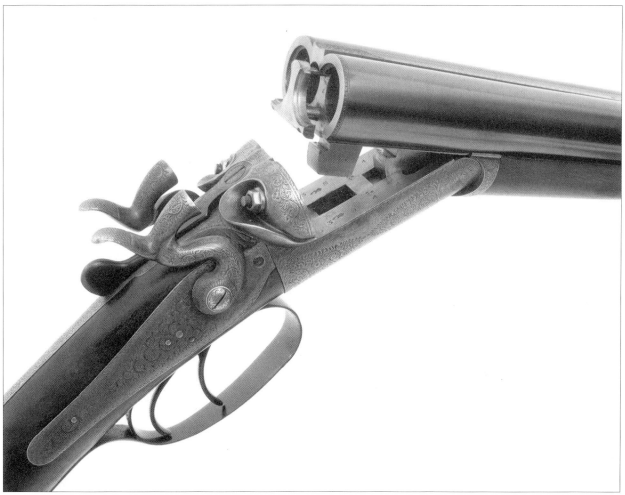

A double-barrel 16-bore top lever hammer gun no. 3544 ordered on 31st March 1879 by Lord Binning to match his previous Boss gun no. 2882. A very slim and elegant gun.

Paste 41.   Tyninghame House
*   Preston Kirk, N.B.*

Lord Binning.
7 Chester St. Grosvenor Place.

1879
March 31st   *Ordered 31st March 1879.*
                         Completed.
№ 3540.

A. C. F. Gun.

Ordered a 16 C.f. gun. top snap.
rebounders, left barrel slightly
choked. to match in every
respect Gun by Boss № 2882.
barrels. 2f 5in.
fitted in Double Tray Case.
Stamped Lord Binning & points outside

Bend at heel   Length.
*   "   "   face   "   Heel.*
Cast off heel   Toe.
*   "   "   Toe*

Rt. lock
Left. do

Gun
Barrels.

The order for gun no. 3544 dated 31st March 1879 from Lord Binning, Tyninghame House, Preston Kirk, East Lothian. This order was to match gun no. 2882 built in 1871 and a new double tray case was supplied. From Boss's order ledgers. Notice the mistake in the serial number – it is incorrectly recorded as no. 3540. Note the contemporary name for Scotland, "N. B.", meaning North Britain.

Side-snap gun no. 3597. See Plate 30.

The illustration right shows a double-barrel 12-bore side snap hammer gun no. 3597 ordered by the Duke of Portland on 7th November 1880. William John Arthur Charles James Cavendish Bentinck, the Duke of Portland of Welbeck Abbey, was born on 28th December 1857 and he succeeded as Duke in 1879. This gun is the No. 1 gun of a pair nos. 3597/8 and uses the side snap action, the preferred snap action of Edward Paddison and built in greater numbers than any other type of snap action.

The history of this gun follows the familiar story of many hammer guns. When hammer guns went out of fashion at the close of the century and the Duke

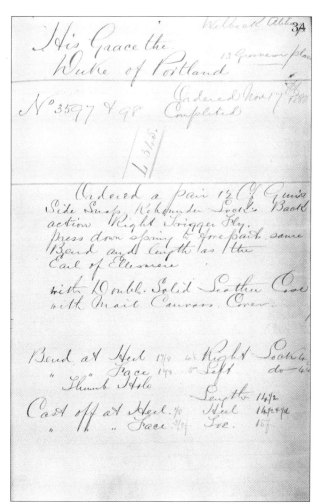

The order for gun no. 3597, the No. 1 gun of a matched pair ordered by the Duke of Portland on 17th November, 1880. From Boss's order ledgers.

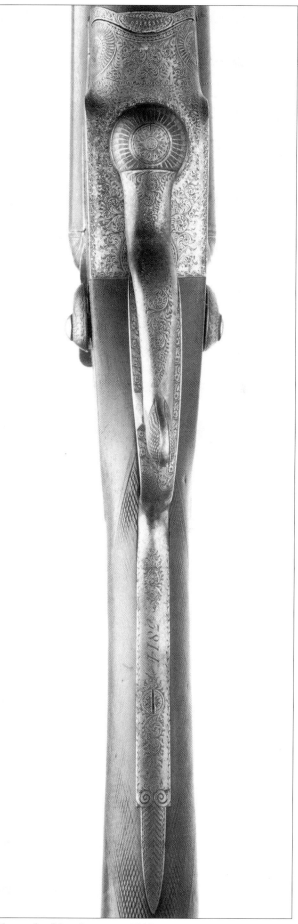

The underside of gun no. 3814.

ordered new Boss hammerless guns, nos. 3597/8 were split up and no. 3597 passed to an estate factor. It was then passed to the estate forester and then to the estate clerk of works and finally to the present owner.

The back action locks are rebounders by Stanton. The hammers remain high and as yet do not lie out of sight when cocked. They are engraved, "Boss & Co.". The 30″ Damascus barrels are engraved, "Boss & Co., 73 St James' Street, London". A No. "1" is engraved upon the top rib. The original barrels must have been damaged because the gun was rebarrelled by Boss in 1889 and the new barrels given the number 4037. An Anson forend is fitted. A gold escutcheon engraved with the Duke of Portland's crest is inlaid into the stock. Originally the guns were fitted in a double leather case with a mail canvas outer cover.

The illustration right shows a double-barrel 16–bore under-lever hammer gun no. 3814 built for A. C. Becher of the 9th Regiment. Andrew Cracroft Becher was commissioned into the Norfolk Regiment. He took part in the Afghan War, 1879–1880 and by the 21st May 1884 he had been promoted to captain. The gun was

The action of gun no. 3814 built in 1885 showing the very fine scroll engraving. See also Plate 31.

ordered on 14th January 1885 and completed on June 1st of the same year. It was built to match gun no. 9407 by J. Parkes, Birmingham but it had to be in a separate case.

The gun has front action locks, very finely scroll engraved and is inscribed, "Boss & Co.". The locks are of the rebounding variety by Stanton and drop points are carved behind them. An Anson forend is fitted.

The Damascus barrels are engraved, "Boss & Co., 73 St James' Street, London". The left-hand barrel has a modified choke, the right-hand barrel improved cylinder. Choke boring advanced the effective range of a shotgun. It also meant that gunmakers could now regulate the closeness of the pattern to suit a customer's requirement. It seems most likely that William Pape of Newcastle was the first to invent and patent the choke in 1866. Just like the pugilists in the old muzzle- vs breech-loading controversy, the introduction of choke boring gave rise to heated debate as to the respective merits of cylinder vs choke guns. The editor of *The Field*, J. B. Walsh, entered into the foray again with a series of public trials to determine the two systems. The trials took place in 1875 and proved conclusively that choke boring produced superior patterns.

Boss, being a very conservative firm, in this period did not promote choke boring. In 1876 a trial of choke and cylinder guns was held at the Gun Club, Notting Hill on live pigeons. A cylinder gun by Boss was used at this trial along with other cylinder guns by Purdey, Lancaster and Grant. The cylinders won by two birds at 27 yards rise and seven birds at 33 yards. These trials were inconclusive since the cylinder guns had by far the best shots on their side. By the 1880s most makers and shooters were converted to choke boring and chokes were increasingly made at Boss from this time onwards.

The first mention of a choke bore in the order ledgers is in the year 1876. How popular the use of choke boring became around this period can be guaged by the number of customers ordering new pairs of choke barrels for their existing guns. The order ledgers are full of such orders in the 1880s.

The gun illustrated overleaf shows a double-barrel 12-bore back action thumb-hole hammer gun no 3860. This gun was ordered on 22nd April 1886 by Mr W. B. Holt-Eardley, 28 Charles Street, London. The gun was to be built to match no. 3491 in every respect to create a composite pair.

This gun is of the highest quality throughout and is of very elegant proportions. The back action rebound-

The order for gun no. 3814 dated 14th January 1885, a double-barrel 16-bore under-lever gun for A. C. Becher. Note the early use of choke boring, the fact that the gun had to match the owner's other 16-bore by Parkes, Birmingham and that the owner gave in part payment, his old gun no. 3468. From Boss's order ledgers.

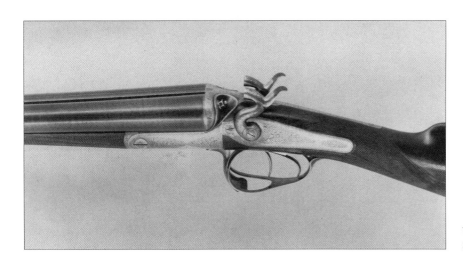

Under-snap gun no. 3860.
See Plate 32.

The order for gun no. 3860 dated 22nd April 1886, for a 12-bore back action under-snap hammer gun. Note that it is to be built to match no. 3491 to create a composite pair. From Boss's order ledgers.

ing locks by Stanton have very fine scroll engraving as has the action body and top lever. The stock is finely figured, has heel plates fitted and the forend is of the lever variety. The 30″ Damascus barrels are stamped "J P", being Portlock barrels and are bored cylinder and choke. A solid leather double case was supplied with a mail cover for the new composite pair. The cost of this gun was £45.0.0. and the case was £7.10s.

It could only be a matter of time until the hammers of a gun were dispensed with altogether. From a pragmatic point of view there was no real need for hammers. Tradition played the major part in their retention since the hammer had been part of the gun since time immemorial. The first hammerless gun built by Boss was a double-barrel 12-bore gun no. 3571 ordered on 17th February 1880 for E. W. Herbert. After 1880 they were built with increasing frequency until the late 1880s when they accounted for the majority of gun production.

George Daw, shortly after he had introduced the centre-fire gun and cartridge in 1861, invented a hammerless gun one year later. It was not particularly attractive and this coupled with a sporting public still reeling over the changeover from muzzle-loader to breech-loader meant that it was too far ahead of its time. The first hammerless gun to achieve any positive success was that of T. Murcott, Haymarket, London in 1871. An under-lever opened the gun and cocked the action. It was efficient, reliable and had pleasing lines. Probably the most famous of the 1870s hammerless actions was the Anson and Deeley, patented in 1875. This was the universal boxlock hammerless gun still made in its thousands today. It was always regarded as a cheap action and since Boss were at the very top end of the bespoke gun trade, they did not make this type of action. It was only when John Robertson took over the firm in 1891 that a few Anson and Deeley's were made in response to customers' demands for keepers' guns. These boxlocks were not engraved, "Boss" they were engraved, "Robertson".

A wide variety of hammerless actions were developed in this period by many makers such as W. & C. Scott of Birmingham, Gye and Moncrieff, Joseph Lang,

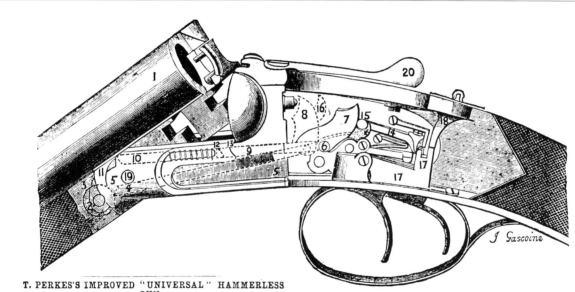

T. PERKES'S IMPROVED "UNIVERSAL" HAMMERLESS GUN.

WE have received the following account of a new action from the inventor:

The accompanying drawing shows a top-lever bar action hammerless gun with doll's head extension and intercepting bolt safety, removed only when the triggers are pulled; the cocking of one of the locks has been effected on opening the breech ends of the barrels (1) by a roller (2) in the fore end (3) pressing against the end of the cocking rod (4), and passing direct through the action (5) to a stud (6) on the tumbler (7) shown at full cock. The tumbler (8) of the other lock is provided with a lever (9) pivoted at one end to the tumbler, the forward end extending along the lock plate into the action (5) where it engages with a short rod (10), the forward end of which is acted upon by the upper part (11) of the fore end (3). When the barrels are being closed, the upper part of the fore end presses the rod backwards against the tumbler lever, which forces the tumbler into full cock; this is done when the barrels are three parts closed; the other part is for the purpose of giving an overdraw so as to ensure the gun being cocked, and to admit of the lever being disengaged from the end of the cocking rod; the lever (9) is disengaged from the cocking rod (10) by a spur formed upon the tumbler lever coming in contact with an abutment (13) formed in the action, and thus throws it out of position to admit of the tumbler falling to discharge the gun, where it remains until the

barrels are opened, when it returns to its former position by the arrangement of the cocking limbs. The gun cannot be loaded until the one lock is cocked, and cannot be closed without cocking the other. Each lock is provided with an intercepting safety bolt (14) which is provided with a hook (15) and engages when at full cock with a hook (16) upon the tumblers to prevent them from falling accidentally upon the striker. Each bolt is removed from the head of the tumbler by the trigger blade (17) pressing against the rear arm of the safety bolt, and thus removes it for firing when the trigger is pulled. The triggers are also provided with an automatic safety slide (18), acted which is upon by the grip lever (20) when the gun is unbolted.

The principle is well adapted for converting hammer guns and rifles into hammerless. The gun can be made with any kind of lever or number of grips, as the cocking arrangements do not interfere with any other part of the gun. By thus dividing the power to cock the tumblers, it enables the user to open and close the gun with the greatest ease, owing to the cocking limbs being worked by the upper and lower parts of fore end.   T. PERKES (Gunmaker).

A description and drawing of the Perkes patent hammerless action as used in all Boss hammerless guns in the Paddison era. From *The Field*, 19th April 1886.

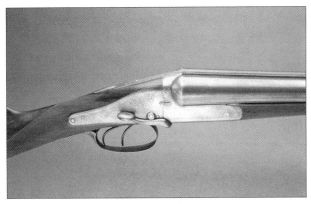

Hammerless gun no. 3892. See Plate 33.

Frederick Beesley, James Woodward, John Dickson, etc. Boss & Co. in the 1880s used a hammerless action in constructing their guns built to Perkes patent. Perkes was a London gunmaker who patented a hammerless action in May 1878 and subsequently improved upon it. All the Boss hammerless guns of the Paddison era were built to Perkes "Universal" hammerless action. For ease of opening, one lock was cocked by the fall of the barrels and the other cocked upon closing the gun.

The illustration left is a double-barrel 12-bore side lever Perkes patent hammerless non-ejector gun, no. 3892 built in 1886/7 for A. G. Bovill, 30 Chester Street, Grosvenor Place, London. This gun is very typical of the Boss hammerless guns of the 1880s. The back action locks are scroll engraved and marked, "Boss & Co.". They were supplied by Chilton. A side lever side action is used. The entire action is very finely scroll engraved and is stamped on the flat, "Perkes Patent, 1968343". An automatic safety is fitted. Some customers did not want automatic safeties; "Automatic safety" had to be specified in the order. The figured walnut stock has iron heel and toe plates.

The 30″ Damascus barrels are bored right barrel improved cylinder and left barrel choke. They are stamped, "C L" being supplied by Charles Lancaster. On the rib "Boss & Co., 73 St James' Street, London" is engraved. A Rigby lever forend is fitted. Originally the gun was supplied in a leather case with mail canvas cover.

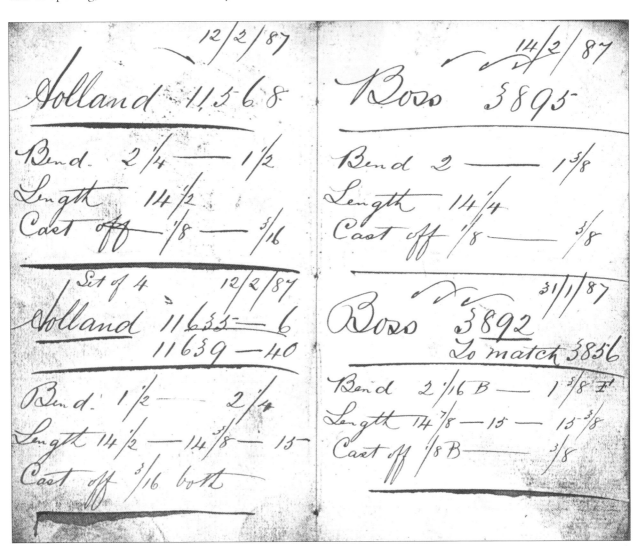

A page from John Robertson's stocking book detailing the order and measurements for Boss gun no. 3892. "To match 3856" means that the stock had to be of the same dimensions and colour as a previous stock fitted by Robertson.

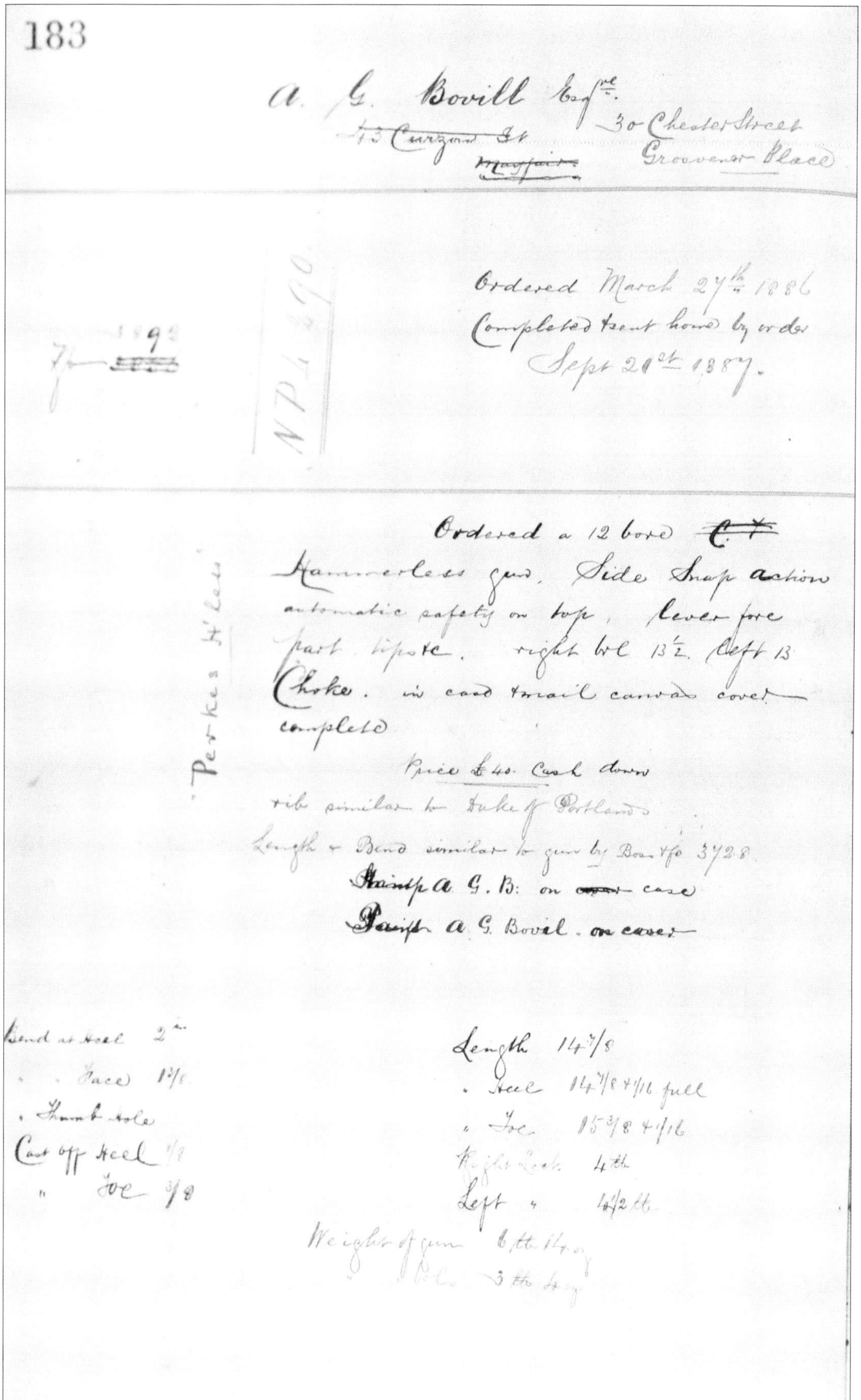

183

A. G. Bovill Esqre
~~13 Curzon St~~   30 Chester Street
~~Mayfair~~   Grosvenor Place

NPL £40.

7—3892

Ordered March 27th 1886
Completed ~~kent home~~ by order
Sept 20th 1887.

"Perkes H'less"

Ordered a 12 bore ~~C*~~
Hammerless gun. Side Snap action
automatic safety on top, lever fore
part tipste. right brl 13½. Left 13
Choke. in case & mail canvas cover
completed

Price £40. Cash down
+ rib similar to Duke of Portlands
Length & Bend similar to gun by Boss & Co 3728
        ~~Stamp~~ A. G. B: on ~~gun~~ case
        ~~Paint~~ A. G. Bovill. on cover

Bend at Heel 2"   Length 14⅞
  " Face 1⅜   " Heel 14⅞ + 1/16 full
  " Thumb hole   " Toe 15⅜ + 1/16
Cast off Heel ⅛   Right Lock 4th
  "   Toe ⅜   Left "   4½ th
                               Weight of gun 6 lb 14 oz
                                     Bls 3 lb 4 oz

The order for gun no. 3892 ordered by A. G. Bovill, on 27th March 1886. Note the length of time it took to complete and the "price £40 cash down". From Boss's order ledgers.

The action for gun no. 3892 showing the side lever snap.

Of great interest to this particular gun is that it was stocked by John Robertson's firm in his pre-Boss days. In the 1880s the Robertson firm stocked most of Boss's guns. The record of no. 3892 in John Robertson's stocking book of the late 1880s survives. Robertson received the order to stock the gun on the 31st January 1887. In addition, the trigger plate is stamped, "J. R." being the work of John Robertson also.

The illustration in plate 34 shows a pair of early Boss hammerless guns nos 3991/3992 ordered on 17th August 1888 for General Digby Willoughby, a keen live pigeon shooter who ordered many specialised guns from Boss for this purpose.

They are built to Perkes patent hammerless action. The back action side locks have superb scroll engraving and are engraved "Boss & Co.". The style of engraving, "Boss & Co." changed around this period to a banner style, a form that has usually been used up to the present day. The 30″ Damascus barrels are engraved, "Boss & Co., 73 St James' Street, London". Rigby lever forends are used. Horn heel plates are used to protect the butts. Just as had taken place in the metamorphosis from percussion to breech-loader, these early hammerless guns are not particularly attractive. Although of the highest quality, the back action locks do not look right – it looks like a hammer gun without hammers, which is exactly what it is after all! Once again Paddison preferred them like this.

The guns are contained in their original leather, wood reinforced double case. The red baize lined case has the "Boss & Co. Gunmakers to His Royal Highness the Prince of Wales" label. Accessories include: a hand roll over tool, a wad rammer, oil bottle, Boss snap caps, cleaning rods and black Moroccan pouch containing a pull through.

Only one final real improvement to the hammerless gun needed to be made to perfect it into the gun we know today – that of an ejector to throw out the empty cartridge case after discharge. The first ejector gun made by Boss was a double-barrel 12-bore side lever no. 3920 ordered on June 3rd, 1887 by Dr G Johnston, 11 Savile Row, London.

Joseph Needham of Birmingham invented an ejector in 1874. It was a well-constructed ingenious device and others would soon follow. In 1881 W. W. Greener of Birmingham used a version of it in his boxlock gun. Charles Lancaster likewise used Needham's principle in his ejector gun of 1879. In all these ejectors the force to fire the ejector was supplied by the mainspring in the action body of the gun. This put undue pressure on mainsprings and meant that they had to be of robust construction thereby hindering the opening and closing of a gun. The ejector set independently in the forend with its own action is the type most frequently

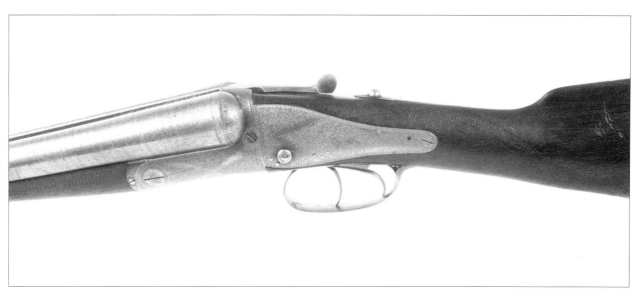

The double-barrel 12-bore back action hammerless gun no. 3991. See also Plate 34.

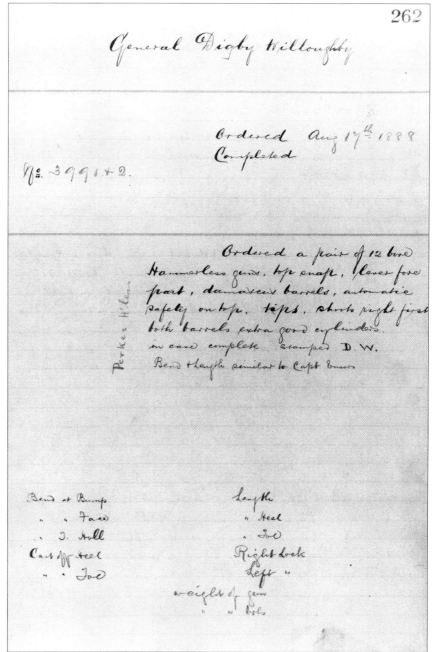

The order for guns nos. 3991/3992 dated 17th August 1888, a pair of Perkes patent hammerless guns built for General Digby Willoughby. From Boss's order ledgers.

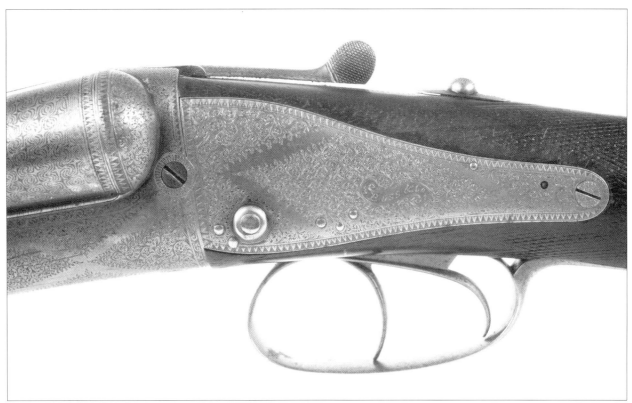

The action of gun no. 3991 showing the very close scroll engraving. Note the banner style of the engraving, "Boss & Co." introduced around this period.

found today. This type of ejector was first patented by Perkes in 1878. Just as Edward Paddison had used Perkes hammerless action, he now used Perkes ejector mechanism. In 1888 Edward Paddison wrote to *Land* *and Water* extolling the merits of the Perkes patent ejector gun. This letter is reproduced below together with the subsequent comment from the editor of 2nd May 1888.

THE BEST EJECTOR.

Sir,—In reply to the letters of "Maltese Cross" and "J. C Robinson, Esq.," I beg to state "the Boss" ejector gun was used last season with very great satisfaction, and if either of these gentlemen will call at 73, St. James's-street, I shall be pleased to show them an ejector which, for simplicity of mechanism and strength, cannot be surpassed. The ejector I use is "Perke's patent," and I can apply it to both hammerless guns and hammer guns with rebounding locks.

The essential points are :—

1st. The gun can be built any action, top, side, or underneath snap with double-grip bolt, as well as the old-fashioned lever over the guard,

2nd. The mechanism is most simple, and not liable to get out of order.

3rd. The barrels are not required to drop any lower than in my hammerless guns, which are not ejectors.

4th. No extra power is required to cock the gun, the springs of the ejectors being compressed ready for action by closing the gun.

5th. Its safety from risk of accident. It is impossible for "the Boss" gun to eject exploded cartridges until after the gun is cocked, and the triggers bolted.

6th. The whole of the ejecting mechanism is in the forepart, and can be entirely removed by taking out one screw, after the forepart is out of the wood.

7th. The gun can be put together quite easily, and both locks and ejectors act independently of each other. E. F. P. Boss.

[The above letter coming from a maker, we think it right to call on Mr. Boss and examine the gun he describes.—Ed.]

MAY 2, 1888.   SHOOTING.

MR. BOSS'S HAMMERLESS EJECTOR GUN.

AS WE WERE NOT ABLE to keep our promise to our readers, Mr. Boss called on us, and brought with him the inventor of his hammerless ejector gun. It is hardly necessary for us to tell our English readers that the workmanship is everything that can be desired.

The mechanism is somewhat distinct from that of every other action which has come before us. The hammerless tumblers are cocked in the most simple way by the pressure of the fore-end on opening the gun against the cocking-rod, which acts upon the tumbler, and it is this rod which, after cocking the tumblers, acts as a finger upon a trigger in the lock action of the ejector movement. This trigger, however, is not pressed until the gun is opened after firing, and in fact it is the trigger in the fore-end which is moved by the fall of the gun, on opening, to meet the rod which is in connection with the tumbler of the hammerless action, having cocked which it then strikes the trigger of the ejector.

The great beauty of this arrangement is that by the unscrewing of a single screw the whole of the two ejector lock movements can be taken away, and the gun acts as an ordinary hammerless, just as it would act if the whole of the ejector lock action broke and became useless. The intention has been so to contrive the gun that it shall be cocked before the ejector has been let off, so that the ejection of the cartridge shall indicate that the gun is cocked. When once cocked, this rod is held so that it cannot act upon the trigger of the ejector action, so that it allows the opening and shutting movement full play without coming into contact with the ejector action of the un-fired barrel.

The hammerless action is extremely neat, and occupies very small space, as the trigger-spring lies within the short arm of the main spring, and the intercepting block action requires the full pressure of the trigger to bring it out of the line of the fall of the tumbler.

A letter written to *Land and Water* by Edward Paddison in 1888 explaining the merits of the Boss ejector gun built to Perkes patent and a subsequent comment by the editor dated 2nd May 1888.

THE GUN CASES AND ACCESSORIES OF THE BREECH LOADING ERA

Boss gun cases changed considerably in the breech-loading era. At first in the 1860s, with the pinfire guns, cases tended to remain much the same as the muzzle-loaders. They were constructed in oak with leather outer covers to prevent damage in transit. Many pinfire cases were of the two tier variety with the top tray used to store cartridges since pinfire cartridges were unstable in transit due to their protruding firing pins.

Breech-loaders did not require anything like the amount of apparatus that muzzle-loaders did. There was no need for the old heavy oak case. In addition with good railway travel, lighter cases were preferable for the increasing distances made possible. Three types of case were used by Boss in this period. These cases are still in use today and have not really changed much in over a century.

The cheapest type was a simple leather case with carrying handle and straps which tended to be used for single guns. It was light and convenient. In the 1860s/1870s the old standard green baize used by Boss in the muzzle-loading period gave way to the more fashionable red baize. Occasionally, the old green was still used.

The second type of case was again a leather case reinforced by wood as illustrated in guns nos. 3991 and 3992. This was altogether a superior, stronger case. For pairs of guns this case really had to be used due to the extra weight involved.

The final type of case was the best of all, although expensive. This was an oak case with a leather outer lining and brass corner protection pieces. Being a heavy case, there was little chance of guns getting damaged due to its solidity and rigidity. They are always referred to as "oak and leather cases". The cases themselves were protected by an outer mail canvas cover.

With pairs of guns, two styles of case were on offer. The most popular was the single-tier type of case as illustrated in guns nos. 3991 and 3992. It was convenient and the contents looked good when the case was opened. The other type was of the old two-tier variety with the top tray containing the barrels and the bottom tray the stocks. Some customers ordered three guns. They would be incorporated into a two-tier case such as this.

The main supplier of cases to the top end of the trade was Robert Bryant, 24 Drury Lane, London, still in business today.

Trade labels were standard in this period. When Boss received the Royal appointment in the 1860s the wording on the trade label remained in use until the turn of the century. This was the label that stated:

Boss & Co.
Gun Rifle and Breech Loader Manufacturer
To His Royal Highness the Prince of Wales
73 St James' Street,
London

Apparatus fitted to cases was considerably simpler. The type of accessories that might be found are listed below:

1. Cleaning rod, jags and brushes.

2. Chamber brush for scouring out the chambers. They were usually made by G. & J. W. Hawksley, Sheffield. They are ebony handled with a brass retainer over the brush.

3. Powder/shot measure. Many shooters preferred to load their own cartridges and adjust their charges. They were supplied by Hawksley or Brazier and have adjustable chargers measured in ozs. for shot and drams for powder. Later examples have a measurement in grains for nitro-powders. The earlier examples are in brass with ebony handles. In the later types, the brass gives way to nickel-plating.

4. Wad rammers. These were made out of ebony and were used to push the cardboard wads down into the cartridges.

5. Rolled turnover tools. After the cartridge was loaded the end had to be crimped. Since most cartridges had a rolled turnover in this period, this tool turned the end of the cartridge over the top wad.

Breech-loading accessories. See Plate 35.

6. Decapping base. This was a turned piece of ebony that the base of the cartridge rested upon. A hole was drilled through the ebony so that the old cap could be knocked out.

7. Oil bottles. They were usually made in pewter and supplied by Hawksley.

8. Snap caps. Centre fire guns can not be fired without a cartridge in the chamber. If the chamber is empty, the lack of cushion provided by the cartridge priming cap might cause the firing pin to jar and break. Spring loaded snap caps enabled shooters to practise without fear of firing pin failure. Early snap caps were made of brass, later ones are nickel-plated.

9. Cleaning pouches. Cleaning pouches were made of finely grained Moroccan leather and contained a hemp pull-through and brush. One end was weighted so that the pull-through could easily slide down the barrel. The weight was usually a small pewter oil bottle. Most were supplied by Hawksley.

Cartridge magazine. See Plate 37.

THE SCOTTISH CONNECTION

In the closing decates of the 19th century, Boss & Co. under the leadership of the Paddisons continued the reputation of the company for building London best quality guns. They tended to concentrate on high quality rather than innovative improvements.

This state of affairs ceased when a new proprietor entered the firm in 1891: John Robertson. John Robertson, in addition to being a first-class gunmaker, had an enormously fertile brain and was responsible for many improvements, notably the construction of the first reliable single trigger mechanism. Under Robertson's directorship, Boss & Co. achieved international renown not only as "builders of best guns only" but also in the perfection of the final stage of the hammerless ejector.

John Robertson came from Haddington in Scotland. Haddington, a Royal Burgh and the county town of East Lothian, is situated sixteen miles east from Edinburgh. It is a very ancient Royal Burgh and even today still possesses its medieval street plan. It has the doubtful notoriety of being the first town in Scotland to be hit by cholera in 1831. The death registers of this period make depressing reading – "cholera" as the certified cause of death being written time and time again. The minutes of the Town Council meetings after this period show them to be obsessed about improving the drainage, sanitation, etc, to prevent a repetition of the catastrophy. It is interesting to note the wide web of cholera in the Boss history. John Robertson's parents were lucky to escape the virulent outbreak in a small market town, and yet Thomas Boss was not so lucky catching cholera in the outbreak in London of 1849.

During the 19th century Haddington's primary function was as a leading agricultural market. East Lothian is famed for the quality and fertility of its land, hence intense agricultural activity occurred in this area. Haddington was the centre of this and a market was held weekly. In addition, there were many industries, ironworks, coachworks, breweries, distilleries, tanneries, and so on; around 1830 the population was 5,883.

As such, Haddington was an ideal situation for the establishment of a provincial gunmaking business. With the large amount of agricultural traffic a gunmaking business would surely find regular trade.

John Robertson's grandfather, William Robertson, was a "wright" (or "wricht" in Scotland). A "wright" is a general term for a craftsman who works in wood. William Robertson was in fact a wheelwright in Haddington. After his marriage to Charlotte Wilson, in 1803 (the parish records state that they were

No. 1 Hardgate, Haddington. The home and business premises of John Ireland Robertson, *circa* 1830–54.

Nos. 42–44 Market Street, Haddington. The home and business premises of John Ireland Robertson *circa* 1854–88.

"irregularly married 1st May 1803 in Edinburgh – they acknowledged each other as man and wife – they paid their dues"), they produced the normal large family.

Their second son, born on 23 June 1807, they christened John Ireland Robertson. It was John Ireland Robertson who founded the Robertson gunmaking business in Haddington. Around 1830, at the age of twenty-three, John Ireland Robertson set up business as a gunmaker at no. 1 Hardgate, Haddington.

To whom he was apprenticed, we do not know – no record exists. In Hardgate in the 1830s, there were an infinite variety of small businesses, wheelwrights, shoe-makers, plasterers, tailors, dressmakers, etc. The building Robertson conducted his business from still stands today substantially unaltered. In June 1834 he married Jean Dudgeon, daughter of a Haddington tailor, Robert Dudgeon.

John Ireland Robertson soon achieved an excellent reputation as a top-class craftsman. He produced many percussion rifles that were renowned for their accuracy and he was one of the first to fit telescopic sights to rifles. His reputation spread far beyond Haddington and he received orders from many parts of the country. In addition, he conducted the normal trade of a provincial gunmaking business, selling fishing rods, etc.

By the 1840s, the "Gunner", as he was known, had built up a remarkably large business. In the 1851 Census he describes himself as "gunmaking master employing ten men". This was equal to Thomas Boss who also employed ten men at St James's Street in 1851. In

addition the Robertsons had prospered sufficiently to employ a local girl Christina Watt as a servant aged eighteen years.

John Ireland Robertson and Jean Dudgeon produced a large family in this period. Their second son, Robert Robertson born in 1837, died aged ten years in 1848 from "water in the head". Fourteen years after his death, another son was born and this son they also christened "Robert Robertson" – obviously not a superstitious family!

However, I digress. Their third son born on 26 June 1839 was christened John Robertson. This was the future partner in Boss & Co. Young John Robertson went to school in Haddington and was brought up in the background of the prosperous family gunmaking business. It was no doubt that it was from his father that he inherited many of his future skills and learned much gunmaking practice.

During the 1850s, the Robertson gunmaking business declined and business fell off. At some time between 1851 and 1854 the business moved to smaller rented premises at 44 Market Street. This building still exists today.

From this period until John Ireland Robertson's death in 1888, the business continued to contract. In the 1861 Census, Robertson was described as a gun-maker employing one man – quite a change from ten years previously. The rateable value for the Robertson shop in Market Street was assessed at £25 per year in 1856. By 1857 it was £17 per year, by 1863 it was £10 per year and in 1868 £5 per year. Obviously the share of the building occupied by the Robertson family decreased as the family left home and business diminished. The servant had long ago been dismissed.

Due to the fact that the building at 44 Market Street was not a single home but really a collection of rented flats, the Robertsons now shared the building with a variety of occupants – a joiner, a painter, a slater, a skinner, etc.

It was probably with this background of declining business that made up young John Robertson's mind to leave the family business and seek his fortune elsewhere. This he did in 1858 at the age of nineteen years.

The "Gunner's" wife, Jean Dudgeon, died on 23 May 1884 within 44 Market Street aged seventy-four from a heart attack. It would not be long until her husband followed her.

John Ireland Robertson, the "Gunner", lived to the ripe old age of eighty years and died on Friday, 10th February 1888 at 44 Market Street. His death certificate states that he died of "senile ulceration for eight months and shock for three days". He left no Will. On account of his notoriety and respect, the local paper the *Haddingtonshire Courier*, published a fairly long obituary on 7th February 1888.

THE LATE MR JOHN ROBERTSON GUNMAKER

On Friday morning last, this old citizen quiety passed away after a comparatively brief illness. Deceased though late of years doing little in the way of busi-ness beyond repairing fishing rods and such like jobs was a remarkably clever craftsman and few better than he could handle his tools.

There are not now many alive who remember our deceased townsman when at his best and before years and infirmities had weakened his energies. In his early manhood, such was his acknowledged skill as a gunmaker that his name was known far and near, the rifles turned out by Robertson of Haddington acquiring almost a national celebrity for their excellence of construction. At one period of his life, his business which he carried on in Hardgate Street in the premises at present occupied by Mr Wright, watchmaker, was of a very extensive character and we have heard him say that at times he would have as many as ten journeymen working for him. But fashions changed and business gradually fell off, till at length the flourishing and successful gunmaker who had had the best people in the county for his customers was constrained to limit himself to the humble premises of Market Street where he closed his long and chequered life. Wherever Haddingtonians are to be found, the initimation of the death of their old friend "the Gunner" will be received with regret for few of the youth of the Burgh have not at times been obliged to the clever fingered and quick witted old man for putting their shooting or fishing or golfing gear in order.

One of his sons, if we mistake not, occupies a position of responsiblity in the gunmaking trade in England. Another son is chief clerk in the Excise at Lincoln.

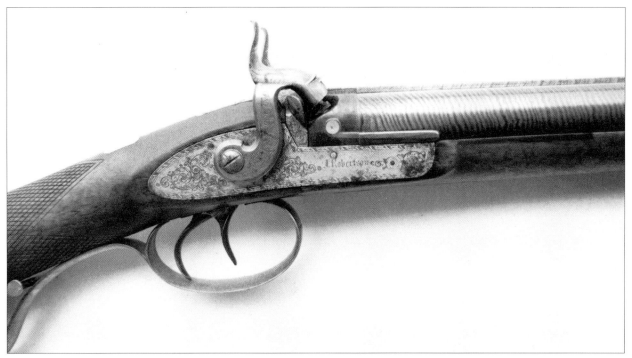

A double-barrel 20-bore percussion sporting gun *circa* 1835 by John Robertson (Snr.), Haddington.

The same gun showing the Gothic engraving "J. Robertson" on the lock plates.

These illustrations (previous page and above) show an early John Robertson (Snr.) double-barrel 20-bore percussion sporting gun *circa* 1835. This gun was built shortly after John Robertson commenced his business at no. 1 Hardgate, Haddington. The gun displays many late flintlock characteristics. The front action locks are engraved in Gothic script, "J. Robertson". There is an acorn finial to the front of the trigger guard and the trigger guard itself is of the scroll guard variety. The twist barrels are 30″ long with an elevated top rib and are inscribed in the same Gothic style of lettering, "J. Robertson, Haddington". It is interesting to note the absence of the no. 1 Hardgate address on the barrels. Platinum vents are fitted. A silver escutcheon is fitted behind the tang into a nicely figured stock. There is no serial number on the gun.

JOHN ROBERTSON LEAVES HADDINGTON

In many respects the early history of John Robertson mirrors that of Thomas Boss. Both their fathers were top-rate gunmakers and imbued in their sons an enthusiasm for gunmaking and both the sons in addition to becoming highly skilled gunmakers were possessed with a drive to reach the top in a very competitive trade.

John Robertson was not content to carry on his father's business in Haddington. There were limits to a provincial gunmaking business and for his drive to succeed he would have to go to the large gunmaking centres in Britain in the Midlands and in London where the new breech-loaders were being developed and

where mechanical anticipation abounded. John Robertson simply could not be a part of this if he remained in Haddington.

His father's main interest was in rifle manufacture, an interest that rubbed off on John Robertson. To enlarge his knowledge of rifle making he joined the leading rifle maker of the mid 19th century, Joseph Whitworth of Manchester. In 1858, aged nineteen years, John Robertson travelled south from Haddington to Manchester to work for Whitworth. It was a bold step for Robertson to make. He had to leave his long-standing girlfriend Margaret Wilkinson behind in Haddington and he must have experienced trepidation at the thought of leaving a small country town for the city of Manchester.

Whitworth was born in 1803, the son of a schoolmaster, and after leaving school aged fourteen years was apprenticed to an uncle who had a cotton spinning business. His main interest was not in cotton spinning but in the machinery of the factory. He left to become a mechanic, a profession in which he excelled, and he became a maker of precision machine tools in 1860 producing standard threads for screws that are known to this day as "Whitworth".

In the middle of the 19th century arms manufacture for the government was concentrated in the government's own factories. In times of war, rapid large-scale production could not take place unless machinery was adopted that would result in rapid and interchangeable output. The production of the new Enfield rifle at this time left much to be desired as regards standardisation of parts and to improve upon these defects the government called in Whitworth in 1854 in an advisory capacity to investigate the adoption of rifle-making machinery. In typical Whitworth style, since he knew little about firearms, he made a thorough study of rifles. Westley Richards was appointed as his technical assistant. Whitworth was impressed by the octagonal bore to improve accuracy and to achieve the flatest trajectory and maximum penetration reduced bore size from the standard .577 to .451. Whitworth rifles were extremely accurate, but for military use their precision manufacture and their tendency to foul meant that they were not adopted by the British government. However for target work, Whitworth rifles reigned supreme and carried everything before them in most of the competitions of their era.

Such then was the immense establishment in which John Robertson immersed himself during 1858. With his previous knowledge of rifles and his intelligence and skill in rifle manufacture, he quickly rose to prominence in Whitworth's factory. The first meeting of the National Rifle Association took place at Wimbledon in 1858 and the opening shot was fired from a Whitworth by Queen Victoria. John Robertson himself played a part in the building of this gun. The Queen did not really fire the gun, since it was clamped in a rest and discharged by the pull of a silk cord! The bullet struck within 1½″ of the centre of the target at 400 yards, showing the remarkable accuracy of the Whitworth rifle.

During his holidays John Robertson always returned to Scotland to see his family and friends. His return to Haddington in Christmas 1860 was of special importance and eagerly looked forward to. On Christmas Eve, 24 December 1860 in Haddington, John aged twenty-two married his girlfriend, Margaret Wilkinson. Her father, Samuel Wilkinson, was a butler originally hailing from Aberlady, East Lothian, a village close to Haddington. Whilst he was in service at Dunbarney in Perthshire, his wife gave birth in November 1838 to a girl christened Margaret, John Robertson's future wife. Margaret was a very attractive woman and strongly supported John in his desire to become a successful gunmaker. Soon after their marriage, they travelled southwards to John's work with Whitworth in Manchester and set up home at 24 Bright Avenue, Ardwick.

One year after this marriage, their first son was born on 7th February 1862 at this address.

This first son was christened John, after his father and grandfather. This John would later serve his apprenticeship to his father and along with his two younger brothers, Sam and Bob, become totally involved in the Boss business, eventually taking it over upon their father's death in 1917. Either to differentiate

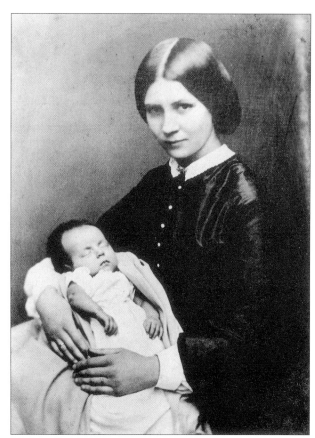

Margaret Robertson holding her first born baby, John Robertson (Jnr), a photograph taken in 1862 in Manchester. John Robertson (Jnr) would eventually take over the business along with his two younger brothers, Sam and Bob.

between father and son, or adopting an Anglicised form of John, the youngest John Robertson would sometimes be known as "Jack".

John Robertson remained with Whitworth for four years. In 1862, having gained all the skill and experience of rifle manufacture of every attainable description, Robertson went to work for Westley Richards in Birmingham. It is interesting to speculate what might have been the results if John Robertson had continued down the line of rifle development and manufacture. A great pace of change occurred in rifle development in the third quarter of the 19th century with the implementation of bolt action systems, magazines, etc. Who knows what might have resulted from Robertson's ingenuity as applied to rifles?

Since Whitworth and Westley Richards had co-operated in Whitworth's trials, John Robertson would have known Westley-Richards. The firm was established in 1812 by Mr William Westley-Richards. Guns were produced at their factory in High Street, Birmingham and retailed through their London agency at 178 New Bond Street, managed by William Bishop, the flamboyant "Bishop of Bond Street". In 1855, William Westley Richards's son joined the business of his father. He had taken an active interest in the business from an early age and it was this Westley-Richards who developed the business into the large scale concern it would later become.

When Robertson joined Westley-Richards in 1862, they were heavily involved in the development of breech-loaders and it is not surprising with John Robertson's thirst for knowledge that he wanted to be part of this. During Robertson's time with Westley-Richards, they were perfecting their top lever fastening connection, the "Doll's Head" connection. Later after Robertson had left, they would achieve further acclaim in the annals of breech-loading development with their Anson and Deeley action of 1875, the ubiquitous boxlock. Thus John Robertson became acquainted with the manufacture of sporting and military firearms as were produced in Birmingham at a time when the Birmingham gun trade was in its most flourishing condition. But like William Boss, who was working in Birmingham nearly a century before, the pull of the Metropolis was great for any gunmaker who wanted to become involved in best gun manufacture. It was a natural progression for John Robertson. His own standards of workmanship were precise and this could only find an outlet in best gun manufacture – this meant London. It was during this spell with Westley-Richards in Birmingham that John Robertson's second son, Samuel, was born on 22nd November 1863 at the family home in 14 Ravenhurst Street, Aston, Birmingham. Sam would become the number two of the trio of Robertson sons who would become gunmakers and inherit the Boss business.

John Robertson only stayed with Westley-Richards for a year or two and then in 1864 he heard of a vacancy in the London gunmaking firm of James Purdey. Purdeys at this time were headed by James Purdey the Younger who took control of the firm in 1858. Their address was 314½ Oxford Street, London, having taken over these premises from Joseph Manton in 1826 when he went bankrupt. Like Boss at this time, Purdeys had established themselves as best makers producing guns highly thought of in terms of construction, quality and durability. They would only employ skilled journeymen and with Robertson's credentials well established with Whitworth and Westley-Richards, it is no wonder he was offered a position with Purdeys.

The Robertsons moved to 47 Princess Terrace, Primrose Hill, at the north end of Regent's Park, London. As was the norm in the 19th century, the Robertsons went on to raise a large family. Alison Black Robertson (Alison Black was Margaret Robertson's mother's maiden name) was born on 7th February 1865, another son, William Robertson, was born in 1867 (he must have died young since there is no later mention of him) and Margaret Robertson was born in 1870. By 1871 the family had moved down the road to number 30 Princess Terrace. With their expanding family, the Robertsons had to move house again and around 1873 they moved to 1 Bernard Street, Regent's Park, London. Here on 11th July 1874, a third son was born named Robert Dobson Robertson. This was the third member of the trio of Robertson sons who would become gunmakers at Boss. John would eventually run the shop, Sam the factory and Bob the shooting ground. In the mid 1870s the family moved again, this time to 25 Enkel Street, Holloway, London. It was here that their last child was born, Annie Lloyd Robertson in 1878. She made a total of seven children born to John and Margaret Robertson – four boys and three girls. Excluding William who died as a young boy in the 1870s, the three sons would share their father's enthusiasm and skill for gunmaking and run the very successful Boss business in the first half of the 20th century.

Robertson worked for Purdey for a total of nine years. During this time, he became one of Purdey's right-hand men and had a position of considerable importance. As a journeyman he was at the pinnacle of his career – the next step must be his own business.

THE ESTABLISHMENT OF JOHN ROBERTSON'S EARLY GUNMAKING BUSINESS, 1873

John Robertson had been in the employ of others since leaving Haddington in 1858. By 1873 he was thoroughly versed in all facets of gun manufacture and had made a great many contacts in the trade in London. He was thirty-four years of age and concluded that it was propitious to establish his own business. Robertson realised that opening a gunmaking business selling guns of his own make to the public would probably be doomed to failure. Competition was more intense than ever in the 1870s – another gunmaking firm with a name unknown to the sporting public would find trade very difficult.

It would be far better to capitalise on his reputation and skill amongst the gunmaking trade and work for the London gunmakers where considerable business would be assured. The similarity with the early history of Thomas Boss is apparent since Thomas Boss had come to the same conclusion and worked for the trade in the 1820s.

In 1873 he rented premises at 101 Great Titchfield Street, just off Oxford Street, and commenced business as a gunmaker working for the trade. During the second half of the 19th century, with increasing wealth and a rising nouveau riche, interest in shooting accelerated. There was a steady demand for sporting guns and British gunmakers produced more guns in this period than ever before. The apprenticeship for skilled journeymen still took seven years and time served men of quality were in short supply. The leading gunmakers usually had to subcontract work to meet demand and this was how the Robertson business flourished. He was well known within the trade for his meticulous approach to gunmaking, and could be relied upon to produce the quality work required by the established makers.

The major gunmakers for whom Robertson worked in the 1870s and 1880s were: Stephen Grant at 67a St James's Street, Joseph Lang at 88 Wigmore Street, Holland and Holland at 98 New Bond Street, Boss & Co. at 73 St James's Street, Henry Atkin at Oxenden Street, William Evans at 95 a Buckingham Palace Road, John Rigby at 72 St James's Street, and many other lesser-known makers.

By far the majority of work done by Robertson at this time was for Stephen Grant and Holland and Holland. Grant received orders and Warrants of Appointment from the Royal houses of France, Spain, Germany, Austria-Hungary, Russia, Persia, Turkey and some Indian Maharajahs. He won the Gold Medal at the Paris Exhibition in 1878. John Robertson stocked, screwed and finished virtually every Grant gun in this period, including the Gold Medal guns. Similarly, with Holland and Holland, who by 1883 had achieved international renown by decisively winning all *The Field* Rifle Trials, Robertson stocked, screwed and finished many of their guns and rifles. Holland's made different grades of guns of varying qualities. The Holland guns on which Robertson worked were for the most part of their best quality. The similarity with the early days of Thomas Boss is again apparent. Thomas Boss essentially built many of the guns of a very well-known maker in the 1820s, James Purdey and now Robertson in the 1870s and 1880s built many of the guns of other well-known makers, Holland and Holland and Stephen Grant.

Boss today are fortunate in still possessing several workbooks detailing much of the work undertaken by the early Robertson business. These workbooks show that Robertson's main work at first in the 1870s was in stocking and screwing guns together. By the 1880s he was producing actions as well. The Robertson actions are unique and can easily be spotted when any gun is dismantled. The strengthening part where the top strap joins the action is not rounded as on most guns, it is angled. This angled part is stamped "J R". Since the gunmakers for whom Robertson supplied his actions did not want it to be publicly known that they were not building their own guns, this "J R" is often filed off. The filing is usually crude and can be spotted.

In the Robertson records the gun numbers of the maker are given alongside details of the work carried out and the price charged. Examples from these workbooks are given below.

Stephen Grant 6th May 1876

No. 4089 Cleaning and chequering butt.	11s 0d.
No. 4102 Stocking and screwing	£1.10s 0d
Nos. 4078/9 Fitting pins, jointing, cleaning and chequering	£1.18s 6d

Holland And Holland 20th November 1886

No. 11598 Stocking and screwing.	£2.0.0d
No. 8626 Silver oval	10d
No. 11071 Making off and chequering with pistol hand.	£1.7.6d
No. 11039 Finishing rifle	£1.8.6d

Edward Lang 11th December 1879

No. 1223 One best top lever action (.400)	£7.0.0d
No. 1217 Stocking and screwing	£2.5.0d
Making off and chequering	£1.4.0d
One pair best rifle barrels	£7.0.0d

William Evans 1st July 1886

Nos. 1925/6 Stocking screwing and finishing in soft	£6.10.0d
Filing tail pipes	3s.0d
Ovals	2s.0d
Forend woods	1s.0d
Stipping and finishing	£2.10s.0d
Regulating locks and gilding strikers	7s.4d

The factory in Great Titchfield Street was not big enough to cope with the increase in business. In 1882 the firm moved to 4 George Yard, Wardour Street, Soho. In the 19th century Soho's reputation differed from today's montage of restaurants, neon lights, distinctly (and more interestingly) non-academic bookshops, and cinemas that discourage patrons under 18 years of age. It was an area with a multitude of small businesses in all its nooks and alleys. Four George Yard contained other gunmaking businesses as well: Frank Squires the well-known gunbarrel-maker was there, as were Southgate and Mears, gunmakers. Southgate went on to achieve fame with the Southgate ejector and Mears was a relative of Thomas Boss who had worked with the firm for a time. Interestingly, the property is referred to as a "Printing Works" in the rate books of the period! For some reason in 1886, 4 George Yard was renamed 4 Dansey Yard.

The three sons of John Robertson, John, Sam and Bob, all entered this gunmaking business. John became apprenticed to his father in 1876, Sam in 1877 and Bob in 1888. For a trade only business the firm was large, probably the biggest in London in the period. Around fifteen gunmakers were employed, a measure of the

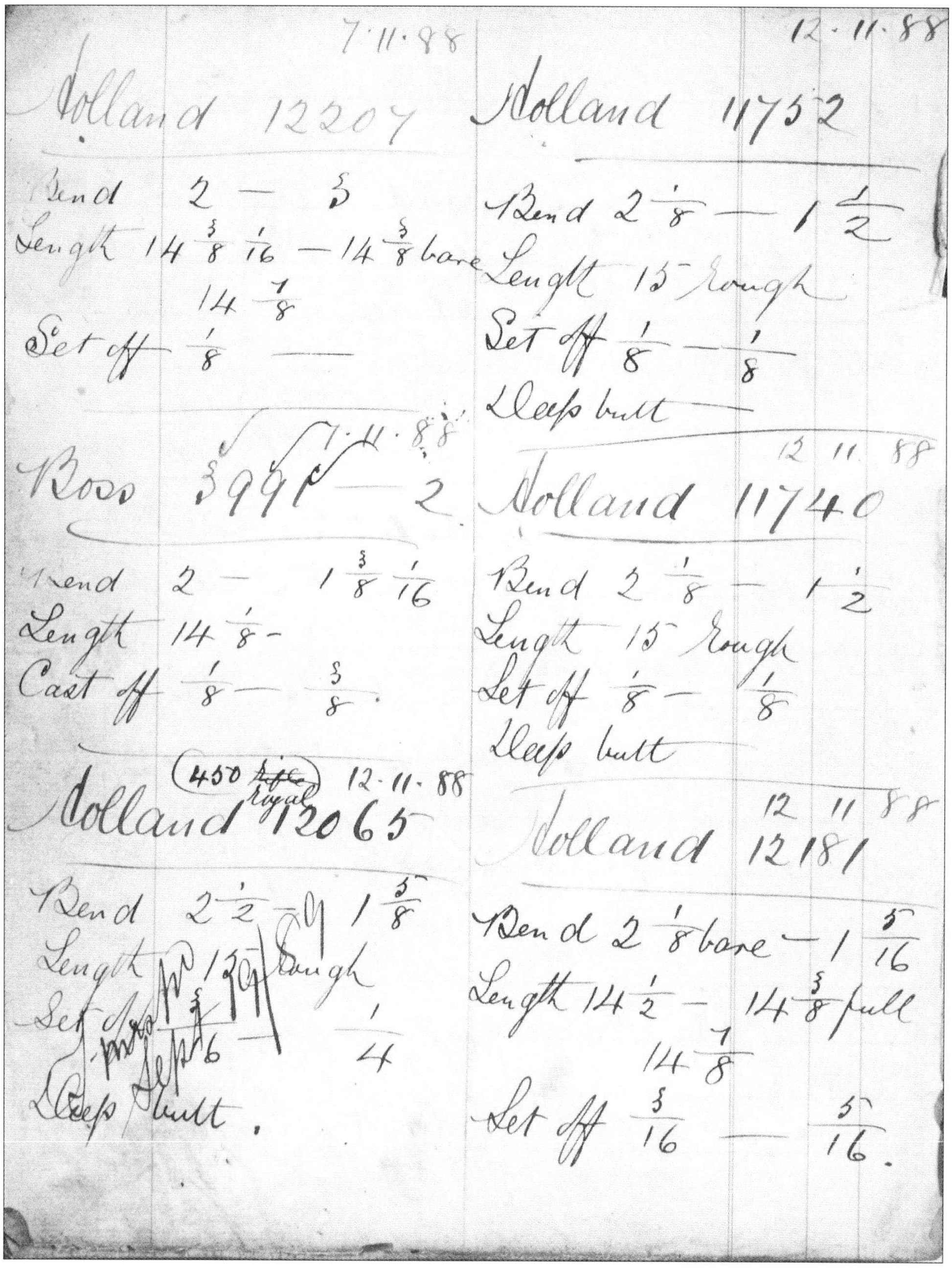

7.11.88   12.11.88

Holland 12207   Holland 11752

Bend 2 — 5
Length 14 3/8 1/16 — 14 3/8 bare
    14 1/8
Set off 1/8 —

Bend 2 1/8 — 1 1/2
Lengh 15 Rough
Set off 1/8 — 1/8
Deep butt

Boss 3991 — 2
7.11.88

Bend 2 — 1 3/8 1/16
Length 14 1/8 —
Cast off 1/8   3/8

Holland 11740
12.11.88

Bend 2 1/8 — 1 1/2
Length 15 Rough
Set off 1/8 — 1/8
Deep butt

(450 life Royal) 12.11.88
Holland 12065

Bend 2 1/2 — 1 5/8
Length 15 Rough
Set off
    4
Deep butt.

Holland 12181
12.11.88

Bend 2 1/8 bare — 1 5/16
Length 14 1/2 — 14 3/8 full
    14 1/8
Set off 5/16 — 5/16.

A page dated November 1888 from John Robertson's workbook, detailing stocking measurements for his stocking contracts with various makers. Of particular interest are Boss guns nos. 3991/2 as illustrated on page 99.

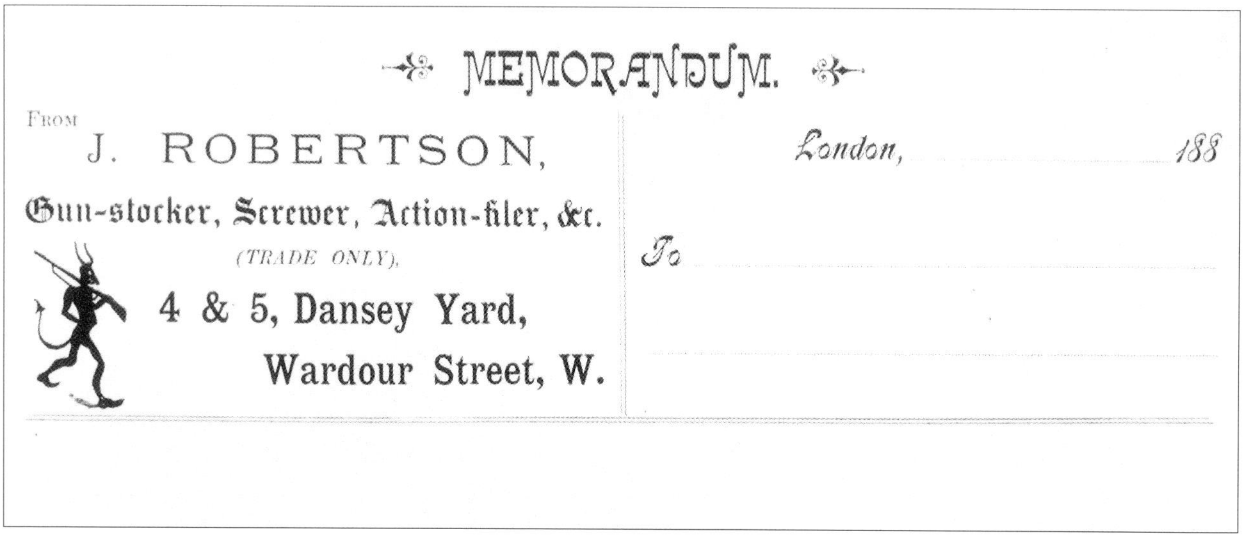

BELOW: A memo from John Robertson's business in the 1880s. Notice the wording, "Trade Only". Sometimes a logo is added underneath the Devil, "not so black as he is painted".

MEMORANDUM.

FROM
J. ROBERTSON,
Gun-stocker, Screwer, Action-filer, &c.
(TRADE ONLY),
4 & 5, Dansey Yard,
Wardour Street, W.

London,   188
To

84 | 1890 | 60

	Jany 4	Jany 11	Jany 18	Jany 25
C Johnson	2 . 15 . 0	2 . 8 . 0		3 . 15 . 0
W. Adams	2 . 10 . 0	2 . 10 . 0	2 . 10 . 0	2 . 13
J. Rowbotham	2 . 9 . 2	2 - 9 . 2	2 . 12 . 6	2 . 14 . 2
J Wyse	1 . 6 . 3	1 . 5 . 0	2 . 4 . 6	2 . 11 . 8
A. Rowbotham	1 . 10 . 0	1 . 10 . 0	1 . 11 . 9	1 . 13 . 6
J.R.	1 . 14 . 0	2 - 19 . 6	2 . 19 . 6	2 . 18 . 6
S.R.	1 . 15 . 0	1 . 15 . 0	1 . 16 . 8	1 . 17 . 6
N. Weaves	1 . 5 . 0	1 . 8 . 6	1 . 8 . 6	1 . 10
G Young	19 . 0		15 . 0	14 . 6
N. Hughes	10 . 2	16 . 0	16 . 0	
L. Adams	14 . 6	11 . 6	14	12
R. R	4 . 6	4 . 6	4 . 6	4 . 6
E. Fraser	5 . 6	5 - 6	5 - 6	5 . 6
J Prentice	2 . 0 . 0	3 . 0 - 0	1 . 0 . 0	1 . 10 .
C Price	1 . 10 . 0			
Sumner			2 . 0 . 0	.
Brider			1 . 4 . 0	1 . 4 .
Sundries	13 - 1	1 . 7 - 5	14 - 1	1 . 5 . 6
J.R.	1 . 8 . 0	2 . 19 . 6	2 . 19 . 6	2 . 18 . 6
	23 - 9 - 2	25 - 9 - 7	25 - 19 - 0	28 . 7 . 10

**A page from Robertson's wages book, January 1890. Notice the abreviations, "J.R., S.R., and R.R."
for the three sons. Bob was still in his apprenticeship and received a low wage. William Adams was
involved with John Robertson in many of his patents. Sumner was an engraver at the top end of the
trade, not actually employed directly by Robertson.**

Sam Robertson – a photograph taken near the end of his apprenticeship *circa* **1884.**

success and demand for Robertson's work. A wages book from this era exists and details the workers employed by Robertson.

In addition to running a successful, flourishing business, John Robertson found time to apply his talents of inventive mechanical ingenuity to perfect the sporting gun.

His first patent was taken out in 1882 and his last in 1915 and during this period he applied for twenty-five provisional patents, although only eighteen were eventually published as complete specifications. All the Robertson patents are described and illustrated in fuller detail in Appendix 8. What is remarkable about these patents, apart from their considerable number and the mental application that must have gone into formulating them, is that none were superflous trivia that inventors can often be prone to. Each patent was very relevant and either used by Boss or sold to other gunmakers. Three of these patents were of such importance in the gun world that they guaranteed John Robertson a position of considerable esteem that is still held today. They are provisional patent no. 22894 of the 26th November 1894, The Boss Single Trigger, provisonal patent no. 2988 of 4th February 1897 The Boss Ejector Mechanism and provisional patent no. 3307 of 10th February 1909, The Boss Over and Under Gun.

The first patent taken out by John Robertson was provisional patent no. 2833 of 15th June 1882. It deals primarily with tumbler safety catches for both bar-

action side locks and Anson and Deeley boxlocks. In addition, it also contains a hammerless action cocked by the front lump.

His second patent was provisional patent no. 23 of 1st January 1883. He co-operated with Henry Holland over this and the patent bears both their names. It was an improved cocking mechanism whereby one lock was cocked by the fall of the barrels and the other upon their closure. Four years later, on 21st April 1887, again in a combined patent with Henry Holland, he took out provisional patent no. 5834 to improve upon ejector mechanisms. A further combined patent between Holland and Robertson of 26th August 1887, no. 11623 improved upon the previous ejector mechanism patent. His final patent whilst working for the trade and incidentally, the final combination of Holland and, Robertson, was provisional patent no. 16691, dated 16th November 1888, again improving upon the two previous ejector mechanism patents. The remaining patents would all be taken out with the Boss address when Robertson became the proprietor.

The year 1888 also saw the first marriage of the three Robertson sons. The eldest son, John Robertson (Jnr), married Alice Trevillion in the Register Office, Islington on 2nd May 1888. He was aged twenty-six and Alice was aged twenty-two. By this time, his father, mother and family had moved out of the family home at 25 Enkel Street, Islington, but John (Jnr) remained at the address to set up home with his new bride. Since 25 Enkel Street, was a good size and to generate extra income, the spare rooms were rented out to an acquaintance from Scotland and his family, James Burns, who was a gunmaker at Boss. One year after their marriage, their only child was born here. This was May Robertson who would marry John Rennie, a relative of Rennie the bridge builder, in 1915. As May Rennie she would be a director of Boss in the 1930s, 1940s and 1950s.

Since the establishment of his business in 1873, John Robertson had built it up into a healthy business, respected and well-known by all the trade in London. Such was the variety of makers he did work for, and the volume of work he produced, the Robertson establishment must take a large part in the credit due to the reputation of London for unsurpassed gun work – the London made gun setting the standard for all others to aspire to.

The future of himself and his three sons was secure. Due to the fact that he worked for the trade only, he might have remained an enigmatic figure to the public and to history had not two events contrived to ensure himself a place in the limelight and in the annals of gunmaking history – two events that enabled him to take over Boss & Co in January 1891.

John Robertson (Jnr) around the time of his marriage, 1888. Taken in a photographer's studio in Seven Sisters Road, just round the corner from his home in Enkel Street.

CHAPTER EIGHT

JOHN ROBERTSON – PROPRIETOR OF BOSS & CO., 1891

During the late 1880s, the fortunes of Boss & Co. under Edward Paddison were declining. The rate of gun production dropped and profits were down although guns produced were still of the highest quality. Paddison remained conservative in his attitude to gun technology and innovation and in addition he was a sick man who found the burden of running the establishment difficult. Acquiring wives was a far more interesting pastime.

He decided during 1890 that he would have to find a partner to assist run the business. This was the first event for John Robertson. It was not every day that a long established first-class gunmaking business partnership was on offer. The benefits to Robertson of becoming involved in the Boss business would be enormous. Firstly, he would have an established clientele and a superb reputation on which he could capitalise and secondly he could continue his trade business in Dansey Yard. The two businesses could combine very easily, the public Boss business and the private Robertson trade business. In addition, by being involved in Boss, Robertson could achieve his ambition and run a best gun establishment.

The only problem was that there might be other contenders for the partnership. This is where the second event comes in. John Robertson had done a great deal of work for Boss since the establishment of his trade business in 1873. His workbooks contain scores of orders from Boss, mainly stocking and screwing. Paddison, knowing the quality of Robertson's work and being very proud of the reputation of Boss guns, need have no qualms about Robertson's involvement. There is a story that goes the rounds at Boss & Co., possibly apocryphal but probably truthful, to further explain why Robertson was offered the partnership. The type of work done by Robertson for Boss, stocking, screwing, actioning, etc was expensive. In the Robertson workbooks, bills to Boss of around £200 are not uncommon, a large sum of money in the 1880s. Due

to Paddison's inability to run the business efficiently, or due to his medical debility, he found difficulty in meeting these bills to Robertson. On account of these debts, Robertson had a rightful claim to the partnership.

During late 1890 Edward Paddison and John Robertson signed a deed of partnership to come into effect on 1st January 1891. John Robertson was to pay £600 to Paddison for a half share in the Boss business, minus £168 for work to be done for Boss by Robertson in the year 1891. This was a very low sum involved for a half share in the Boss business and helps to lend credence to the story that Paddison was under an obligation to offer Robertson a partnership at a below market valuation. In addition the fact that Edward Paddison only left £23.10s.0d. in his Will when

John Robertson *circa* 1891, a photograph taken around the time he became proprietor of Boss & Co.

he died in September 1891 lends more weight to the story. His funeral expenses of £3.18s.6d. could not even be paid and Boss & Co. had to pay for them.

Just before he died, Edward Paddison transferred his share of the partnership to his nephew Walter Fields Paddison. His nephew subsequently enjoyed a half share in the profits drawing around £5 every week. This partnership arrangement obviously was a drain on the Boss business and John Robertson was keen to end it. On 31st December 1893, by mutual consent, the partnership was dissolved. It was agreed that John Robertson would pay £1,501.9s.2d. to Walter and Emily Paddison in compensation for the dissolution. To find this sum, Robertson had to take out a £1,200 mortgage at 10% to be repaid not later than 1st January 1903. The mortgage was eventually paid off on 26th March 1903, by which date John Robertson owned the Boss business outright.

On 1st January 1891, Robertson took over the running of Boss and in addition he kept on the Robertson trade business at Dansey Yard. The trade business employed around fifteen gunmakers and the Boss business around the same, making a total of thirty gunmakers under Robertson control – a sizeable concern. In the wages books, the Boss business is referred to as "The Next Shop" being a very different connotation from any other establishment today.

At first little changed. The Robertson workers remained at Dansey Yard and the Boss workers at 73, St James's Street. Robertson continued to do a massive amount of work for the trade and by this time had expanded from stocking and screwing into making actions for the trade. As time went on circumstances did change. The personnel at Boss at 73 St James's Street declined slightly. Around ten gunmakers remained there. In November 1897, Bob Robertson transferred from Dansey Yard to 73 St James's Street, to become his father's assistant. Later his particular charge was the fitting of guns and instruction in shooting with them. The two elder brothers, John and Sam, remained at the factory.

Sam Robertson had married by this time. He had in fact married on 11th May 1891, shortly after the takeover of Boss. He was twenty-seven and his bride of twenty-six years of age was Annie Eliza Johnson, the daugther of a builder living at 14 Roden Street, Islington. Sam and Annie would later sire three sons, Jack, Alec and Tom, but only Alec came into the company to become the third generation of Robertsons to run Boss. The present Robertson at Boss today is, however, the grandson of the youngest brother, Tom.

With the great innovations of Robertson, the single trigger and such like, the Boss side expanded considerably. More and more of the factory work went into

building Boss guns, whilst the trade business diminished somewhat. In the late 1890s the workforce in the factory increased to around thirty-six, making a total of around forty-five gunmakers employed by Robertson.

THE BOSS SINGLE TRIGGER

The firm of Boss & Co. are synonymous with single trigger guns, whereby one trigger can fire both barrels one after the other on a double-barrel gun. More than any other maker, they have perfected and promoted the single trigger and are regarded today as the leading manufacturer of single trigger guns. The firm have always exclaimed this fact, "Speciality – Single Trigger Guns – Absolutely the Safest Guns Made" appears time and time again in Boss advertisments both past and present.

It was John Robertson in his very early days as proprietor of Boss in the early 1890s who studied and perfected the single trigger. It was his single trigger that was widely described and acclaimed by the sporting press that really brought fame to Boss & Co. The old established reputation of "Builders of Best Guns Only" and now builders of highly innovative guns was a winning combination that guaranteed Boss a world famous name.

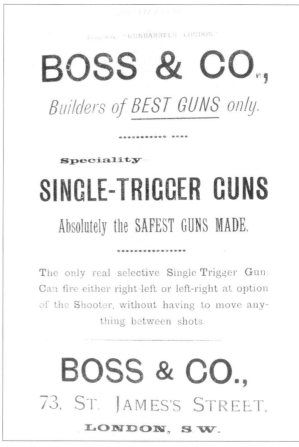

An advertisement *circa* 1900 promoting the speciality of Boss – their single trigger guns.

An advertisement *circa* 1900 showing how the single trigger was acclaimed by the contemporary sporting press.

The importance of the single trigger to Boss must never be underestimated. Many of the improvements to hammerless guns in the late 19th century were not immediately obvious to sportsmen, such as ejectors, hammerless actions, because they were "out of sight". A single trigger was obvious to all and although many sportsmen did not like single triggers, its virtues and vices were much discussed in the late 19th/early 20th centuries whereby the name "Boss" would frequently be mentioned. Its operation was intriguing and, like it or not, all sportsmen found it fascinating how one trigger could fire both barrels, either barrel first.

Single triggers on double-barrel guns were nothing new. For over a century gunmakers had wrestled with the problem. A single trigger can have many advantages over two triggers.

1. The length of stock and position of the hand and finger is the same when using either barrel.
2. A second shot can be got off more quickly.
3. The inconvenience suffered as the result of recoil jarring fingers on the trigger guard and triggers is negated.
4. Wearing gloves is a possibility due to the greater space within the trigger guard because one trigger occupies the same space as two triggers.

Against these advantages must be set the following objections.

1. The increased complexity of the trigger mechanism makes for possible reliability problems.
2. Increased cost of a single trigger gun.
3. The shooter does not have the same freedom to choose which barrel he will discharge first. Even though a selector is fitted, the selection process takes longer than it does on a gun fitted with two triggers.

Over one hundred patents have been taken out on single trigger guns, the earliest patent no. 1707 taken out in 1789 by James Templeman, a gunmaker in Salisbury. In 1797, John Manton of 6 Dover Street, London, took out patent no. 2178 for breeches and locks in firearms. Although without drawings part of his patent states: "I have constructed a tricker for double guns and pistols on an improved principle." William and John Rigby of Dublin produced many double pistols and rifles with single triggers in the 1840s. Like most of the patents they were unsuccessful in that the principles of the single trigger were not fully under-stood and that a double discharge could take place.

The first single trigger patent taken out by John Robertson was provisional patent no. 20873 of 3rd November 1893. This was a fussy, delicate single trigger

working on the two pull system and unsatisfactory in that it could lead to a double discharge. The two pull system was the norm of most single trigger patents up to and including this patent. A first pull of the trigger fired the first barrel, some sort of mechanism was then brought into action to enable the second barrel to fire and in the second pull this second barrel could be fired. This was the theory but, for reasons that will shortly be explained, in practice no matter how well thought out and how well made the early two pull single trigger device was, a double discharge could take place. Until the double discharge problem was sorted out, the single trigger would never gain favour. On 21st March 1894 Robertson brought out provisional patent no. 5897, another attempt at producing a single trigger. It failed for similar reasons as in the previous patent.

As so often happens in the history of inventions, more than one mind seems to have conceived the solution to the problem at roughly the same time. It dawned on one or two gunmakers that a simple two-pull system could not work. When the shooter pulls the trigger, and the gun discharges, the gun recoils, and moves backwards. As the gun moves backwards, the shooter's finger does not and comes off the trigger. Instinctively, the shooter realises his finger is not on the trigger and immediately renews his grip on the trigger. Consequently, on firing the first barrel he does not make one pull, but two pulls. The first pull is voluntary, and the second pull involuntary. This is where the problem lay in the single trigger and explains why gun-makers were baffled by the double discharge. To over-come the problem, two methods could be used. In the first method, a delay could be introduced between the firing of the first and second barrel to render impotent

The single trigger patent no. 22894 of 26th November 1894.

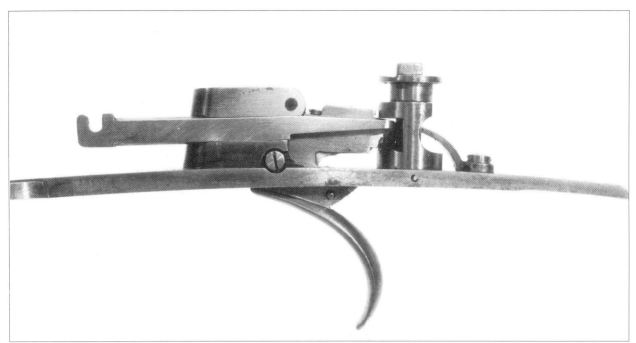

A single trigger assembly showing the revolving turret (right) and cocking lever (left).

the second involuntary pull. This is known as "the delayed action system". In the second method, three distinct pulls could be introduced, the first pull firing the first barrel, the second pull being the involuntary pull and the third pull firing the second barrel. This is known as "the three-pull system".

The famous Robertson three-pull single trigger system was provisionally patented on 26th November 1894, provisional patent no. 22894. It is this patent number that will be found engraved on early Boss single trigger guns. Patent no. 22894 bears the title, "Improvements in Drop Down Arms". The reason that it does not mention the term "single trigger" is that because several gunmakers had begun to understand the three pull system, they were all working feverishly to patent a system upon its principles. The date on Robertson's provisional patent is 26th November 1894. Until the complete specification was submitted and published, in this case on 19th October 1895, the contents of the patent remained secret apart from the title. Robertson was deliberately vague in his title lest other makers found out what he was up to and quickly submitted rival patents.

Although the patent bears the name of John Robertson only, it is known that his foreman, William Adams who co-operated with Robertson on other patents, had much to do with it. John Robertson was a stocker to trade and had to have the assistance of others in working out and building his designs. The patent itself is extremely complex and covers many facets of the three-pull system. There are one 101 drawings and the patent specification runs to twelve pages. The complexity and minutae of detail contained in the

patent make it obvious that Robertson had made a very thorough study of single triggers.

Although various three-pull systems are described, the central core of the patent is the revolving turret that combines safety and simplicity and made the Boss single trigger the best known and most popular.

The following description is very brief. For a detailed description on how the system works, consult Appendix 8. On the trigger plate, there is a revolving turret (g) with various notches cut into it. Contained within the turret is a watchmaker's coiled spring, constructed in gold to resist corrosion. When the trigger (b) is pulled on the first pull, the first barrel fires and the turret revolves a predetermined distance. Upon the shooter inadvertently making the second pull, the turret again revolves a set distance. The second barrel cannot fire at this point because the position of the turret bolts the

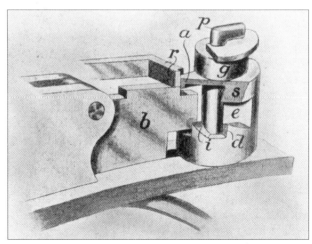

Diagram of the Boss single trigger showing the revolving turret (g) and the trigger blade (b).

lock of the second barrel. When the shooter releases his grip after this second involuntary pull, the turret again revolves and is now ready to discharge the second barrel upon the third pull. Throughout the cycle, the turret revolves in very carefully controlled movements, making accidental or premature discharge of the second barrel impossible.

The shooter is quite unaware that he has actually pulled the trigger three times to fire two barrels. Only when the gun is dry fired, with snap caps in the chambers, is it obvious that three distinct pulls have been made.

Robertson's successful single trigger caused a great sensation when it appeared. To capitalise on his achievement and to maximise publicity he organised the first of several public trials to convince the public and sporting press of the superiority of the Boss single trigger. In December 1894 a number of representatives of the sporting press and others journeyed to the London School of Shooting at the Old Oak Common, Willesden. Five Boss single triggers were used. Cartridges loaded with a variety of loads were used at clay birds simulating rocketing pheasants, running rabbits, etc. By 2 o'clock in the afternoon one thousand

cartridges had been expended. To quote Dudley Watson, *Land and Water's* correspondent in their edition of 22nd December 1894, "In a word it (the single trigger) emerged from the ordeal with undoubted success. During the whole course of the trial, there was not a single case of jarring off of the left barrel . . . very little practice, if any, was required to become throughly accustomed to the working of the single trigger . . . before the trial was half over it was easily seen and generally admitted that the ingenious inventor (Mr Robertson) had successfully overcome all defects of the previous one trigger guns . . . the one trigger gun is at last an accomplished fact."

There then followed over the next year or so lively debate in most of the sporting periodicals about the single trigger. Most were concerned about its reliability and safety. To dispel any doubts, Robertson again organised another public trial. On the 2nd June 1896, a public trial of the Boss single trigger took place at the London Shooting School, Willesden, before an influential body of press representatives and expert sportsmen. A single trigger gun with the pulls reduced to 1 lb was produced. Blows with a 4 lb hammer to the butt failed in moving either lock. The same gun was fired

---

May 23, 1896

THE SHOOTING TIMES AND BRITISH SPORTSMAN.

BOSS AND CO.'S SINGLE TRIGGER GUN.

TO THE EDITOR OF THE SHOOTING TIMES.

SIR,—From the correspondence that has recently taken place in some of your contemporaries there seems to be a doubt in the minds of many sportsmen as to the efficiency and safety of single trigger guns. As it appears difficult to make our simple mechanism understood, and with a view to inspire your readers with confidence, we propose to hold a public trial at the London Shooting School, Willesden Junction, on Tuesday, June 2nd, at twelve o'clock. We shall then practically demonstrate, not only the efficiency and reliability of our mechanism, but the absolute safety of our single trigger over guns with two triggers. To show this properly we propose to reduce the left pulls of a single and a two-trigger gun to about 1 lb. or so (not that such pulls are required in actual shooting), but to prove that our one trigger gun is safe to shoot with at this weight, and must, of course, be more so with ordinary pulls.

The timely suggestion in SHOOTING TIMES of April 25th we shall be pleased to follow, and any charges can be used not dangerous to an ordinary game gun. We shall afterwards strip the gun, show the mechanism, explain the working, and answer all questions relating to it. We cordially invite you to be present, and any other test you would like the guns put to during the trial we shall be pleased to carry out. Kindly let us know whether you will be represented and oblige,

BOSS & CO., per A. S. EMBLETON.

73, St. James's-street, London, S.W., May 20th, 1896.

P.S.—We invite you to bring a two trigger gun with the left pull this weight to test for safety. As we wish this trial to be public, will you kindly convey the invitation through your columns and oblige?

[We shall be pleased to accept the above invitation and report the result in the issue following the event—ED.]

Boss & Co.'s letter to *The Shooting Times* advertising their public trial of the single trigger on 2nd June 1896.

Although Messrs Boss and Co. were amongst the first in the field with this idea (see the *Field*, April 4, 1896, p. 498), owing to some misunderstanding, for which we think they were to blame, their one-trigger gun was not tried by us until this year. The trials were as severe as we think the circumstances warranted, and the mechanism proved thoroughly reliable. We tested guns of 10, 12, 16, and 20-bore with the heaviest and lightest charges, both with heavy and light trigger pulls, and triggers of the shortest draught ; so that when releasing the trigger after the involuntary pull the finger had not to move forward more than one-tenth of an inch, and no variation in the pulls nor in the charges used made any difference to the mechanism.

In order to judge what effect the weather might have upon the mechanism, we immersed the single-trigger tumbler, with spring fitted, in water, and exposed it at intervals to the air for a couple of months, without causing any perceptible difference in its action.

An excerpt from *The Field*'s test of the Boss single trigger as reported on 20th November 1897.

with various loads, yet a double discharge did not take place. A two trigger gun with a 1lb lock pull received similar treatment but it jarred off every time. This reinforced Boss's claim, "Absolutely The Safest Guns Made". A finished gun, no. 4391 which had never previously been shot, was tried in every way and worked perfectly.

Land and Water of 6th June 1896 stated after its report on the trials, "In conclusion we have to add that in our opinion throughout the trial Messrs Boss & Co. acted with absolute fairness, that those who were present applied and verified the tests with strict impartiality and at lunch afterwards agreed with the opinion expressed by the Editor of *Land and Water* for the claim that a distinct advance had been made in gunnery and our knowledge of it. These opinions were confirmed by representatives of *The Times*, *The Shooting Times*, *Rod and Gun* and others." *The Field* in particular gave the mechanism a very thorough test and reported the results to its readers on 20th November 1897.

Another public trial used a double-barrel 4-bore rifle with 16 drams of black powder and a 4 oz bullet. It is probably hard to envisage a greater recoil, yet the jar could not possibly discharge the second barrel. The same gun was loaded with an ultra light load of 2 drams of powder and 1 oz of shot. The minimal recoil was quite sufficient to effect the three pull system.

Guns that had been through entire shooting seasons were publicly examined and tested and all came through with flying colours showing that there had been no perceptible wear on the mechanism. Some commentators had reservations about the strength of the mechanism and foresaw that it could fail very easily. To dispell any doubts about this, John Robertson constructed a convincing experiment. The normal material used in the single trigger was of course best quality hardened steel. In this experiment, Robertson substituted the steel with boxwood. Boxwood is a dense wood and capable of intricate working, yet it is still wood and many times softer than steel. A great many

shots were fired from the gun in rapid succession with absolutely no problem at all.

The first single trigger guns sold were nos. 4305, 4306 and 4308, double-barrel 12-bore top lever hammerless ejector guns with Damascus barrels ordered by H. H. Islam on 2nd April 1894. All were chased in gold with stocks inlaid with gold. The single trigger mechanism is termed "The Thistle" single trigger. I think this refers to Robertson's early single trigger patent no. 5897 of 21st March 1894. Altogether six "Thistle" single triggers were constructed. Probably the first single trigger constructed under the famous patent no. 22894 of 26th November 1894 was a double-barrel 12-bore top snap hammerless ejector pigeon gun no. 4369 ordered on 17th December 1894 by J. H. Denny, Pittsburgh, Pennsylvania. Very rapidly afterwards, thanks to the enthusiastic and positive response of the press and the public, single trigger guns were made in increasing quantities. By the late 1890s they accounted for around two-thirds of Boss's output.

In a booklet produced by Boss *circa* 1920, they described the advantages of their single trigger, thus:

The single trigger gun was introduced mainly to afford the shooter confidence in his weapon – to relieve him of all such acts as might be calculated to distract his attention from the object of the chase. In the single trigger gun, the sportsman has only to think of this solitary object. He has not to shift from one trigger to another to fire his second barrel, and the length of his gun remains the same for his left barrel as for his right. The bruising of the middle finger is entirely obviated by the use of a one trigger gun. A double trigger gun which is of the precise length for his first barrel, cannot with two triggers be correct for the second, or vice-versa. There are, of course, other advantages, but the single trigger gun has long since proved its superiority over the orthodox weapon.

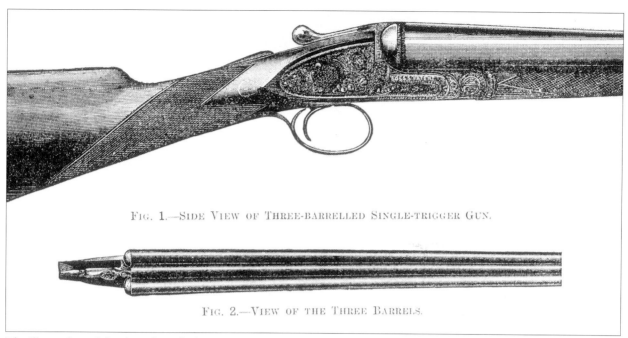

FIG. 1.—SIDE VIEW OF THREE-BARRELLED SINGLE-TRIGGER GUN.

FIG. 2.—VIEW OF THE THREE BARRELS.

The illustration of the three-barrelled gun as it appeared in most of the sporting periodicals in the year 1898.

During the years 1898–1901, John Robertson constructed two three-barrelled 16-bore guns fired by single triggers. Multiple-barrelled sporting guns were nothing new. Flintlock guns so designed had been built and, more recently, Charles Lancaster had brought out a four-barrelled gun in 1882. His gun was not a real success. It worked on the revolver principle with the difference that the barrels remained static while the hammer revolved within the action, hitting each striker in turn. The pressure on the trigger was considerable due to the fact that it had to cock and rotate the hammer each time. In addition, it was an ungainly and clumsy gun.

In the Boss gun, the three barrels were laid side by side. Being a 16-bore, the width of the three barrels was not much more than a normal double 12-bore. It was light, too, weighing just under 7 lbs. The weapon was by no means clumsy – from the side it looked like any other gun.

What was remarkable was that the three barrels were fired by a single trigger. A modification to the revolving turret enabled the single trigger to be used and indicators were fitted to show which of the barrels had been fired. To get the ejector mechanism to work without hitch of any kind was no slight undertaking. Only two triple-barrel guns were built and both survive today. Robertson intended that this gun should be used with driven game, whereby three birds could be brought down from a covey, almost an impossibility where a gun has to be changed. At the London Sporting Park, Hendon, one well-known game shot was successful in breaking all three clay birds in the air thirteen times in succession without a miss, a near impossible feat with a

change of guns in the ordinary driving manner. Yet the triple-barrel gun never caught on. The double-barrel side-by-side was the standard game gun and always would be. Repeating shotguns were being developed at this time and many sportsmen regarded anything other than a double-barrel as unsporting.

Probably the main reason that Robertson developed the gun was the one-upmanship that was necessary to keep gunmaking firms in the limelight when the hammerless ejector had been developed to its practical limit at this time. It was something different and it would certainly set the sporting public talking. The other reason for it could be that it was the ultimate demonstration of the single trigger. A single trigger and three barrels was a mechanical triumph and demonstrated the superiority of the Boss single trigger. One of these guns is illustrated below.

Triple-barrel gun no. 4690. See Plate 61.

THE SINGLE TRIGGER PATENT DISPUTE 1906

Immitation is the most sincere form of flattery and this was the ambivalent emotion that John Robertson now experienced. Such was the popularity and demand for the single trigger at the close of the 19th century that many leading gunmakers invented and adopted their own single trigger actions.

How popular the single trigger became can be judged from the list of patents brought out 1894–97 after Robertson's patent no. 22894 of the 26th November 1894. The list is not conclusive.

DATE PATENT NO PATENTEE

1894	23751	H. W. Holland and T. Woodward
1895	1844	W. P. Jones and W. Baker
1895	3420	T. Perkes
1895	4005	E. Harrison
1895	5517	H. A. A. Thorn (Charles Lancaster)
1895	5543	W. P. Jones and W. Baker
1895	10133	F. Beesley
1895	13063	R. Hill and J. V. Smith
1895	21346	F. J. Penn and J. D. Deeley
1895	24426	W. Cashmore
1896	2422	T. Southgate
1896	2769	H. W. Holland and T. Woodward
1896	3337	L. Barrett
1896	7570	J. Hourat and J. Castadere
1896	11068	H. W. Holland and W. Mansfield
1896	12234	G. Bouckley
1896	13492	J. W. Smallman
1896	20088	H. W. Holland and T Woodward
1896	27310	F. De W. Granger
1897	301	J. Rigby and L. E. Atkins
1897	2955	T. Southgate
1897	3988	J. W. Smallman
1897	4893	H. W. Holland and T. Woodward
1897	5110	E. J. Bland
1897	5404	F. Beesley
1897	6141	F. T. K. Baker
1897	9897	Aug. Francotte & Co.
1897	14592	W. Nobbs
1897	14877	E. C. & F. Green
1897	22624	L. E. G. de Woolfson & S. Smallwood

And so the single trigger patents continue in the swansong of the 19th century. A great many mechanisms are contained within these patents, "one pull", "two pull" and "three pull".

Of all the mechanisms Boss's single triggers were the best known and had the best reputation and John Robertson regarded the three-pull system as his own. This was confirmed by the American Patent Office. "Priority of Invention" for the three-pull single trigger was awarded to Robertson on 19th January 1897. American patents were only issued after thorough investigation and John Robertson's claim "to be the inventor and patentee of the first reliable hammerless

A letter from John Robertson to *Land and Water* dated February 13th 1897 stating that priority of invention of the first reliable single trigger gun had been granted to him in the United States of America.

single trigger gun" received corroboration by the decision of the American patent officials.

Due to the fact that the Boss single trigger working on the three-pull system caused such a sensation, considerable debate ensued as to the inventor of the three-pull system. From the outset it must be made clear that John Robertson did not claim to be the inventor of this system. What he did claim was:

1. He patented the first three-pull system, and
2. His single trigger was the first reliable single trigger mechanism.

A Birmingham gunmaker, William Baker, claimed to have invented the three-pull system in 1882/3. Under provisional patent no. 4766 of 1882, William Baker in conjunction with David Bentley produced a single trigger mechanism. Several guns were built to this patent yet, as usual in the early single trigger days, a double discharge occasionally took place. Baker then modified one of these guns on to a three-pull system and this cured the double discharge. Baker supplied such a single trigger mechanism on 3rd May 1883 to another Birmingham gunmaker W. Jones who then fitted it to the gun of a leading gunmaker, Carr of Huddersfield. He then supplied a similar mechanism to Carr on 22nd August 1883. The provisional patent lapsed due to the fact that Bentley and Baker never thought a single trigger would come to much and in any case they did not have sufficient funds to complete the patent specification.

There the matter would appear to have rested until Robertson's three-pull system of 1894 generated such interest and excitment. Baker immediately claimed anticipation and that he not Robertson invented the three-pull system. It seems odd that he was disinclined to pay the patent fees amounting to only £5 for his earlier 1882 patent. It also appears odd that the well-known gunmaker Carr of Huddersfield did not recognise the supposed merits of his three-pull system. In total only two guns were built upon his original three-pull system. In addition, the fact that one of these guns mysteriously surfaced after Robertson's success must be viewed with scepticism. It could easily have been altered to a three-pull system after 1894. Upon seeing the success of Robertson's single trigger, Baker in conjunction with W. P. Jones brought out single trigger patents no. 1844 and 5543 in 1895.

The invention of the three-pull system is indeed murky, yet it did play an important part in the patent dispute of 1906. The particular problem as far as Robertson was concerned was the Purdey single trigger. In March 1897 Athol Purdey went to see John Robertson to discuss who had actually invented the three-pull system. Athol displayed an arrogance in his approach and roundly condemned Robertson's success. Purdeys had been caught on the hop with the single trigger. They regarded it as a fad and never really paid much attention to it. Upon realising the genuine popularity of the single trigger, they resurrected a supposed three-pull system patented by a Purdey actioner, William Nobbs in patent no. 13130 of July 1894. This patent pre-dated Robertson's by four months.

John Robertson claimed that Mr Nobbs's patent was vague. He wrote to *The Field* on 9th May 1896, "As to Mr Nobbs's patent, if your correspondents think that there are three pulls in the mechanism therein described and specified, I should simply ask them to make a gun from the drawings and descriptions, when they will have absolute demonstration of the fact that the patent is decidedly on the two-pull and not the three-pull system." From the foregoing, I feel myself justified in saying it will be clearly seen that the first patented system of three pulls with a single trigger belongs to John Robertson (Boss & Co.) 73 St James's Street, London.

This was it in a nutshell. Robertson believed that the Purdey single trigger was not built exactly to the Nobbs's patent, but was a copy of his own three-pull system.

On Saturday, 15th December 1906, John Robertson took Purdeys to law in the Chancery Division of the High Court before Mr Justice Parker for alleged patent infringement of the Boss single trigger. In the years prior to the litigation, John Robertson had made large wooden models of his mechanism and most professional and gunmaking opinion was on his side.

The battle between two leading gunmakers, Boss and Purdey, fighting it out publicly made exciting reading at the time. Some recent published work insists that Purdey won the case, other works are not so sure. A

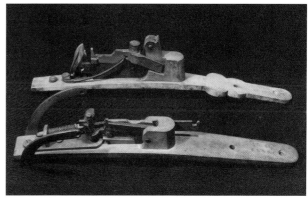

Patent dispute wooden models. See Plate 38.

careful study of the case comes out in favour of the latter. Neither Boss nor Purdey won the case outright in reality, although costs were awarded to Purdey and Robertson's litigation failed.

Boss were represented by Mr T. Terrell, K.C. and Purdeys by Mr A. J. Walker, K.C. Essentially, Robertson sought an injunction restraining Purdeys from infringing upon his three-pull single trigger patent. Purdeys presented evidence to show that patent no. 13130 of July 1894 had been granted to William Nobbs, an actioner with Purdey, for an alleged three-pull system. This was supposedly the single trigger as used by Purdey. This pre-dated Robertson's system by four months. Purdey's also showed that a three-pull system had been invented in 1883 by William Baker, a manufacturer of gun actions in Birmingham. He never patented this because the patent fees were too costly and he did not think three-pull single trigger guns would be a success. Some of the Baker guns were produced in Court.

The action for infringement turned upon the broad question whether or not the existance of the three-pull system was known before Robertson's patent of 1894. The evidence was very lengthy and it was not until Tuesday, 26th February 1907 that Mr Justice Parker delivered his judgement. He stated that, although not patented, the Baker three-pull system had received publication and some of his guns had been used from 1883 onwards. Consequently Robertson could not claim to be the inventor of the three-pull system. In addition, Mr Justice Parker stated that the alleged three-pull system patented by Nobbs and used by Purdey some four months earlier than Robertson's was, in the patent specification, insuffient and inaccurate. (The late Mr Newton who drafted the specification was blind!) This Purdey patent was therefore deemed invalid on account of its vagueness.

In many respects, the whole case was unsatisfactory. Robertson knew that Nobbs's 1894 patent was poorly drafted and explained, and felt that its vagueness meant that it ought to be challenged. In addition, no single

A pen and ink drawing by Dorofield Hardy of no. 73 St James's Street, *circa* 1895. Robertson had perfected the try gun in this period, an adjustable gun for measuring up shooters. John Rigby, gunmakers, were next door at no. 72. From The Survey of London (Supplementary Portfolio 11 nos. 1 & 2).

trigger by Nobbs had been seen in public before Robertson's guns appeared, and Robertson felt that this fact, coupled with a vague patent, meant that Purdey were attempting to emulate Robertson's success. The fact also that the gun developed in 1883 by Baker, yet never patented, was taken in evidence, must have really rankled. It took the gun trade many years to get over this case due to the fact that sides had been taken. Robertson had to amend his specification and this can be seen in the title to patent no. 22894 in Appendix 8.

In years subsequent to the Boss single trigger patent of 1894, Robertson took out various other patents to improve upon it. One of the problems of the 1894 patent single trigger was that it did not offer a selective device whereby the shooter could choose which barrel to fire first. Provisional patent no. 10949 of 13th May 1898 offered such a device. A lever on the right-hand lock selected which barrel to fire first. *Rod and Gun* of 5th July 1898 commented upon this improvement. "With this new selective action, the last objection to the use of single triggers seems to me to have been removed, for even the mixed shooter who fires one shot at a duck and another at a snipe can fire either barrel at

will, right or left, or left right as well as right left throughout a whole day's shoot."

On the outside of the lock plate, just above the trigger, is a small slide actuated by the finger. In its normal position this leaves exposed upon the lock plate a letter "R" and the gun fires right left. By moving the slide back a very short distance, the "R" is covered and an "L" revealed when the gun fires left right.

The Sporting Goods Review of 15th July 1898 commented favourably, "We fired a number of shots from a gun so fitted and were most favourably impressed. Messrs Boss & Co. are to be congratulated on their success in the solution of the chief remaining objection urged against single-trigger guns."

A criticism of the revolving turret in the single trigger mechanism was that the spring could fail. If this happened, the gun would be rendered inoperative. Robertson was alive to this potential problem and provisional patent no. 241 of 5th January 1903 tackled this. A new type of revolving turret was introduced devoid of a spring. A series of inclined planes on the turret, operated by the trigger blade, turned the turret. For ease of operation, the turret ran on ball bearings.

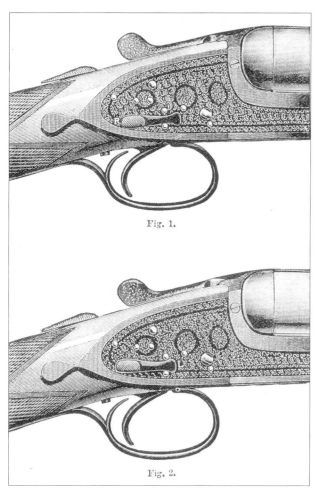

Fig. 1.

Fig. 2.

The selective device patented in 1898. Figure 1 shows the lever pushed forward to fire right left and figure 2 shows the lever pushed backwards to fire left right.

This improvement never found favour – it was very complicated and expensive to make; it would require frequent maintenance to ensure that the ball bearings ran smoothly. It was far simpler to construct the spring from gold to combat corrosion and it is this method that has been in use from the beginning of this century to the present.

The final real improvement to the single trigger mechanism was contained within patent no. 11278 of 30th May 1905. If a lock sear was not properly engaged for some reason, the slightest pull on the trigger could discharge the gun. On account of the fact that the revolving turret required the full lift of the trigger, its mechanism could be upset and the other barrel could fire prematurely. To overcome this, Robertson fitted a safety device to the trigger blade. This locked the turret until the full lift of the trigger blade had taken place. This patent number is engraved on a great many Boss single triggers. Interestingly, the engraving of single trigger patent numbers on the trigger plate can be haphazard. Even with the improvement of the 1905 patent, the patent number 22894 of 1894 will be found to be engraved. Engravers copied the number of the

most readily available trigger plate – hence the reason that the number often does not relate to the mechanism inside!

THE BOSS EJECTOR 1897

The capacity for John Robertson to work intellectually, administratively and physically, seemed to know no bounds. Intellectually, he had a stream of patents to his name and was regarded as one of the most erudite gunmakers at the turn of the century. Administratively, he had turned the fortunes of Boss around from having a comparatively small turnover in 1890, to over six times that by 1900. Physically, success had not changed his habits much. He was to be found most of the day at his bench, in his shirt-sleeves engaged in gunmaking, wearing as all the gunmakers did in this period, a white apron. He was unusual in that he harked back to an earlier era as a working master gunmaker, running his own business. Such had been the expansion in gunmaking by the turn of the century that most of the owners of the big gunmaking establishments were simply administrators now. They could not build guns and had not the consummate skill and knowledge of guns that only a practical gunmaker could. John Robertson employed Mr A. F. Embelton, an old

John Robertson at his bench circa 1905 in 73 St James's Street, wearing the white apron contemporary to most gunmakers during this period. Note the electric switch to his left – an early use of electricity.

employee of Boss under Edward Paddison, to administer the day-to-day affairs of the business for him.
Most of the contemporary commentators praised
Robertson for his style and bemoaned the demise of the
working gunmaker and the rise of the administrator.
That Robertson realised the importance of this is
apparent in that he made his three sons, John, Sam and
Bob, go through thorough gunmaking apprenticeships
before branching out into their own particular fortés.

Soon after the 1894 single trigger, John Robertson
co-operated with William Adams again to bring out
provisional patent no. 18135 on 28th September 1895.
This patent, an improved safety mechanism for locking
the sears of the locks, bore both their names on the
actual patent specification.

On 4th February 1897, Adams and Robertson co-
operated again to bring out patent no. 2988. This is the
second in the trio of major Boss innovations, The Boss
Ejector. In the early breech-loaders, when the gun was
opened, the fired cartridges were extracted a small
distance, whereupon the shooter then had to remove
them from the breech by hand. In an ejector, the fired
cartridge is automatically ejected when the gun is
opened, making for more rapid loading. Ejectors had
been on the scene since the 1870s. John Robertson (in
co-operation with Henry Holland) had played a part in

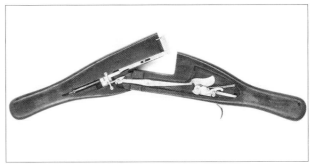

Wooden Boss ejector model. See Plate 39.

their development, bring out three patents concerning
ejector mechanisms in the late 1880s.

The great virtue of the Boss ejector of 1897 is its
simplicity, its ability to withdraw unfired cartridges considerably further than in any other guns and its help in
the work of opening the gun (only when the gun has
not been fired).

Due to the small number of parts used in this system,
the ejector is easy to regulate and is very reliable in
addition to the advantages given above. As was very
popular at the turn of the century in an era of manda-
tory classical education, Robertson gave a pseudo Latin
name to this ejector, "the Desideratum Ejector",
desideratum meaning "something desired or much
wanted". Such titles were much in vogue at this time
eg, Woodward's "Automaton" hammerless gun, W. W.
Greener's "Facile Princeps" opening action. The term
"Desideratum" had been used before in Cogswell and
Harrison's hammerless gun of 1882.

The Boss single trigger and Boss ejector contrived
to give a major fillip to the Boss business. By 1900 the
turnover and volume of gun production was so great
that the factory at 4 Dansey Yard had become over-
crowded. Larger new premises were sought and, in
1899, Robertson rented 1 and 2 Ham Yard, off Great
Windmill Street, Soho, London. Here the Boss factory
would remain until the outbreak of World War I. It is
remarkable how incestuous the gun trade was in
London at this time. At Dansey Yard, Southgate and
Mears, gunmakers and Frank Squires, barrel-maker
were there beside Robertson. Not only at 12 Ham Yard
did John Rigby the gunmaker have a factory, they also
ran their business at 72 St James's Street right next to
Boss at no. 73.

On 27th May 1901, the youngest in the trio of
Robertson gunmaking sons, Bob Robertson, his father's
assistant at 73 St James's Street, married in the Register
Office, West Ham, Mabel Knapman, a laundry proprietor's daughter from 315 Densingham Avenue,
Manor Park, London. Bob was twenty-six and Mabel
twenty-three. Bob and Mabel would eventually produce
two daughters, Maisie and Ruby. Sam alone out of the
three Robertson brothers produced three sons, one of

Another view of John Robertson *circa* **1905.**

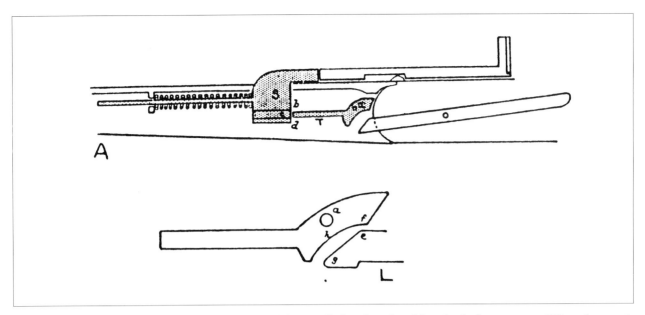

Contained within the forend is a slide (S) operated by a coiled spring that drives back the extractor. When the gun is opened unfired, the power of this spring pushing against the slide and the extractors assists in the opening of the gun due to the fact that the extractors are hard against the breech. Because the extractors are powered by the spring, the extractors are pushed out a considerable distance. As the motion of the spring is gradual, the extractor is not flicked backwards so as to produce ejection. This is the main virtue of the Boss ejector. Unfired cartridges are withdrawn this distance and they are easy to grasp and remove with a cold or gloved hand. In an ordinary ejector gun, most extractors are operated by a cam, not a spring as in the Boss action and are unable to push the extractors any real distance.

When the gun is fired, a cocking lever (L) rises and forces the tipper (T) downwards until its point comes opposite the point (d) on the slide. When the gun is opened, the cocking lever pushes the tipper up slightly until it comes opposite a hole (c) in the slide. The slide has now nothing to contain it, moves forward rapidly under power of the spring and rapid ejection takes place.

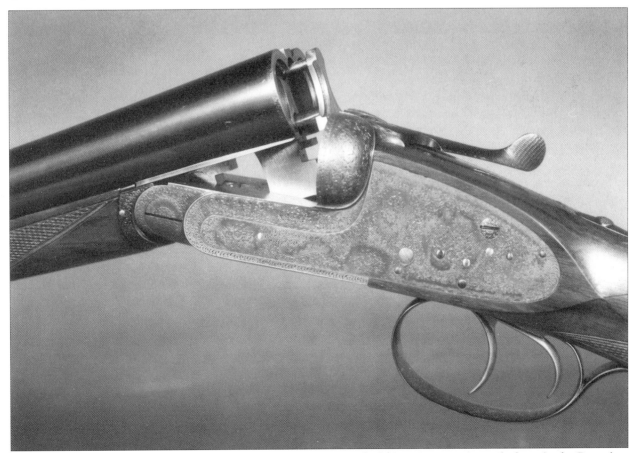

A gun broken open in the unfired position showing the extent to which the extractors are pushed out in the Boss ejector.

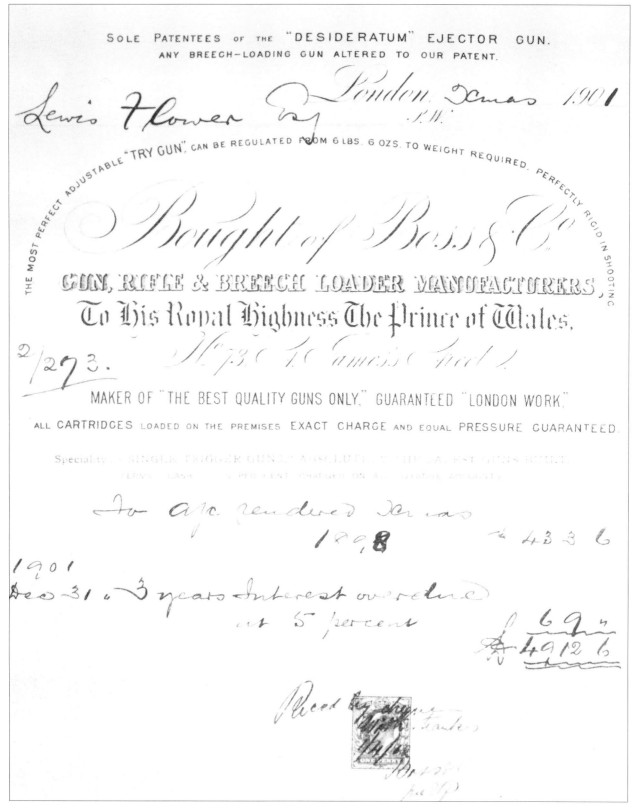

Boss bill dated 1901 with the heading "Desideratum" ejector gun. This bill shows that Robertson suffered from the same problem as Thomas Boss and Paddison had before, unpaid bills.

whom Alec was to carry on the gunmaking business at Boss. By this time John Robertson senior had moved house to 25 Uplands Road, Hornsey in North London.

On 31st May 1905, Robertson brought out two more patents, provisional patent no. 11400 and pro-

visional patent no. 11400B. The first of these patents altered trigger pulls. When the trigger is pulled, it is not pulled directly backwards, but backwards and sidewards at the same time due to the angle of the shooter's finger. Robertson foresaw that this sideways movement

instruction, Boss sent their customers to Mr Watts of the London Shooting School. By this time, many of the leading London gunmakers had their own shooting grounds and it seemed desirable that Boss should follow suit.

In the spring of 1903, Boss & Co. opened up their shooting school, the Regent Shooting Ground. This early shooting ground was off the Finchley Road and relatively close to the centre of London. Customers took the tube to Finchley Road station and then had to drive or walk about two miles to the shooting ground that lay well back from the highway on agricultural land. Suburban sprawl had not yet reached this area. To make the ground as realistic as possible, ponds were created and cover planted. Clay bird traps were set up which attempted to simulate as realistically as possible actual field conditions.

By late 1907, house building requirements evicted Boss from their Finchley Road site. The Hampstead Garden City Company intended to build in the area, and Boss had to go further afield for a new site to Hendon. In early 1908, a new shooting ground covering some fifteen acres was opened up at Shire Hall Lane, Hendon. Lest customers be unable to find it, "Opposite the Royal Oak, Finchley Road" was always printed on any correspondence. Here the shooting ground would remain until once again housing demand meant that it was compulsorily purchased in 1929.

John Robertson and his three sons *circa* **1900. Standing left to right, Bob and Sam. Sitting left to right, John (Jnr) and John (Snr).**

might cause a trigger to bind. He altered the angle of the trigger blades to ensure they were pulled directly backwards to obviate any malfunction. The second of these patents improved upon the safety mechanism of previous patent no. 18135 of 28th September 1895. This locked the lock sear of the unfired barrel making it impossible to fire.

THE REGENT SHOOTING GROUND
In the past there seemed to be no real need for shooting schools. People brought up in the country were familiar with guns from an early age. By the late 19th century with increasing urbanisation, increased interest in shooting and the fact that many people enjoyed country pursuits only in times of leisure meant that a demand for instruction in shooting arose. The introduction of clay pigeons in the 1880s made effective instruction possible.

Many shooting schools sprang up to cater for this demand in and around London. At first Boss had no shooting ground of their own. In the old muzzle-loading period their guns could be tried at the Red House, Battersea. "Tried" is apposite since it was hardly a school in the accepted sense of the word. In the 1880s and 1890s, to cater for the demand for proper supervised

John Robertson's house at 25 Uplands Road, Hornsey, North London *circa* **1900. On account of the fact that this house was on the corner of Uplands Road and Ridge Road, the address of it is sometimes given as 81 Ridge Road.**

An early clay pigeon trap *circa* **1900 of the type used at the Regent Shooting Ground.**

The Hendon ground was an attractive area pre World War I. Agricultural landscape with the river Brent meandering through it and an extensive view of Harrow formed the backdrop due to the fact that the shooting ground stood on high ground. This ground was far more modern than the old Finchley Road ground. A lofty tower was installed which fired clay pigeons at great height, traps were carefully concealed against brush wood from which clay partridges un-expectedly sprung and driven clay grouse came right at one and over one. Static metal targets were set up for testing shot patterns and for rifle practice.

Bob Robertson's particular specialisation now became the fitting of guns and instruction in shooting with them at this shooting school. For the rest of his life, until his death in 1951, Bob would remain at the shooting schools building up no mean reputation as a first-class shot and coach. Early practice targets were glass balls filled with feathers, but by the time the Regent School was established, the "inanimate bird" (clay pigeon) as it was then termed, fired by a spring trap, had been perfected.

In the 1890s, try guns for use at shooting schools were developed by many makers. This was a gun that could be adjusted to fit the varying measurements of shooters. Once the shooter was satisfied with the fit after adjusting the try gun, his measurements could be taken and his gun could be built to his own particular requirements.

As usual, great rivalry between gunmakers developed as to who had the best try gun. John Robertson con-sidered that the Boss "patent try gun" was the best. There were so many articulations in the Robertson try gun to cope with every individual measurement, that there was no room for a safety catch. Robertson claimed on account of the multitude of articulations that it was the "most perfect try gun ever produced". On 16th

March, 1895 he wrote to *The Field* with a suggestion that did not meet with their approval.

Boss & Co., 73 St James's Street
13th March.

With what has been written regarding the utility of the try gun as well as the advantages obtainable at the London Shooting School, we are in thorough agree-ment. There are however, try guns and try guns. We think we are not over estimating the advantages of our patent try gun when we state our conviction that it has never been equalled in efficiency by that of any other gunmaker; and Mr Watts of the London Shooting School (who has seen other try guns in existence) is so satisfied on this point that we are building one for use at the school with additional improvements . . . we would respectfully suggest your aid in enabling the sporting world to decide as to the most useful and com-plete try guns. A trial by some recognised and undoubted authority in shooting circles would be an interesting as well as instructive experiment.

John Robertson's single trigger trial by *The Field* was very favourably reported on, and he knew his try gun would receive a similar report, hence his goading of *The Field*. *The Field* would not take him up saying that "the

Bob Robertson, the shooting instructor, with a loader at the Regent Shooting Ground, Shire Hall Lane, Hendon, 1925.

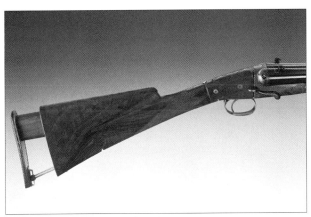

Side lever try gun. See Plate 40.

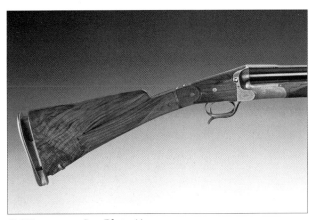

O/U try gun. See Plate 41.

try gun is a technical instrument used by practical gun-makers for the purpose of carrying out their work with good effect…".

The Robertson try gun speaks for itself. Boss's records detail many try guns being built for leading makers to engrave and call their own.

In their booklet produced *circa* 1920 describing their guns and business, the Boss try gun was specifically mentioned.

One of the most important adjuncts to gun fitting is of course a try gun – that is a gun that can be altered instantly in length of stock, bend, cast off and cast on to suit the physical and optical variations in the persons to be fitted and at the same time is a practical and useable weapon. There are numerous types of try guns, but few which really handle like an

ordinary gun and the consequence is that the shooter is often ill at ease when using them. This fact was kept rigidly before us when constructing the guns which are in use at our grounds, the result being that we have try guns which possess features not found in any others including single and double trigger, 12-bore and 20-bore and the only O/U try gun made.

All try guns are of the same weight as our game guns; the cast off or cast on is effected at the juntion of the rib with the action and not as is commonly the case in the centre of the hand or below the action strap.

The bend is alterable at this point; thus the perfect outline or symmetry of the gun is preserved, and the balance is kept perfect – indeed only upon the closest examination does it appear to differ from an ordinary weapon.

CHAPTER NINE

CHATTELS AND CHOCOLATES

Thomas Boss had moved into 73 St James's Street in March 1839. By 1908, 73 St James's Street had been home to Boss for some seventy years, a very long period for a gunmaking business to remain at a single address. The premises were leasehold not freehold and by 1908 the chattels were due to come up for renewal. The landlord decided not to renew the lease to Boss & Co. He could make a far better profit if he tore down the old Georgian building, replace it with what he regarded as something more opulent and modern and thereby demand a greater return on the lease.

Boss & Co. had to find new premises, new premises that would continue to befit their reputation and remain close to the environs of their clientele. John Robertson searched around and eventually found that the lease on 13 Dover Street, very close to St James's Street, was on offer. Thirteen Dover Street was literally across the road from St James's Street, the road in question being Piccadilly.

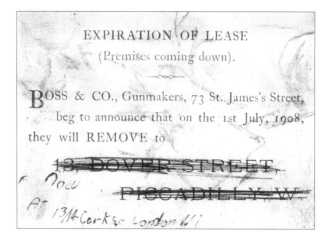

Dover Street was a far smaller street than St James's Street. Unlike St James's Street, it had never really been home to many gunmakers. The notable exception to this was John Manton and his successors who were in business at 6 Dover Street from 1781 to 1878. The building that Boss & Co. transferred to on 1st July 1908,

at a rent of £75 per quarter, was very different to the previous building. Seventy-three St James's Street, was a large establishment on four floors with a basement that was totally involved from top to bottom in gun manufacture. All the Boss guns of Thomas Boss and the Paddison era to 1891 were produced there.

In contrast, Boss at 13 Dover Street had the ground floor and basement only. Although there were gunmakers on the premises, guns were not actually manufactured in the new building, they were manufactured at the factory in Ham Yard. There simply was not enough room in Dover Street. The building was entered by a side door on the left which entered into a room from where the bulk of the firm's business was conducted. In this room at the front window overlooking the street, a couple of gunmakers' benches were set up, where parts like the single trigger were constructed and repairs done. Jack Sumner, the engraver, also worked in front of this window. Two or three small rooms led off where other gunmakers worked. Steep stairs led to a basement where there were storerooms and where there was a strong room to keep guns secure. Due to the compactness of the building, guns, cases, ledger books, gun cabinets, gunmakers were everywhere, a veritable hive of activity and fascinating clutter. Hundreds of thousands of cartridges were loaded every year by hand in the basement.

In one part of the basement directly below the pavement in Dover Street was a small room filled with sand at one end. This was where guns were tested if there was not time to take them to the shooting ground.

Here Boss & Co. would remain for around twenty years, until 1930 when they moved to 41 Albemarle Street. In 1922 a young Fred Oliver joined Boss at 13 Dover Street as a cartridge loader. Today Fred is still with Boss as a director and company secretary. What is remarkable is that in 1982 when Boss were at 13/14 Cork Street and the lease was about to expire, Fred walked out of Green Park underground station and happened to notice a sign above 13 Dover Street "Lease

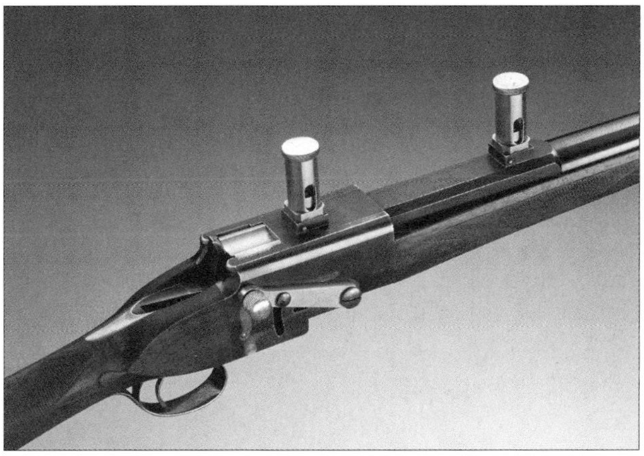

Pressure gun. See Plate 42.

for Sale". The company promptly took the lease and today are back in the old 13 Dover Street building that they vacated in 1930! Externally and internally, the building is much as they left it in the pre-war period – even the strong room is there. Even the basement room filled with sand is still used for testing. I wonder if the shoppers who perambulate Dover Street and who hear muffled explosions know that there is a shotgun going off directly beneath them!

As for the old 73 St James's Street building? It was demolished in 1908 and one year later, in 1909, a handsome sandstone building on six floors to a very French design was completed. What was now produced at no. 73? – Chocolates! It was home to Rumpelmayer's celebrated chocolaterie. Today a Japanese restaurant conducts its business from the premises. *Tempus adax rerum!*

THE OVER AND UNDER GUN 1909

On 10th February 1909, John Robertson filed provisional patents no. 3307 and no. 3308, his over-and-under gun and its particular ejector. This is the final in the trio of major Boss innovations. Robertson's over-and-under gun is regarded by many to be the finest of all British O/Us and represented for Robertson the culmination of an important career as a gunmaker.

Like his single-trigger invention, Robertson could not lay claim to be the inventor of the over-and-under gun. They had been in use for centuries, but what he could claim was building a radically new O/U gun that was strong, very light and graceful in contrast to exist-

13 Dover Street, home to Boss & Co. from 1908 to 1930 and 1982 to the present. This photograph was taken in the 1920s. Alex Robertson can just be made out at the window working at his bench constructing single triggers.

The new building at 73 St James's Street, *circa* **1910, home to Rumpelmayer's Chocolaterie.**

situated on top of the other as opposed to the usual side-by-side arrangement. Building breech-loading O/U guns was difficult due to this barrel arrangement and it was Robertson's simple but carefully thought out system that ensured the popularity and acclaim of the Boss O/U. Various advantages are claimed for the over-and-under.

1. By sighting along a single barrel it is easier and quicker to take aim.
2. Better balance. There is usually more metal in the action body of the gun and this means there is less inertia at either end making the gun easier to balance.
3. The forend wood is much deeper and this makes for a better grip.

The chief disadvantage of the O/U gun is its appearance. In comparison to a best side-by-side gun it can look ungainly and clumsy. This was the defect of the existing German O/Us. The chief merit of Robertson's gun was that he managed by careful design and construction to obviate any clumsiness and produce an elegant, slender gun.

Robertson was very much alive to the criticism of the German over-and-unders. He was determined that the Boss O/U would be build in accordance with the highest principles of best gun manufacture and not just be a fad of something different to keep in the forefront.

ing O/U guns. At the beginning of the 20th century, Germany dominated the manufacture of O/U guns. An over-and-under gun is a gun whereby one barrel is

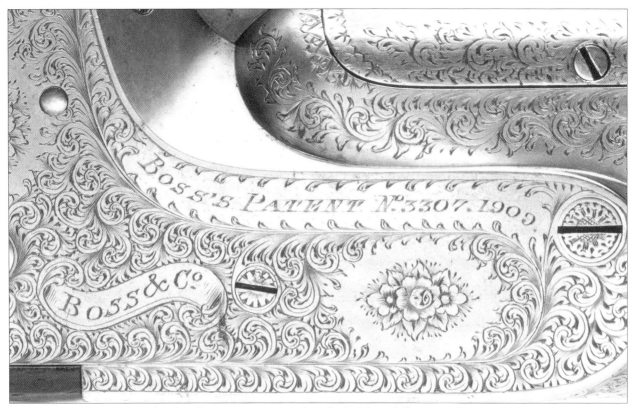

The O/U patent no. 3307 of 10th February 1909 engraved on both sides of all O/U actions.

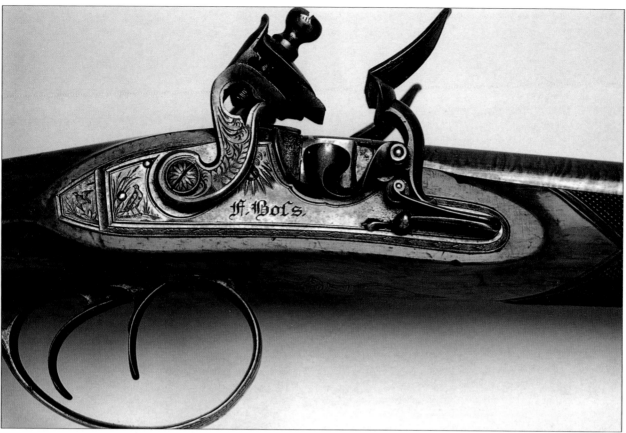

1. A double-barrel 20-bore Flintlock sporting gun by Fisher Boss *circa* 1810.

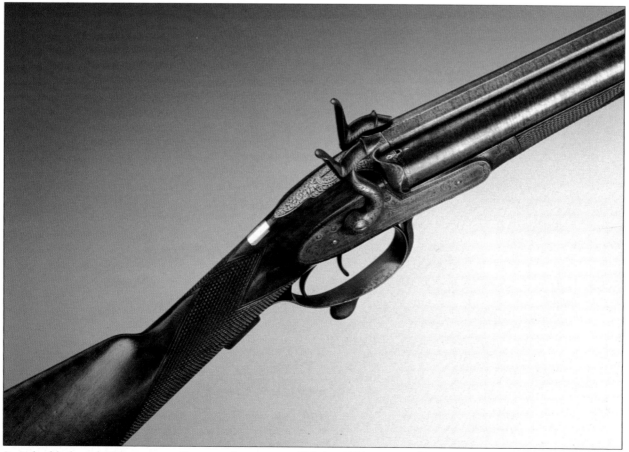

2. A double-barrel 19-bore percussion sporting gun no. 196 *circa* 1835, converted to pinfire *circa* 1860. This is the earliest Boss gun extant to date.

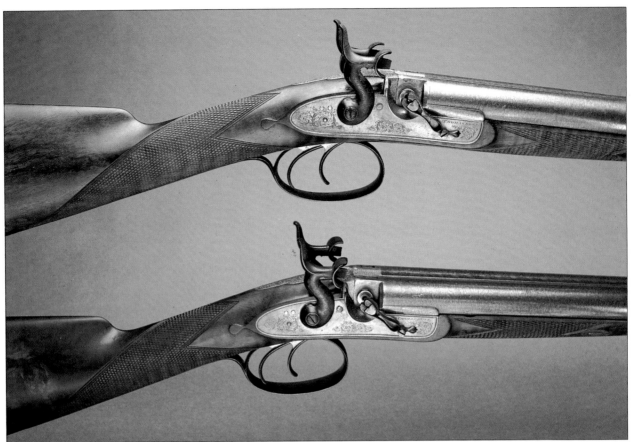

3. A pair of double-barrel 14-bore tube-lock guns nos. 682 and 683 built in 1846 for the Marquis of Blandford. By the mid 1840s tube-locks were out of fashion although some sportsmen preferred them for the certainty of ignition.

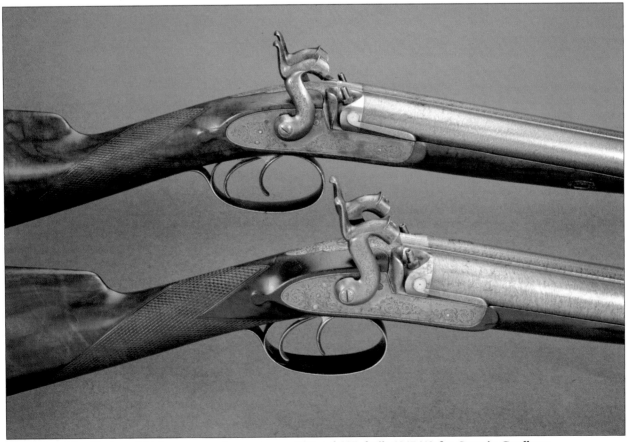

4. A pair of double-barrel 14-bore percussion guns nos. 763 and 827, built 1847/48 for Captain Goulburn.

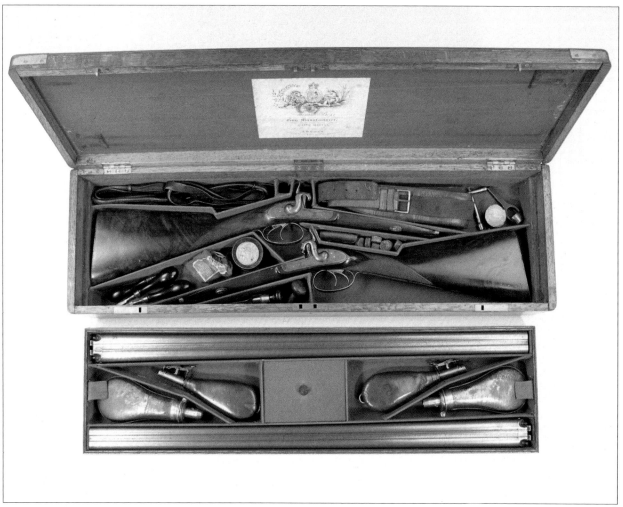

5. Nos. 763 and 827 in their original oak two-tier case with all accessories. The barrel tray shown lifted out.

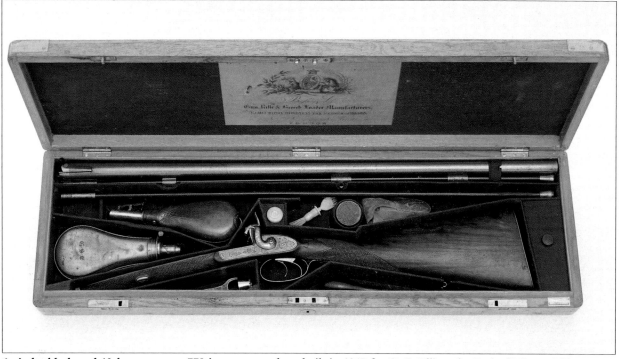

6. A double-barrel 13-bore gun no. 778 in case complete, built in 1847 for G. S. Elliot, the Earl of Minto. Of interest is the non original later 19th-century Boss label. This has been pasted over the original label probably when the gun went for repair or servicing to Boss in the late 19th century.

7. The double-barrel 13-bore gun no. 778 built in 1847. It is unusual in that it does not have Parkin barrels, the barrels being made by Christopher Aston, a barrel-maker little used by Thomas Boss.

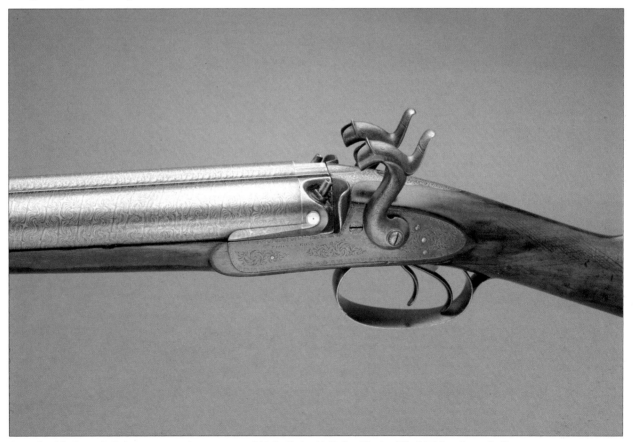

8. A double-barrel 12-bore percussion gun no. 813 built in 1847 for Sir Archibald Islay Campbell.

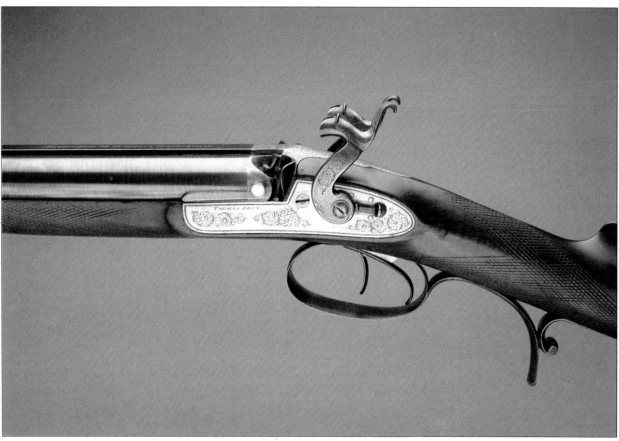

9. A double-barrel 16-bore percussion ten groove rifle no. 1037 built in 1853.

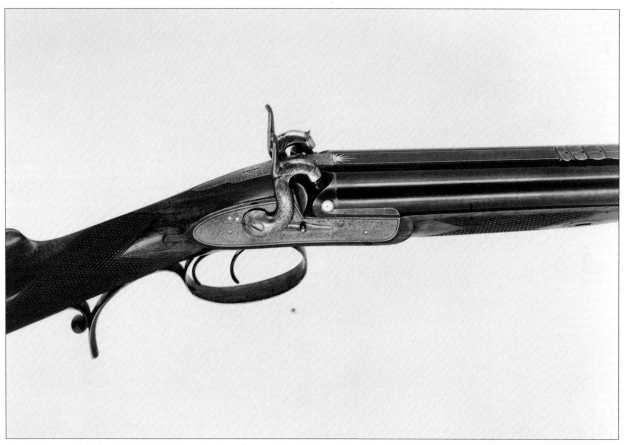

10. Rifle no. 1098 built in 1851. Note the Brazier-made platinum-lined leaf sight sighted to 250 yards, the grip tail guard and bolted locks.

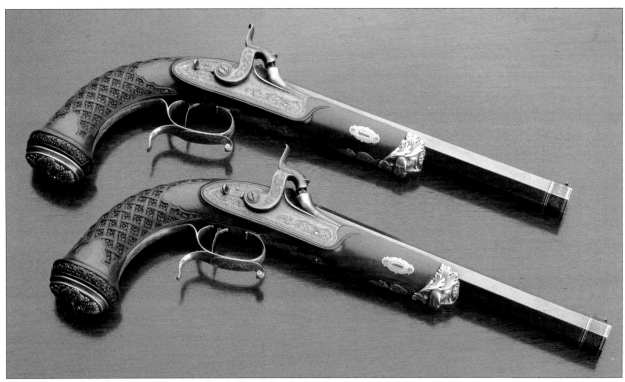

11. A pair of pistols of exceptional quality built probably for the Great Exhibition 1851.

12. The pistols showing the unusual checkering of lattice work infilled with roses.

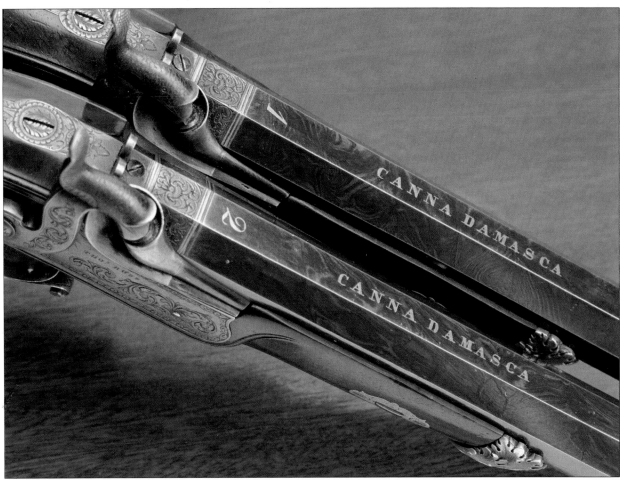

13. The extraordinary Damascus barrels inlaid with the lettering, "Canna Damasca" being in reference to the internal steel barrel tubes.

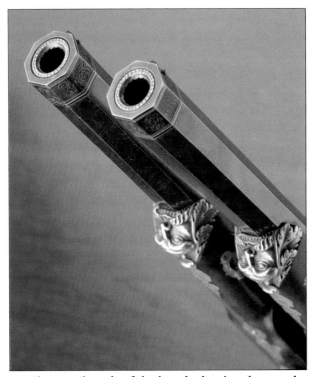

14. The muzzle ends of the barrels showing the muzzle-locking nuts to which are attached the internal steel barrel tubes. Note the sharp multi-groove rifling and grotesque man silver forend finials.

15. The superb quality silver mounts, the butt caps in the shape of a grotesque bearded man.

16. Double-barrel 12-bore percussion gun no. 813 built in 1847 with Thomas Boss's Letters Book of the same period.

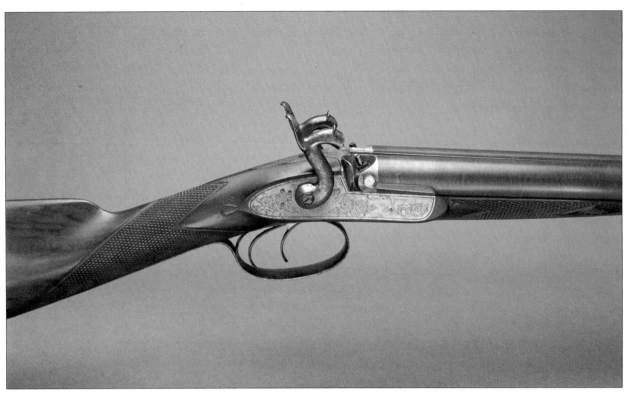

17. A double-barrel 12-bore percussion sporting gun no. 1198 built in 1852 for Hedworth Williamson.

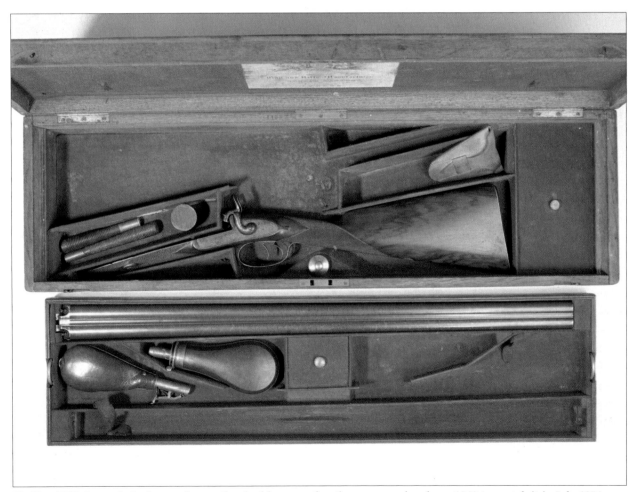

18. No. 1198 shown in its later oak two-tier double case, after the owner ordered no. 1342 to match it in July 1854.

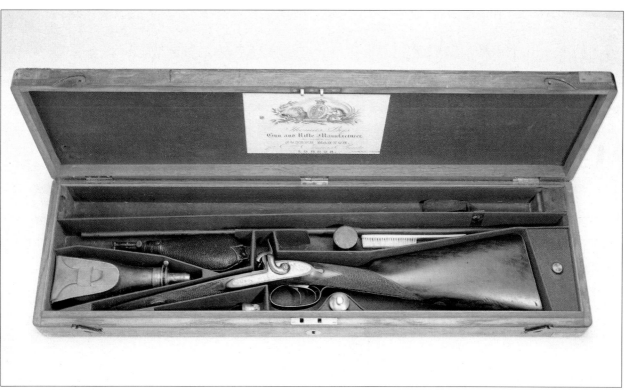

19. A double-barrel 14-bore percussion gun no. 1380 built in 1855 for Sir Massey Lopes. This gun is contained in its original oak case with most of its original accessories. The barrels are missing.

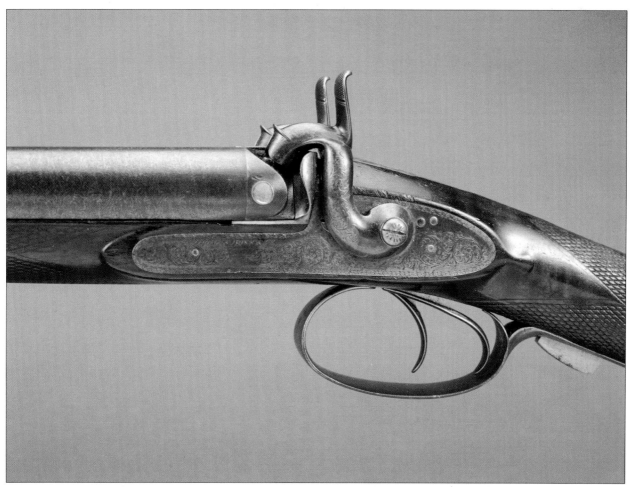

20. A double-barrel 13-bore percussion gun no. 1673, the No. 1 of a pair, built in 1859 for Captain Long. Note trigger guard safety.

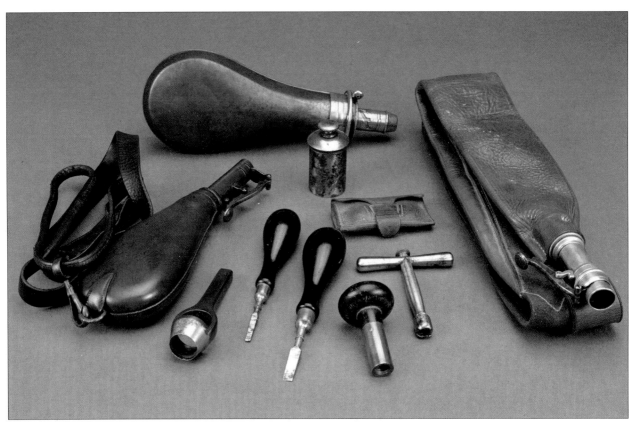

21. The original accessories as supplied to guns nos. 763 and 827, showing leather shot pouch, steel–bodied powder flask, wad punch, turnscrews, oil bottle, pigskin leather pouch, loading rod end, nipple key and leather shot belt.

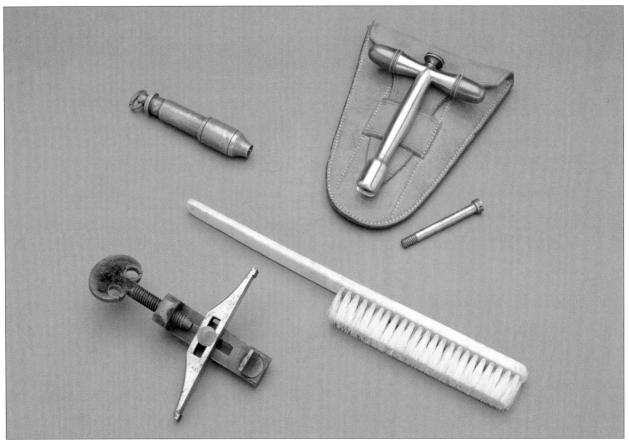

22. Other accessories as found in Thomas Boss percussion gun cases. Brass nipple primer and pricker. Nipple key with pricker in the centre and compartments for spare nipples on either side of the handles. The nipple key is contained in a pig skin leather pouch. Another part of this pouch houses a spare side nail. An ivory handled rib brush. A main spring clamp.

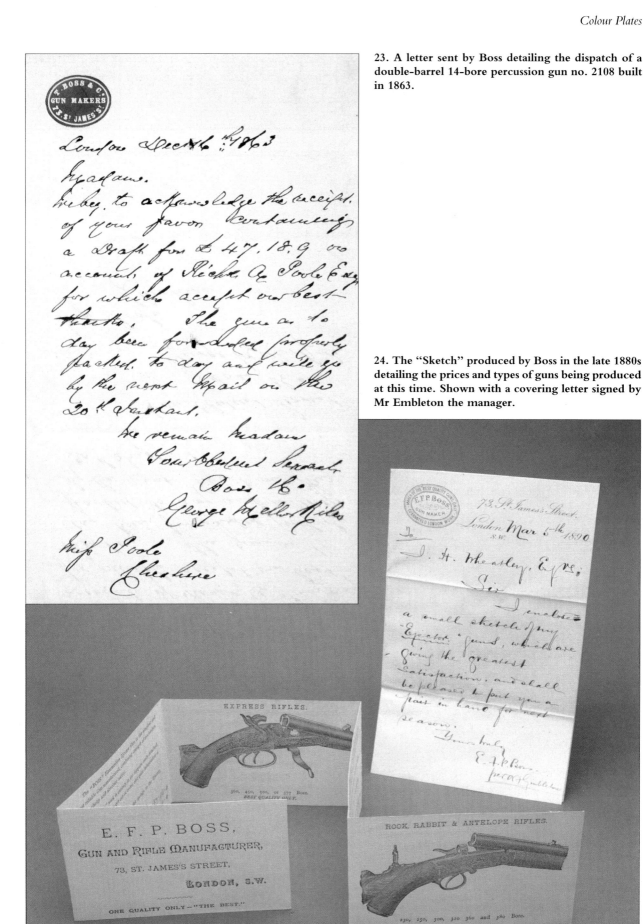

23. A letter sent by Boss detailing the dispatch of a double-barrel 14-bore percussion gun no. 2108 built in 1863.

24. The "Sketch" produced by Boss in the late 1880s detailing the prices and types of guns being produced at this time. Shown with a covering letter signed by Mr Embleton the manager.

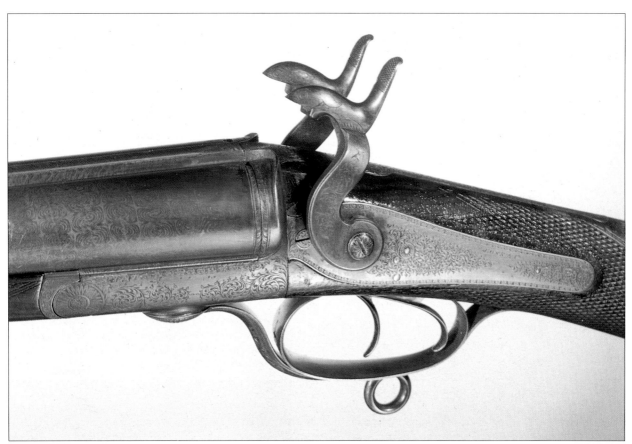

25. A double-barrel 12-bore pinfire gun no. 2135 ordered on 9th February, 1864 by M. A. Bass. This gun is the No. 1 gun of a matched consecutively numbered pair. Pairs of pinfires are very rare.

26. A double-barrel 12-bore under-lever hammer gun no. 2857 built in 1870 for R. E. Crompton. This gun displays an early use of rebounding locks.

OPPOSITE PAGE:

27. TOP: A single-barrel 16-bore back action under-lever hammer gun built for a boy *circa* 1870. There is no serial number on this gun.

28. CENTRE: A double-barrel 12-bore top lever hammer gun with rebounding locks no. 3403 built for R. Hutton Squire in 1877.

29. BOTTOM: A double-barrel 12-bore thumbhole hammer gun with rebounding locks no. 3455, the no. 1 gun of a pair, built for Captain V. Montagu R.N. in 1877.

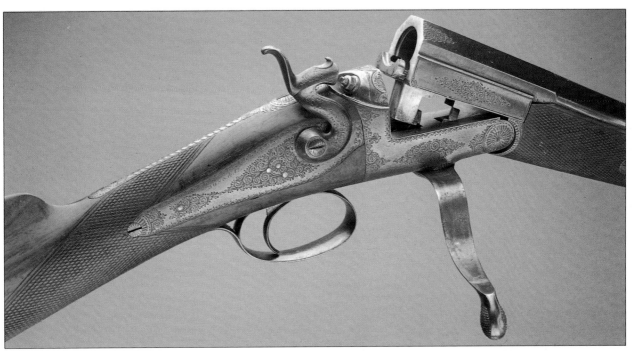

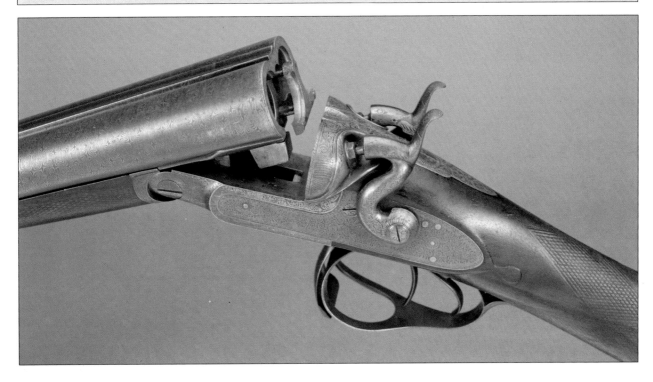

30. A double-barrel 12-bore side snap hammer gun no. 3597 built in 1880. More side snaps were built than any other type of snap action by Boss in the Paddison era.

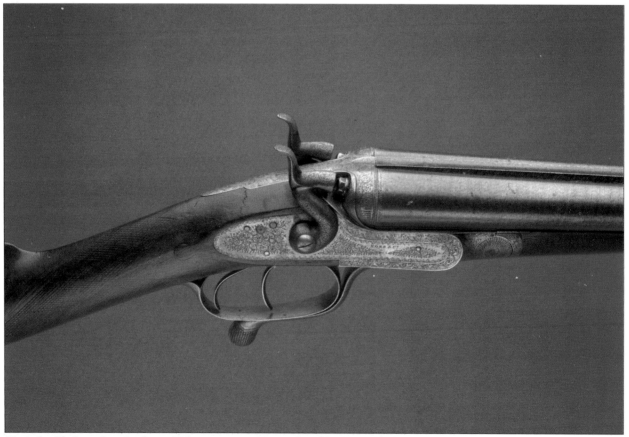

31. A double-barrel under-lever 12-bore gun no. 3814 ordered by A. C. Becher on, 14th January 1885. This gun with bar action rebounding locks and hammers out of sight when cocked, is a late use of the under-lever action.

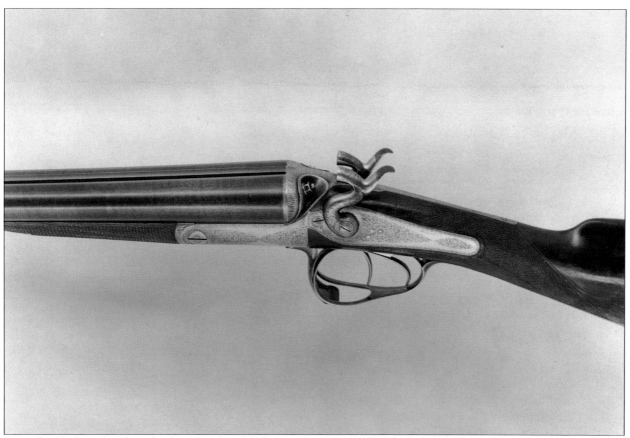

32. A double-barrel 12-bore back action thumbhole hammer gun no. 3860 built to match no. 3491. This gun was built in 1886 for W. B. Holt-Eardley and is of superb quality throughout.

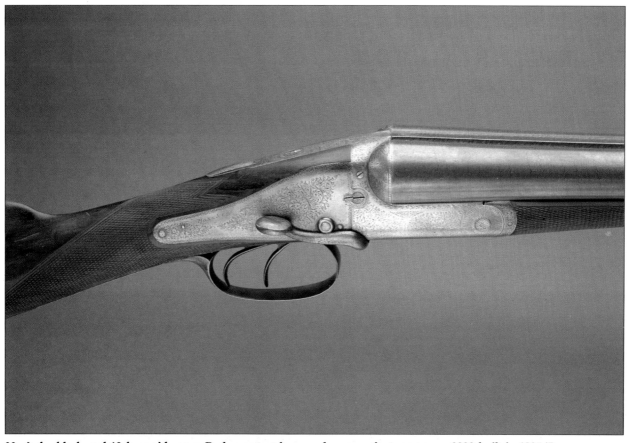

33. A double-barrel 12-bore side-snap Perkes patent hammerless non-ejector gun no. 3892 built in 1886/7.

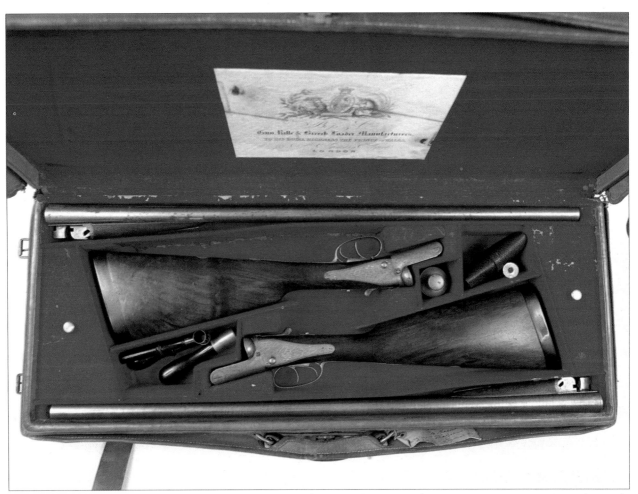

34. A pair of double-barrel 12-bore back action hammerless non-ejector "Perkes Patent" guns nos. 3991 and 3992 in original case with accessories. Built for General Digby Willoughby.

35. Accessories as found in breech-loading Boss guns in the 19th century. From left to right: brush, pull-through and oil bottle (all contained in the cleaning pouch behind), chamber brush, rolled turnover tool, decapping base (centre), three snap caps, wad rammer, powder and shot measure.

36. ABOVE: No. 4690, the second of two triple-barrel 16-bore single trigger hammerless ejector guns built in 1899–1901.

37. LEFT: A leather cartridge magazine retailed by Boss & Co *circa* 1890. This magazine was probably supplied by Robert Bryant, 24 Drury Lane, London.

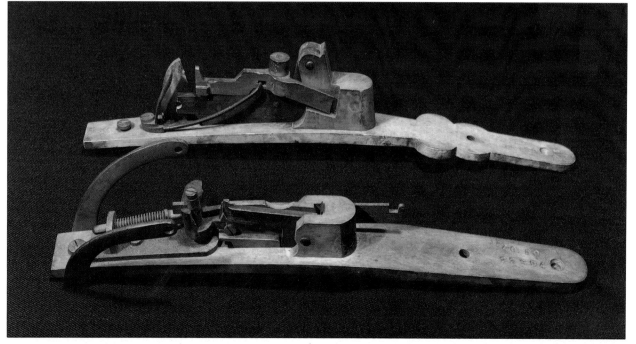

38. Two of the wooden models used in the High Court patent dispute 1906. The lower wooden model is built to Robertson's patent no. 22894 of 26th November 1894 and the upper wooden model is built to Nobb's patent no. 13130 of July 1894. Note the patent numbers stamped on the wood at the trigger plate finial.

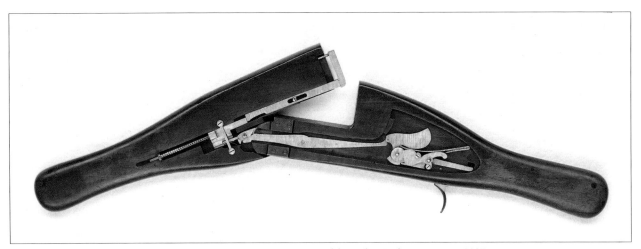

39. A working wooden model of the Boss ejector, constructed by John Robertson *circa* 1897.

40. A double-barrel 12-bore side lever Boss try gun *circa* 1895 showing the multitude of articulations possible.

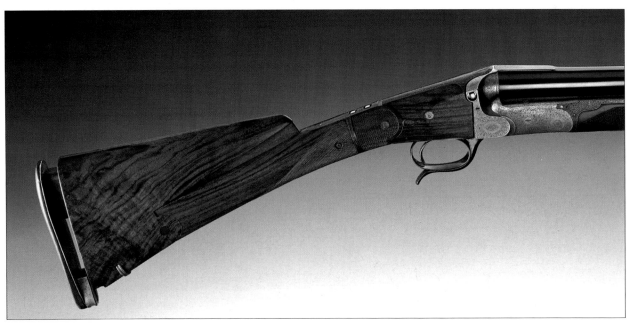

41. An O/U under-snap Boss try gun *circa* 1910.

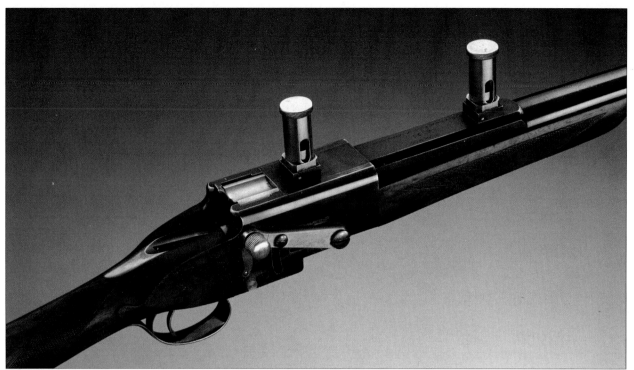

42. A single-barrel Boss 12-bore gun used for testing cartridge pressures. Hundreds of thousands of cartridges were hand loaded in the basement in Dover Street and this gun was used regularly in a cellar under the pavement to ensure consistency in hand loading. Pressures were tested against the powder manufacturer's calibration tables. Lead pellets were inserted in the two upright pistons situated 1″ and 6″ respectively from the breech. When fired, the pellets would be crushed, the depth of which would then be measured and the pressure read off against Boss's own tables. The greatest explosive pressure took place at the 6″ position.

43. A Boss O/U dating from the 1920s.

BOSS & COMPANY, LIMITED, 41, ALBEMARLE STREET, LONDON, W.1

ALL CARTRIDGES ILLUSTRATED BELOW ARE GUARANTEED ACCURATELY
HAND LOADED WITH ONLY THE BEST COMPONENTS

NEW WADDING.

We recommend the new Air Cushion Wads (12 bore only). These new wads ensure better penetration, less recoil, and more regular patterns, especially in barrels bored cylinder or slight choke.

Before Firing. After Firing.

Unless otherwise ordered, Air Cushion Wads will be loaded in all our 12 bore cartridges this season.

Air Cushion Wads make shooting more comfortable.

A

A $\frac{3}{4}''$ brass head, metal lined, gastight case, absolutely waterproof.

Per **20/-** 100

D

A $\frac{5}{8}''$ brass head, metal lined, gastight, water resisting case, specially loaded to give just that extra range without undue recoil, regularity of pattern guaranteed. Strongly recommended for high pheasants.

Per **19/-** 100

THE **SPECIAL** WATERPROOFED CARTRIDGE WITH LARGE CAP.
For 12 Bore Only.

B

$\frac{3}{4}''$ BRASS HEAD, METAL LINED.

Per **19/-** 100

E

A thoroughly reliable case with a $\frac{7}{16}''$ brass head.

Per **15/6** 100

C

A $\frac{5}{8}''$ brass head, metal lined, gastight, water resisting case.

Per **19/-** 100

F

A metal lined case, of excellent quality, with a $\frac{5}{8}''$ brass head.

Per **18/-** 100

All Powders used are specially blended and periodically tested at our own Shooting Grounds. Individual Loads a Speciality.

44. Boss's cartridge catalogue from the 1930s.

45. RIGHT: The shop front of Boss & Co. today, 13 Dover Street, London, its appearance virtually unaltered since the firm's first move there in 1908.

46. The back shop in 13 Dover Street today where stock polishing and general repairs are done.

47. Side-by-side barrels being brazed in the gas fired forge.

48. An O/U 20-bore action, machined and locks fitted.

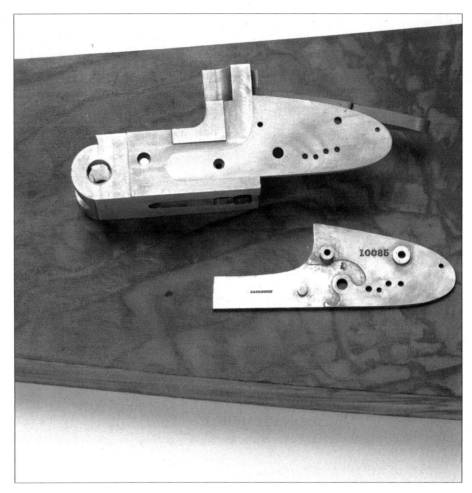

49. A pair of walnut stock blanks and a single best blank. The O/U gun is prior to the stock being "made off" and the action finished.

50. Stocking in the factory.

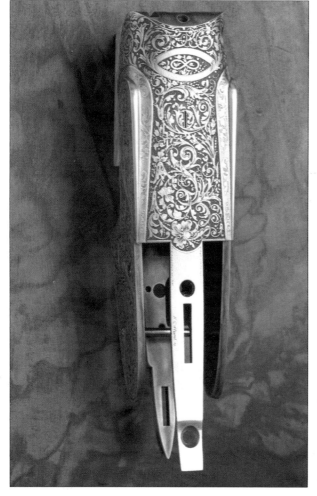

51. A 12–bore single-barrel trap gun engraved by Ken Hunt after hardening and finishing.

52. The old and the new. A Boss O/U dating from the 1920s and a brand new Boss O/U prior to finishing.

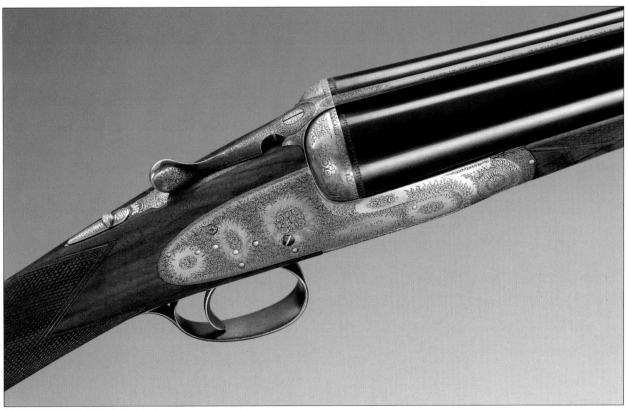

53. A round action Boss. This type of action was introduced by John Robertson in the 1890s as part of his intention to streamline his sporting guns.

54. The graceful lines of the Boss O/U.

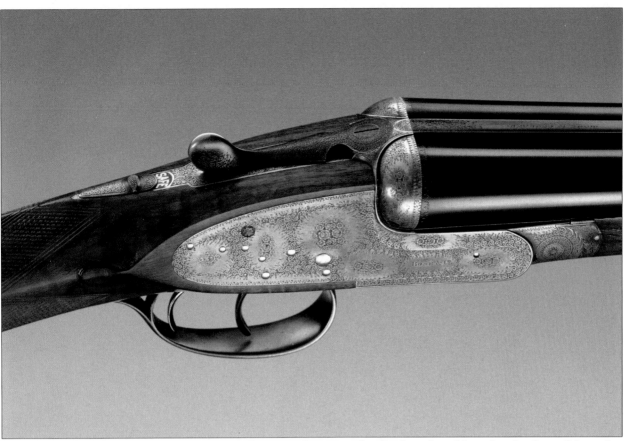

55. A 20-bore gun showing the Boss standard of construction. Note the slim barrels and breech, crisp lines of the action and elegant side locks.

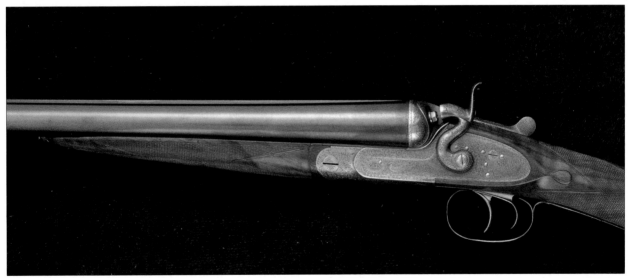

56. A double-barrel 12-bore top snap hammer pigeon gun no. 4495 built in 1897 with the banner style engraving of "Boss & Co".

57. A double-barrel 12-bore side lever hammer pigeon gun no. 4124 constructed in 1892, a very elegant late built hammer gun.

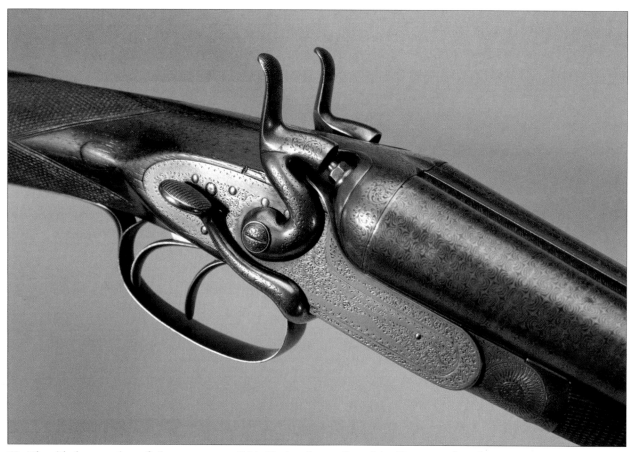

58. The side lever action of pigeon gun no. 4124. Notice the quality of the Damascus barrels.

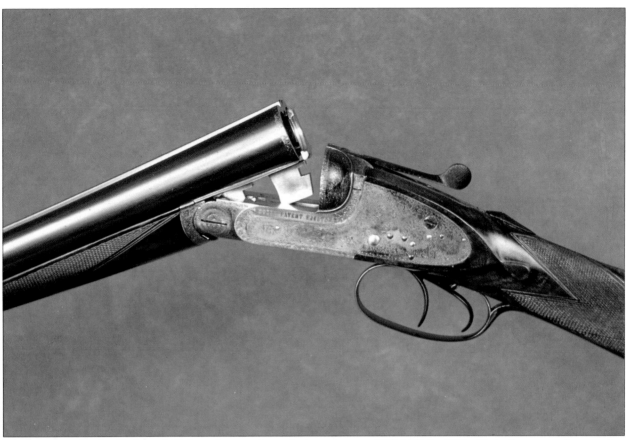

59. A very early double-barrel 12-bore hammerless ejector gun no. 4247 built in 1893. Note the unusual engraving proclaiming, "Boss' Patent Ejector".

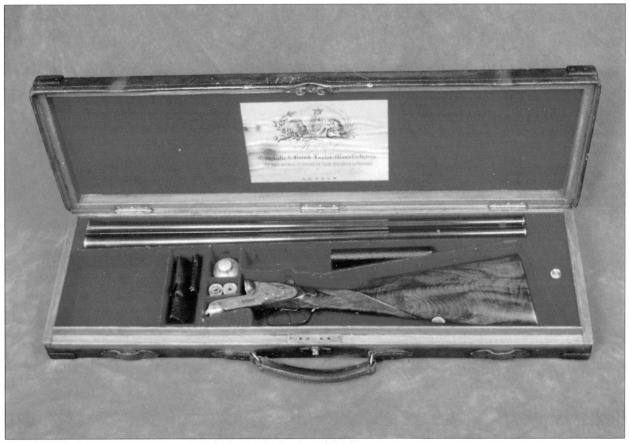

60. The early hammerless gun no. 4247 in its original oak and leather case.

61. A triple-barrel 16-bore single trigger hammerless ejector gun no. 4690 built 1899–1901. One of only two such guns built.

62. A .295/300 boxlock ejector rook and rabbit rifle no. 4817 in its original case built in 1900 for Viscount Castlereagh's wife. Boss produced very few such rifles.

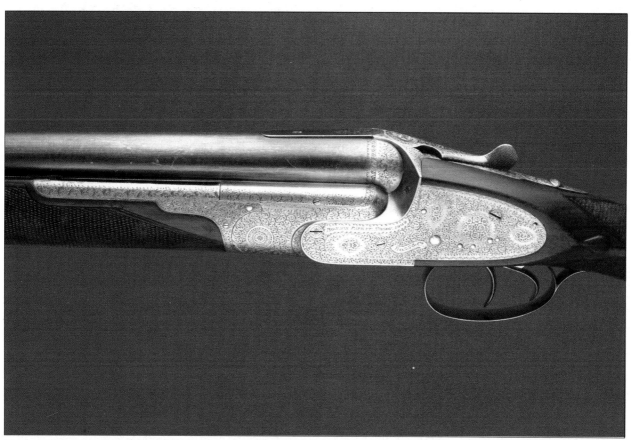

63. A double-barrel 12-bore O/U gun no. 6148, the No. 2 gun of a pair built in 1913.

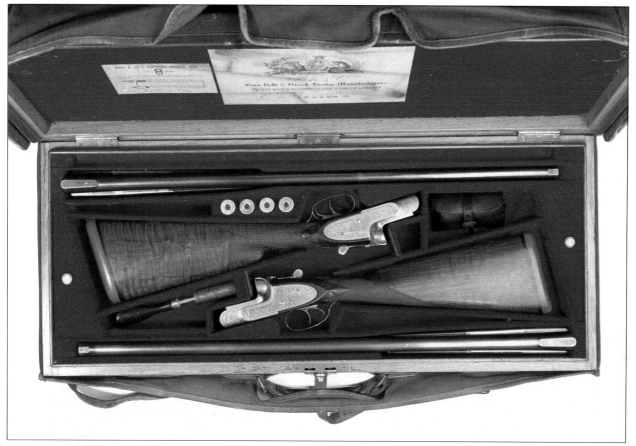

64. A pair of 12-bore O/U guns nos. 6147/8 built in 1913 in their original oak and leather case with mail canvas cover and accessories.

65. RIGHT: "The O/U design coupled with the slim rifle barrels must make this weapon one of the most elegant rifles every produced."

66. BELOW: O/U rifle no. 6179 built in 1913 showing the folding platinum-lined leaf sight and extended top strap.

67. BOTTOM: O/U rifle no. 6179.

68. BELOW RIGHT: O/U rifle no. 6179 in its original leather reinforced canvas case. Note the "incorrect" 73, St James's Street label.

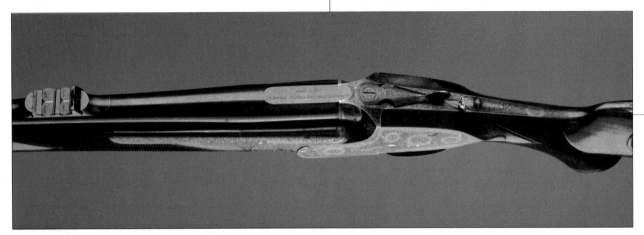

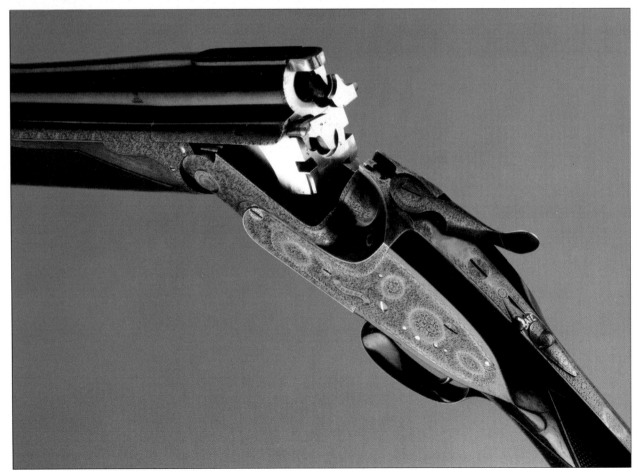

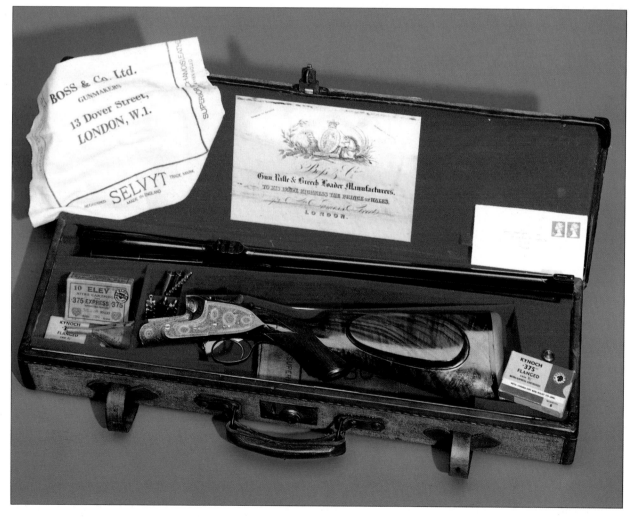

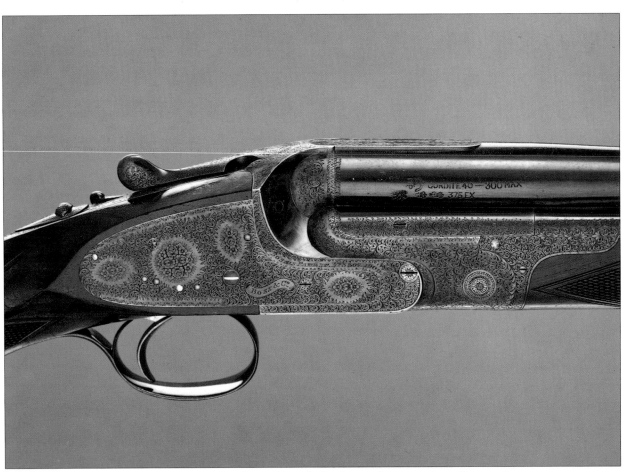

69. The action of O/U rifle no. 6179. Notice the quality of John Sumner's rose and scroll engraving.

70. A single trigger 12-bore O/U gun no. 6452 built in 1913/14. This gun was originally the no. 2 gun of a trio nos. 6451/2/3.

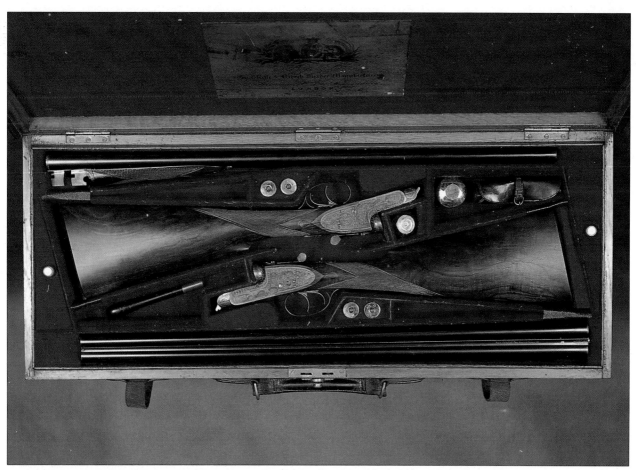

71. A pair of two trigger 12-bore hammerless ejector guns nos. 6597/8 in their original oak and leather case with accessories built in 1919.

72. A double-barrel 12-bore two trigger hammerless ejector gun no. 6597, the No. 1 gun of a pair built in 1919.

73. **A trio of single trigger O/U 12-bore hammerless ejector guns nos. 7261/2 and no. 7256, built in 1926/7. Note over-stamping of the label with the new address update.**

74. The trio of O/U guns nos. 7261/2 and no. 7256 contained within their original oak and leather treble case.

75. A very rare and unusual O/U combination 20-bore gun and .256 rifle no. 7755 built in 1929. Like the previous rifle no. 7667 there is little engraving present.

76. The action of O/U combination gun/rifle no. 7755. Notice the rounded O/U action.

77. A pair of single trigger round-bodied 12-bore self-opening guns nos. 8491/2 built in 1937. This pair was built with 25″ barrels and relatively recently extra barrels of more conventional length were supplied by Boss.

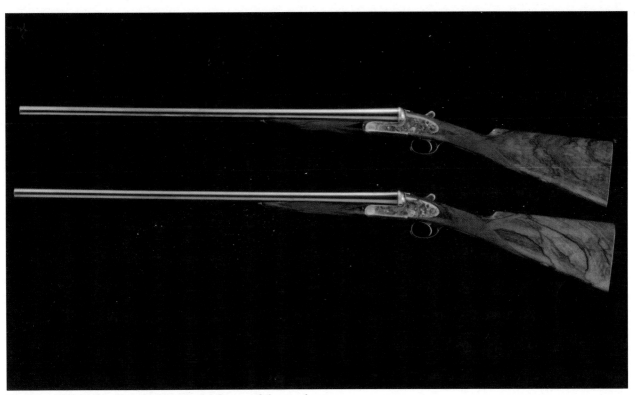

78. Nos. 8491/2 showing the wonderful figure of the stocks.

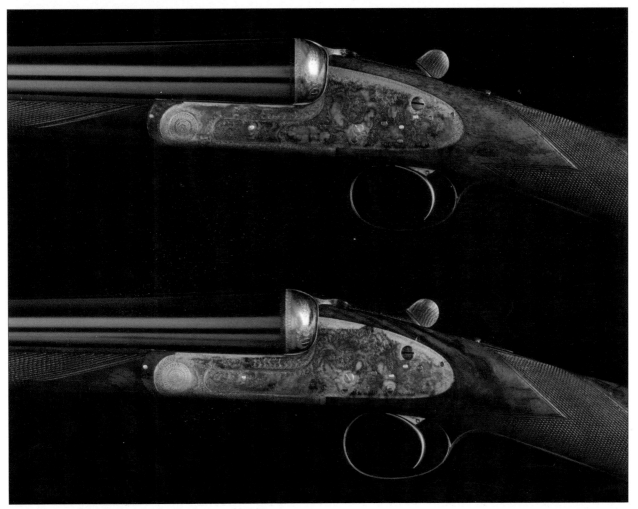

79. The round-bodied actions of pair nos. 8491/2.

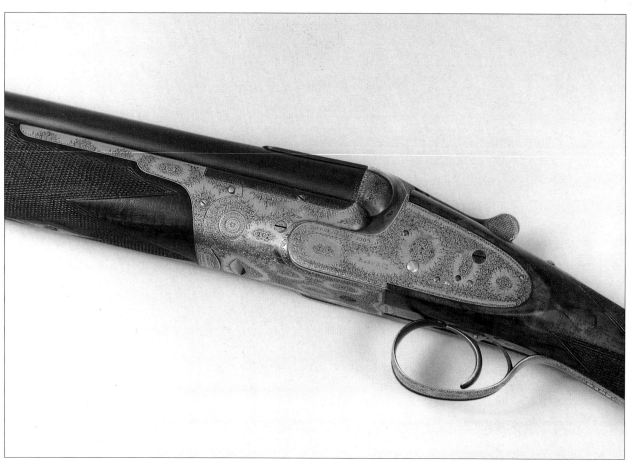

80. A single trigger 12-bore O/U gun, no. 8127 built in 1946/7.

81. A recently completed .410 over and under no. 10000. This gun has 3″ chambers and a ventilated top rib. A single trigger is fitted. Engraving by Ken Hunt. This is the no. 1 gun of the trio of .410s, nos. 10000/1/2.

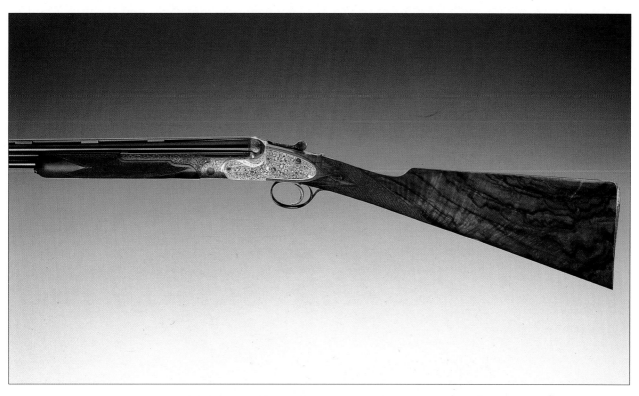

82. No. 10000, the .410 over-and-under.

83. No. 10000, the .410 over-and-under.

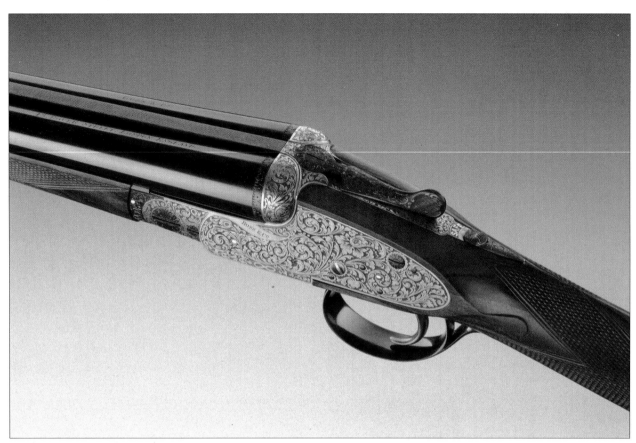

84. No. 10001, the second in the trio of .410s. The no. 2 gun is a square-bodied side-by-side with 3″ chambers and single trigger. Engraving by Ken Hunt.

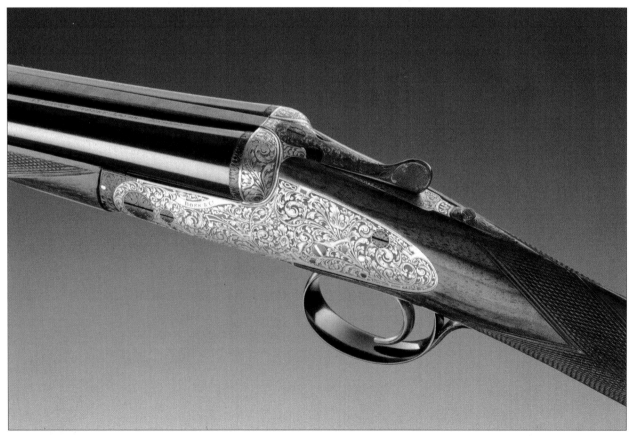

85. No. 10002, the third in the trio of .410s. The no. 3 gun is round-bodied side-by-side with 3″ chambers and single trigger. Engraving by Ken Hunt.

86. A recently completed double-barrel 12-bore sporting gun, round bodied with single trigger and specially ordered ornate carving, no. 10025 the No. 1 gun of a pair. These guns are engraved by Keith Thomas to the customer's specifications. "Boss & Co." is engraved in gold relief on the underside of the action.

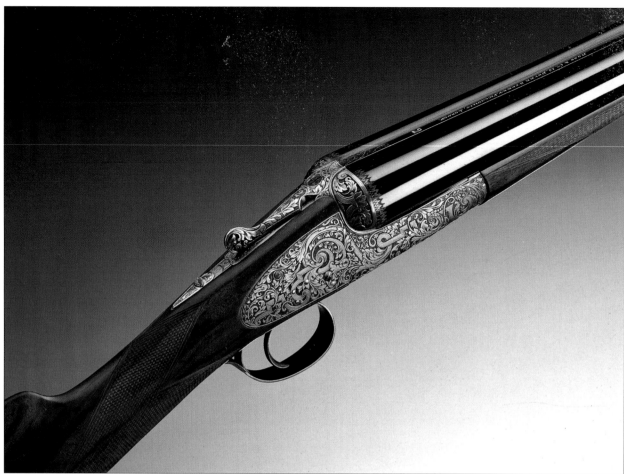

87. The No. 2 gun of the pair no. 10026.

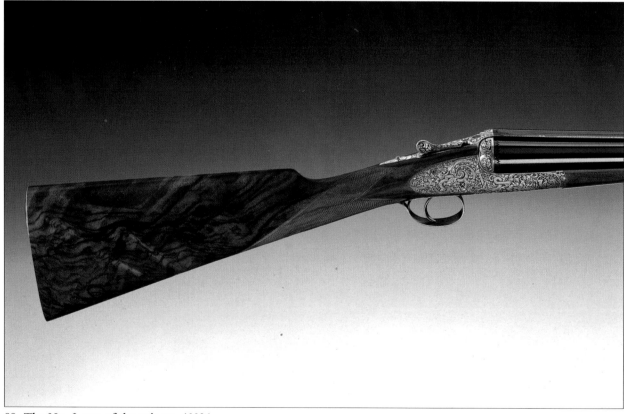

88. The No. 2 gun of the pair no. 10026.

89. A pair of recently completed double-barrel 12-bore single trigger O/U sporting guns.

90. A recently completed double-barrel 12-bore square bodied two trigger sporting gun.

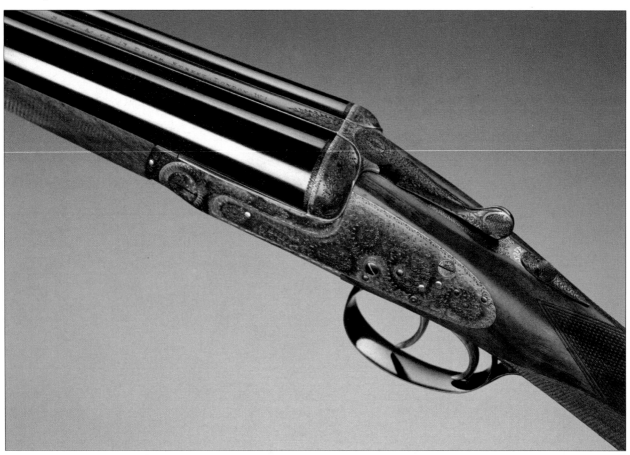

91. A recently completed double-barrel 20-bore rounded action two trigger sporting gun.

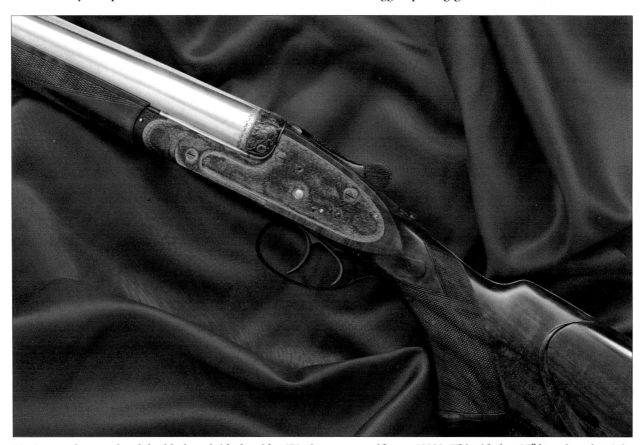

92. A recently completed double-barrel side-by-side .470 nitro express rifle, no 10090. This rifle has 25″ barrels and weighs 10 lbs 10 oz. This rifle has still to be regulated and the barrels blued.

The breech end of the barrels on a Boss O/U. Notice how the bottom barrel has become the lump at the breech end. This is one of the main virtues of Robertson and Henderson's O/U design. A gun with a very slim depth of action is the result.

The O/U reproduced best gun standard conditions of construction. In a typical Boss O/U, the 29″ barrels weigh 2 lbs 15⅛ ozs, the stock and action 3 lbs and the forend 7⅛ ozs. The barrels balance at 9″ from the breech and the stock and action at a trifle over 3½″ from the same measuring point. These figures prove that the weapon was designed in strict accordance with the recognised specification of a best gun of a light style.

In developing his gun, John Robertson was assisted by Bob Henderson, the factory manager at Boss. Bob Henderson, "The Scotsman", played a major part in designing the O/U, to the extent that he probably played the most important role in its design and development. His name does not appear on the patent itself, only "John Robertson". Bob Henderson, rankled at not achieving due credit and recognition for his role, left Boss after World War I and went to work for John Rigby. Boss found difficulty in making O/U guns after he left and it took a great deal of diplomacy to get him to return. Like his single trigger, and his ejector, Robertson's O/U is simple and well designed. On most other O/Us, the lumps are placed underneath the barrels, meaning that the action must be very deep. This increases the weight and makes the gun look ungainly. In the Boss gun, studs are fitted on either side of the lower barrel and the lower barrel in effect becomes the lump. These studs fit into corresponding slots in the breech. Due to the fact that the breech end of the lower barrel is the lump, the depth of the action is considerably reduced being but little greater than on an ordinary gun and it is this practice that gives the Boss O/U its handsome lines. Due to this slender action, the gun is light, weighing around 6½ lbs. Thanks to the barrel arrangement a special ejector had to be developed.

The ejectors were fitted on either side of the forend.

Apart from the virtues of the gun being light and attractive, its other virtue is that it is a very strong gun. The action is specially forged to ensure that the grain of the metal follows the shape of the action. The grain

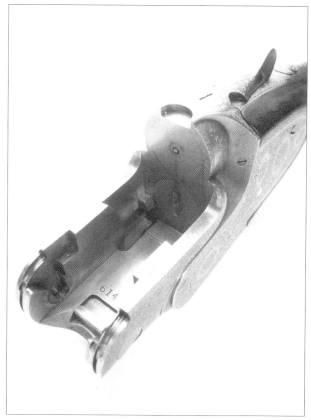

The action of the Boss O/U. One barrel locking bolt can be seen at the bottom end of the action face. The barrel bolt slots are cut into the bottom of the action, not the centre, where the greatest strain takes place. This makes the Boss O/U action very strong.

ABOVE: **A Boss O/U dating from the 1920's. See plate 43.**

runs along the action, then curves up the breech face, then curves again along the top strap. In addition, the barrel bolt slots are cut into the bottom of the action, not the middle as in most O/U's where the greatest

LEFT: **The O/U ejector patent no. 3308 of the 10th February 1909 engraved on the forend of all Boss O/Us.**

BELOW: **The instruction label pasted into the lids of O/U cases explaining how to cock the ejectors before assembling the gun.**

BOSS & CO.'S VERTICAL BARREL GUN.

OVER & UNDER

Should ejector hammers of fore-part get forward accidentally, they must be pushed back to position before putting on the barrels.

Fig. 1.

Fig. 2.

Fig. 1.—Ejector hammer forward.
Fig. 2.   do.   do.   in position.

ABOVE: **John Robertson in the year 1910 examining his recently introduced over-and-under gun of 1909.**

BELOW: **The first page of the explanatory booklet on the O/U gun** *circa* **1910.**

strain takes place.

In an article in *The Field* of 1913, they summed up very accurately the Boss O/U gun.

An extraordinarily graceful effect was produced by the mounting of one barrel over the other, with all the aids to appearance that high class workmanship and finish are capable of giving. Flowing lines and sweeping curves existed in complete harmony with the general scheme of construction. There was no suggestion of meaningless outline in any part of action, barrels or wood. This is a lot to say for a newly developed design that departs from the conventions of an earlier construction.

To popularise and advertise their O/U guns, Boss brought out an explanatory booklet *circa* 1910.

The booklet runs to some twenty-four pages on the history, the working and the favourable response to the gun. Various sections from this booklet are reproduced below.

…Mr Bob Robertson, an excellent shot and at the same time a practical gunmaker, discovered that a large number of sportsmen when taking aim with an ordinary double-barrelled gun at a bird – particularly a crossing bird – took a transverse view of the object from the left breech to the right barrel in the case of a bird crossing from right to left, and in consequence

Boss & Co.'s
O.U. GUN

BOSS & CO.
Builders of Best Guns only,
13, DOVER STREET,
PICCADILLY,   W.

Telegrams :   Telephone :
" Gunbarrels, London."   4711 Gerrard.

of this all too common habit invariably got behind the bird. …Persons trying the over-and-under gun for the first time are amazed at the rapidity with which they get on to their mark. …The effect is like pointing with one finger instead of three – the two barrels and the rib – and quicker shooting follows…

Sporting writers have wittingly or unwittingly with one accord paid tribute to the wonderful shooting of our forefathers, and particularly in these days when single-barrel guns were the vogue and Joe Manton was famous as a gunmaker. Some critics have attributed the fine shooting and heavy bags of days gone by to the length of stubble and the tameness of the birds, but our experience leads us to the conclusion that the use of a single barrel had very much to do with it . . . our object in introducing the over-and-under gun is to combine the advantages of single-barrel guns with the convenience of an ordinary double-barrel gun . . ..We offer a gun which is neater, handier and even more secure than the orthodox two-barrel gun. The depth of our action, the bulk and the weight of our Over-and-Under Special are the same as in an ordinary gun . . ..

A hundred thousand shots can be fired from our over-and-under gun without the least danger of the action being loosened . . ..We cordially invite your inspection of our new gun, many of which are in process of construction to the order of some of the most prominent shots of the day.

The importance of a perfect ejector mechanism in guns with superimposed barrels cannot in any way be over estimated . . ..There is we maintain no ejector mechanism upon the market so simple, so effective and so reliable as ours. We have long since abandoned the shibboleths adhered to by many gunmakers and our guiding principle in the ejector mechanism has been to maintain the direct drive . . ..

The O/U gun received great acclaim from the press:

The Field stated: "*A Vertical Double-Barrel Gun*"

A thorough shooting test confirmed the general good opinion which had previously been found concerning the handling properties of the weapon.

The Shooting Times stated: "*A Much Needed Improvement In Shotguns*"

Never since the introduction of the three-pull single trigger gun, which inspired so much emulation in the gun world, has any improvement in drop down sporting guns roused our interest so much as the

Fingers below Line of Sight.

Bob Robertson demonstrating the O/U gun *circa* **1935.**

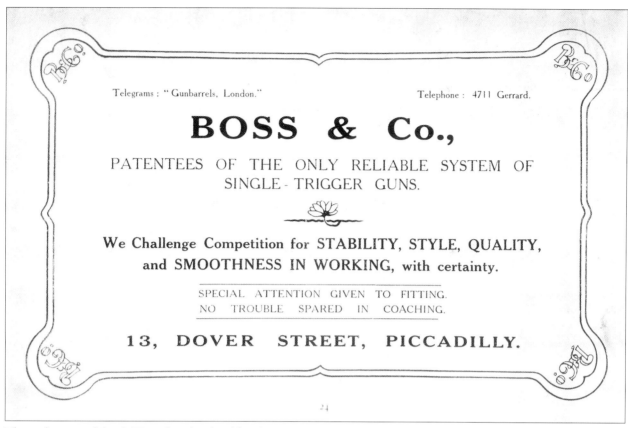

The end cover of the O/U explanation booklet circa 1910.

improvement just effected by Mr John Robertson of Messrs. Boss & Co., late St James's Street and now of Dover Street, W.

The Country Gentleman stated: "*A Striking Innovation In Modern Gunnery*"

We have seen the same design in German weapons, but so bulky and clumsy that there was no advantage shown in them to the user. The neatness of the action and barrels together is very marked, the workmanship being in the usual Boss superior style and finish.

Country Life stated: "*The New Double 12-Bore*"

What appealed to us most was the fact that this renewed attempt to develop the over-and-under principle avoids these drastic changes to which sportsmen, after years devoted to adapting themselves to a certain order of things, very naturally entertain objections.

BUILDERS OF BEST GUNS ONLY

As in the days of Thomas Boss, John Robertson would only employ first-class craftsmen. To these men, the "builders of best guns" must be due every credit for the work that they produced. Such men were not easy to

come by and when their merits were recognised they were valued and some remained in Boss's employment for many decades.

In the Edwardian era, Boss employed around forty men. Some nine men were in the shop in Dover Street, the rest were at the factory at 1 & 2 Ham Yard. The pre-war era was one of considerable industrial strife coupled with a growing awareness of the need for workers' protection in employment. The Liberal Government of this time worked hard to ameliorate working conditions in such areas as sweated industries, workers' contracts and trade union reform.

The type of gunmaker employed by Boss was never a victim of the sweated industry model that was prevalent by the late 19th century. Gunmakers were skilled craftsmen in short supply. This meant they could demand good wages and if conditions of employment were not to their liking, it would be easy to find another employer. In the first decade of the 20th century, the average weekly wage for a time served journeyman was around £2.15s.0d. This was a reasonable living wage ahead of many other skilled tradesmen at the time. Wages paid out by John Robertson to his employees amounted to a not inconsiderable amount each week. For example, on 20th April 1912, the weekly wage bill came to £102.8s.10d. The men were on piece work, that is to say a certain sum was decided upon for a particular piece of work. When the piece of work was finished, it was inspected by the foreman. There was no point in trying to rush a job and finish as many "pieces" as possible, for if the piece was rejected it would have to be done again in the workman's own time.

The journeyman tended to specialise in one particular aspect of gunmaking eg, barrel-making, actioning, stocking, finishing, single trigger, etc. For the rest of his working life he would continue to make one part of the gun. There were exceptions to this when, on occasion, there would be a craftsman of such skill that he could make more than one part of the gun. The advantage of such specialisation was speed. A man would become very proficient in his own field, this would result in higher wages for him and increased output for the firm.

Of the forty or so gunmakers, around eight were apprentices. Many of the apprentices were in fact the sons of some of the experienced journeyman at Boss. Apprentices usually began at the age of fourteen and their indenture was of seven years duration. In the early years they received around seven shillings per week and thereafter this gradually rose as the apprenticeship was completed. The first thing an apprentice did was to make his own tools, tools that in many cases would last him for the rest of his working life. Making his own tools would develop the type of skills needed and provide the specialised tools required that in many cases could not be bought off the shelf in an ironmongers. Apprentices under their gaffer would be taught his own particular specialisation. Good apprentices could greatly assist their gaffer in cutting down the amount of time necessary to complete a piece.

Boss & Co. still possess the wages books for the firm at the turn of the century. Separate wage books were used for the personnel in the shop in Dover Street and the gunmakers in the factory at Ham Yard. Taking 1910 as a sample year, these books give us the following information on who worked for Boss in this year:

EMPLOYEE AND WEEKLY WAGES

The Men Listed Below Worked in the Shop at 13 Dover Street

Robert Henderson £4.0s.0d

This was Bob Henderson a gunmaker of extraordinary skill. He was the factory manager. Bob Henderson, known as "The Scotsman" had been apprenticed to Daniel Fraser, the rifle maker in Edinburgh. He had gone to London and joined Boss in the 1890s. He had a terrific interest in gunmaking and gave great encouragement to any with a similar interest.

He fell out with the Robertsons after World War I over his failure to achieve recognition for the part he played in developing the O/U gun and left to work with Rigbys. Boss were keen to have him back. Similarly, Bob was keen to work for Boss again, but he refused to approach them. Obstinate pride on both sides was the stumbling block. Young Alec Robertson took the initiative and acted as peace negotiator. He suggested to his uncle Bob Robertson that they should go for a pint after work. Alec had said exactly the same thing to Bob Henderson! After their initial surprise at meeting, the ice was broken and Bob Henderson returned to Boss where he remained until the 1950s when he emigrated to Australia at a comparatively advanced age.

His love of Boss guns nearly cost him his life one day. He was out shooting with John Wilkes the gunmaker on some coastal flats. Bob had picked up a brand new O/U from the factory for the outing. As he walked over some marshland, he suddenly disappeared up to his waist in slimy mud. John Wilkes rushed to help him and pull him out, but Bob exclaimed, "Take the bloody gun first, take the bloody gun, it's going to get covered in mud." At home he still retained his air of authority. He had a chalk line drawn on the floor in front of his chair and woe betide his sons if they crossed it when he was sitting in that chair!

Bob was a rare breed, a gunmaker of extraordinary skill. He could turn his hand to virtually any aspect of gunmaking from barrel-making to stocking and it is to him that credit must go for playing a major part in developing the O/U gun with John Robertson in 1909, regarded by many as the finest sporting gun ever. His talents other than gunmaking ranged from taxidermy to playing the violin. He was a hard task master, something of a tartar even, and men trembled under his outrage if standards were not high enough. The many apprentices he trained were always known as "Bob Henderson's Boys".

In later life Bob went bald and as many men have done before him and many men will no doubt do in the future, he grew his hair long at the sides and combed it up to cover his barren patch. When he bent over the bench his lengths of hair would stand out and he was known as "the devil"! Bob had some sort of problem with his feet for a while. At break time he used to bathe them in methylated spirits. This treatment and the fact that Bob was a chain smoker did not auger well. The inevitable happened, a minor conflagration occurred in the nether extremities of his body and Bob ran screaming to dunk his feet in a trough of cold water. The gunmakers fell about the place – "you see, we told you – you are a bloody devil!"

H. Paice £2.0s.0d

Bob Robertson £4.0s.0d

Bob was now in charge of the Regent's Shooting School at Hendon.

A. F. Clement £3.0s.0d

Clement was the shop manager at 13 Dover Street.

A. Temple £1.15s.0d

S. Clinton £1.12s.0d

F. Peart £0.11s.6d

E. Peart £0.9s.0d

A. F. Embleton £4.0s.0d

Embleton had been with Boss in the days of Edward Paddison. He was the manager of the firm.

The Men Listed Below Worked in the Factory at Ham Yard

C. Johnson £3.5s.0d

Johnson was a senior man at the factory and had been with John Robertson in his early days working for the trade at Dansey Yard. He was nicknamed "Tiger".

W. Pither £3.13s.0d

Pither was the foreman at Boss pre-1891. Robertson retained him as foreman.

J. Vyse £3.0s.0d

Vyse was a finisher, another old employee dating back to Robertson's trade business and was now a senior man at Ham Yard.

J. Ranger £2.12s.6d

Ranger was an employee of Boss pre-1891 retained by Robertson.

R. Adams £2.13s.0d

Adams was a finisher, an old employee of Robertson in his trade only days. His nickname was "Papa".

L. Adams £2.12s.6d

H. Parry £2.12s.6d

Parry was an old employee of Boss pre-1891.

H. Reeves £2.10s.0d

Reeves was another workman who followed Robertson from his early trade business.

E. Westley £2.10s.0d

Westley worked for Boss pre-1891.

Cullum £2.10s.0d

C. Padgett £2.10s.0d

His nickname was "Ghandi". He worked for Boss as late as the 1940s.

Ernest Sanderson £2.14s.0d

Robertson's nephew, A. G. Sanderson joined the firm in May 1913 as a boy and was to play a large part in the running of Boss, eventually becoming a director in 1955.

W. Perkins £2.5s.0d

W. Johnson £2.5s.0d

Dewen £2.5s.0d

Adam Speaight £2.5s.0d

Adam Speaight joined Boss aged 13 in 1897. He worked for Boss all his life eventually retiring about 1965.

G. Limby £1.15s.0d

Urie £1.13s.0d

Guppy £1.0s.0d

Smith £1.0s.0d

Sherry £0.9s.0d

Shepherd £0.7s.6d

Alec Robertson £0.7s.0d

Alec Robertson was the third generation Robertson to work at Boss. His father was Sam Robertson, his grandfather John Robertson. Alec was born on 18th October 1894 at 15 Dalmeny Road, Islington, London. He began his apprenticeship in early 1910 and the above wage of £0.7s.0d per week reflects his position as an apprentice. His father Sam died in 1934 and Alex became a director of Boss' the following year.

John Robertson (Jnr) £4.0s.0d

Sam Robertson £4.0s.0d

John and Margaret Robertson *circa* **1910.**

William Johnson, a stocker with Boss, stocking a side by side in the factory in Lexington Street, *circa* 1920.

William Baker, a finisher with Boss, finishing an O/U gun in the factory in Lexington Street, *circa* 1920.

The three sons of John Robertson, John, Sam and Bob all received a standard wage of £4.0s.0d per week reflecting their interest in the business. This was the top wage paid out by John Robertson. When he died in 1917, the three brothers inherited the business, became equal partners and enjoyed the profits of the enterprise. But not in 1910 – they were gunmakers receiving a weekly wage. John Robertson ensured that his sons knew their place in life. He drank in the St James's Tavern and made it clear to his sons that since they were his employees, he did not wish to drink with them!

Every year in late August or early September the entire Boss workforce went off on an annual outing. In the Edwardian period they went to the Warwick Castle Hotel, Clacton-on-Sea. On Saturday, everyone assembled at Liverpool Street Station and caught the 10.20 am train to Clacton. Dinner was served at "2 o'clock prompt". A programme and menu for their 89th Annual Dinner on Saturday, 28th August 1909 survives to tell us about this social outing. On the menu was:

Boiled Salmon, Lobster Sauce
Cucumber

★ ★ ★

Roast Sirloin of Beef, Yorkshire
Roast Lamb and Mint Sauce
Vegetables in Season

★ ★ ★

Roast Chickens
Roast Ducks
York Ham

★ ★ ★

Custards
Wine Jellies
Stewed Fruits

★ ★ ★

Cheese and Salads

★ ★ ★

Toast = The King

The dinner was followed by tea at 5.30 pm. At 7.00 "precisely" a Smoking Concert took place. This concert in pre-instant entertainment times was a serious affair. The players were all Boss employees and

The Boss factory outing at the Warwick Castle Hotel, Clacton-on-Sea, August 28th 1909. Unfortunately very few personnel can be positively identified. Front row, fourth left John Robertson (Jnr), sixth left Bob Robertson, seventh left Sam Robertson. Second row, sixth left John Robertson. Third row, far right Bob Henderson.

⇥| Programme |⇤

OVERTURE ... Band and Chorus of 40 Voices (of a sort)	SONG ... ... R. J. COLLETT
SONG ... ... H. PARRY	SONG ... ... J. FOWLER
SONG ... ... A. CLEMENT	Toast: "The Young Governors."
SONG ... ... A. F. EMBLETON	A. F. EMBELTON, W. PITHER, C. JOHNSON.
Toast: "The Governor." THE VICE-CHAIRMAN.	SONG ... ... E. BALLARD
SONG ... ...J. TREVILLION	SONG ... ... E. WESTOBY
SONG ... ... C. PADGETT	Response: JACK, SAM, and BOB.
Response: THE CHAIRMAN.	SONG ... ... J. LEITCH
SONG ... ... F. SQUIRES	Toast: "Outdoor Workmen and Visitors." THE CHAIRMAN.
SONG ... ... J. ROBERTSON, JUN.	SONG ... ... R. ROBERTSON
Toast: "The Manager." THE CHAIRMAN.	Response: F. SQUIRES, J. HARRISS, J. DONCASTER, J. TREVILLION, J. LEITCH.
SONG ... ... J. HARRISS	SONG ... ... SELECTED
SONG ... ... J. ROBERTSON, SEN.	Toast: "The Chairman." THE VICE-CHAIRMAN.
Response: THE VICE-CHAIRMAN.	SONG ... ... SELECTED
SONG ... ...S. ROBERTSON	Response: THE CHAIRMAN.
SONG ... ... G. LIMBY	⚹ ⚹ ⚹ "Auld Lang Syne" ⚹ ⚹ ⚹ CHAIRMAN AND CHOIR.
Toast: "The Indoor Workmen." THE CHAIRMAN.	
SONG ... ... R. HENDERSON	
SONG ... ... A. AMSDEN	Ambulance, 5s.
Response: C. JOHNSON, R. HENDERSON.	

Boss & Co.'s Annual Dinner programme for the Smoking Concert at the Warwick Castle Hotel, Clacton-on-Sea, Saturday, 28th August 1909. The Vice Chairman was A. F. Embelton, the manager of the firm. The Chairman was John Robertson. F. Squires was the barrel-maker who supplied barrels to much of the trade. R. J. Collett was a barrel-browner to the trade.

they must have rehearsed assiduously for many weeks prior to the event. The programme is illustrated on the previous page.

Well fed and well watered, they all returned from Clacton at 8.35 am on Sunday morning, a rather uncivilised hour considering the nature of the previous day!

The menu of the next year's annual outing, 1910, made several alterations to the normal fare of the Warwick Castle Hotel.

Fish
Boiled Imitators and Unparalleled Sauce

Roasts
Roast Sirloin of Beef, Single-trigger Pudding
Roast Lamb and Ejector Sauce
Vegetables in Season

★ ★ ★

Roast Meeklings of the Press
Our Ducks – God Bless Them – Spinach
York Ham and Birmingham Savoury

★ ★ ★

Custards, Wine Jellies, Stewed Fruits

★ ★ ★

Cheese and Salads

Dessert
O/U Guns and Sour Grapes

John Robertson obviously could not resist a cynical swipe at the single trigger copyists, Birmingham guns, and the fact that the recently brought out O/U gun achieved such acclaim!

A notable change that John Robertson made, in contrast to other gunmakers, was a decreased dependence on outworkers. Robertson employed far more gunmakers than did Paddison and on account of the fact that these men encompassed all skills of gunmaking, there was no need for him to contract out. Nowhere is this change more evident than in barrel-making. Barrel-making was always regarded in the 19th century as something of a labourer's job – hard, dirty work. This was undoubtedly true in the days of twist and Damascus barrels that required a great deal of heating and hammering. Most gunmakers did not have the facilities to manufacture such barrels and bought them from specialists like Parkin. In the 1890s and the early part of the 20th century, Boss used the barrels of Frank Squires,

3 George Yard, Wardour Street, Soho, London. The Squire family had been in business as barrel-makers for most of the 19th century beginning with J. Squires at 12 Newcastle Street, Whitechapel in the 1830s, then his son Henry Squires at 3 George Yard, followed by the third generation, Frank Squires. The advent of steel barrels in the late 19th century changed barrel-making considerably. Good gunmakers could now buy in rough finished steel tubes from say, Vickers or Armstrong-Whitworth, finish, fine bore and joint them. This involved great skill and barrel-making rose in precedence. Robertson employed several such barrel-makers and dependence on makers like Squires ceased.

One aspect of gunmaking, engraving, a particular skill, remained the domain of outside specialists. The leading engraver, John Sumner, now of 15 Bateman Street, Soho, London, engraved most of the leading makers' best guns of this period. His family had been in business for a considerable length of time and had engraved Boss guns for some seventy years. The Thomas Boss percussion guns were engraved by Sumner.

Fairly recently a fire broke out at 15 Bateman Street, and large sheaves of engraving instructions to Sumner from many of the best makers were discovered. Giles Whittome of Brevex Gunmakers kindly let Boss & Co. examine the Boss engraving instruction sheets that they rescued from this fire. The sheets are from the years, 1909 to 1911 and cover virtually every Boss gun in late 5,000 to 6,000 serial number range, eg:

From J. Robertson, Gunmaker
1 & 2 Ham Yard Great Windmill Street, W.
4th August 1909

Mr Sumner,
Please engrave Boss gun no. 5689 usual best style to be numbered "1" in gold, put these barrels in hand at once so we can get them in brown tonight and oblige.

John Robertson

The average cost of engraving such a gun in "best style" was £1.0s.0d. "Full cover", that is to say engraving a gun completely, was sometimes demanded within two days. The total cost of a gun was about £70.0s.0d. so the engraving costs, considering the skilled nature of the work, were very low.

Jack Sumner's father had begun business in the 1830s at 10 Queen Street, Soho, London. Around 1885 he had moved to 15 Bateman Street, Soho. In late 1915 Jack Sumner shut up shop and as private J. G. Sumner no. 94332 he joined the R.A.M.C. He spent much of the war at the Convalescent Depot, Mustapha, Alexandria, Egypt. When he returned from the war, he decided that a regular weekly wage was preferable to the vagrancies of running his own business and he joined Boss as their own engraver working for the firm for many decades. In the 1920s and 1930s Jack Sumner was the man responsible for organising all the firm's annual outings.

Poor old Jack Sumner ended his days destitute. In these days there were no works pension schemes. Things did not work out for Jack and he found great difficulty in making ends meet. Such was his standing that his fellow gunmakers, in particular Bob Robertson, rallied round and persuaded The Gun & Allied Trades Benevolent Society to make some sort of a provision for him.

On 25th November 1940, the secretary of the Society, Bill Dover, replied to Bob Robertson concerning Jack:

My Dear Bob,

I have your letter of the 23rd inst. and am very sorry to hear of the misfortune of old Jack Sumner.

You may rely on my putting his case up to the Committee and I think you may count upon him getting some help.

Now Bob under our rules no man may receive more than £25 in any one year but as a subscriber I wish you would let me know whether it is a case where we should send a lump sum say £10 now or at Christmas, then later on a further amount, or would you think say £2 per month is preferable.

On hearing from you I will put the wheels in motion.

My kindest regards
Yours as ever
Bill

Other specialist work had to be done outside the factory. A. C. Haynes of 23 Lisle Street, Leicester Square, was an inlayer who inlaid any gold inlay on guns. J. R. Collett was a barrel-browner who had the tanks and chemicals necessary for browning and blueing.

Apart from this specialised work, all other aspects of Boss guns were built at the factory in Ham Yard. This meant that under the meticulous eye of John Robertson and Bob Henderson the factory manager, quality control of Boss guns was assured and their reputation as the Rolls Royce of gunmakers would never be tarnished. Many of the other leading London gunmakers subcontracted a considerable amount of work to outworkers of all descriptions but, under the Robertsons, a Boss gun was a Boss gun.

1910 saw the fiftieth anniversary of John and Margaret Robertson's marriage. To celebrate this anniversary, the Boss gunmakers presented John and Margaret with a special signed scroll in recognition of

A drawing for a Jack Sumner engraving of the underside of an action.

his talents as a gunmaker. This framed scroll hangs today in the shop in Dover Street.

In 1913 the factory moved again. From Ham Yard the gunmakers, vices, benches and tools moved very close by to 6, 8 and 10 Lexington Street, Golden Square, Soho, London, at a rent of £50 per quarter. The Boss factory would remain at this address for some twenty-five years, until the outbreak of World War II.

"WE DON'T WANT TO FIGHT BUT BY JINGO IF WE DO . . ."

Gavrilo Princip's shots of 28th June 1914, assassinating the Arch Duke Franz Ferdinand and his wife at Sarajevo in Bosnia, probably hardly merited talk by the gunmakers at work in Lexington Street. An assassination in

The "Illuminated Address" presented by the Boss gun-makers to John and Margaret Robertson on the occasion of their Golden Wedding Anniversary, Christmas Eve 1910. This scroll hangs in the front shop of Boss today.

John and Margaret Robertson on the occasion of their fiftieth wedding anniversary, 24th December 1910.

an area known for its instability was not headline news and nobody could foresee the appalling consequences that would follow. However in the weeks that followed, the system of alliances automatically operated, old animosities hardened, armies mobilised and when the German Schlieffen Plan rolled into operation, Britain was drawn into the war on 4th August 1914 due to her treaty obligations with Belgium.

Nobody could envisage the scale of the war nor consequent carnage that would ensue in the next four years. "A thunderstorm to clear the air over Europe" was the general feeling. The war would be over by Christmas and, in the great surge of patriotism that occurred in the autumn of 1914, thousands of men rushed to join up lest they miss the excitement. The Boss workers were no exception to this general feeling. A large number of them left to join the colours. In August 1914, forty-six gunmakers were on the Boss payroll, yet one year later in August 1915, exactly half that number, twenty-three remained.

Not all the gunmakers who disappeared from the payroll joined up. One result of the European war was a dimunition in the number of gun orders. European customers embroiled in war naturally could not order and back home demand for guns in the luxury sporting gun market dropped as the exigencies of war created other pressures. Many of Boss's customers had joined up and had no time for leisure pursuits. Other customers lost their inclination for the battue due to the nature of the slaughter that was occurring in Europe. Organised shoots diminished and the main form of shooting that took place during World War I was rough shooting of the type that Boss did not really construct guns for. Many factors played a part in the virtual cessation of organised shooting. Due to the fact that many keepers and estate workers had taken the King's Shilling, pheasant rearing was difficult. Game bird cover decreased as marginal land was brought into cultivation and forests were cut down. Cartridges were in short supply as munition manufacture took top priority and, to cap it all, the increased taxation necessary to cope with war expenditure meant that

customers would postpone ordering new guns until the cessation of hostilities.

When war was declared in August 1914, gun orders all but ceased. In 1915 only fourteen guns were ordered and in 1916 a mere ten guns. For example the Earl of Rocksavage, 25 Park Lane, London, ordered a trio in 1916. In 1917 and 1918 only one or two guns were ordered. Most of the these guns would have been made from stock guns already partially built. I doubt whether all these wartime orders were actually delivered. Most customers would have to wait till after the war.

These combined effects of a changed pattern of demand and a war economy could have had disastrous effects upon the business of Boss & Co. as net profits dropped alarmingly. They were left with no option but to dismiss some gunmakers. In addition, John Robertson realised that some sort of alternative work associated with the war effort was necessary to keep the company going and for Boss to do their bit for the Great War.

Even though John Robertson was an old man in his late seventies, war weaponry was a new challenge. Once again he applied his talents to devising new weapons of war. He concentrated on designing a grenade thrower, patenting his invention on 26th August 1915, provisional patent no. 12298. In the early years of the war, grenades were rather primitive devices, whereby a fuse was lit and the bomb thrown. Robertson's grenade thrower was a device to propel such a grenade far further than could be thrown by hand.

The bomb was fitted on a carrier to which was attached two lengths of rubber. A ratchet handle pulled this carrier back under tension of these rubber springs. The bomb was lit, the trigger pulled, and the bomb propelled a given distance. Although it sounds simple, Robertson added a degree of sophistication to this device. The bomb rested against a lever (j) on the carrier. As the carrier and the bomb neared the end of

LEFT: **The immediate Robertson family on the occasion of John and Margaret Robertson's Golden Wedding, 24th December 1910. Front row left to right: Charlie Stone, Billy Mansfield (first child), Molly Mansfield (second child), Bobby Mansfield (third child), Maggie Mansfield, Alison Cousins, Margaret Robertson, Kitty Stone (baby), Sam Mansfield (boy), John Robertson, Elsie Stone (girl on his knee), Annie Stone, Ruby Robertson (girl in the foreground), Maggie Stone, Alice Robertson, Sam Robertson, Maisie Robertson. Back row left to right: Tom Robertson, Alec Robertson, Kitty Robertson, William Mansfield, Bob Robertson, Mabel Robertson, Jack Robertson, May Robertson, John Robertson, Annie Robertson.**

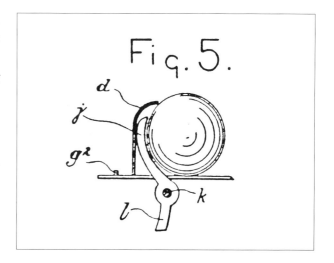

their travel, a trip block struck the lever (l) which then whipped forward and gave the bomb extra impetus to travel further. Calibrations were included in the mechanism to enable the bomb to be thrown a precise distance.

On 13th March 1915, *The Field* published a report entitled:

A Boss Grenade Thrower

Mr John Robertson, whose success with the Boss single trigger pronounces him a mechanic of high order, has been turning his attention lately to the design of a grenade-throwing apparatus for use in trench warfare. A private view of his apparatus was accorded to a member of this staff, and although its details necessarily cannot be disclosed, the general principles observed may be noted without entering into details. Elastic is the chosen medium of propulsion. A sliding carriage receives the bomb and hurls it with adjustable velocity in a predetermined and repeatable direction. The rubber springs are set by winding a cable on a drum till a catch springs into a notch. The bomb itself is of about the size of a cricket ball, made of light metal and having a hole which communicates with the interior cavity.

The chosen explosive mixture is passed in through this hole, the same being afterwards blocked with a suitable length of time fuse. No detonator is employed. The general scheme of design is arranged so that the time fuse may be ignited at the moment preceding discharge, the time of flight introducing the necessary safety margin. This is of extreme importance, since the bomb may by adjustment be made to explode within a second or less of its time of arrival, so minimising the chance afforded to the enemy of taking cover or even of pitching the spluttering bomb out of harm's way. More may not be said, other than to congratulate the veteran inventor on having found seasonable employment of his versatile faculties.

There is no record as to whether these grenade throwers found actual front line use in the trenches. In any case, these early hand lit bombs were superceded by the Mills Bomb, a far better and more reliable weapon.

The year 1915 also saw Robertson family events that would ensure family involvement in the Boss business for the next two generations. May Robertson, the only daughter of John Robertson (Jnr), married John Cameron Rennie, an electrical engineer, on 10th March 1915 at the Register Office, Islington, North London. May was twenty-five years of age and lived at 454 Camden Road, Islington and John Rennie was twenty-eight and lived at 28 Oxford Road, Putney, London.

John Rennie was a great grandson of John Rennie, the famous civil engineer and bridge builder of the late 18th and early 19th centuries. May Robertson, now as May Rennie, would become a director of Boss after the death of her father in 1929. On 23rd December 1915, at 17 Alba Gardens, Golders Green, London, May Rennie gave birth to her first son, John Donald Rennie. This John, known as "Jack" Rennie would become a gunmaker, primarily a barrel-maker and work all his days at Boss becoming a director in 1951. The Rennies augmented the Scottish connection at Boss. John Rennie the bridge builder hailed from East Lothian, the same county as John Robertson. "Robertson" is a very Scottish name as is "Rennie".

THE DEATH OF JOHN ROBERTSON, 1917

The penultimate year of the war witnessed the death of John Robertson. In late March 1917, John Robertson developed an appendicitis and had to go into the Hendon Cottage Hospital. He was an ageing man of seveny-seven years. Complications set in and he died in hospital on 24th March 1917. His family were with him when he died. Some four days later, on 28th March, he was cremated at the Golders Green Crematorium.

John Robertson was ahead of his time in his religious philosophy. As a boy he had been subject to a strict Scottish Calvinist upbringing where Sunday was indeed a day of rest with nothing permitted except Bible reading and church attendance. He had reacted strongly against this discipline and when he left home he formed a diametrically opposed opinion. Just as his mother and father had been dogmatic about imposing a strict religious faith, he became dogmatic that religion would not feature at all in his family's life.

He was influenced by Charles Bradlaugh, a rationalist lecturer who created a Constitutional dispute in 1880 when he was elected MP for Northampton and refused to swear the Oath upon entering Parliament. Bradlaugh was a "free thinker" who had an unenviable reputation for his advanced views, and this was the philosophical approach to religion that Robertson adopted. Robertson's free thinking approach is evident in that he forbade his sons and daughters to marry in church. Even near death he did not relent and left specific instructions that he was to be cremated without religious ceremony. In the early years of this century cremation was not common.

Just before he went into hospital he made a will, on 20th March. He left around £15,000, a large sum of money, the profits from his success as a gunmaker. Like many people who had surplus funds at this time, he had bought up speculative plots of land on the outskirts of

London. He owned eight leasehold cottages and five freehold plots of land at Bell Road, Enfield and he gave these to his daughter, Annie Stone. As for the Boss business, he left it to his three sons, John, Sam and Bob "in equal shares as tenants in common".

John Robertson's time with Boss, 1891–1917, was probably the most important period in the history of the company. To him must be due the credit for making the firm into a great gunmaker, for making the name "Boss" revered throughout the world as builders of very handsome, well designed and highly original guns. Such was his notoriety and respect, *The Field* printed on 31st March 1917 one of the longest and most detailed obituaries ever published on a gunmaker (below):

The *Shooting Times* also published an obituary in late March 1917:

OBITUARY

JOHN ROBERTSON (BOSS & CO)

It is with regret that we record the death, at the ripe old age of 77 years, of Mr John Robertson (Boss & Co.), a figure well known in the world of gunmakers. Mr Robertson took an active part in his business up to the end of last year, but recently he had been ailing and after an operation for appendicitis he passed away on the 24th inst. The funeral took place at Golders Green on Wednesday when there was a representative gathering of gentlemen connected

---

THE LATE MR JOHN ROBERTSON.

WE HAVE TO ANNOUNCE with great regret the death of Mr John Robertson, proprietor of the gun-making firm of Boss and Co. Though he had attained the great age of seventy-seven years, his habits of life never changed. Much of the celebrity of Boss guns was earned by the work of his own hands. This is not so much to say that he engaged in the processes of actual manufacture, though his skill would have been fully equal to the task, but that he performed the final titivation, adjustment, and inspection which insured the perfection of every detail. As a critic of workmanship all processes were included in his " view." His speciality was the adjustment of single triggers. As inventor of the system which bears his name, he knew every manifestation of which it was capable, not only on its own account but when influenced by the divers personalities of users. This has been the secret of his great success in a problem of gunmaking which admits of no royal solution, but is susceptible only to the kind of personal treatment which a doctor applies to a patient whose constitution he lays himself out to study. In spite of mature years, and notwithstanding the differences between sporting and military firearms, Mr Robertson has with his own hands made parts of the service rifle during the present war. Though the methods he adopted were naturally not those of the rifle factory, the skill he was able to bring to bear on his task enabled the work he did to pass gauge tests the severity of which is supposed to outclass hand work altogether.

In Mr Teasdale-Buckell's book *Experts on Guns and Shooting*, published in 1900, a full and sympathetic account is given of the firm of Boss and Co., and in particular of Mr Robertson, its proprietor at the time and since. From that source we learn that Mr Robertson was a native of Haddington, his father having carried on a gun business in that town for a period of sixty years. John Robertson left Haddington at the age of nineteen to enter the employment of the late Sir Joseph Whitworth at Manchester. This association enabled him to learn much about rifles under one of the foremost authorities of the day. He next took service with Westley Richards, of Birmingham, and for ten years after that was in the employment of Mr Purdey. He then started on his own account, "working for the trade," to use a well-known expression in the gun business. Mr Stephen Grant was his first principal customer, but others soon learnt to appreciate the quality of his work. Quoting from another source of information, this portion of his career extended over a period of twenty years, and it came to an end in the year 1891. An opportunity had arisen for acquiring the business of Boss and Co., and this Mr Robertson did, leaving his sons, who by that time had acquired mastery of their father's trade, to carry on the old workshop. As time went on, and Boss guns acquired a new fame in consequence of Mr Robertson's talents and energy, the family workshop became more and more absorbed in the production of these justly celebrated weapons. In due course the sons took a more and more active share in the routine of the Boss business, the diversity of their talents enabling them to specialise in its sundry branches. One found his *métier* in gun fitting and instruction, another supervised construction, and so on, the father all the while pursuing his own bent in the little room upstairs, where only very favoured visitors were allowed to invade his privacy. Of business cares he had practically none, for he was lucky enough to find in Mr Embleton, who died but a short while since, a worthy representative for the "front shop."

Mr Robertson always wore an apron, thus carrying on in his own person a tradition sanctified by Westley Richards's former manager, the "Bishop of Bond-street." Whether any gunmakers remain who wear aprons and work at the bench we are not certain. Atkin, of Jermyn-street, was one of this sort, but Mr Robertson has survived him by a substantial margin of years. The young Robertsons, as they have been called during a sufficient number of years to enable them to outgrow the title, no doubt still carry on the tradition, but in most other establishments even the vice has disappeared, with its curious assortment of decrepit-looking tools. The above remarks are, of course, not intended to suggest that knowledge and skill have departed from the higher personnel of modern gun businesses, but rather that the ever-increasing extent of operations has transferred practical work to other and less highly rented premises. Till a few years ago the business of Boss and Co. was carried on in old-fashioned premises in St. James's-street, where a noble corner site was devoted from cellar to garret to the firm's affairs. Rebuilding operations evicted guns in favour of chocolates, and the firm found fresh quarters in Dover-street, Piccadilly.

The technical achievements of the late Mr John Robertson are alike a tribute to his practical knowledge, to his restless ingenuity, and to the patience which enabled him to pursue a difficult undertaking until perfection had been secured. Webley, of Birmingham, took over the rights of one of his earlier inventions for an intercepting safety, and he collaborated with Mr Holland in the production of several important improvements to hammerless guns during the development of the modern system. The Boss single trigger he produced and marketed off his own bat, and the greatness of this achievement can only be appreciated by those possessing full knowledge of the difficulties to be over-come and appreciation of all that was involved in making the single trigger a standard part of the firm's gun as distinguished from an optional extra ordered at the purchaser's own risk.

Many supposed that the opportunities for radical invention in sporting-gun construction had long ago been exhausted, and yet the firm of Boss a few years ago asso-ciated their name with the under-and-over arrangement of the barrels. The gun which Mr Robertson and his co-workers produced was a marvel of ingenious construction, departing as it did from well-ordered conditions which had been standardised for centuries. As with the single trigger, such questions as whether he was the precise first to give form to the idea, and whether the new system will supplant the older type, stand apart from the ability and originality displayed in both instances in giving sound mechanical form to ideas which exist at the start merely as brain images. Inventing has two widely dissimilar aspects—first, the idea pure and simple, and, second, realisation of the idea in supremely workable form. To be acclaimed as one of the world's inventors requires a clear opening as well as the faculty for finally evolving the perfect form. John Robertson was certainly a great inventor, but he was subject to the limitations imposed by lack of virginity in the territory to which fate had limited his efforts. Had he stuck to rifles such qualities as he possessed might have made of him a British edition of Mauser. Military rifles, including even the Mauser, need at this day the titivating attentions of a hand and brain such as John Robertson possessed.

with the trade to pay their last respects to the deceased.

Mr Robertson hailed from Haddington where his father was a gunmaker. Leaving his native town in 1860, he worked in the firm of Sir Joseph Whitworth of Manchester for a few years, leaving there for Birmingham: but his residence there was not of long duration as he journeyed to the Metropolis and joined the staff of Messrs Purdey. Here he stayed about ten years and on resigning he commenced business on his own account, working for the trade until about twenty-five years ago when he became a partner in the firm of Boss & Co. It was not long before Mr Robertson took full control of the firm and he has carried on the business ever since. To his inventive faculties may be attributed the successful single trigger gun manufactured by Boss & Co. which has gained renown throughout the shooting world. Mr Robertson leaves a widow and three sons to whom we offer our condolences in their loss.

We understand the business will be carried on by the sons all of whom have been on the staff for many years.

Arms and Explosives published a lengthy obituary in their edition of 2nd April 1917 (right):

To conclude on John Robertson, I can do no better than quote from an article which appeared in *Arms and Explosives* on 1st May 1902. The object of the article was stated in the frontspiece:

The name of Boss is probably as well known to sportsmen of this generation as was that of Manton to their predecessors, but in the modern instance the working proprietor, Mr John Robertson is to some extent over-shadowed by the name under which he works. This small brochure is intended to identify the individuality of the man with the work he has done under another name, and if it achieves this purpose, the labour involved in its preparation will not have been undertaken in vain.

"A Typical Gunmaker – Mr John Robertson"

But to his gifts as a mechanician must be added a genial, kindly personality before the portraiture is complete. Thorough in everything, thorough in his work, thorough in his opinions and thorough in his friendships, is "Jack" Robertson as he is familiarly termed by everyone in the London gun trade. Working gunsmiths respect and regard "Jack" Robertson as a workman who has strenuously toiled throughout his life, and throughly deserves the

THE LATE
MR. JOHN ROBERTSON.

WE learn with regret of the death of Mr. John Robertson, proprietor of the firm of Boss & Co., Dover Street, Piccadilly, on the 24th ult. He had been ailing for some time, but the malady only took a severe turn a few days before his death, and he died under the operation that was attempted. He would have completed his 78th year had he lived till June. Throughout the gun trade he commanded the highest respect on account of his supreme ability as a gunmaker and the steady persistence with which he always strove for perfection. The London gun trade is an asset to the entire industry on account of the high standard of workmanship which it associates with the name of British guns, and no individual worker of the present generation has strived more earnestly than Mr. Robertson to keep the flag flying, nor has anyone achieved a higher quality of success.

No man was better qualified for the task of maintaining the reputation of London guns than Mr. Robertson when,

position he has secured by his own perseverance and talents. Master gunmakers, on the other hand, recognise in him an addition to their ranks, whose mastery of gunmaking greatly helps to uphold the reputation of London gun manufacturers. Mr. Robertson finds his greatest recreation in mechanical experimenting at his bench, where, from morning to night, he can almost always be found enthusiastically devoting himself to the solution of some problem in gunmaking; or examining in minute detail the work done by his large skilled staff. If he takes an occasional day off it is likely to be spent gun in hand in the field, or among the spectators at a football or cricket match, or driving in the country. But his holidays are few, no one in his establishment working harder than he does, his greatest pleasure appearing to consist in being among his staff and superintending their work, in the year 1891, he took up his quarters in the St. James's Street premises. He was always proud of having worked under the late Sir Joseph Whitworth at the time when this versatile mechanical genius was engaged in investigating problems connected with rifled small arms. A gunmaker bred and born, at the age of 19 he left his native town of Haddington, where his father carried on business as a gunmaker for no less a period than sixty years, to make his own way in the world. As he did not desire to abandon shot guns wholly in favour of rifles, he left Manchester in due course and proceeded to Birmingham, where he took service with the firm of Westley Richards. Later on he came to London, and his qualifications were by this time so high as to enable him to find employment at Purdey's, where he stayed for ten years.

His department of work was stocking, screwing and finishing, his double mastery over wood and metal being thus explained. So complete were his qualifications and so great his ambition that he finally decided to start in business for himself, not as a retailer but as a worker for other gunmakers. The firm of Stephen Grant gave him his first orders, but the quality of work he was able to turn out soon enlarged his clientele, and in a very short time he was employed by all the best firms in the trade who were in the habit of availing themselves of outside assistance. Robertson's services were in special demand when unusually high quality was required. The result was that his workmanship figured more than once in exhibitions, where it earned appropriate recognition.

His career really began when he took over the business of Boss & Co., for which he had previously done a considerable amount of work. He promised the previous proprietor that so long as he directed the firm's fortunes they should never sell any but best work. This promise has been faithfully kept, notwithstanding the profit that would have attended the sale of other grades of weapon under a name that had justly become famous. He did a bold thing in at once initiating his experiments with single-trigger guns. Though already no novice in invention he here found himself up against a very difficult problem. He discovered the involuntary pull, and although subsequent events showed that he had been forestalled so far as strict originality was concerned, his solution was the pioneer of practical devices. His mechanism led the new fashion, largely owing to the unexampled skill and care which he devoted to the adjustment of every gun sold. Rivals arose in number, and very little else was discussed in connection with guns for the next ten years.

There were two schools; the one utilised the intermediate involuntary pull, whereas the other sought by timing gear to render it inoperative. Robertson's mechanism was of the former type, being known as three-pull, which means that the involuntary pull due to recoil formed a necessary link in the chain of operations which switched the trigger from engagement with one sear to the other. Though single triggers have not established themselves in sporting favour to the extent which at one time appeared likely, the Boss gun has by its success proved that, given the necessary standard of workmanship, the theoretical advantages of the

system can be fully realised in practice. Statistics show that more than 75 per cent. of the guns sold by the firm have been fitted with single triggers. The most celebrated customer of the Boss business was Mr. R. H. Rimington-Wilson, whose reputation as a shot and whose ownership of the wonderful Broomhead moor, near Sheffield, imparted a unique value to his example and recommendation.

In later years Mr. Robertson has given us the under-and-over gun, which has aroused an amount of interest nearly equal to that occasioned by his single-trigger gun. There is, of course, the difference that, whilst everybody could experiment with single triggers, the comprehensive re-arrangement of the whole gun's mechanism which was involved in placing the barrels one over the other limited the number who essayed to do likewise. Several of the leading firms have produced models, but the war intervened and the practical test of the system on the considerable scale that was provided for has had to be postponed. Robertson's system of under-and-over gun, like everything else he produced, makes a strong appeal to the student of firearms. His schemes were always realised in bold outline and the details filled in with a loving care that left nothing to chance.

Fortunately for the future of the fine business he had established, the problem of succession presents no difficulties. Three sons, all practical and experienced workmen, have shared the responsibilities of direction for many years. The accompanying group photograph, which was taken fully ten years ago, shows that the heirs had even then arrived at years of discretion. Jack, Sam and Bob, as they are respectively known, have been fully trained by their father, and each has developed specialities on his own account. Their united period of service now covers the respectable period of one hundred years.

'Driving in the country', John and Margaret Robertson *circa* 1910.

severely criticising where he considers such criticism is called for, and praising enthusiastically where praise is due, with the result that the best guns of Boss & Co., having passed the minutest inspection in every part, from start to finish, by one of the most keen and critical judges of fine work, himself a workman of consummate skill, are rightly regarded as second to none in the world.

CHAPTER TEN

THE "YOUNG GOVERNORS"

Whenever John Robertson died, the Boss business was left in the very capable hands of his three sons. John (Jnr) was fifty-six years of age, Sam was fifty-four years of age and Bob was forty-three years of age. The three Robertson "boys" were rather tongue-in-cheek known as the "young governors"! During the 1920s and 1930s in rather difficult times, they would run the business very efficiently producing the guns developed by their father.

When the celebrations diminished after the 11th November 1918, Boss reverted to producing guns for the sporting market once more. Most of the workforce returned and orders started to come in. On 29th September 1920, the lease on 13 Dover Street was re-negotiated to run for fourteen years at £450 per annum. The following year on the 25th March 1921, the lease on the factory at 6/8/10 Lexington Street likewise was re-negotiated to run for eighteen-and-a-half years at £280 per annum.

In 1922, as a young boy, Fred Oliver, who would later become secretary of Boss in 1940 and a director in 1965, joined the company. Today in his 80s Fred still puts in a full day's work in the shop at Dover Street. He began his days with Boss as an assistant cartridge loader. Wally Walters also loaded cartridges and George Felix was responsible for boxing them. Hand-loaded cartridges were in big demand pre-War and Boss loaded and supplied thousands upon thousands. The cartridges

The annual outing of Boss & Co *circa* 1920. The Young Governors are standing at the rear – left to right, John, Sam and Bob. This photo was discovered recently at Boss & Co, underneath a drawer, making it stiff to open.

were loaded in the basement in rather unpleasant surroundings and in our safety conscious days there was always an element of danger associated with this loading. In the room where the cartridges were boxed was a fire for warmth. "Dangerous – oh no," says Fred." We had to keep warm and in any case the cellar is still intact today!"

Some four years later in 1926 Fred was promoted to the front shop as a junior clerk. The reason for his promotion was that the previous incumbent was given the sack for stealing insurance stamps. As a junior clerk Fred was responsible to Arthur Clement the shop manager. At 10.45 am precisely each day, Fred had a very important duty to perform for Mr Clement. He had to run up to Regent Street to a pub named "Mrs Ponds" and bring back Guinness for Mr Clement and the other senior staff – and woe betide Fred if the Guinness was not in 13 Dover Street before 11.00 am. This is a tradition that has carried on at Boss since this period. If you ever visit 13 Dover Street today, I recommend around 11.00 am when you will find the management at their most convivial!

In 1922 the young governors decided to put the business on a more formal footing and drew up Articles of Partnership between them. This Indenture was duly signed by all three on the 1st March 1923. Apart from the usual clauses pertinent to a private partnership, the chief object behind the indenture was to formalise what financial benefits would accrue to their wives in the event of a partner's demise. Any widow was to receive a one-third share of the business.

John Robertson (Jnr) *circa* 1922.

worked in the City. Very generously he gave the firm £1,000 to secure its future. It was not a loan, it was a gift. Without the benefaction of Mr Turner, it is highly possible that Boss would not have survived.

By this time, the three brothers had established themselves in their own particular domain within the company. John Robertson was in charge of the shop at 13 Dover Street.

Apart from his managerial tasks and dealing with customers, John's job was chequering guns. John worked at this in the back shop. The only toilet in the shop was an outside affair, open to the elements and the pigeons (as it still is today!). When nature called John had quite a walk from his bench to this toilet. Usually he found it more convenient to walk to the cellar under the pavement in Dover Street where there was an open drain. The drain is still there today complete with original rusty grill!

Like many a gunmaker before and after him, John Robertson enjoyed a dram. There was always a bottle of whisky in the shop in Dover Street. When a customer was prevaricating over a decision to buy a gun, John would very civilly offer the customer a chair and join him in a dram. "Don't bother to rush your decision – you can take your time – can I top up your glass, Sir?" The customer would be terribly impressed at John Robertson's hospitality and coupled with a sensory perception now somewhat more relaxed, an order would be secured. Later when the customer came back to buy something trivial, for example cartridges or oil, out would come the whisky again and gradually word went round about the generous, genial gunmakers in Dover Street. But what the customer did not know was

For some reason in the early 1920s, Boss experienced financial problems with their business. There was a cash flow problem and it looked as though the firm might go under. Word of this quickly spread amongst their customers and one good customer in particular was concerned that for want of a relatively small sum of money, the firm of Boss with its auspicious reputation should not face liquidation. This was A. G. Turner who

The Articles of Partnership signed between John, Sam and Bob on 1st March 1923.

that the price of his gun had been upped ever so slightly to take account of this benevolent hospitality!

Sam Robertson was in charge of the factory in Lexington Street. Sam was of a stern disposition and made it his business to ensure that the factory ran efficiently. With this in mind he constructed a central glass office amidst the gunmakers to counter any lackadaisical leanings upon their part. Sam's specialisation within the factory was in stocking forends.

Bill Wise, who rose to become the foreman at Boss's factory in the 1950s and 1960s, had the misfortune to encounter Sam's rather unforgiving disposition early on in his career. As a boy apprentice in the 1920s, one of his chores was to carry guns from the factory to the shop in Dover Street. Sam in his drive for efficiency piled as many guns as he could on top of poor Bill and off they trotted down the street. Bill simply could not keep up with Sam. Sam let fly at the top of his voice a torrent of invective abuse at the hapless Bill. "Come on, get a move on you idle boy – pick these feet up, left, right, left, right – hurry up." At that moment a policeman heard this rough hectoring, stopped Sam and severely chastised him for haranguing the boy in public in such a manner. "Now, Sir, you carry some of the guns and be a little more civil and understanding. Come on now, off we go, pick these feet up, left, right, left, right." And off this odd trio walked to the shop in Dover Street – the policeman poker faced, Sam even more stern faced and Bill smirking from ear to ear.

Upon the policeman leaving, Sam exploded at young Bill, "You bloody fool – a fine bloody mess you caused showing me up like that. Get out – you are fired!" Fortunately Sam cooled down, saw sense if not the humour and Bill carried on to produce a lifetime of work for Boss.

The youngest of the three brothers, Bob, was in charge of the shooting ground at Shire Hall Lane, Hendon. Apart from being a first-class shot himself, Bob was well suited to dealing with the general public day in day out as befitted the nature of his work. Bob was very much a live wire, an outgoing personality, ideal for building up a good rapport with customers and as a salesman for Boss. He was well known as a raconteur, amusing, enlightening and entertaining.

Bob's rapport and sales technique sadly failed him on one famous occasion. Boss had always been disappointed that they had never received the Royal Warrant. Bob had always intended that he would approach the Monarch when a convenient time presented itself. Such a time did occur on a Yorkshire grouse moor in the late 1930s. Bob had been invited along to coach a member of the nobility and present at this shoot was King George VI. Bob sidled up to the King and asked, "Excuse me, your Majesty, have you never thought about buying a Boss gun?" The King instantly retorted, "A Boss gun, a Boss gun, bloody beautiful but too bloody expensive!"

In addition to his gunmaking and shooting skills, Bob

Sam Robertson with Peggy Robertson (his daughter-in-law) beside him and Eileen Robertson (his daughter-in-law) behind him alongside his wife Annie. The occasion was the marriage of Bob Robertson's eldest daughter Maisie in June 1925.

was no mean sportsman. He was a keen racing cyclist and won many prizes in big road events. He was an accomplished amateur boxer and boxed to a very close decision (the casting vote) against one of the best amateurs of the turn of the century, Nat Smith. He was the principal founder of the Hendon Boxing Club, still boxing there in the 1920s around the age of 50. He excelled at football and formed the Boss & Co. team – the team that found fame in the 1920s when they reached the final of the Battersea Cup.

In the Boss gun catalogue of the 1920s, Bob's work at the shooting ground was thus described:

> The Grounds are under the personal control of Mr Bob Robertson, who is not only an excellent shot but is also a practical gunmaker. This latter qualification is a necessity in a good instructor: for not only can he bring a technically trained mind to bear upon the actual task of gun fitting, but he can arrive at the particular needs of each case with more directness and certainty.

> Mr Robertson is frequently engaged as coach to large shooting parties: and his swiftness in detecting and correcting errors on the part of sportsmen has been of considerable advantage and service to our clients.

A note followed after this lest some customers be put off:

> Any make of gun can be used at our grounds and clients using guns not of our manufacture can feel assured of every possible attention. The Regent Shooting Ground is in no sense an establishment for inventing faults in other people's guns for the purpose of additional trade. It is a school for instruction and practice pure and simple.

One of the big changes instituted by the Robertsons was a far greater emphasis placed on sales abroad. Due to the vagrancies of transport and communication in the 19th century, very few Boss guns were sold to customers outside Great Britain. Before the First World War rapid communication particularly with the United States became possible and American gun orders began to appear. The single trigger and to a greater extent the over and under excited the American market and the Robertsons were determined to exploit this vast potential. In addition it was a market that could not afford to be ignored. Economically, the effect of World War I on Great Britain would be felt for many years. Taxation was still high and estates neglected during the war required investment. This meant that home demand

for sporting guns was lower than in pre-war days. Profits went down accordingly – hence Boss's desire to seek customers in a part of the world not affected to any real extent by the ravages of the Great War.

Bob as the shooting instructor and with his extrovert personality was the natural choice to visit the United States to drum up business. After World War I, America was enjoying an economic boom and affluent American sportsmen were demanding best English guns. Messrs. Von Lengerke and Detmold, 200, 5th Avenue, New York, a sporting goods store and acknowledged authority on all sporting activities in the U.S.A., despatched a representative to Boss in the post-war period. A business deal was concluded and Von Lengerke and Detmold were appointed agents for Boss guns in the U.S.A. To promote the guns, Bob Robertson visited the U.S.A. for three months every year in the 1920s and 1930s. He coached at Von Lengerke and Detmold's shooting ground, demonstrated Boss guns and the end result was a great deal of business secured for Boss in America.

Later in the 1930s Boss's agent in the U.S.A. became Messrs. Abercromby and Fitch of Madison Avenue, New York. During the 1920s and 1930s American orders accounted for around 50% of Boss sales.

Bob Robertson *circa* **1929. Bob was in charge of Boss's Regent Shooting Ground.**

the safety and single trigger selector device had to be in Japanese. This must have caused Jack Sumner the engraver a few problems!

THE LONG SUFFERERS' ASSOCIATION, 1926

John Robertson was one of the founding members of the Long Sufferers' Association and in recognition of this role was elected its first chairman in 1926. The Long Sufferers' Association was open to any gunmaker with twenty-five or more years in the trade. John Robertson felt that the established gunmakers never really got together for a social event that would promote greater intercourse among them. In particular, he thought that the Birmingham and London gun trades were worlds apart and that an annual dinner and get-together would improve relations.

The upshot was the Long Sufferers' Association, founded in 1926 and holding its inaugural dinner in a hotel in London. Although I do not know where this first dinner was held, a menu exists for the second annual dinner which took place on Saturday, 15th January 1927 at the Florence Restaurant (King George Room). On the front of the menu, W. J. Booker wrote a poem to explain the reasoning behind the association:

> Ye merry men of Ammunition fame,
> Upon the Empire's history ye have writ your name,
> And by the Gods! you have a special right,
> To have a jolly time on Veterans night,
> The viands sit before you are both rich and rare,
> Let every "Long Sufferer" for the feast prepare,
> Shew your capacity and prove your worth,
> Give yourselves over to jollity and mirth.

During the evening a collection was made for the Gun and Allied Trades Benevolent Society. The chairman was in office for one year. Pre-war, the following gunmakers served as chairman:

1926	J. Robertson
1927	C. S. Rosson
1928	H. Whitehead
1929	H. Whitehead
1930	H. W. R. Tarrant
1931	A. G. Redfern
1932	Theo Rigby
1933	G. V. Powell
1934	C. J. Hellis
1935	M. S. Marson
1936	T. Blomeley
1937	C. Gardner
1938	R. D. Robertson

Bob Robertson demonstating how to change guns at the shooting ground, Shire Hall Lane, Hendon in 1925.

American customers tended to prefer double triggers and purchased most of the O/U guns. Very few pairs were ordered.

In their orders the Americans tended to go in to more detail specifying the exact type of engraving, the figure of the wood, chequering pattern, etc. The guns ordered were more ostentatious too – guns chased and inlaid were preferred to traditional English rose and scroll engraving. Often on top of the barrel inlaid in gold would be wording similar to "Built especially for . . . by Boss & Co., London, England."

Bob Robertson would usually take a large collection of completed guns over to the United States himself on his yearly visits. If this was not possible, completed guns would be dispatched by fast steamer. In the records, "sent by *Aquitania*, June 2nd 1931", or "sent by *Queen Mary*, May 3rd 1937" often appears.

The Japanese market was sizeable. A great many Boss guns of more traditional workmanship were ordered by Japanese customers in the 1920s and 1930s. The orders for these Japanese guns always state that the lettering on

The menu of the second annual dinner of the Long Sufferers' Association at the Florence Restaurant, Saturday, 15th June 1927.

The Gunmakers' Association 1929 with no. 32 Alec Robertson, no. 33 Bob Robertson, no. 20 Sam Robertson, no. 21 John Robertson.

Arthur Sanderson (centre) shop manager at 13 Dover Street, on a factory outing *circa* 1930 with Jack Sumner the engraver (left).

The Long Sufferers' Association proved to be a great success. The annual dinner and the pre- and after-dinner drinks certainly made for a very enjoyable evening and led to a far greater bond between the long established gunmakers throughout the length and breadth of the land. The association still flourishes today, true to its original concept as devised by John Robertson.

In 1926 Arthur Sanderson was promoted to shop manager at 13 Dover Street. He was intensely proud of working for Boss and would remain with the firm until his retirement in the early 1970s. He was an excellent choice for shop manager, listening to customers' problems and serving them in a genial, efficient manner.

The young governors' control of Boss & Co. did not survive for long after the death of their father in 1917. On the 26th January 1929, John Robertson died at his home at 60 Freegrove Road, Holloway, London. He was sixty-seven years old. He had been ill with a disease of the kidneys for some time. When getting up from bed one night, he missed his footing and fell down the stairs in his house. He fractured his arm, this aggravated his illness, and as a consequence he died shortly afterwards. As is required by law in the case of accidental death, an inquest was held by the Coroner of Central London on the 30th January 1929 who confirmed the cause of his death. In his Will proved on the 11th March 1929, he left nearly £11,000, the entire proceeds going to his only daughter May Rennie. John was careful in his will to stipulate that the presentation watch given to his father by a Mr Rimmington Wilson of Broomhead was to go to Sam and Bob for them to fight it out over possession! This watch was a great source of pride to both the John Robertsons. Rimmington-Wilson was a wealthy aristocrat who owned a famous grouse shoot at Broomhead, Sheffield. He ordered countless Boss guns and, as a token of appreciation, presented a watch to John Robertson Snr. With May Rennie's inheritance she now became a partner in Boss & Co. along with the surviving two brothers Sam and Bob. May would remain a director of Boss until 1953.

On 2nd February 1929, *The Shooting Times* wrote an obituary for John Robertson:

> On 26th January the death took place of Mr John Robertson of the well known firm of Boss & Co., of Dover Street, London. Mr Robertson was a practical gunmaker of exceptional ability whose pre-eminent skill and scientific knowledge were justly held in high repute among all sportsmen. It is men such as he was who have played a worthy part in making British guns the best in the world, men of whom it can be said that they brought the highest qualities of art and science to bear upon their work. Mr Robertson was born in January 1862: he commenced work in 1876 and continued it to the date of his death. He had thus the fine record of fifty-three years of notable service in British Gunmaking. It should be mentioned that he was one of the prime movers in the establishment of the Long Sufferers' Association and he was its first chairman. His genial temperament and kindly nature endeared him to all his colleagues and the news of his death will be received with profound regret both at home and abroad. Life's work well done and now – Requiescat.

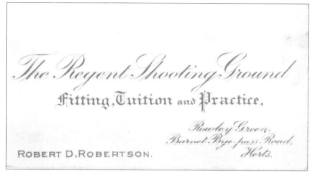

The trade card of Bob Robertson *circa* 1930.

SUBURBAN SPRAWL

During the early part of 1929, the house building boom of the 1920's threatened the Green Belt around Hendon. Boss & Co.'s shooting ground at Shire Hall Lane, Hendon was compulsorily purchased due to this voracious suburban sprawl. It was getting more and more difficult to find a shooting ground remotely close to central London and Boss found that they had to go further North to near Barnet in Hertfordshire.

At Rowley Green, just of the Barnet by-pass, the Regent Shooting Ground was re-established. This is the present day site of Boss & Co.'s shooting ground. The thirty-three acre site, considerably larger than the old Hendon site, was purchased on 29th August 1929 for

The new Regent Shooting Ground at Rowley Green, Hertfordshire – a photograph taken shortly after its purchase in August 1929.

The early accommodation at the Rowley Green shooting ground *circa* **1935!**

£5,356.5s.9d, the bulk of the land being previously owned by the Earl of Stafford. The new ground was quickly converted into an excellent shooting ground with Bob Robertson in charge.

In a gun catalogue of the 1930s, Boss describe their new ground thus:

THE REGENT SHOOTING GROUND

Rowley Green (Barnet By-Pass Road)

These grounds are fitted with every modern device necessary for practice, coaching and fitting. They may easily be reached by electric train to High Barnet (Hampstead Tube) or by road (see route diagram on back of cover).

WALKING-UP

Our arrangements for practice in walking up include concealed traps for bolting rabbits, springing clay birds and afford exciting sport, under the nearest natural conditions possible. All the mechanical arrangements are invisible, and each event is a surprise. The whole ground may be beaten without a shot, or the sport around one may be fast and furious, when the necessity for quick loading presents itself with natural reality, and no imagination is needed to recall similar conditions which all sportsmen have experienced in the field.

DRIVEN BIRDS

The arrangements for driven birds are as natural as human skill can make them, and the ground is provided with pit butts, now considered the correct thing on many big shoots, as well as the old-time butts. It will therefore be seen that nothing has been left undone to make the school thoroughly efficient from every point of view.

BOSS & CO. LTD, 41 ALBEMARLE STREET, PICCADILLY, LONDON

In the year 1930, Boss & Co. experienced two major changes. Firstly they moved shop again, this time from 13 Dover Street to 41 Albemarle Street, and secondly they became a limited company.

Compared to 73 St James's Street, 13 Dover Street was very small. The Robertsons were always on the look-out for a larger shop. In addition the lease on 13 Dover Street had only another four years to run. In the spring of 1930, the Robertsons found out that 41 Albemarle Street was on offer leasehold. In May 1930 a deal was concluded and the lease was purchased for £5,000. Albemarle Street was parallel to Dover Street, in Piccadilly and virtually directly opposite St James's Street. Forty-one Albemarle Street had been home to Harrison & Hussey, gunmakers, who had been taken over by Stephen Grant and Joseph Lang in that year.

A Boss trade card *circa* 1935.

Boss would remain at Albemarle Street until the lease ran out in 1960 and they moved to 13/14 Cork Street.

The Albemarle Street shop was far bigger than the old 13 Dover Street shop. The shop was reminiscent of an earlier era being very Victorian in character. Like 13 Dover Street, gunmakers' benches were set up in the windows. In these windows Alec Robertson constructed single-trigger mechanisms and cleaning and repairs were done. Jack Sumner the engraver and his assistant Freddie Epps came over from the factory in Lexington Street to work in another window in this spacious shop. Freddie Epps was an engraver with Boss in the 1920s and 1930s. During World War I, as no. 293092 Gunner Epps, he had served with a Howitzer Battery.

For a while Bob Henderson the foreman worked in Albemarle Street. He worked in the basement that he promptly termed "The Mines". His displeasure in this area was exacerbated by the fact that he took out the electric lighting and reverted to the old gas lights! It was not long before he returned to the factory in Lexington Street.

The autumn of 1929 witnessed the end of the post-war American economic boom. The crash on Wall Street heralded the onset of the Great Depression that was to permeate the economies of all countries in the Western World. Interestingly, the American market for best guns did not really diminish rapidly although home demand and European demand did. The order books for 1931/32 are full of red lines on gun orders reading "cancelled". Luxury sporting gun makers felt keenly this diminution in demand and the future did not appear healthy for Boss & Co.

One result of this unfortunate economic climate was that the Robertsons intended to put Boss & Co. onto a sounder financial footing by seeking to secure limited liability status. From 1857 to 1930 the firm had been a private company. In addition to the uncertainty as to what the 1930s might bring, there was also the problem of the death of John Robertson in January 1929. His only child, May Rennie, had inherited his share of the business and as a non-gunmaker it appeared

more sensible for her interest to be best served by limited liability.

On 19th June 1930, Boss & Co., 41 Albemarle Street, London, was incorporated as a private limited company under the 1929 Companies' Act. The nominal capital was £20,000 divided into 10,000 preference shares at £1 each and 10,000 ordinary shares also at £1 each. The directors appointed were Sam Robertson, 54 Manor View, Church End, Finchley, London, Bob Robertson, 17 Graham Road, Hendon, London and May Rennie, 17 Alba Gardens, Golders Green, London. Both Sam and Bob received an annual salary of £750 and May an annual salary of £50. The worth of the company was assessed at, stock in trade, plant, etc £8,410.5s.2d, actual business, £13,358.14s.5d and the freehold shooting ground, £5,356.5s.9d.

The object behind the company in the Articles of Association were defined as, "to carry on the business of gunmakers and armourers and to manufacture, purchase, sell, repair, overhaul, and generally to deal in guns, rifles, pistols, firearms and weapons of every description, cartridges, ammunition, explosives and accessories and equipment materials and things of all kinds required or used in connection with shooting and the preservation and rearing and capture of game and other forms of sport, and to carry on a shooting school and to teach shooting and to test guns, rifles and firearms and other weapons and ammunition of every description."

In common with a great many other businesses and factories, the gunmakers were forced in the harsh economic climate of the early 1930s to take a cut in wages. A 10% drop in wages was endured by all in the firm but at least it enabled the company to keep going when orders were down and very few men had to be laid off. The "Census of Production" statistics for the 1930s as required by the Board of Trade, show how the 1930s presented difficult times for Boss in the depression years.

These statistics give a very detailed insight into the firm in the 1930s. During the early years of the Depression, the firm was hardly affected at all, some 112 sporting guns being made in 1931. Three years later in 1934, the full blast of the Great Depression was keenly felt. Seven gunmakers had to be laid off and gun production was more than halved to fifty guns per annum. What is interesting is that sales of cartridges were not affected in the slightest. As can be seen from the value of cartridges sold, cartridge sales were important to the Boss business and in reality in the mid-1930s they kept the firm going when sporting gun demand dropped off. There was no let up in shooting during the Depression. The curtailment of the high disposable income of customers caused a drop in demand for new guns until

Year	Workforce	Coke consumed	Electricity consumed	Cost of materials	Sporting guns made	Barrels made	Cartridges loaded	Repair work
1931	43	4 tons	8,866 units	£8,430	112 value £14,566	22 value £798	506,000 value £5,843	£1,462
1934	36	N/A	N/A	£7,038	50 value £6,500	13 value £350	639,635 value £5,553	£1,637
1935	37	N/A	N/A	£6,997	69 value £8,280	15 value £396	716,300 value £5,978	£1,273
1936	39	4.5 tons	7,900 units	£6,815	67 value £8,560	20 value £450	710,819 value £6,167	£1,572
1938	39	4.5 tons	8,540 units	£5,329	71 value £10,312	18 value £400	549,300 value £5,953	£1,298

more prosperous times ensued. Repair work and servicing remained constant proving that shooting remained continuously popular during the 1930s.

Gun demand picked up gradually in the later 1930s as countries threw off the shackles of depression. However it was not until 1939, with the onset of war, that full recovery became reality with the advent of war-related work.

In the early 1930s Jack Rennie entered the firm as an apprentice barrel-maker. John Donald Rennie (known as "Jack" in the Boss business but "Don" in the family) was the fourth generation descended from John

Three generations of the family firm on a work's outing in the 1930s. Alec Robertson, third generation (left), Bob Robertson, second generation (centre), Jack Rennie, fourth generation (right).

Robertson (snr). Jack's mother, May Rennie, was originally May Robertson, the only daughter of John Robertson (jnr). Jack worked for Boss all his life as a barrel-maker and occasionally as a coach at the shooting ground. Although retired he remains a director of Boss today.

On 22nd May 1934, the second of the "young governors", Sam Robertson, died. He died from a cerebral haemorrhage, experienced three months earlier, aged seventy at his home at 54 Manor View, Finchley, London. He died intestate and as a result Letters of Administration were granted to two of his sons, Jack Robertson, laundry proprietor, and Tom Robertson, bank clerk. His estate was valued at £8,075.1s.1d. Sam's one-third share of the business passed to these two sons, Jack and Tom. It would not be until June 1945 that these shares were reallocated to include his third son, Alec.

The *Shooting Times* published a lengthy obituary on Sam Robertson in their edition of 26th May 1934.

It is with very deep regret we have to record the death of Mr. S. Robertson which occurred on Tuesday last, May 22nd. He was a partner in the universally well known firm of Boss & Co., Albemarle Street, London.

Born in 1864, he commenced to serve in 1877 under his illustrious father the late Mr. John Robertson from whom he inherited the skill of a master craftsman – in fact one could but say of him that he was a working master gunmaker and a worthy representative of the older generation of gunmakers of the Joe Manton type – and an asset to the industry on account of the high standard of workmanship he earnestly achieved, and which is associated with the name of Boss, which firm he joined when it was taken over by his father in the early nineties.

His ability as a gunmaker was supreme and allied to it was a steady persistence for perfection, which was evidenced by his supervision of the unsurpassed workmanship connected with Boss guns. He was a member of the Gunmakers' Association for many years and also a Freemason of the Brent Lodge for over a quarter of a century. At the time of his death he was their senior lay partner and he will be sadly missed by the brethren of that Lodge.

In this age of machinery and mass production the loss of such a craftsman is doubly deplored. Quiet and kindly, we can not recall every having seen him ruffled and for his many kind acts done in the same unostentatious way, his memory will be revered. He was ill but for a short time – three months – and leaves a widow and three sons – VALE.

The cremation took place at Golders Green Cremetorium on Thursday, May 24th and in addition to the family mourners the following were present:

Messrs. Robson senior and junior (Stephen Grant and Joseph Lang Limited), E. Redfern (Messrs Westley-Richards & Co., Limited), Mr Mansfield (Messrs Holland & Holland), Messrs Dickens and Dover (Imperial Chemical Industries), H. Varge (Salter & Varge), J. Wilkes (Messrs Wilkes & Co.), G. F. Whitfield (William Evans & Co.), W. Howe (Grant & Lang), F. A. Redmond (*Shooting Times*), Messrs Brown, Stillman, Henderson, Claudoir, Thompson, Harman and the whole of the staff of Boss & Co. The following Brethren from the Brent Lodge were also present:

R. Moore, A. E. Taylor, J. H. Thomas (New Normal Ammunition Company), W. C. Dickson, H. C. K. Rogers, H. Griffiths, J. T. Meek, G. Hancock, W. T. Sweet, E. C. P. Clow, J. I. Moore, E. G. Steward, M. Goldstone and A. J. Delnevo.

To replace Sam and to ensure family continuity, Sam's second son, Alec Robertson, a gunmaker at Boss, was appointed a director of Boss & Co., on 28th May 1935. This meant that the directors were now Bob Robertson, the remaining "young governor", May Rennie and Alec Robertson.

During this period, around thirty-eight men were employed at Boss. By the Workmen's Compensation Acts and Factory Acts, Boss had to fill in a return regard-

The photograph of Sam Robertson which appeared in the *Shooting Times* of 26th May 1934.

A Boss & Co outing in the late 1930s. Known personnel are: 1. G. Bates, 3. E. Pither, 4. Bill Lees, 5. Bill Lees (snr), 6. Charlie Austin, 9. Mr. Lawrence (Bryants Gun Cases), 10. Harry Parry, 11. Bill Wise, 15. Ernie Nobbs, 17. Arthur Sanderson, 19. Adam Speaight, 20. Alec Robertson, 21. Mr. Dover (ICI representative), 24. George Felix, 25. Bob Robertson, 27. Bob Henderson, 29. Fred Oliver, 31. Len Adams, 35. Jack Sumner, 36. Jack Rennie.

ing men employed, wages and hours worked. Some of these returns still exist to give us a very accurate picture of the firm in the mid to late 1930s. In 1937 for example:

Occupation	Numbers employed	Total salaries/ wages
Clerks	2	£416
Gunmakers	33	£6,915
Cartridge loaders	3	£345
	—	—
	38	£7,676

Of these workers, nine were employed at 41 Albemarle Street and twenty-nine at the factory in Lexington Street. Seven of these workers were aged under twenty-one. The ordinary hours of labour were fifty-four hours per week. About one-quarter of the workforce did regular overtime amounting to an extra seven hours per week. The nature of the work is described as in 41 Albemarle Street, "cleaning and repairing sporting guns and cartridge loading", and in

the factory in Lexington Street, "building and repairing sporting guns". To us today, the regular hours of work appear very long but, by the standards of the time, they were the norm for skilled workers.

One happy event of the late 1930s was a celebratory dinner which took place in 1938 to celebrate 50 years of gunmaking by Bob Robertson. Bob had begun his apprenticeship in 1888 under his father pre-Boss days in the factory at 4 Dansey Yard. On the 11th July 1938, a "Jubilee Dinner" was held at the Holborn Restuarant, to which all Boss employees and selected guests were invited. Entertainment was provided by Cyril Shields, conjurer, Jock Walker, Scottish comedian, and at the piano Tommy Best.

In late 1939, the lease was up on the factory at 6/8/10 Lexington Street. Once again the factory had to move. A new site was found at 34 Osnaburgh Street, off Euston Road, and here the factory would remain until 1953. The factory was shared with Bill Wakefield, who used to be a barrel-maker with Boss. Bill Wakefield, when he worked for Boss, primarily made O/U barrels. He asked for a wage rise and casually inferred that, if he were to leave, Boss might find difficulty in making O/U barrels. Bob Henderson the factory manager was the wrong type of person to try that tack with and Bill was forced to put into practice his inference. He then set himself up as a barrel-maker working in the same yard as Boss in Osnaburgh Street.

Trade depression was not the only cloud to permeate the decade of the 1930s. This was the era of the belligerent dictators espousing an evil avarice dressed up in a new political creed termed fascism. Faced with such blatant aggression, appeasement seemed the panacea to a Western world still reeling from the trauma of World War I. High appeasement at Munich in 1938, and the subsequent debacle in its aftermath, caused a widespread change in attitude and a realisation that Hitler could only be stopped by force – a pragmatic *vis contra vim*. Rearmament was speeded up and the country prepared for a war, the only question now being when would that war actually begin.

This time the country was under no illusion as to what this would involve. There would be no "over by Christmas" optimism as prevailed in the Great War, it would be out and out total war requiring the participation of all in resolve and resources to win.

In the Great War, at first Boss attempted to carry on as usual. In the second war there could be no question of this in an economy geared to maximum wartime effort. Bob Robertson devoted much time and energy in writing to the Ministry of Supply, Royal Small Arms Factory, aircraft firms, etc., to ascertain whether Boss with their intrinsic skills could be of assistance. He was very successful. All the pre-war staff were kept on, working on military contracts, and demand was such that an additional Boss factory had to be opened up in Euston Road.

Boss managed to continue building sporting guns for the duration, albeit on a much reduced scale. War work came first and in any spare time the gunmakers reverted to their original trade. In their returns to the Ministry of Labour, war work was recorded as being 99% of total Boss output. Cartridges likewise continued to be loaded, again much reduced, and there are many orders detailed for serving officers abroad.

With their gunmaking skills, the factory in Osnaburgh Street received a contract for manufacturing blades and foresights for the Lee-Enfield No. 1 rifle. In addition they made extractors for the Lee-Enfield No. 4 rifle, e.g. on 16th February 1942 Boss received an order value £77,850 for extractors at 1s.6/7d. each. Magazines for various rifles were also constructed. Work of a more mundane nature included assembling Hotchkiss machine guns, assembling Lanchester machine guns and degreasing and reconditioning Pattern P.14 rifles.

To cope with the increased war production, new machinery had to be installed. New lathes and milling machines were supplied as were auto-saws, electric welders, etc. Much of this equipment was used by Boss until very recently, easily recognisable by the War Department arrow stamp! During the early part of 1942 it was apparent that the Osnaburgh Street factory was not big enough to satiate Boss's wartime production. A new factory was opened up closeby at 143 1/2 Euston Road. This factory did work of a very different nature. The work done here was blacking metal parts like aircraft instrument panels by the Brunofix method. Similar work was in anodising and dipping aeroplane parts to resist corrosion. In the latter process, Boss did much work for the De-Havilland Aircraft Company. Equipment entirely new to Boss & Co was installed for the blacking and anodising. Large gas heated tanks, degreasing tanks, cold washing tanks, paint dipping tanks and hot air ovens filled the new factory. Most of the blacking work was sub-contracted by the Metal Box Co., Chequers Works, North Circular Road, Palmers Green, London. On account of the fact that much of this work was relatively unskilled, females entered the Boss factory for the first time!

Around eight women worked in the factory on this blacking process. One of these girls, nicknamed "Bubbles" for some reason, was pregnant in mid-war. Jim Iredale, the single trigger specialist, had transferred his skills to helping with finishing bayonets. Carrying a load of bayonets one day from one part of the factory to the other, he inadvertently bumped into "Bubbles". "Watch out!" some wag shouted, "Bubbles is going to burst."

In the autumn of 1940 the German airforce began to bomb London as part of a change in tactics, the infamous Blitz initiated by Goering to sap the will of the civilian populace and thereby bring an end to the war. The Blitz lasted some eight months from September 1940 to May 1941. Day raids became infrequent and night attacks commonplace. London was bombed virtually every night in late 1940 by an average of 200 aeroplanes. The loss of life was smaller than had been anticipated, but damage to buildings was extensive. There were several raids in early 1941 culminating in a major attack on May 10th in which the Chamber of the House of Commons was destroyed and all but one of the main-line railway stations temporarily put out of action. It was during the May 10th raid that Boss's factory in Osnaburgh Street suffered a fair amount of damage. The Germans were using high explosive bombs designed to blow in windows and blast off roofs to let in the elements and cause widespread damage. Such a bomb dropped in the early hours of the morning in the vacinity of Osnaburgh Street and blew in all the skylight windows and knocked off several slates on the factory roof. Boss were indeed very lucky to escape from major damage during this Blitz. Forty-one Albemarle Street was unscathed although there was extensive damage in Albemarle Street itself.

Promoted in 1940 as company secretary of a firm engaged in war work, Fred Oliver assumed he was in a reserved occupation. However, in the spring of 1944, the inexorable steamroller in the shape of the War Office sent Fred his call-up papers. Bob Robertson was furious on account of the war work in which the firm were engaged and wrote a letter to the War Office requesting the deferrment of Fred because he worked single handed in connection with book-keeping, wages, income tax, etc for the two factories. He stressed that Boss would find it practically impossible to continue if he were lost. The War Office replied that it now understood the situation and Fred's call-up was deferred.

Most of the gunmakers were deferred due to the nature of the work in which they were involved. This was by no means automatic and the position was regularly reviewed. As a result, Jack Rennie was called up and spent much of the war in the army in Egypt. Bob Henderson's son, Roy, was an early conscript and became one of the veterans of Dunkirk.

In the early days of the Home Guard, when they were known as the Local Defence Volunteers, they were regarded with a certain amount of derision due to their paucity of arms and the resultant improvisation to which this led. Arms supply naturally had priority with the regular forces. To ameliorate this shortfall, the length and breadth of the country was scoured for arms which could have a belligerent use. Boss & Co., as gunmakers, were viewed as a cornucopia. On the 5th November 1941, the following items were requisitioned from the shop in Albermarle Street and the factory in Osnaburgh Street: 12 rifles, 5 revolvers, 19 12-bore shotguns and 2800 rounds of .22 ammunition, worth in total £777.12s. Out of interest, guns nos. 4683/4, nos. 4261/2, no. 5649 and no. 4496 were part of this requisition order.

An unfortunate incident occured during the war which could have had very serious consequences. Alec Robertson liked a drink after work and one evening in a jovial frame of mind was waiting on the platform of the underground for the tube to take him home. A couple of Canadian soldiers, enjoying a night out in much the same frame of mind as Alec, struck up a conversation with him. A bit of banter ensued as to the relative fighting merits of the British and Canadian armies and the end result was that one of the Canadians punched Alec. Alec staggered back and fell onto the track. The Canadians ran off but fortunately one or two onlookers managed to pull Alec off the track before a train appeared. Unfortunately this was not the end of Alec's troubles. His foot had jammed in the track as he

fell over and his ankle broke. He was taken to hospital and his ankle set in plaster. For some reason the ankle did not set properly, complications set in and the end result was that Alec had to have his foot amputated. A wooden foot was fitted and for the rest of his life this wooden foot was a Godsend to the Boss gunmakers. Whenever Alec visited the factory they could hear the clump of his foot before he opened the door – naturally Alec was always impressed by the constant industrious attitude of his gunmakers!

Exactly who did what at Boss during the war is listed in a questionaire required by the Ministry of Labour and National Service dated 17th August 1943. "Please forward full details to cover all employees on staff list giving name, date of birth, hours of work and precise duties of each employee."

Name	Nature Of Work Done	Average No. Of Hours Worked Weekly
Bob Henderson	Gunmaker	47
G. Griffin	Porter	57
Fred Oliver	Secretary	59
Sidney Earl	Blacking and Anodising	59
Lilian Plaskett	Blacking and Anodising	53
John Carroll	Blacking and Anodising	53
John Middleton	Blacking and Anodising	53
Eliza Cole	Blacking and Anodising	60
Sylvia Holloway	Blacking and Anodising	60
Bridget Hayes	Blacking and Anodising	60
Emmy Downing	Blacking and Anodising	60
Lilian Winderbanks	Blacking and Anodising	53
Mary Deverill	Blacking and Anodising	53
Mary Middleton	Blacking and Anodising	53
Jim Iredale	Setting and Operating Shaping Machine	56 1/2
Arthur Walters	Filing Extractors	60
Walter Grant	Milling Machine Operator	56 1/2
William Walters	Milling Machine Operator	60
Charlie Austin	Milling Machine Operator	56 1/2
Bill Lees	Boring	53
Dick Adams	Filing Extractors	47
Charlie Padgett	Milling Machine Operator	59
Bill Wakefield	Tool Maker	57
Edwin Pither	Milling Machine Operator	56 1/2
John Perkins	Assembling Lanchester Machine Guns	56 1/2
Bill Johnson	Filing Extractors	47
William Baker	Assembling Lanchester Machine Guns	53
George Steggles	Milling Machine Operator	56 1/2
Arthur Sanderson	Milling Machine Operator	56 1/2
Henry Edwards	Milling Machine Operator	59
Sydney Gall	Milling Machine Operator	56 1/2
Matthew Busuttell	Drilling Machine Operator	56 1/2
Bill Wise	Charge Hand	68
Adam Speaight	Foreman	68

Only Bob Henderson remained building guns. Due to his superior skills, he built most of the guns from start

Year	Employers	New guns built	Cartridges sold	Cleaning guns	Repairs	Shooting ground income
1948	21	14 value £4,645	186,000 value £3,284	£1,305		£1,917
1949	21	17 value £6,125	£3,915	£1,444	£1,590	£1,754
1950	21	19 value £6,996	£4,631	£1,551	£2,272	£2,001
1951	23	21 value £8,813	£6,822	£1,571	£2,995	£1,200
1954	19	18 value £8,496	£3,268	£1,788	£2,789	£2,102

to finish during the war. The administrative staff were cut right down to four, eg, Arthur Sanderson the shop manager now operated a milling machine. All the blackers and anodisers were extra unskilled staff, mostly women, brought in for the duration. Compared to the World War I situation, when around half the Boss workforce disappeared, hardly any of the gunmakers were lost due to the skilled nature of war work in which they were involved.

At the beginning of 1945 it was obvious that it would only be a matter of time before the war ended. The Ministry of Supply began to run down its war-time contracts and when the German forces surrendered unconditionally on the 7th May 1945, the need for war work came to an end. Blacking and anodising ceased, the women employed released and the gunmakers returned to the business that they knew best of all. It would not be an easy metamorphosis – the world of the late 1940s was very different from the pre-war world. The remaining young governor, Bob Robertson, realised that selling best quality guns in this different world would not be easy. In July 1945 he wrote a letter, shown opposite, to all previous customers to drum up potential business.

This was the "Age of Austerity" and demand of luxury items like sporting guns was low. During the war financial limits were not to stand in the way of physical war effort – the war was to be financed as far as possible out of taxation rather than borrowing. Income tax increased rapidly during the war and new taxes like purchase tax were introduced. Post war, the Labour government of Clement Attlee, returned to power in 1945, continued this high taxation policy. Due to the fact that it was a socialist government with a highly progressive income tax, some of Boss's customers in higher income brackets were paying 19s.6d. in the £1. Harold Nicholson, in his *Diaries*, was shocked to think that he would "have to walk and live a Woolworth life hereafter". This was an absurd exaggeration but undoubtedly the gist was an underlying fear for many of the wealthy at this time. This high re-distributive taxation, coupled with the Labour Party's commitment to nationalisation and a policy of greater social justice, meant that Boss & Co. could never revert to the pre-war situation. It was indeed fortunate that

Boss & Co. had been successful during the war to tide them over the difficult post-war period.

The upshot was that when Boss reverted to gun production, orders were far fewer than in the pre-war period. In addition to the problems of the home market, European market demand was low due to the ravages of war and American demand was poor due to the extent to which America participated in the war. The Census of Production Statistics show the changes which had taken place (see above).

As a comparison, approximately forty people had been employed and around seventy guns produced per annum pre-war.

Bob Robertson went off to the United States to renew his pre-war contacts. The price of a Boss gun after taxes and import duties was too high for most Americans and orders were not as profligate as before.

Another effect of the war that would continue for serveral years was a trade imbalance. The United States alone was able to produce commodities which the rest of the world wanted and destruction elsewhere did not allow other countries to offer much in return. This resulted in a rampant dollar shortage. Dollars became "hard currency" and it became impossible for Britain to achieve a trade balance. In July 1947, as part of a loan agreement with the U.S.A., Britain agreed to make sterling "convertible". The exacerbated the trade imbalance as the rest of the world immediately began to convert sterling into dollars. Due to the size of Britain's deficit, she was forced to devalue the pound in September 1949, a staggeringly high devaluation reducing the pound from £4.03 to £2.80. This encouraged inflation with the result that new gun prices had to be increased. Coupled with the purchase tax this further reduced home demand. On the credit side exports of guns became a better proposition with the new exchange rate.

To take account of these new changes Alec Robertson wrote to Boss's sole agent in the U.S.A., Abercrombie and Fitch of Madison Avenue, New York. The price of new guns was adjusted to £300 for a side-by-side, £420 for an O/U gun, new side-by-side barrels £75, O/U barrels £110, full pistol grip £6.10s., gold name plate £8.10s., rubber recoil pad £5, ventilated rib £20, matted top rib £10, selective single

Boss & Co Ltd
GUNMAKERS.
DIRECTORS:
R. D. ROBERTSON.
M. RENNIE.
A. ROBERTSON.

SHOOTING GROUND:
BARNET BY-PASS,
ROWLEY GREEN, HERTS.
TELEPHONE: BARNET 3287

FACTORY:
34, OSNABURGH STREET.
N.W. I.

TELEGRAMS: GUNBARRELS, PICCY, LONDON.
TELEPHONE: REGENT 0711.
" " 1127.

41, Albemarle Street,
London,
W.1. July, 1945.

SPECIAL NOTICE.

The European War having now been successfully concluded we are released from Government Contracts and are, once again, able to turn our attention to the manufacture and repair of Sporting Guns.

In view of the approaching Shooting Season we respectfully suggest that it would be to your advantage to have your guns overhauled, and we should be most pleased to carry out this service for you. We have been permitted to retain our highly skilled Staff and all orders will receive the same high standard of work and the same prompt attention as in the pre-war years. We also hold a good selection of second-hand guns which we should be pleased to show you.

Our Shooting Ground on the Barnet By-pass, which has been carried on in a limited way during the war, is now operating and coaching by Mr. Bob Robertson and the old staff can be arranged by appointment.

We should like to have the opportunity of being of service to you in these respects and can assure you of our personal attention to all your requirements.

R. D. ROBERTSON,
Managing Director.

The letter written by Bob Robertson to customers in July 1945 to generate business after the conclusion of World War II.

trigger £35, restocking side-by-side £35, restocking O/U £45. For the home market only, Boss were now forced to charge £40 extra for a single trigger – previously this was at no extra cost. For the American market, it was felt that they could not justify this extra charge and in reality a Boss single trigger was some £40 cheaper than single trigger guns produced by other makers. Another departure in the unstable economic climate was that Boss were forced to ask for a deposit when a gun was ordered – such was the cost of materials involved in best gun manufacture.

The late 1940s were indeed an age of austerity with

The certificate issued to Boss after they were chosen to display their sporting guns in the Festival of Britain, 1951.

rationing, shortages in the shops, etc., whilst at the same time people were being continually urged to work harder. Many people agreed with Herbert Morrison when he said in 1950 that people deserved a pat on the back for what they had done and for what they had suffered in the immediate post war years. This was the justification for the 1951 Festival of Britain. At first this

was intended as a commemoration of the Great Exhibition of 1851, but some people saw it as a chance to show the hard-pressed British many of the new materials and goods that would soon be available. It was decided to build a Festival Hall and display on the South Bank of the Thames in London. On 3rd May 1951 King George VI, speaking from the steps of St Paul's, declared the Festival open on a grey drizzly day. When the Festival ended on 7th October 1951, over 8 million people had gone to see this display of Britain's future.

Just as Thomas Boss had exhibited in the 1851 Great Exhibition, so did Boss & Co., in the 1951 Festival of Britain. Side by sides and O/U's were displayed to prove to the world that even after the ravages of war, British gunmaking was still the best in the world.

On 15th August 1951 the remaining young governor, Bob Robertson, died. He died in the hospital of St John's and St Elizabeth's, Marylebone, London from a peptic ulcer. He was seventy-seven years of age and lived alone in the family home at 17 Graham Road, Hendon, his wife Mabel having pre-deceased him on 18th January 1950. Bob and Mabel had two daughters, Ruby and Maisie, hence this line of the gunmaking family did not continue. In his Will of 4th April 1950, he gave his bowling woods to his friend Francis Harman, and devided his estate valued at

Bill Lees (shooting coach), Bob Robertson and Jack Rennie at the shooting ground 3rd April 1951.

£17,155.0s.3d equally between his two daughters, Maisie and Ruby.

With Bob's demise, a new director would be required. Before his death, he had nominated his friend Francis Harman, who was Boss's accountant, as new director. This new directorship took effect on 11th September 1951. Francis Harman would remain a director of Boss until his death in 1965. On the same date Jack Rennie was made a director of the firm. At this time Jack lived in London Colney near St Albans, Hertfordshire and was working as a shooting instructor at the shooting ground.

With Bob's death, the young governors were no more and so ended the second generation of Robertson gunmakers at Boss. It had been an auspicious period at Boss since the young governors had taken over from their father in 1917. All three sons, John, Sam and Bob, were fully trained gunmakers and had continued the tradition established by their father and Thomas Boss of building best guns only. The fact that they were trained

Bob and Mabel Robertson in the garden of their home, 17 Graham Road, Hendon, North London, *circa* **1948.**

gunmakers in charge of their own business was unusual in the first half of the 20th century. Most gunmaking businesses by this time were run by administrators. It would now be up to Alec Robertson, the third generation, to run the firm.

CHAPTER ELEVEN

HORSE SHOE ALLEY AND BEYOND

During the year of the Coronation, 1953, the Boss factory had to move again. The lease on the old factory at 34 Osnaburgh Street was up. New premises were found South of the River Thames at Southwark, in an old Victorian factory situated in Horse Shoe Alley. Here the Boss factory would remain for some twenty years until 1973.

Dave Cox was employed by Boss as an actioner in this factory from 1954 to 1968. It is to him that I am indebted for much of the information contained within this chapter on the gunmakers and the techniques employed in building Boss guns in the 1950s and 1960s.

Dave Cox began his gunmaking career in 1950 as an errand boy cum dogsbody with Holland and Holland. He then progressed to their workshop and learned the rudiments of gunmaking. He decided that he would like to work for Boss and against all advice applied for a position. Boss at this time had such a reputation that legend had it that they would only employ members of their own family, relations of existing gunmakers, or gunmakers upon recommendation. To work for Boss was analagous to going to the correct school – there was a certain snobbery associated with them. Three tries later, Dave procured an interview with Alec Robertson in 41 Albemarle Street. The interview turned out to be something of an anticlimax – "You want to work here, Cox – right start on Monday morning at 8 am", was the crux of the interview. Dave has always remarked on the happy nature of the factory at Horse Shoe Alley in the 1950s and 1960s. Even in the trade it was known as "the happy factory". Today Dave has a pedigree labrador called "Boss" – so called due to its combination of pedigree and genial temperament!

The factory at Horse Shoe Alley was on the south side of Southwark Bridge. It was a private alley owned by Barclay's Brewery. The factory itself was situated on the top floor of an old Victorian warehouse and, even though it was the second half of the 20th century, the factory and machinery harked back to the Victorian era.

When you entered the factory the first thing that became very evident was the incessant clattering and tick-tocking of the machinery. The reason for this constant background noise was that all the machinery was driven in an antiquated manner by one electric motor turning two shafts at ceiling height. Pullies and belts led off these shafts to drive lathes, milling machines, power saws, grinders, etc. To turn on a particular machine, you pulled the appropriate wooden lever that would then engage the belt from the overhead shaft. This system was so antiquated that, when Boss left the factory in 1973, a museum asked them if they could have all the old shafts and machinery. Unfortunately, before anything could be agreed, the building burned down and all was destroyed. Somehow or other nobody objected to this antique machinery. The guns were being produced in exactly the same way as they had been at the beginning of the 20th century, exactly the same skills were required and on account of the fact that the machinery had been so well made, it was still quite up to the job. To give an example of this machinery, the milling machine bought in 1909 for milling O/U actions was still known in the 1960s as "the new machine"! The hours in the factory, 8 am to 6 pm, were typical of the period.

The following men worked in the Horse Shoe Alley factory *circa* 1955. It is remarkable how many of them or their relations feature in the earlier list of the Edwardian era in Chapter 9:

Bill Wise, the factory foreman worked on bolt and lever work. Bill was full of life and well known as a raconteur and for his wit and sense of humour. There was never a dull moment in the factory with Bill. He joined Boss after World War I and became their foreman around 1955. Bill was an excellent teacher and imparted his gunmaking knowledge in a very thorough manner to all his pupils. Unfortunately, Bill would not take on apprentices in the 1950s because he regarded them as being too much trouble. Later in the 1960s, when it was pointed out that this would cause problems for the future of gunmaking, he relented and apprentices were taken on.

Jim Iredale's speciality was single triggers and ejectors. Jim had begun with Boss in November 1915. His father had connections with the gun trade being a tool and accessory maker.

Charlie Austin was an action filer and like Jim Iredale he had a very long career with Boss beginning at the end of World War I. He had a reputation as a first-class filer and for some odd reason always wore carpet slippers whilst at his bench. He was a keen golfer and believed in the merits of self education, assiduously studying the *Readers' Digest* in his breaks!

Edwin Pither was another action filer. Edwin's father, William Pither, had been the foreman at Boss during the 1880s in the era of Edward Paddison. Edwin himself had joined Boss as an apprentice in 1913. Regarded as one of the cleanest filers in the trade, he returned to Boss after a long absence in 1956.

Doug Baylis was a stocker. He began his career in the late 1930s and left in the early 1960s.

Ernie Noble, a barrel filer, began with Boss in the late 1920s. He came from the Nobbs family that had worked for years with Purdey. His grandfather, William Nobbs, had invented the Purdey single trigger, the subject of the Robertson/Purdey patent dispute of 1906. To comply with a Will he changed his name to Noble. Once when a top strap was being forged he told the story that he saw his father break one off with his bare hands. Ever ready with the fast retort, Bill Wise proclaimed, "I am not surprised, your father was known as the butcher of Purdey's!"

Alf Grant was a machinist. Like Ernie Noble, Alf had been with Boss for a considerable number of years eventually retiring in the late 1950s. The gunmakers at Horse Shoe Alley were fond of finding soubriquets for one and all due to some past misdemeanour or unfortunate incident. Alf's was "Bush Ranger" due to a failed emigration attempt to Australia!

Adam Speaight was another machinist. He began with Boss in 1897 as a boy aged 13. He must have machined every O/U action from 1909 until he retired around 1965. He was known in the factory as "the mate", in typical Cockney rhyming slang. He was incorrigible, full of apocryphal stories and a salesman's dream for Scotch whisky. The Gaelic word for whisky "Usige Beatha" meaning water of life was very apt since Adam

The presentation to Adam Speaight, 17th October 1957, to mark his sixty years with Boss. From left to right, Roy Henderson, Bill Wise, Edwin Pither, Charlie Austin, Adam Speaight, Jack Rennie, Dave Cox, Arthur Sanderson, Bill Allen, Doug Baylis, Jim Iredale, Sid Gaul, Ernie Noble.

remained as fit as a fiddle when he retired aged around 85. In addition he was an avid snuff-taker that helped contribute to the spit and sawdust style factory. Some of the gunmakers put chalk rings on the floor round the results of Adam's nebular activity. Adam very genuinely complained to one and all about the "bloody mess" that was being made on the factory floor!

Everything that Adam did was "special". He went on special holidays, and even though he was completely bald his original hair was special. He came to work one day with an ex army shirt on and upon everyone admiring it, mentioning that it would be ideal for work and, asked from where he had obtained it, he said, "Oh no, you won't get one like this, it's a special officer's shirt."

To mark his sixty years with Boss, a presentation was made to Adam in the factory on 17th October 1957. He was presented with an inscribed gold wrist-watch. Two directors, Jack Rennie and Arthur Sanderson, made the presentation. Adam, well into his seventies in the early 1960s, had got into the habit of coming into work late, around 10 am. By then he was the owner of two special caps, one was for wearing at work and the other was for going home in. He would open the door at 10 am, bang his shoulder on the door-post to give him momentum to reach the hat and coat racks, whereupon he would change caps in one special two-handed movement. On the day he retired in 1965, he entered in his usual manner at 10 am. After changing caps he looked around and said to Dave Cox, "Bugger it old son, I've had enough." At that he changed caps again and went home.

Sid Gaul was a finisher. He had begun work with Boss in the late 1920s and had retired by the 1980s.

Roy Henderson's forte was in stocking, primarily forends. He was the youngest son of Bob Henderson. Roy's nickname was "Poopdeck". When boys, in the 1930s, Roy along with his brother visited the factory wearing sailor suits. In addition Roy's brother had some medals pinned to his chest. Up went the cry, "Blimey, it's Captain Poopdeck and the Grand Mussolini." Just as Roy was known for ever more as "Poopdeck", his brother was always known as "Musso"! On one occasion, Bob Henderson came to Horse Shoe Alley and looked at his son "Poopdeck" who was making hard work out of a simple job. Bob said, "Son, the night your mother gave birth to you she must have eaten a crab, and you have been crabby ever since then"!

Bill Allen was a stocker who was the grandson of William Adams who co-invented with John Robertson the Boss single trigger. He served his time at Purdeys because of rivalry between his grandfather and Bob Henderson. He came to Boss around 1956 and was known as "Corncap" because he resembled the scruffy character in the Carnation corncap advert!

Harry Clark was a finisher. At one stage he introduced his elder brother into the firm. This brother lasted one day under Alf Grant, then resigned. His reason was, "I'm not working there any more, it made me sweat." Consequently his soubriquet was "Sweaty".

The final man in the factory was *Jack Rennie* who specialised in barrel-making. Jack was the grandson of John Robertson Jnr. By this time Jack was a director of the firm, having taken his turn at every aspect of the Boss business. He had worked at the shooting ground firing clay traps and maintaining the grounds. He was strong and well built and was always in demand when a new ditch or pond had to be created. He had even worked in the shop loading and doing general gunsmithing.

So much for the men in the factory. At the shop in 41 Albemarle Street, the following men worked:

The infamous *Bob Henderson* now worked in the shop. Getting on a bit, he found it difficult to climb the stairs in the factory in Horse Shoe Alley, so he transferred to the shop to build his share of the guns. Still highly skilled, still hot tempered and still very enthusiastic about the guns he produced, it would not be long until he retired and emigrated to Australia.

Alec Robertson, in addition to his managerial tasks as director, built the single trigger in the shop. Alec was regarded by one and all as a very decent chap. He

Arthur Sanderson, *circa* **1960, the shop manager.**

Fred Oliver, the President of Honda and Arthur Sanderson *circa* 1955 in the Albemarle Street shop.

visited the factory every day at 3 pm. Round about 2.30 pm, the phone would ring, Bill Wise would pick up the phone and Alec would say, "I'm on my way." "He's on his way," Bill would shout to all the gunmakers. Some time later they would hear the clump of Alec's artificial foot, the door would creak open and Alec entered to find all the men hard at work!

Arthur Sanderson, known as "Sandy", was the shop manager having been with the firm since 1913. He was regarded by everyone as a good fellow and was very well liked. He wore a white apron in the shop and had the habit of stroking his chin when he anticipated some event. Carrying on the very important tradition of shop manager at Boss, at 11.00 am he would rub his hands briskly on the bib of his apron, stroke his chin and say, "Well, Bill, time for the Guinness!"

Bill Harris started with Boss in the 1930s working in the shop and, apart from running for Guinness, loaded cartridges. Bill was very impressed by the clientele of Boss & Co. and even when answering the telephone Bill would bow – "Yes, M'lord (bow), very good M'lord (bow)". The grander the title, the deeper the bow!

And last but not least there was *Fred Oliver* the Company Secretary. By the 1950s Fred had clocked up over thirty years with Boss. Today in his eighties Fred still works in the Dover Street shop having now recorded over seventy years.

The control of Boss by the third generation of Robertson in the personage of Alec Robertson did not last long after the demise of Bob Robertson, the second generation, in 1951. On 13th December 1954 aged sixty, Alec Robertson died from a heart attack in the Middlesex Hospital, London. He had suffered a heart attack at his home at 2 Beechwood Hall, Regent's Park Road and had been rushed to hospital. The heart attack had been massive and nothing could be done.

In the 31st December edition of the *Shooting Times,* his death was noted:

Death of Mr A. Robertson. It is with profound regret that we have to record the death of Mr Alexander Robertson, the chairman and managing-director of Messrs, Boss & Co. Limited, the well known gunmakers of 41 Albemarle Street, London.

In his Will, Alec left £3,178.19s.3d., the entire proceeds going to his wife, Phyllis, on account of the fact that they had no children. To make good the loss of Alec, Arthur Sanderson the shop manager was created a director on 27th January 1955. With no Robertsons now in the firm, it was felt that Boss & Co. lacked the family continuity and direction so vital to its existence. Accordingly a nephew of Alec Robertson, John Gilbert Robertson, was appointed a director on 8th November 1956. John Robertson was a chemical sales manager with no gunmaking background, but he felt that he had to take on a directorship of the firm to ensure the continuation of Robertson involvement. His commitment was part time and he did not actually work in the shop. It was a wise decision and would lead directly to his son Tim Robertson becoming a director of the firm in 1990 and subsequently managing-director in December 1993.

The year 1960 saw the Boss shop having to move again. The lease on 41 Albemarle Street had run out and was not to be renewed. New premises were found close by, parallel to Albemarle Street, and on the 15th July 1960 Boss & Co. moved to 13/14 Cork Street. The old Albemarle Street shop was demolished and in its place a new building was erected in typical design of the swinging sledge hammer sixties. The Cork Street shop was an impressive shop with a superb eye-catching frontage. It was larger than the Albemarle Street premises and afforded spacious accommodation for the cornucopian clutter accumulated over the last one hundred and thirty years. Fortunately this shop still survives today, albeit in the very different guise of a wine bar!

In November 1965, Francis Harman, the accountant and a director of Boss, died. His place was taken by the company secretary, Fred Oliver, who became a director on 1st December 1965 – not bad for a lad who had begun loading cartridges for Boss in 1922! In the mid 1960s, change of major proportions occurred when it was decided to stop making the O/U gun. It was expensive to make and Boss were finding it difficult to get gunmakers skilled in O/U production to build them. It was also the time when cheaper foreign O/Us were flooding the market primarily for clay shooting and the O/U tended to be associated with this type of gun and shooting. Consequently there was a drop in demand for it.

Although not as a consequence of the demise of the

13/14 Cork Street, *circa* 1965.

O/U, but rather as a part of the general trend at Boss, the 1970s and 1980s were rather depressed years. Many of the old hands like Bill Wise and Bill Allan reached retirement age and left. Due to the fact that hardly any apprentices had been taken on, there was a real problem in trying to obtain skilled gunmakers. The number of gunmakers employed by Boss dropped to around eight. Very few new guns were constructed in the 1970s and 1980s and it was really only repair work and cartridge sales which kept the firm going.

On 31st January 1973, Arthur Sanderson resigned, having been with Boss since before World War I. For a short time, Jack Rennie's brother, Alastair Rennie, was a director, before he too resigned to live in Australia. Clearly someone else was required to help manage the business and, on March 13th 1981, Tony Lokatis, a friend of the Robertson family, was appointed as director.

One factor that caused the firm grave problems in the 1970s was the high inflation particular to that decade. Because hand-built guns took so long to make, it was impossible to quote a firm price and many customers backed out as the costs continually spiralled.

In 1973, again due to the expiration of the lease, Boss had to leave their factory in Horse Shoe Alley. They moved very close by to 8 Holyrood Street, Southwark, the factory that they still occupy today. Some ten years later, in 1982, the lease on the shop in Cork Street

expired. Incredibly, new premises were found in Dover Street, no. 13 to be precise, the exact same shop the firm had occupied between 1908 and 1930. To this well-known address the firm moved on 26th March, 1982 (see plate 45).

In reality in the 1980s Boss were trading on past reputation. There was every possibility that the firm would go the way of many other famous gunmaking names and be bought up or considerably changed into some outlet for clothing and country pursuits with the building of guns definitely second best.

Alec Robertson died in 1954 and until Tim Robertson entered the firm in 1990, there had been no day to day involvement by a family member of the

---

BOSS & CO. LTD.
owing to the expiration of our lease
we are now moving to

13, Dover Street,
London W.1.

As from 26th March 1982

A trade card informing about the move to Dover Street in 1982.

shareholders. Tim Robertson is the great nephew of Alec Robertson, son of Sam Robertson, son of John Robertson. Despite his father being the Chairman of Boss & Co., Tim had only vaguely known of the gun firm as a young boy and instead pursued a business career in science. In the late 1980s, Tim became aware of his father's concern for the future of the firm, manifested by the possibility of both the executive directors retiring and no successor to continue the business. The fact that his family had played such an important role in the history of Boss, coupled with the name of Boss in gunmaking, meant that it was a challenge he found irresistable.

A hands-on approach to the firm was adopted with daily visits to the factory to encourage, chastise and learn the business of gunmaking. After consulting the workforce, the factory tools and machinery were suitably modernised without inherently changing the handmaking techniques. The majority of the original hardened steel guages are still in use today. These are used in conjunction with modern micrometers and any innovations that the young workforce have developed. The original barrel boring bench is still in use. Of all the "best gunmakers" in Britain today, Boss are by far the most traditional, using techniques that would be entirely familiar to John Robertson at the turn of the century. Boss guns today are hand built, not "hand built".

One very fortunate factor in the turn around of Boss has been a revival of interest in O/U guns. Sportsmen the world over have now revised their opinion of O/U guns for game shooting and they are in good demand. On account of the fact that the Boss O/U gun is regarded as the best O/U, there has been considerable interest in it. It is heartening to know that the Boss O/U is very much back in production, accounting for the majority of Boss gun orders today. There was a time in the 1980s when second-hand Boss O/Us achieved very high prices because it was thought that they would never be made again. O/U rifles are also being produced in virtually any calibre required by a customer.

The renaissance of the Boss O/U has only been possible after a considerable amount of thought, time and investment. The nature of the Boss over-and-under design allows for the smallest margin of error in their manufacture of any of the best English sporting guns. This ensures that the gun is hand-made throughout, taking a very high number of man hours to produce, whilst making each one entirely individual. At the time it was designed, labour charges were relatively lower than they are today. In addition the competition to make the best over-and-under was extremely fierce among the rival gunmakers, not only in regard to their function but also concerning overall beauty and low weight. The

Boss design has concentrated on these aspects, above all else sacrificing time, difficulty and commerciality. This would explain why fewer than 500 have ever been produced – always demanding very high prices – either new or second-hand, selling predominantly to North America.

Tim Robertson is adamant that Boss is all about guns and quality. They might sell you a cleaning rod or gun case in Dover Street today, but you will not find a waxed jacket or chocolate cartridges anywhere. Very few guns per year are built – usually around ten. Prices begin at £26,000 for a side-by-side and £42,000 for an O/U. The guns take many months to make, yet the waiting list is long. Other firms will produce guns cheaper and in less time. The reason for this is simple. Boss guns today are made to exactly the same standards as in the past with absolutely no compromise on quality. The majority of the so-called hand-built English guns today make considerable use of machinery in their construction. From the outside, they appear to be the perfect hand-built article, yet strip any gun down and it is apparent why their costs are less.

The shop in Dover Street typifies an old establishment steeped in tradition. When the firm returned to Dover Street in 1982 after having last vacated it in 1930,

Tony Lokatis, displaying a Boss O/U, with Fred Oliver in the background, in 13 Dover Street. This photograph appeared on the cover of *The Telegraph Sunday Magazine* of July 20th 1986. Diligent observers will be able to give the precise time when this photograph was taken – 11.15 am. – notice the half consumed Guinness on the desk.

the interior and exterior of the shop were virtually unchanged from the first period of occupation. If John Robertson walked into the shop today he would immediately recognise that same shop into which he first walked in 1908. It is remarkable that in the intervening period between 1930 and 1982, considering the foibles of fashion, no real changes were made. In one of the cellars, even the sand into which guns were fired was still there. Consequently the interior and atmosphere of the shop is very Victorian. There are glass-fronted gun cases circa 1860 bearing the wording, "T. Boss, 73 St James' Street", and John Robertson's large roll-top desk sits in one corner piled high with correspondence. One cabinet is stuffed full of order ledgers going back to the 1850s, another is full of bits and pieces of old guns. Dusty antlered heads look down on you and the floor is strewn with gun cases, stock blanks, etc. In the far corner sits Fred Oliver busy book keeping, his seventy years with the firm adding to the general ambience of the shop. No fancy window displays, no suited salesmen and no inferiority complex when you enter without £42,000 in your bank balance.

Through the back shop is a gunmaker's bench with all its associated paraphernalia. Here a gunmaker works on general repairs and deals with the technical aspects of customers' guns. The smell of gun oil and linseed oil permeates the shop and emphasises to one and all that this is a gunmaker's shop not an effete front for selling guns. Downstairs are several basement rooms each one filled to capacity with customers' guns, old gun-cases, old ledgers, boxes of cartridges, etc.

The shop could be regarded as a time warp and yet it would be totally wrong to describe it as such. The ambience is of a firm steeped in history for nearly two centuries where a product can be bought utilising the best materials and employing the highest skills – quality in a era of mediocrity. See Plate 46.

CHAPTER TWELVE

BUILDING A BEST GUN ONLY

Today Boss guns are built in their factory in Southwark, London. They are built in the same tradition and using the same skills as practised by Boss for over a century. The guns are virtually entirely hand built to the exact specification demanded by customers. Due to the fact that building a Boss gun is so labour intensive, they take many months to make and they are expensive to buy. Even so demand is high and there is a waiting list for placing a gun order. Unusual in today's consumer market, brand new Boss guns, carefully looked after, are an investment.

Entering the factory, you climb up a flight of stairs. At the top, a door with the wording, "Boss & Co." scrawled in marker pen might lead the ignorant to assume that nihilism prevailed. Open the door and immediately a large, light, noisy factory with several men beavering away becomes apparent. Long benches line the walls adorned with vices, files, gas burners, etc. For the most part, the gunmakers are stooped over these benches, filing, polishing, checking and rechecking their work. Where this factory stands apart, from the normal conception of a factory, is in the paucity of machinery. There are a couple of drills, a milling machine, a lathe, and barrel boring machine, but little else. Best guns are built at benches.

Two very different types of gun are produced at the factory, the O/U and the side-by-side. The construction of both types of guns differs considerably. On account of this, the gunmakers tend to specialise in one particular type, eg, one barrel-maker will mostly make O/U barrels whereas another barrel-maker will construct side-by-sides. Due to the skills involved in all processes of building a best gun, such specialisation is necessary. Individual specialisation encompasses the following branches: single trigger construction, O/U barrel-making, side-by-side barrel-making, O/U actioning, side-by-side actioning, O/U ejector work, side-by-side ejector work, stocking and finishing.

When a gun order goes to the factory, the gun will be built in the following manner. The first part of the gun to be built is the barrels. Taking the side-by-side first. Rough chopper lump tubes are bought in, from a supplier in London. Boss only use chopper lump barrels on account of the fact that they are by far the strongest and best. In a chopper lump barrel, the lump is an integral part of the barrel. In cheaper barrels, a separate lump is brazed on after the barrels have been joined together. Such a joint with inherent weakness is not used in best gun construction.

The barrels supplied are longer than the finished product, being around 30 inches in length. The muzzle end can easily be damaged in manufacture – this extra length is for safety. Later the barrels will be reduced in size to the customer's requirements. In addition to the barrels being "over long", they will also be "over choked". All barrels supplied have long full chokes. The barrel-maker will shorten and alter the chokes once again to the customer's specification.

This is the first task that the barrel-maker will do to the rough tube. Using a cutter on a lathe, the chokes will be reamed out to their desired requirements. The lathe used in barrel manufacture at the factory has given Boss good service. Originally it was a treadle lathe, now of course it is powered electrically!

Having finished the choke the barrel-maker must now grind the inside of the barrel to the correct bore size. This is done on the lathe using the lead lapping technique. The lead lap is made in the following manner. A six- to eight-inch hole, exactly the same size as the intended bore size, is drilled in a piece of metal to create a mould. Molten lead is poured into this mould. When cool, the length of lead is removed and attached to a long metal rod. The barrel is clamped to one end of the lathe and the metal rod with lead tip inserted into the revolving chuck at the other end. Grit soaked in neatsfoot oil and paraffin is smeared on the lead. The lathe is switched on and the lead lap is pushed up the barrel by hand. Gradually the grinding paste will

Rimming the exterior of a barrel tube on the lathe to reduce it to the correct barrel diameter.

lap the barrel to the correct size. When the correct bore size has been achieved, the barrel is fine bored to remove any scratches. Very fine emery paper is used attached to another rod that the barrel-maker pushes up the barrel. The interior of the barrel is now virtually finished.

The exterior of the barrel must now receive attention. Boss barrels are distinctive and different in shape to most other gunmakers' barrels. They are slimmer at the breech end. As stated previously, this was a deliberate design by the Robertsons to ensure that Boss guns were as slim and graceful as possible. Several ring guages are used which fit over the barrel at intervals along its length. These ring guages check that the barrel diameter is correct from muzzle to breech. Should the dimension be incorrect, or if there are any ripples, bumps, etc, a striker is used. A "striker" is a flat piece of metal with emery paper over it. This process is termed being "struck down". The thickness of the barrel is crucial to its strength and weight. The barrels should not be less than 30/1000 of an inch and never more than 35/1000 of an inch, unless a customer gives contrary instruc-tions. The exterior of the barrel is now virtually complete.

The barrels must now be jointed together. This is by no means a simple task and calls for great skill in getting the correct muzzle convergence angle and then brazing and soldering the barrels together. The first thing that must be done is to machine the chopper lumps so that the bores are the correct distance apart and that they converge correctly at the muzzle end. After this has been done, the barrels must be joined together prior to their brazing and soldering. The insides of the lumps are blacked to ensure a good even flow of the brass in the brazing process. Most gunmakers wire the barrels together for this purpose. Boss do not practise this technique, believing that there is scope for movement, not to mention the fact that the wire can get in the way. Boss rivet the barrels together at the chopper lump. This makes for better rigidity. The breech end of the barrels are then brazed together. The barrels are not brazed their entire length – the heat of the brazing would distort the metal of the barrels and in any case the subsequent soldering is quite strong enough to hold them together. The barrels are then left over night to cool down gradually.

After brazing the barrels together, the barrels are rough chambered at the breeches to enable them to accept the cartridge. The barrel lumps are now cut to roughly the correct size. In cutting away this excess metal, the rivets that held the barrels in position prior to brazing will be removed since they were deliberately using a file and emery cloth to remove any bumps and scratches.

The barrels for the O/U gun go basically through the same stages of manufacture. Where O/U barrel construction differs from side-by-side lies in the jointing technique. Chopper lump barrels again are used. The chopper lumps dovetail into each other on account of one barrel being above the other. For brazing together, the barrels are not riveted. It is impossible to find any surplus metal in which to insert a rivet. Instead the barrels are wired together. Putting the ribs on the O/U is more complicated and for this reason O/U barrels go to proof first. There is no point in spending a long time finishing the barrels if something shows up in the Proof House.

At the same time as the barrels are being made, the action of the gun receives attention. The actions of different guns vary considerably. Is the action to be round bodied, or square bodied? Is a single or double trigger to be fitted? Is it an O/U action? etc. In addition, each action will be individually built to take into account the measurements of the customer regarding the bend, drop, etc of the stock. Actions are supplied in the form of rough forgings by J. B. Phillipson, who have specialised in this field for many decades. The metal used is mild steel EN 32 B.

To get the action close to a workable shape, it is machined, drilled and spark eroded. In addition it is annealed to leave the action soft and workable. The action now begins to look like the completed model. This basic action now has the holes roughly cut for the cocking limbs, the top lever, trigger plate, furniture, etc. Boss still use the original turn-of-the-century guages made for O/U and side-by-side manufacture.

Barrel brazing. See Plate 47.

put in such a position on the lumps. The loop (attachment that the forend is secured to) is soldered onto the bottom of the barrels. On Boss easy openers, the loop is brazed on due to the fact that it takes a far greater strain. The bottom and top ribs are now placed in position and soldered along their entire length. The surplus solder must then be cleaned away and then the barrels are ready to be "struck up". "Striking up" means

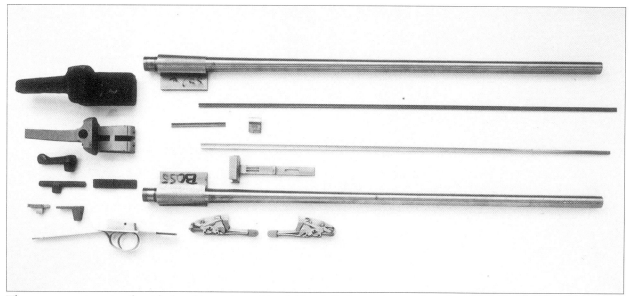

The component parts of a side-by-side part machined. Top left shows the rough action forging and below it the same forging part machined. Other parts include the barrels, top and bottom ribs, forend iron, top lever, safety catch, single trigger and locks.

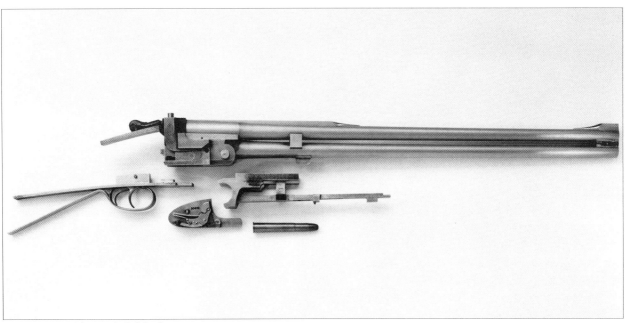

A .470 O/U rifle semi-finished.

The next stage is to joint the gun, ie to fit the barrels to the action. Before jointing, further work will have been done on the barrels. The extractor holes will have been drilled, the extractor beds machined, extractors installed and under cocking slides fitted and barrels machined at the breech end. The inside of the action is polished in readiness. Jointing is a very skillful process. The barrels are dropped into the action and the action filer must use smoke from an oil lamp to assist him in filing the joints to ensure an exact fit. The fit will be so exact that, when finished, it is impossible to close the gun with a sheet of rice paper between the barrels and action. At first actions are tight, but after a small amount of use the action will settle down. Thereafter, the work-

manship is such that although thousands of shots will have been fired from the gun, and many decades have passed, the action will remain tight.

The forend of the gun is now fitted. Forends and ejectors are made up separately and then individually fitted to the gun. Slightly harder steel EN 9 is used for forend metal due to the greater stresses involved. Holes are drilled in the forend for the ejector rods. The ejector rods and springs are fitted, together with the ejector sears. The forend snap fastening will also be fitted.

The top strap of the action until this stage is bent upwards at a very odd angle. This is to get it out of the way so that the actioner can machine and drill the

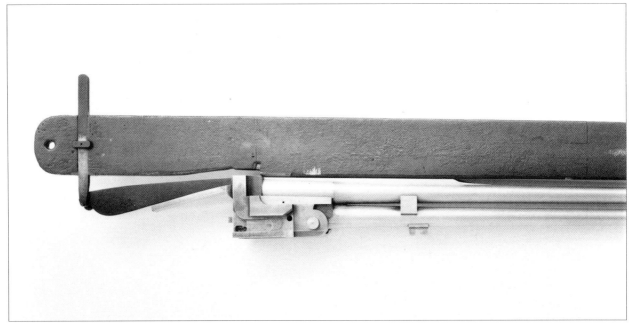

The special jig used to set the correct angle of bend on the top strap.

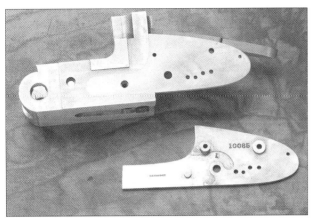

O/U action. See Plate 48.

Walnut stock blanks. See Plate 49.

action. The top strap is now heated and bent to the desired bend. A special jig is used for this purpose which works off the barrels to give the correct angle of bend as desired by the customer.

After the top strap is bent into position, the top lever, spindle and barrel locking bolts are chiselled out, drilled and fitted. The hand-made locks are now fitted into the action, the striker holes drilled and strikers fitted and the trigger plate and the hand-made trigger plate fitted. The action is then filed up and roughly shaped. Some gunmakers, for example Purdey, use the term "detonating" for shaping. The gun now closely resembles the finished product. At this stage the gun is sent to the Proof House in Commercial Road, near the Tower of London, for proof.

When the gun returns from proof it is block stocked. Walnut for gun stocks in the 19th century always came from France. The ravages of two World Wars seriously depleted this source and it is now necessary to travel further afield to obtain comparable quality wood. Only

a small part of the walnut tree can be used for a best gun. The most sought after part of a tree is the trunk at ground level where the trunk joins the roots. The straighter grain of the trunk is used for the hand of the stock. This grain then flows into the fine figure of the root as used in the butt.

Customers can inspect stock blanks and select their own particular preference as regards colouring, figuring, etc. It usually takes around three to four years for a "wet" stock blank to dry out thoroughly. If drying has not taken place properly shrinkage and cracking of the stock can occur. The stocker, using gouges and chisels, will inlet the tang and action, then fit the locks and trigger guard. To ensure as close a fit as possible, lamp black is again used. The gun is now termed rough-stocked or block-stocked.

If a single trigger is required this can now be fitted into the gun, calling for great skill on account of the fact that the angles on the revolving turret must be cut exactly to connect with the lock sears.

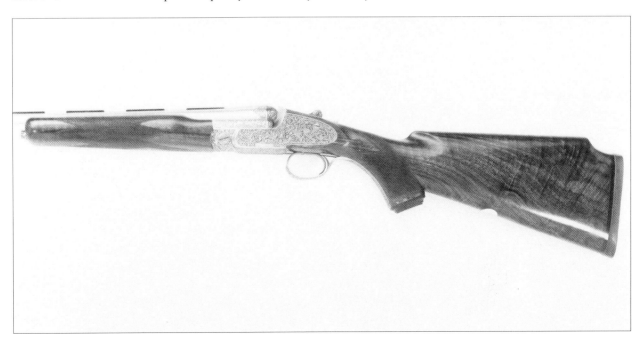

The single-barrel trap gun.

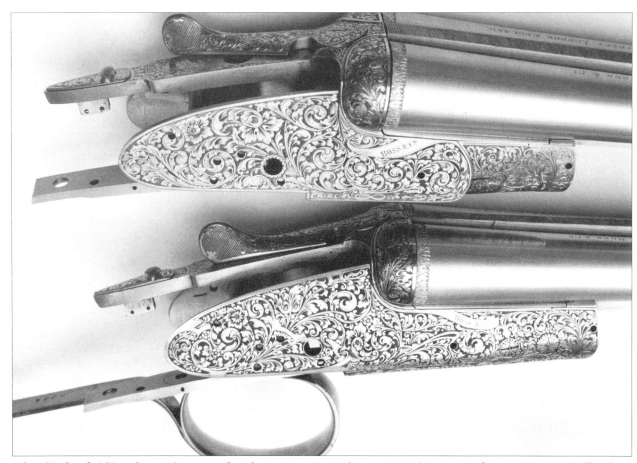

After this fine finishing the gun is engraved to the customer's requirements. Various types of engraving are on offer, from traditional English rose and scroll to sporting scenes or chiselled relief work. The guns illustrated above have just returned from the engraver. They are a pair of .410 shotguns no. 10001, square bodied, and no. 10002, round bodied, "in the white" after engraving. Engraving by Ken Hunt.

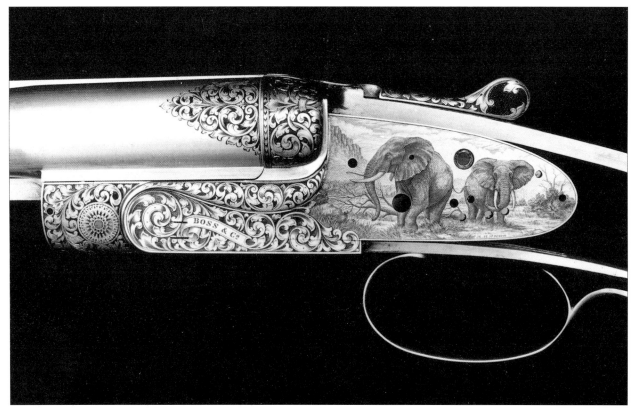

.470 Express Rifle "in the white". Engraving by Brown Brothers.

The stock is now "made off", shaped and rough chequered. The single trigger and ejectors are regulated to ensure that they work correctly. The action is checked to ensure that it closes properly.

The last part of building a best gun is finishing. Finishing is a very important process. It is after all the finish that the customer sees. The gun must look right and the quality must be readily apparent. Gun finishers are highly skilled and must be adept at the whole gun making process.

The action will be fine finished. It will be smoothed with a file and a burnisher to give a very high standard of finish. All the metal parts receive this treatment. The gun will be chequered at wrist and forend and a silver or gold escutcheon fitted. The grain of this stock is filled and the stock is oil polished by hand. A tiny drop of oil is rubbed into the stock by hand at regular intervals. This hand rubbing produces a wonderful lustre which appears from within the wood. Quickly applied cheaper varnishes provide a surface finish only.

After the gun has been engraved, the action and working parts must be hardened to obviate wear. Guns are made from mild steel, a soft and inherently flexible material designed to cope with the stress of explosions. Unless it is hardened on the exterior, wear would be very rapid. The metal parts intended to be hardened are heated until red hot. They are then plunged into a metal trough filled with bone meal. The bone meal imparts a fine layer of carbon onto the metal, that not only gives the metal a very tough skin, but also gives it an attractive colour. The barrels will be "blacked". Barrel blue is achieved by the traditional rusting process. After being degreased thoroughly, wooded plugs are inserted in the barrels and blueing solution is applied. Overnight the barrels will have developed a layer of rust. This is rubbed off with steel wool and the process repeated. Once the desired colour is achieved, any remaining chemicals are killed off and the barrels oiled. Apart from the attractive colour of the blue, barrel blackening prevents rust. The completed gun now goes back to the finisher who checks over the entire gun – sometimes the working of the gun can alter after hardening. He must ensure everything functions properly and that the finish of the gun is perfect.

The gun now goes to the shooting ground to be shot and regulated. It will be thoroughly tested to ensure the ejectors work correctly, the single trigger functions, etc. Regulating the gun is an art and very important for the correct shooting of the gun. Shots are fired at a paper pattern and the spread and density of the pattern checked. If the pattern is not satisfactory, the gun will

RIGHT: .470 Express Rifle "in the white". Engraving by Brown Brothers.

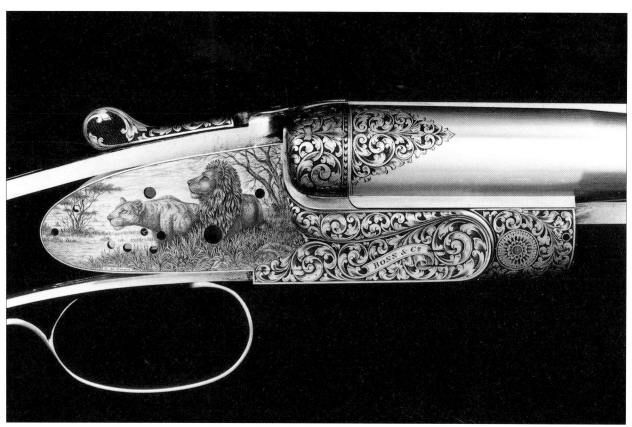

.470 Express Rifle "in the white". Engraving by Brown Brothers.

go back to the factory for slight alteration to the chokes. It is up to the tester to make these recommendations and it is his skill that will eventually result in the gun giving even and regular patterns.

If the customer so demands, a case individually fitted to the gun will be supplied. Many types of cases are available from lightweight motor cases to the traditional best oak and leather. Finally finished, the gun will be picked up from the factory or shooting ground and delivered to 13 Dover Street. At the shop the management of Boss will give the gun a final thorough inspection. Is the stock properly filled? Does the action close correctly? Has the gun been finished to the usual high standard? Having passed this final test the gun can then be handed over to its new owner.

CHAPTER THIRTEEN

THE GUNS AND RIFLES OF THE ROBERTSON ERA

Whenever John Robertson took control of Boss in 1891, a subtle but very important change occurred in the guns and rifles produced by the firm. Some of the breech-loaders produced pre-1891 under the direction of Edward Paddison, although of superb quality, often looked inelegant. Back action locks were prevalent and underlevers very common. Paddison's approach to gunmaking tended to be pragmatic – he used the mechanism he thought to be the best and most reliable. Aesthetic considerations came second. However, it must be borne in mind that the era of Paddison at Boss, the late 19th century, was one of considerable metamorphosis in gun design. The bar action top-lever type of design did not become the standard best gun pattern until the close of the 19th century.

John Robertson was determined to change this. He desired a combination of aesthetic beauty and function and it is to him that we owe the debt for designing the classic Boss hammerless ejector that has been produced from the beginning of the 20th century. John Robertson talked about "streamlining guns". The lines of a Boss gun had to be lean and elegant and it was with this aim in mind that he devoted considerable energy into designing very graceful sporting guns. He knew full well that a very handsome gun would be in high demand.

Robertson's streamlining is apparent in the design of all aspects of Boss guns. In barrel manufacture he insisted that the barrels must be very slim at the breech. Many other gunmakers used extraneous metal in this area which gave their guns a swollen appearance. Robertson perfected in the 1890s a new type of action, particular to Boss guns, that is still used today – "the round action". The round action is a conventional sidelock that is rounded off at the bottom along with the locks and stock. The Boss round action certainly makes for a very slim and elegant design.

Robertson's O/U gun of 1909 was a triumph of functional beauty. The clumsiness of existing O/Us completely disappeared in his design. Great attention was paid to the lines of the gun and the end result was that the Boss O/U achieved acclaim as the model to which all other O/U's aspire.

Even John Robertson's three-barrel 16-bore gun looked elegant for a triple barrel. By using his method of barrel manufacture, he managed to achieve a barrel width of not much more than a normal double 12-bore.

In the building of the guns Robertson changed practices too. He was intent that the actions of the guns should stand out clean and sharp. Boss are virtually unique in this approach to action making. Look at any Boss gun in excellent condition and compare it with that of any other maker. Robertson achieved this sharpness by forbidding the action filers in the finishing process to use emery cloth. Emery cloth would roll off the edges and give a cheap look. Very fine, no. 8 files, virtually impossible to obtain today, and the use of burnishers gave the actions such clean crisp lines. James Woodward, when in business, used the same technique and this partly accounts for the high reputation of Woodward guns.

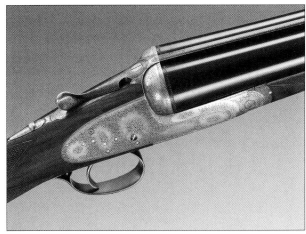

Round action gun. See Plate 53.

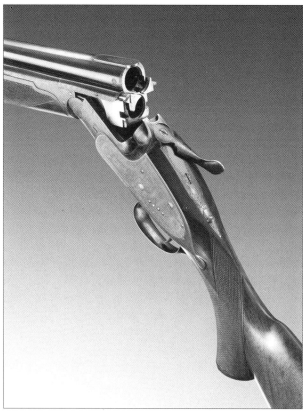

Boss O/U. See Plate 52.

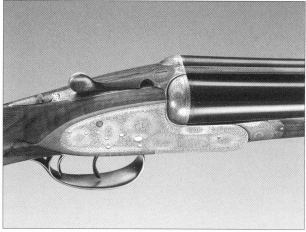

Boss standard of construction. See Plate 55.

Another important factor that gave the guns their superb quality was that standard cutters and turning tool bits were not used. All the cutters and bits used in Boss gun construction were manufactured in the factory itself to a very high standard. The machinists made these cutters and bits from high speed steel. After they were turned and cut to the correct size, they were heated in the forge until white hot and then plunged into a mixture of paraffin and oil. In addition, the action filers and stockers made all their own taps and dies.

In an article in *Arms and Explosives* published on 1st May 1902, specific reference was made to the Boss style:

> The distinctive quality of the Boss gun, granting the finest workmanship and best materials, is style. This is a somewhat elusive property, the equivalent of quality in a good racehorse or beauty in a fine yacht – in a word, the absence of lumber. The metal is in the right place and none of it in the wrong; the sweeping lines of the stock satisfy the artistic eye, leading to strength as well as handiness and accurate balance. The gun looks well and shoots well, the use of it being a continuous pleasure to the shooter. Colonel Hawker termed Joe Manton not only a gunmaker but an "artist in firearms", an expression thoroughly correct; and in pronouncing Mr John Robertson's work in gunmaking as not only fine but artistic, sportsmen are only giving him a verdict to which he is entitled.

By far the majority of guns produced were double-barrel shotguns. A surprisingly large number of trios were ordered and a fair number of quartets. Before World War I the British market was dominant but this changed to the American market after the war. Some boxlocks were produced for the first time in the history of the firm. These boxlocks, of superb quality, were usually sold bearing the name "Robertson".

Inflation, to a lesser extent in the 19th century and to a greater extent in the 20th century, meant steadily rising prices for the guns. The prices below are average prices for Boss guns:

1890s

Hammer ejector in case	£50.0s.0d.
Pair of Damascus barrels	£12.0s.0d.
Pair of hammerless ejectors in case	£126.0s.0d.
Hammerless ejector, single trigger in case	£63.0s.0d.

1910

Hammerless ejector, single trigger in case	£70.0s.0d.
Trio of hammerless ejectors, single triggers in cases	£220.10s.0d.
Pair of hammerless ejectors, single triggers in case	£147.0s.0d.
O/U single trigger in case	£89.5s.0d.
Pair of O/Us, single triggers in case	£175.0s.0d.
O/U pigeon gun, single trigger in case	£100.0s.0d.
Pair of hammerless ejectors, two triggers in case	£147.0s.0d.

1920s

Hammerless ejector, two triggers	£135.0s.0d.
Oak and leather case	£16.10s.0d.
Pair of hammerless ejectors, single triggers	£240.0s.0d.

1940s

Hammerless ejector, single trigger	£259.0s.0d.
Pair of hammerless ejectors, two triggers in case	£532.0s.0d.

O/U single trigger	£288.0s.0d.
Pair of O/U barrels	£95.0s.0d.

1960s

Pair of hammerless guns, single triggers in case	£1,125.0s.0d.
O/U single trigger	£640.0s.0d.

1970s (early)

Pair of hammerless ejector guns, two triggers	£5,000.00

1970s (late)

Pair of hammerless ejector guns, single trigger	£15,000.00

1990s

Hammerless ejector gun, single trigger	from £26,000.00 + VAT
O/U single trigger, from	£42,000.00 + VAT
Rifles	Price on Application

Note the increased cost of the O/U gun and how the single trigger was fitted at no extra cost in the early days.

Like all the gunmakers, and his predecesors at Boss, Robertson used outside suppliers for specialist items. The following list gives some of these specialist suppliers as used by Boss in the early years of this century:

E. Chilton & Son, Lock Makers – 40/41 Northampton Road West, Wolverhampton.

S. B. Mansfield, Lock Makers – 63 Sherwood Street, Wolverhampton

J. Stanton, Lock Makers – Kensington Works, Merridale Road, Wolverhampton.

Joseph Brazier, Lock Makers – Wolverhampton.

Armstrong-Whitworth, Barrel Tubes.

Robert Bryant, Gun Cases – 24 Drury Lane, London.

C. R. Johnstone, Snap Caps, Brushes, Rods – 11 Clarendon Place, Seymour Street, London.

G. & J. W. Hawksley, Turnscrews, Brushes, Oil Bottles, Snap Caps – Carver Works, Carver Street, Sheffield.

The gun illustrated above right is a double-barrel 12-bore side lever hammer pigeon gun no. 4124 ordered by Captain E. A. Brooke, on 16th February 1892. Edward Alston Pierrepont Brooke, born on 6th August 1858, joined the Queen's Own Cameron Highlands on 23rd July 1879 and had been promoted to Captain on 17th January 1889.

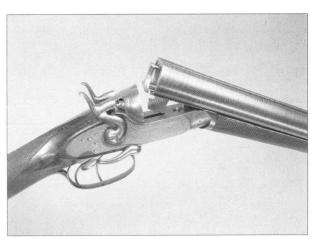

Top and Above: Side lever gun no. 4124. See Plates 57 and 58.

There is obviously some confusion in Boss's records over the number of this gun. It appears with the number 4191, a mistake by a clerk. No. 4124 was built at the time that John Robertson took over Boss. It is a very elegant late built hammer gun that already shows the influence of John Robertson in Boss gun design. The 30″ Damascus barrels are engraved, "Boss & Co. 73 St James' Street, London". They are stamped underneath, "C.L." being made by Lancasters, have 2¾″ chambers and are proofed for 1¼ ounce shot, this being the standard combination for pigeon guns. A side lever of the type preferred by Paddison is still used. The scroll engraved locks are by Joseph Brazier and are engraved, "Boss & Co.". The hammers lie back out of sight when cocked and a Rigby lever forend is used. This gun is in excellent original condition and this coupled with its elegant style makes for a very attractive gun.

A very early Robertson influenced 12-bore hammerless ejector gun no. 4247 is illustrated on page 192. No. 4247 was ordered by Captain E. A. Brooke (who had previously ordered no. 4124) on 24th January 1893. Like Robertson's hammer guns, this gun displays the "streamlining" that Robertson introduced to Boss. Gone are the unsightly back action locks and in their place a very elegant bar action side-lock ejector is the result.

Capt E. A. P. Brooke

No. 4191.

Ordered Feby 16th 1892
Completed

Ordered a 12 bore C.F. Hammer gun, side snap action, lever forend fore action locks, hammers below line of sight, brls 30 in long, right extra good cylinder, left choke 1⁴⁄ usual rib, not too thin in the hand weight as near as possible 6 lb 14 oz. well balanced

Bend at Heel 1⁵⁄₈ full   Length 14³⁄₁₆ f
  " " face 1¼+¹⁄₁₆ f   · Heel 14³⁄₈
Cast off Heel ¹⁄₄+¹⁄₁₆   · Toe 14⁵⁄₈
  " " Toe ½ f

Bend at Bump 1⁵⁄₈ f   Length 14³⁄₁₆ f
  " " face 1¼+¹⁄₁₆ f   · Heel 14³⁄₈
  " S. Hole   · Toe 14⁵⁄₈
Cast off Heel ¹⁄₄+¹⁄₁₆   Right lock
  " " Toe ½ f   Left "
Weight of gun   Weight of brls

The order for gun no. 4124, incorrectly numbered 4191, dated 16th February 1892. From Boss's order ledgers.

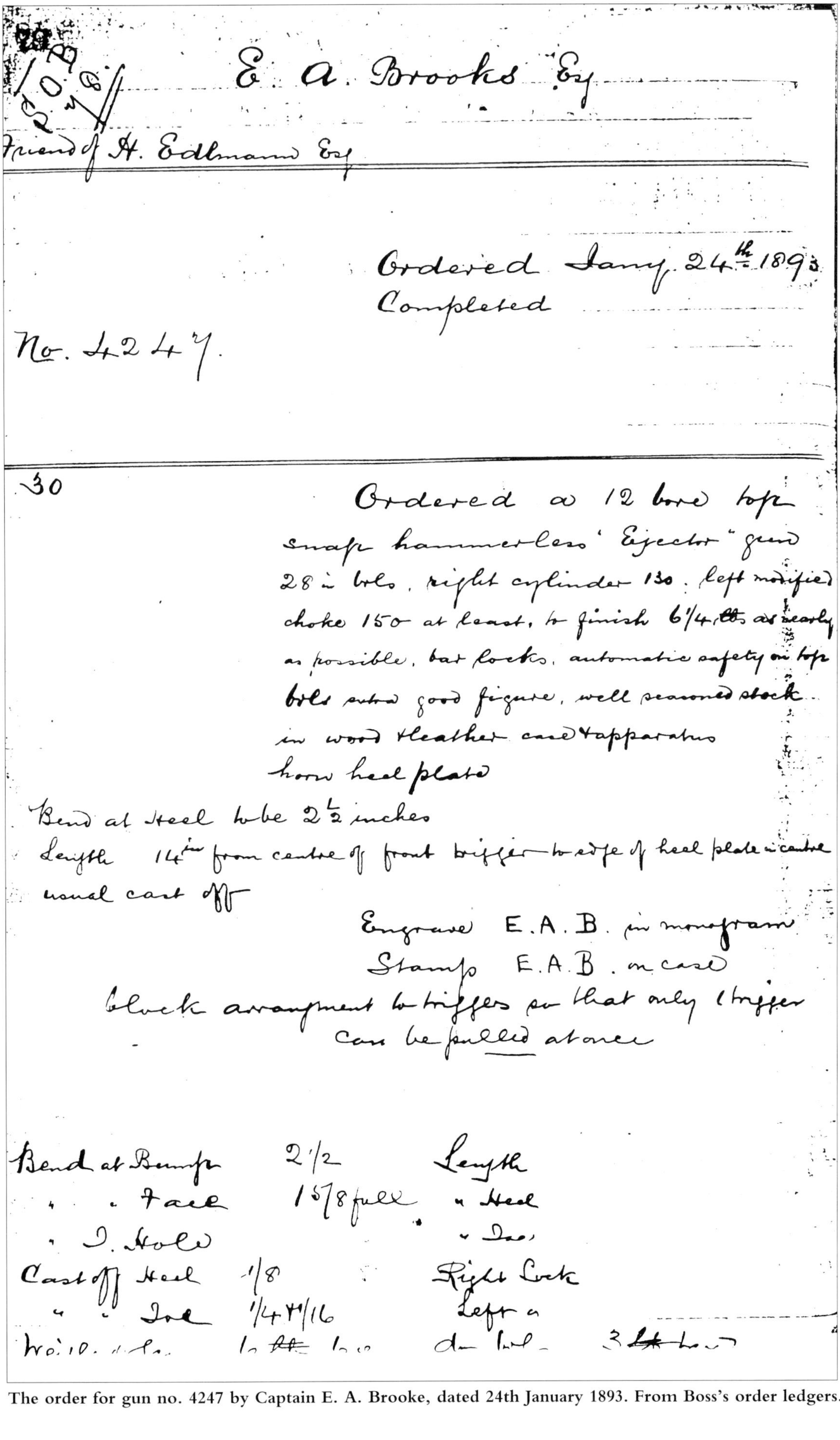

E. A. Brooks Esq

Friend of H. Edlmann Esq

Ordered Jany. 24th 1893
Completed

No. 4247.

30

Ordered a 12 bore top snap hammerless 'Ejector' gun 28 in brls, right cylinder 130. left modified choke 150 at least, to finish 6¼ lbs as nearly as possible, bar locks, automatic safety on top brls extra good figure, well seasoned stock in wood + leather case + apparatus horn heel plate

Bend at Heel to be 2½ inches

Length 14 in from centre of front trigger to edge of heel plate i centre usual cast off

Engrave E.A.B. in monogram
Stamp E.A.B. on case
block arrangment to triggers so that only 1 trigger can be pulled at once

Bend at Bump	2½	Length	
" " Face	1⅝ full	" Heel	
" I. Hole		" Toe	
Cast off Heel	⅛	Right Lock	
" " Toe	¼ + 1/16	Left "	
Weight			3

The order for gun no. 4247 by Captain E. A. Brooke, dated 24th January 1893. From Boss's order ledgers.

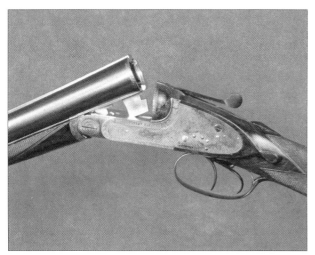

Hammerless ejector gun no. 4247. See Plates 59 and 60.

Triple-barrel gun no. 4690. See Plate 61.

The Damascus barrels engraved, "Boss & Co., 73 St James's Street, London", are 28″ long and are bored right cylinder and left modified choke. An automatic safety is specified on account of the fact that they were not as yet universal and a block arrangement is fitted to the triggers so that only one trigger can be pulled at once. The gun is contained in an oak and leather case with 73 St James's Street label.

An unusual feature of the gun is that the sides of the action proudly proclaim, "Boss' Patent Ejector". This is in reference to John Robertson and Henry Holland's ejector patent no. 16691 of 16th November 1888 pre-dating the famous Boss ejector of 1897. Guns with the wording, "Boss' Patent Ejector" are comparatively rare on account of the fact that after the more important single trigger invention of 1894, this took engraving precedence on guns.

Next, facing page, comes another early Robertson influenced gun – a double-barrel 12-bore hammer pigeon gun, no. 4495 ordered on 26th January 1897 by James Denny, Pittsburgh, Pennsylvania. In the closing decades of the 19th century, orders from the U.S.A. for Boss guns began to develop and this gun represents an early example of this new market.

No. 4495 displays all the characterists of the hammer gun at the pinnacle of its development. The barrels are made from steel and are 28″ long. Both barrels are full choke, chambered for $2\frac{3}{4}$th″ cases and the rib is flat and roughed, designed for pigeon shooting. Mr. Denny ordered several guns from Boss for pigeon shooting. The locks are bar action rebounders with the hammers lying well back out of sight when cocked. A top-lever snap action is used and the action is profusely scroll engraved in traditional rose and scroll pattern. The stock is finely figured and the forend is fastened by an Anson snap. Robertson's influence in the design of this gun is very apparent. The gun is very elegant and graceful, an early example of Robertson's streamlining.

The gun above is no. 4690 ordered in 1899 and completed in 1901, one of two triple-barrelled 16-bore single trigger, hammerless ejector guns. Many gunmakers in the London trade were jealous of the success of Robertson's 1894 single trigger. They threw every single possible criticism at it: it was unreliable, it was dangerous, it was delicate, etc. As described before he answered all these questions with convincing demonstrations of the single trigger's superiority. To cock a final snoot at the jealous detractors, he built the three-barrel single trigger. The first gun built was no. 4605 built in 1898. This gun was a prototype and, due to the fact that it was never actually ordered, no reference appears in Boss's records. It was subsequently sold to Herbert Lawton on 3rd July 1922. A keen customer of Boss, W. Baldi from Florence, heard of this gun and ordered a similar example for himself. This was no. 4690 ordered on 3rd July 1899. The gun is a 16-bore with 28″ steel barrels, each barrel bored cylinder. The barrels are engraved, "Boss & Co., 73 St James' Street, London". A single trigger is fitted, modified to fire the three barrels. The ejectors likewise had to be modified to cope with the extra barrel. To deal with the additional strain, double lumps are fitted.

The barrel firing order is right, centre, left. The two outer barrels are fired by conventional side-locks and the centre barrel is fired by an action set upon the trigger plate. The action is slightly wider than normal, but not by a great deal. A pistol-grip stock is used and a gold oval fitted. The forend is fastened by an Anson snap. The gun is fitted in an oak and leather case with mail canvas outer. The case is lined in green velvet, a full compliment of accessories is supplied and the usual 73, St James' Street label is pasted into the lid.

Considering that the gun has three barrels, it is surprisingly light, weighing 6 lbs 14 oz. The barrels themselves only weigh 3 lbs 7 oz. The triple-barrel never really caught on and Boss did not build any more

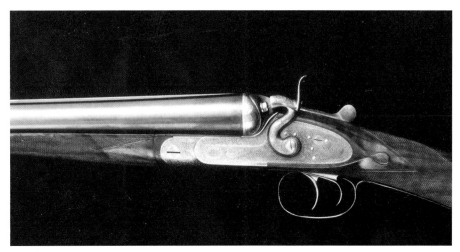

**Hammer gun no. 4495.
See Plate 56.**

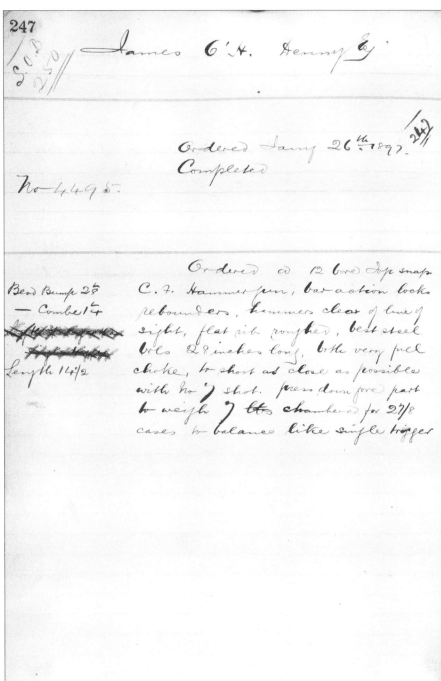

**The order for gun no. 4495 dated
26th January 1897. Note the
remark at the bottom, "to balance like single trigger". From
Boss's order ledgers.**

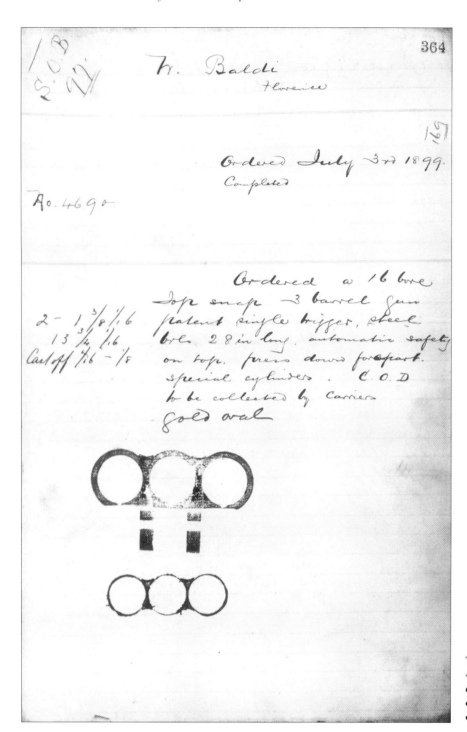

364

W. Baldi
Florence

Ordered July 3rd 1899.
Completed

No. 4690.

Ordered a 16 bore
top snap 3 barrel gun
patent single trigger, steel
brls 28 in long. automatic safety
on top. press down forepart.
special cylinders . C.O.D
to be collected by carriers
gold oval

2 - 1 3/8 /.6
13 3/4 /.6
Cast off 7/16 - /8

The order for triple barrel no. 4690 dated 3rd July 1899. Note the double lumps shown in the print of the breech end. From Boss's order ledgers.

such guns after no. 4690. It was perhaps too unorthodox and in addition it was difficult to make and expensive. No. 4690, ordered on 3rd July 1899, was not completed until 21st June 1901, the length of time betraying the complexity of building the gun.

The gun illustrated above right is a .295/300 top-lever boxlock ejector rook and rabbit rifle no. 4817 built in 1900. This is a rare item in that Boss produced very few rook rifles. Several other firms specialised in these popular small-bore rifles and most customers would patronise them.

Viscount Castlereagh, Charles Stewart Henry Vane-Tempest-Stewart ordered two rook rifles no. 4817 and

no. 4818 in the year 1900. He was born on the 13th May 1878, later joined the Royal Horse Guards and eventually would be elevated to become Lord Londonderry. He bought this particular gun for his wife Edith and her monogram appears on the gold escutcheon on the butt. The Londonderry family were excellent customers of Boss and there are frequent references to them in Boss's order ledgers. Hence their desire to purchase a Boss rook and rabbit rifle.

The 26″ hexagonal barrel is marked with "73 St James' Street, London" and ".295 or .300". The top flat of the barrel is file cut behind the rear sight which has a standing leaf marked 50 yards and two folding leaves

Rabbit rifle no. 4817. See Plate 62.

for 100 and 150 yards respectively. The flat is also file cut behind and in front of the foresight. The barrel is rifled six grooves right-hand twist.

The colour case hardened action is finely scroll engraved and the serial number 4817 is engraved upon the trigger guard. A pistol-grip stock is fitted. The gun is contained in its original red-baize-lined leather case with the 73 St James' Street label. The brass escutcheon in the centre of the case is also engraved with Viscount Castlereagh's wife's monogram.

Robertson's O/U gun of 1909 won immediate acclaim from the public and the press. There was a terrific demand for it, even though it took slightly longer to make and was more expensive. One of a pair of early O/U guns is illustrated below. These guns are

RIGHT: **The gold escutcheon in the butt engraved with Edith Castlereagh's monogram.**
BELOW: **The action of O/U gun no. 6147 built in 1913. Engraved by John Sumner. See also Plates 63 and 64.**

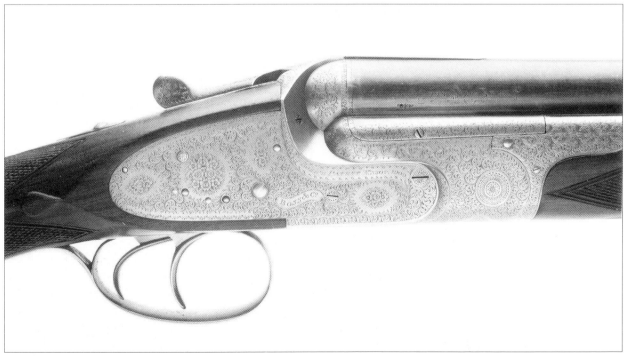

277

V. ℰ. C. Vickers

Ordered   March 11th 1913
Number   6147 + 8
Hammerless ejector pair of guns
One or two triggers 2 triggers   "OU"
Bore   12 bore
Barrels   29" steel
Shooting right   regular
    „   left   do
Weight gun   6.10
    „   barrels
    „   pulls
Stock No.   ~~2184~~ + ~~2348~~   2358 - 2398
Bend   1½" + 1¼"
Length   15"
Cast off   ¼
~~Oval~~   Gold V's
    uses very light charge of 6 shot

Remarks   nice stocks   Safeties to work very easy
    As early in July as possible
        Stamp. V. C. Vickers
            44 Charles St. W. } on cover
        V. C. V. on case)

                D. 40.

Case + cover Stamps
    17775 . 17891.
Completed

The order for O/U guns nos. 6147/8 dated 11th March 1913. Note the early completion date of July required by the customer. From Boss's order ledgers.

nos. 6147/8, a pair of 12-bore two trigger guns ordered by V. C. Vickers, 44 Charles Street, London on 11th March 1913. Although dating from 1913, the guns are in excellent original condition with original case and accessories.

The barrels are made of steel and are 29" long. The relevant "1" or "2" is inlaid in gold on top of the barrels and the engraving reads, "Boss & Co., 13 Dover Street, Piccadilly, London, W.", the firm having moved to this address in 1908. The actions, with rose and scroll engraving, have the banner style, "Boss & Co." and are engraved on both sides with the O/U patent no. "Boss' Patent No. 3307 1909".

The stocks, fitted with gold ovals, have rubber recoil pads and in the order "nice stocks" is specified. The forend has the O/U ejector patent number engraved upon it, "Boss' Patent No. 3308 1909". The guns weigh 6 lbs 10 oz each.

The guns are cased in their original red-baize-lined best oak and leather case. An outer mail canvas cover protects the oak and leather case and this outer case is stamped, "V.C.Vickers, 44 Charles Street, W". The case was probably supplied by Robert Bryant, 24 Drury Lane, London, who supplied most of the best cases for the top makers. Contained within the case are four plated snap caps stamped, "Boss & Co", an ebony-

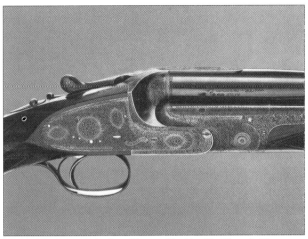

O/U rifle no. 6179. See Plates 65, 66, 67, 68 and 69.

handled chamber brush by Hawksley, cleaning rods and a combined pull-through/oil bottle again by Hawksley in a Moroccan leather pouch. The trade label bears the 73 St James's Street address, even though by the time this gun was built the firm had vacated St James's Street some five years previously. This discrepancy is by no means unusual – existing supplies of trade labels were used up before new ones printed. Quite commonly, the address is over-printed by a rubber stamp bearing the firm's then current address. An instruction label explaining how to cock the ejectors, should they be accidentally discharged, is also pasted onto the lid.

A very interesting O/U rifle no. 6179 is illustrated above. No. 6179 is a single trigger .375 Express Rifle built in 1913. Like the first of the three-barrel guns, there is no reference to it in Boss's order ledgers. The reasoning is the same. This was probably a demonstration or prototype O/U rifle and as such was not individually ordered by a customer. It would be built for stock to demonstrate to potential customers the suitability of the O/U system for rifles. Later on it was sold to a Commander Elia.

The gun is in superb original condition and in its original case with accessories. The 26″ steel barrels are chambered for the .375 nitro express cartridge. A platinum-lined folding leaf sight, sighted to 300 yards, is fitted. The barrels are engraved, "Boss & Co., 13 Dover Street, Piccadilly, London. W". A single trigger is fitted. The top strap is extended over the wrist to the top of the comb for extra strength. The pistol grip stock is of very finely figured walnut with a carved cheekpiece. A rubber recoil pad is fitted and a gold escutcheon inserted. The entire gun has superb fine rose and scroll engraving throughout executed by John Sumner, 15 Bateman Street, Soho, London. The O/U patent number is engraved on both sides of the action and the ejector patent number engraved upon the forend.

The gun is contained in its original red-baize-lined leather reinforced canvas case. The trade label fitted

is the old St James's Street label. No. 6179 surely represents Boss at the pinnacle of their achievement. The workmanship is second to none, the entire gun reeks of quality. The O/U design coupled with slim rifle barrels must make this weapon one of the most elegant rifles ever produced. Not a great many O/U rifles were produced by Boss; it is heartening to know that the Boss O/U rifle is currently back in production.

Another early O/U gun is illustrated below. This gun is no. 6452, the no. 2 gun of a trio nos. 6451/2/3 ordered, in October 1913, by Richard Hennessy. Mr Hennessy had previously purchased a pair of O/U guns nos. 6071/2 in 1912 and traded in these guns for his new trio one year later.

No. 6452 is a 12-bore with 29″ steel barrels. The barrels are engraved, "Boss & Co., 13 Dover Street, Piccadilly, London. W". A single trigger is fitted. The action and locks are finely engraved with rose and scroll engraving executed by John Sumner. The O/U patent number is engraved on both sides of the action and the ejector patent number engraved on the forend. The stock is finely figured and a gold oval is fitted. Originally the trio were supplied in a triple case. In the order book, the following instruction is given:

> Coming to town about May 28th, to try guns in rough, if not done will use try gun. Keep old guns in case new not ready for season.

After World War I, Boss very rapidly reverted to gun production again. Orders quickly picked up and such a post-war order was for a pair of 12-bore hammerless ejector guns nos. 6597/8 ordered on 17th May 1919 by Col. Greig.

The barrels are 28″ long and both barrels are bored improved cylinder. The barrels bear the address "Boss & Co., 13 Dover Street, Piccadilly, London. W", and have their relevant "1" or "2" inlaid in gold on the rib. These guns are of the highest quality. A great many writers

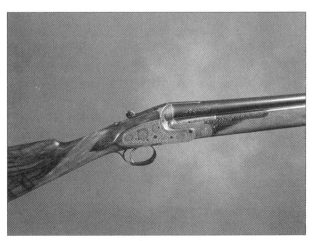

O/U gun no. 6452. See Plate 70.

The order for gun no. 6452 dated 1913. Nos. 6071/2 had been previously built for Mr Hennessy and Boss have used the old order to detail his measurements. From Boss's order ledgers.

have talked about the 1920s and 1930s as being the vintage years of best gun manufacture. Even taking into account the Great Depression of the early 1930s, Boss retained a highly skilled workforce of some forty men in the inter-war period. Orders for sporting guns were plentiful for most of this period and the best materials were easily obtainable. Due to the fact that there was this large reserve of skilled labour and that Boss built best guns only, it is reasonable to assume that the guns of the 1920s and 1930s deserve the charisma that permeates this era.

The stocks of nos. 6597/8 are of a matching figure

with an excellent pattern. The actions are engraved with traditional rose and scroll engraving and are colour case hardened finished. The guns are contained in their original red-baize-lined oak and leather double case. Originally a mail canvas cover was supplied to fit over this case. The label bears the 13 Dover Street address, the company having used up its old 73 St James's Street labels at long last! Contained within this case are four nickle-plated snap caps stamped, "Boss & Co.", a nickle-plated oil bottle likewise stamped and a Moroccan leather pouch containing a pull-through.

During the first quarter of this century Boss con

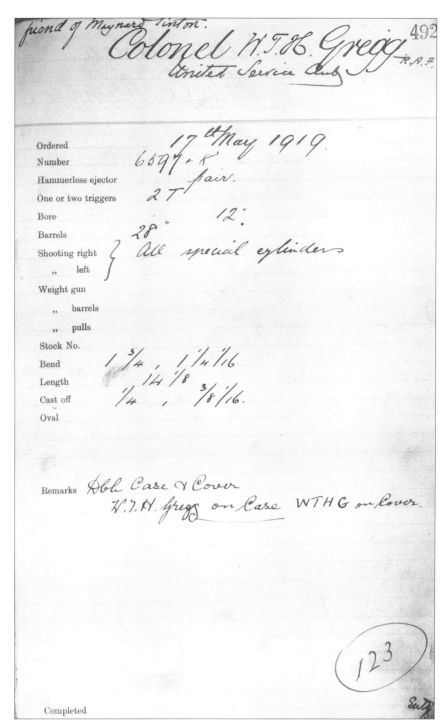

friend of Maynard Tinton.

Colonel W.T.H. Gregg 492

United Service Club R.A.F.

Ordered	17th May 1919.
Number	6597 + 8
Hammerless ejector	*pair.*
One or two triggers	2 T
Bore	12".
Barrels	28"
Shooting right	} *All special cylinders*
„ left	
Weight gun	
„ barrels	
„ pulls	
Stock No.	
Bend	1 3/4 , 1 1/4 7/16.
Length	14 7/8
Cast off	1/4 , 3/8 /16.
Oval	

Remarks *Dble Case & Cover*
W.T.H. Gregg on Case WTHG on Cover.

(123)

Completed

The order for guns nos. 6597/8 dated 17th May, 1919. From Boss's order ledgers.

Hammerless ejector guns nos. 6597/8. See Plates 71 and 72.

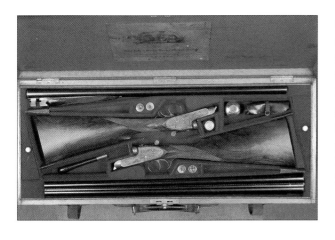

structed many trios of guns and a few trios had been constructed in the hammer gun era. However, by the turn of the century, sets of three guns were being regularly built. On the organised shoots of the Edwardian era, a shooter and two loaders using three guns had a certain elitist appeal in the field. In addition, three guns were a real asset when shooting driven grouse. Unfortunately a great many of these trios have been split up over the intervening decades. This is fortunately not the case with the guns illustrated here.

Sir Albert Bingham ordered a pair of double-barrel 12-bore single trigger O/U guns on the 25th October

1926. Shortly after placing this order, he placed another order on the 3rd February 1927 for a single gun to match the pair, thereby creating a composite trio, illustrated left. The pair are numbered nos. 7261/2 and the third gun no. 7256. Albert Edward Bingham was born on the 30th June 1866 and died on the 6th November 1941. He was a brother of the Earl of Lucan.

The barrels of all three guns are 28″ long with modified chokes. The barrels are engraved, "Boss & Co., 13 Dover Street, Piccadilly, London. W", and have the relevant, "1", "2" or "3" inlaid in gold on the top rib. The actions have very fine rose and scroll engraving, being engraved by John Sumner. The stocks are finely figured with gold ovals and the owner's initials in gold inlet into them. The guns are contained within their original red-baize-lined treble oak and leather case with mail canvas outer cover. The order states "a best oak and leather treble case with M. C. cover and fittings complete". The label bearing the 13 Dover Street

LEFT: O/U trio nos 7261/2 and 7256. See Plates 73 and 74.

BELOW LEFT AND BELOW: The orders for the O/U trio nos. 7261/2 and no. 7256 dated 25th October 1926 and 3rd February 1927. From Boss's order ledgers.

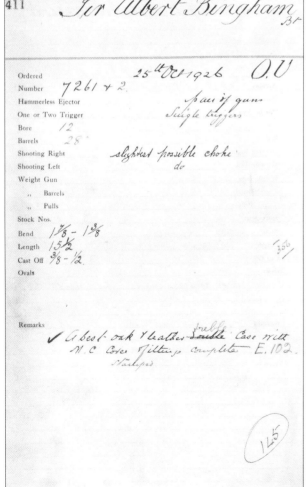

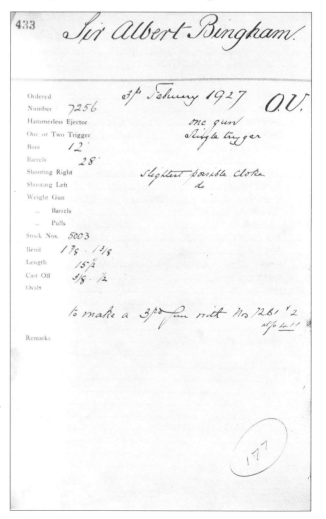

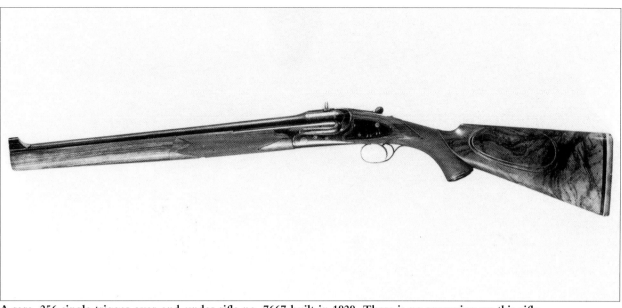

A rare .256 single trigger over-and-under rifle no. 7667 built in 1929. There is no engraving on this rifle.

address is fitted. These guns must have gone in for repair or servicing to Boss later on, because the 13 Dover Street address has been overstamped, "41 Albemarle Street" to update the address.

Illustrated above is a very unusual single trigger over-and-under rifle no. 7667. This rifle, in calibre .256, was ordered by Boss's agents in America, Abercrombie & Fitch on the 18th April 1929 for a customer of theirs. The barrels are 20″ long and are sighted to 150 yards with a standard sight and 250 yards with a folding leaf sight, both sights being fine gold lined. An ivory bead foresight is fitted at the muzzle end. The rib was matted just in front of the foresight.

A finely figured pistol-grip stock with cheek-piece was fitted and contained within a cavity in the pistol-grip is a spare sight. The forend wood is extended right up to the muzzle.

The bottom of the action is rounded and what is unusual is that there is no engraving on the rifle. The entire metal work was black finished. Two telescopic sights are fitted to the rifle, one of 2¾ power the other of 4 power. A best oak and leather case was supplied to complete the outfit. Later in 1933 an extra pair of 24″ barrels in .303 calibre were supplied to fit the rifle. The whereabouts of this rifle are unknown today. The reason for the lack of engraving is that the action of the rifle is made of steel to cope with the high pressures experienced. Due to the hardness of the material, there is minimal engraving.

No. 7755, illustrated right, is a very unusual weapon for Boss. It is an O/U combination gun/rifle, the upper barrel being a 20-bore shotgun and the lower barrel being a .256 rifle. It was ordered by Abercrombie and Fitch in April 1929 and was almost certainly intended for the same customer as the O/U .256 rifle no. 7667.

The barrels are 26″ long, the 20-bore shotgun barrel chambered for the 2¾″ cartridge and bored full choke. For the rifle, there is a 150 yds standard sight and 250 yds folding gold-lined leaf sight. An ivory bead foresight is fitted. The top rib is matted over its full length. The action is unusual in that it is well rounded in contrast to normal O/U actions. This was specified in the order.

A pistol-grip stock is fitted and contained within the cavity in the grip is the spare sight. A cheekpiece and rubber recoil pad complete the stock. A telescopic sight of 2¾ power is supplied, being so mounted that the open sights remain visible. The weapon is housed in an oak and leather case bearing the 13 Dover Street label.

Like rifle no. 7667, this weapon is unusual in that there is little engraving, being border engraved only. A black finish is the preferred option. Guns and rifles with little or no engraving involved a very high degree of craftsmanship. Engraving can cover a multitude of small blemishes – a bare gun must be perfect as is evident in no. 7755. In addition, due to the action being made from steel again, minimal engraving is present.

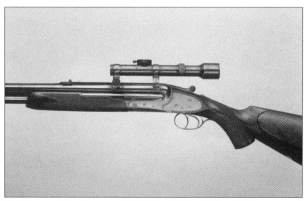

O/U combination no. 7755. See Plates 75 and 76.

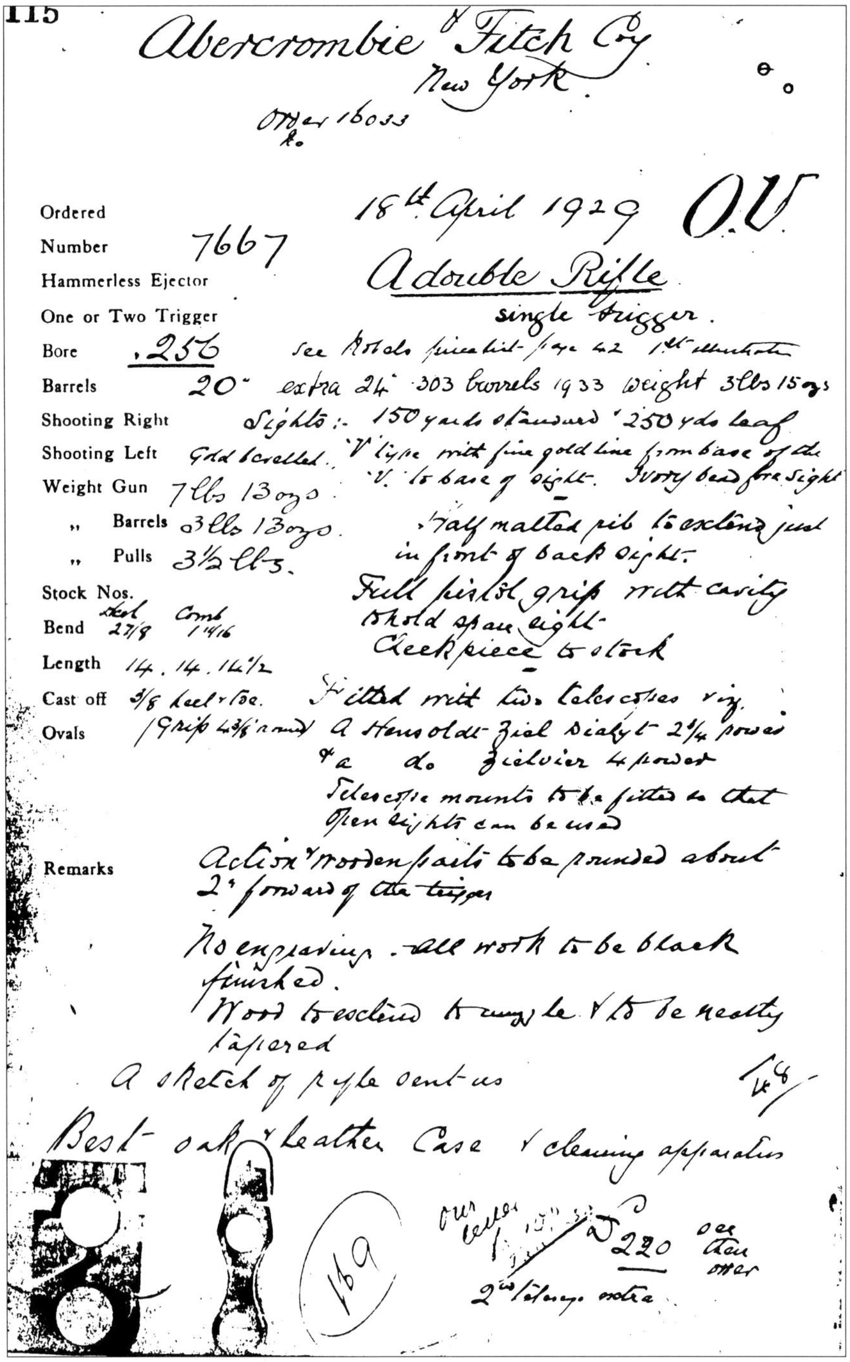

115

Abercrombie & Fitch Co
New York

Order to Boss

Ordered
Number **7667**   *18th April 1929* ***OU***
Hammerless Ejector
One or Two Trigger   *A double Rifle*
Bore   **.256**   *single trigger.*
Barrels   20" extra 24" .303 barrels 1933 weight 3lbs 15ozs
Shooting Right
Shooting Left
Weight Gun   7lbs 13ozs
   „   Barrels   3lbs 13ozs.
   „   Pulls   3½ lbs.
Stock Nos.
Bend
Length   14.14.14½.
Cast off
Ovals

Remarks

The order for rifle no. 7667 dated 18th April 1929. Note the high cost of the rifle, £220 plus the two telescopes extra. From Boss's order ledgers.

A very unusual single trigger O/U gun no. 8208 is illustrated right. This gun was ordered on 22nd May 1934 through Abercrombie & Fitch by C.W. Kress, 485 Park Avenue, New York. Mr Kress had previously ordered many Boss O/Us and later went on to order a composite pair nos. 8279/8338 built in similar style to this gun. No. 8208 was probably designed for trap shooting. The 28″ Whitworth barrels are both bored full choke. Where the gun is unusual is in its unorthodox stock as ordered by the customer. A special wooden hand-grip is fitted in front of the forend and a Monte Carlo stock is used with a very low toe. The stock is of a very finely figured walnut. The whereabouts of this gun are unknown today.

Mr Kress was an avid Boss O/U enthusiast with a penchant for eccentricity in gun design. He had his own shooting ground where he practised with his various gun designs.

He was an excellent customer of Boss in the 1930s. He would order a Boss O/U to his own specific design, have it shipped over and then test it out at his private ground. He would then "improve" on the design of the Boss O/U and order another one to his own very individual requirements. This explains the extraordinary appearance of gun no. 8208. Several similar shaped guns were ordered and if any remain extant today, they will be Kress in origin.

116

Abercrombie & Fitch Coy

Order No 16091

Ordered	April 1929 O.U.
Number	7755
Hammerless Ejector	Combined Gun & Rifle
One or Two Trigger	2 triggers
Bore	20 gun & .256 Rifle - same cartridge as specified
Barrels	26"
Shooting Right	Full Choke 2 3/4 chamber
Shooting Left	150 yards standard sight 250 leaf fold

Weight Gun 6lbs. 10 1/2 ozs. barrels V with fine gold line from base of the V to tip of sight. Ivory bead foresight

Barrels 3lbs 8 1/4 ozs

Pulls 3 1/2 lbs & 4lbs Full length Matted rib

Stock Nos.
Bend 2 7/8 (Heel) 1 7/8 (Comb) — Full pistol grip with cavity to hold spare sight
Length 14, 14, 14 1/4 — Cheek piece to stock
Cast off 3/8 heel' toe — Rubber pencil pad
Ovals left & right hand — Fitted with a Hensoldt-Ziel Dialyt Telescope 2 3/4 power. Mounts to be fitted so that open sights can be used

Action 'Wottenhaus' to be rounded some 2" forward of the trigger

Remarks No engraving. All work to be black finished

Best oak & leather Case & fittings

The order for combination gun/rifle no. 7755 dated April 1929. This weapon was probably ordered by the same customer as no. 7667. From Boss's order ledgers.

A single trigger O/U 12-bore hammerless ejector gun no. 8208 built in 1934 with an extraordinary stock and forend.

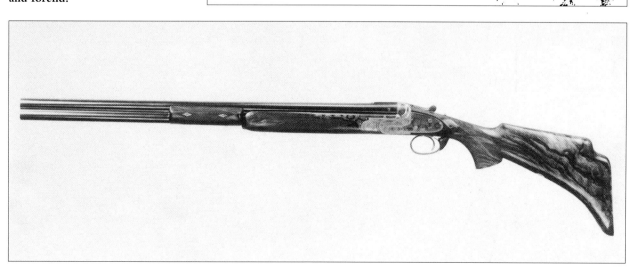

3974

C. W. Kress

Sent to Abercrombies

Ordered   22ⁿᵈ May 1934

Number   8208

Hammerless Ejector   one gun

One or Two Trigger   single trigger

Bore   12

Barrels   28"   Whitworth   2⅝" chambers.

Shooting Right   both full choke to make a 70%

Shooting Left   or better, pattern at 40 yards with

Weight Gun   3 drams of powder & ⅞ oz of 7½ shot

„ Barrels   2-15   with hand piece

„ Pulls

Stock Nos. M.C.   *Self opening*

Bend   1¾ - 1¼ - 3½

Length   12¼ - 13⅜ 13¼ 15, Depth of Butt M.C to toe 7⅞ heel to toe 6¼

Cast off

Ovals

Remarks

To have a special wooden hand grip on the barrels and have his own particular shape stock with Monte Carlo and low toe. Same measurements as photos supplied for re-stocking O.Us except that it is to be ¼ straighter. To have a double trigger guard.

126

The order for O/U gun no. 8208 dated 22nd May 1934. Note the "remarks" pertaining to the unorthodox stock. From Boss's order ledgers.

O/U gun no. 8127. See Plate 80.

The gun illustrated right is a 12-bore single trigger O/U gun no. 8127 built in 1946/7. This gun is interesting on two counts. Firstly, the serial number 8127 should date it about 1934. For some reason this number was not used pre-war. This only goes to prove again that it is impossible to be dogmatic about dating guns from their serial numbers. Secondly, this gun represents one of the very first guns built after the war when Boss were struggling to get back into normal production. It might well be that no. 8127 had been started as a stock gun or as a cancelled gun in the 1930s and kept in reserve and only completed after the war

E. F. Hutton.

²ᶜ⁴
R. D. R.

Ordered : 24ᵗʰ *April* 1937

Number 8491-2.

Hammerless Ejector

One or Two Triggers : *pair of Guns*
Single triggers

Bore : 12

Barrels 25"

Shooting Right No1. Right: Improved Left: modified

Shooting Left : No 2 Right: modified Left: nearly full.

Weight Gun : about 6th 2g. finished 6lbs 3ozs

" Barrels 2lbs 12ozs *Regular actions* '5⁵/

" Pulls : 3½ lbs round bodies

Stock Nos. :

Bend : 2" - 1½"

Length : 14½"

Cast Off : ⅛"

~~Ovals~~ : none E.F.H inlayed in gold in stocks

444E

Remarks :

A best double R.N. Case to # 374 ✓
obtained E.F.H
Taken by E.F.H. on 2ⁿᵈ Sept 1937.

205

The order for pair nos. 8491/2 dated 24th April 1937. Note at the top left-hand corner the initials, "R. D. R.", showing that it was Bob Robertson who secured this order on one of his many trips to the U.S.A. From Boss's order ledgers.

BELOW RIGHT: Hammerless ejector pair nos. 8491/2. See Plates 77, 78 and 79.

when building new guns from scratch was difficult due to changed circumstances.

No. 8127 was ordered on the 19th March 1946 by the Comte Charles de Gramont, 23 Rue de la Paix, Paris. It was completed on the 10th April 1947. The barrels are 29″ long bored full and ¾ choke. The gun weighs 6lb 10oz. The records state that the gun was picked up by a friend of M. Gramont who worked in Whitehall and delivered to the British Embassy in Paris.

One of the nicest pairs of round-bodied Boss I have examined are nos. 8491/2 illustrated right. Nos. 8491/2, a pair of single trigger 12-bores, were ordered by an American customer, E. F. Hutton on the 24th

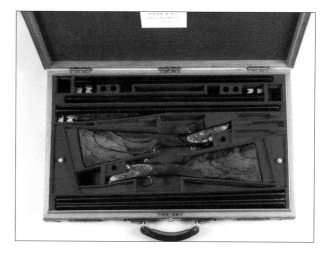

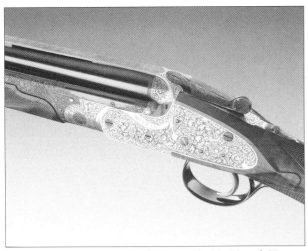

O/U gun no. 10,000. See Plates 81, 82, 83, 84 and 85.

April 1937. Not only are these guns extremely attractive, they are of the highest quality possible and in excellent condition. Unusual for a Boss, they were ordered with 25″ barrels. These short barrels contribute to their lightness, each gun weighing a mere 6lb 3 oz. The relevant No. 1 or 2 is inlaid in gold on the top rib. The colour case hardened round-bodied actions emphasise their grace and lightness. The locks are engraved, "Boss & Co." and have a simpler form of scroll engraving. In addition to the unusual barrel length, the pair are also unusual in that the actions are self-openers. Boss built very few self-openers. The stocks are of the highest possible quality with the most wonderful figure. Originally the pair was supplied in a lightweight double case. Twenty-five-inch barrels are not to everyone's liking and the present owner ordered some years ago additional pairs of barrels of 28″ length. A new oak and leather case was supplied to accommodate both the original barrels and the additional barrels.

Boss & Co. recently completed a trio of .410s nos. 10000/1/2. The trio are of great interest on account of the fact that Boss have never made a trio of .410s before. They are also of great interest in that they differ from a normal trio whereby the three guns match. This trio consists of the three different types of gun that Boss currently produce. Including this trio, Boss have only made seven .410s in total.

No. 10000, illustrated above, is an O/U gun. It has 26″ barrels with 3″ chambers and a ventilated top rib. A single trigger is fitted. No. 10001 is a square-bodied side-by-side, again with 3 inch chambers and single trigger, and no. 10002 is a round-bodied side-by-side with similar specifications. All three guns were engraved by Ken Hunt.

Hammerless ejector gun 10025. See Plates 86, 89, 90, 91 and 92.

Pair of O/U guns. See plate 89.

Square bodied gun. See plate 90.

Round bodied gun. See plate 91.

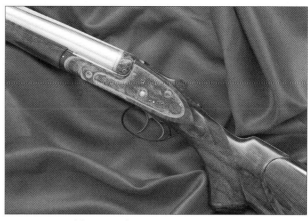

.470 express rifle. See plate 92.

At the time of writing (the early 1990s) Boss & Co., are in the 10,000 serial number range. Serial number 1 began circa 1830 with the first gun produced by Thomas Boss. Bearing in mind the fact that replacement or extra barrels are allocated a separate serial number, it goes to show how, in comparision to other makers, Boss & Co. have produced a relatively small number of guns and rifles since gun no. 1 around one hundred and sixty years ago. Boss & Co. are "builders of best guns only".

APPENDICES

Appendix 1A
The Family Tree of the Boss Family

		William Boss B. 1722 Woodthorpe Leics. M. Oct. 1752 Seagrave Loughborough, Leics.	: Parnell Newberry B. 1727 Loughborough Leics.

William Boss	: Catherine Seymour	John Boss	Parnell Boss
? B. 1757, Narborough Leics. M. 14.11.1784 St Matthews Bethnal Green London D. June 1809 White Hart Place Kennington Lane London Gunmaker Working for Joseph Manton	D. Feb. 1808 White Hart Pl. Kennington Lane London	B. 1759 Narborough	B. 1761 Narborough

William Boss (Jnr)	Fisher Boss	Thomas Boss	: Amy Chapman Fields	Mary Boss
B. 25.2.1787 Cumberland St. Shoreditch London Gunmaker 9 Crown St. London	Bapt. 23.11.1788 St. Ann's Blackfriars London Gunmaker	Bapt. 13.6.1790 St. Ann's Blackfriars London M. 10.9.1837 St Georges Bloomsbury, London D. 17.8.1857 3 St. George's Rd. Brighton Founder Boss & Co.	B. 1.6.1795 Louth D. 29.7.1872 73 St James's St. London Owner/partner Boss & Co.	

N.B.   Individuals underlined denotes a direct connection with the Boss gunmaking business

Thomas Boss
B. 1764
Narborough

Mountjoy Boss
B. 1765
Narborough
D. 1826
London
Coachplater

Thomas Boss
B. 1767
Narborough

Parnell Boss
B. 6.9.1796
White Hart Pl.
Kennington Lane
London
D. 1867
13 Rawstorne St.
London

Catherine Boss
B. 8.5.1798
White Hart Pl.
Kennington Lane
London

Jane Boss
Bapt. 4.1801
White Hart Pl.
Kennington Lane
London

Henry Edward Boss
Bapt. 6.1803
White Hart Pl.
Kennington Lane
London

Jane Charlotte Boss
B. 6.8.1804
White Hart Pl.
Kennington Lane
London

APPENDIX 1B
THE FAMILY TREE OF THE PADDISON FAMILY

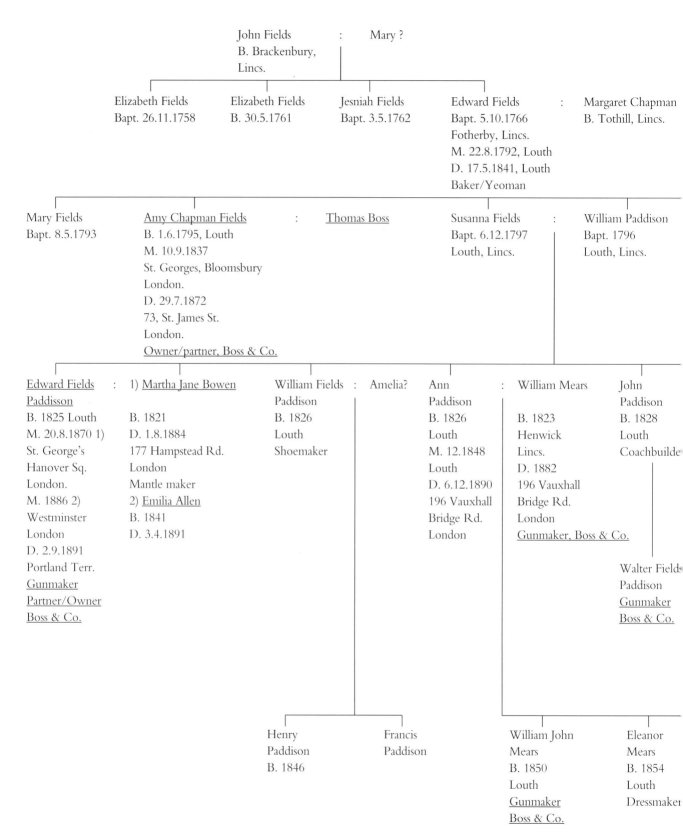

John Fields
B. Brackenbury,
Lincs.

:   Mary ?

Elizabeth Fields
Bapt. 26.11.1758

Elizabeth Fields
B. 30.5.1761

Jesniah Fields
Bapt. 3.5.1762

Edward Fields
Bapt. 5.10.1766
Fotherby, Lincs.
M. 22.8.1792, Louth
D. 17.5.1841, Louth
Baker/Yeoman

:   Margaret Chapman
B. Tothill, Lincs.

Mary Fields
Bapt. 8.5.1793

Amy Chapman Fields
B. 1.6.1795, Louth
M. 10.9.1837
St. Georges, Bloomsbury
London.
D. 29.7.1872
73, St. James St.
London.
Owner/partner, Boss & Co.

:   Thomas Boss

Susanna Fields
Bapt. 6.12.1797
Louth, Lincs.

:   William Paddison
Bapt. 1796
Louth, Lincs.

Edward Fields
Paddisson
B. 1825 Louth
M. 20.8.1870 1)
St. George's
Hanover Sq.
London.
M. 1886 2)
Westminster
London
D. 2.9.1891
Portland Terr.
Gunmaker
Partner/Owner
Boss & Co.

:

1) Martha Jane Bowen
B. 1821
D. 1.8.1884
177 Hampstead Rd.
London
Mantle maker
2) Emilia Allen
B. 1841
D. 3.4.1891

William Fields : Amelia?
Paddison
B. 1826
Louth
Shoemaker

Ann
Paddison
B. 1826
Louth
M. 12.1848
Louth
D. 6.12.1890
196 Vauxhall
Bridge Rd.
London

:   William Mears
B. 1823
Henwick
Lincs.
D. 1882
196 Vauxhall
Bridge Rd.
London
Gunmaker, Boss & Co.

John
Paddison
B. 1828
Louth
Coachbuilder

Walter Fields
Paddison
Gunmaker
Boss & Co.

Henry
Paddison
B. 1846

Francis
Paddison

William John
Mears
B. 1850
Louth
Gunmaker
Boss & Co.

Eleanor
Mears
B. 1854
Louth
Dressmaker

N.B.   *Individuals underlined denotes a direct connection with the Boss gunmaking business*

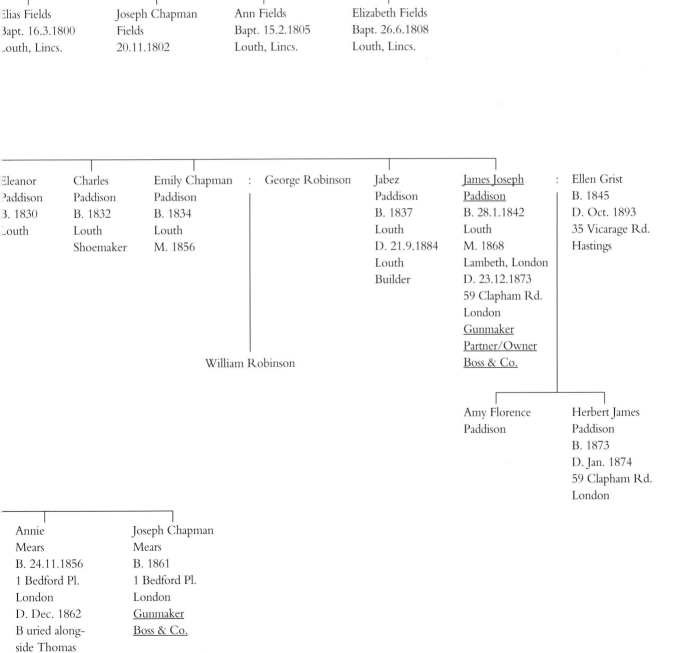

Elias Fields
Bapt. 16.3.1800
Louth, Lincs.

Joseph Chapman
Fields
20.11.1802

Ann Fields
Bapt. 15.2.1805
Louth, Lincs.

Elizabeth Fields
Bapt. 26.6.1808
Louth, Lincs.

Eleanor
Paddison
B. 1830
Louth

Charles
Paddison
B. 1832
Louth
Shoemaker

Emily Chapman
Paddison
B. 1834
Louth
M. 1856

: George Robinson

Jabez
Paddison
B. 1837
Louth
D. 21.9.1884
Louth
Builder

James Joseph
Paddison
B. 28.1.1842
Louth
M. 1868
Lambeth, London
D. 23.12.1873
59 Clapham Rd.
London
Gunmaker
Partner/Owner
Boss & Co.

: Ellen Grist
B. 1845
D. Oct. 1893
35 Vicarage Rd.
Hastings

William Robinson

Amy Florence
Paddison

Herbert James
Paddison
B. 1873
D. Jan. 1874
59 Clapham Rd.
London

Annie
Mears
B. 24.11.1856
1 Bedford Pl.
London
D. Dec. 1862
Buried along-
side Thomas
and Emma Boss

Joseph Chapman
Mears
B. 1861
1 Bedford Pl.
London
Gunmaker
Boss & Co.

APPENDIX 1C
THE FAMILY TREE OF THE ROBERTSON FAMILY

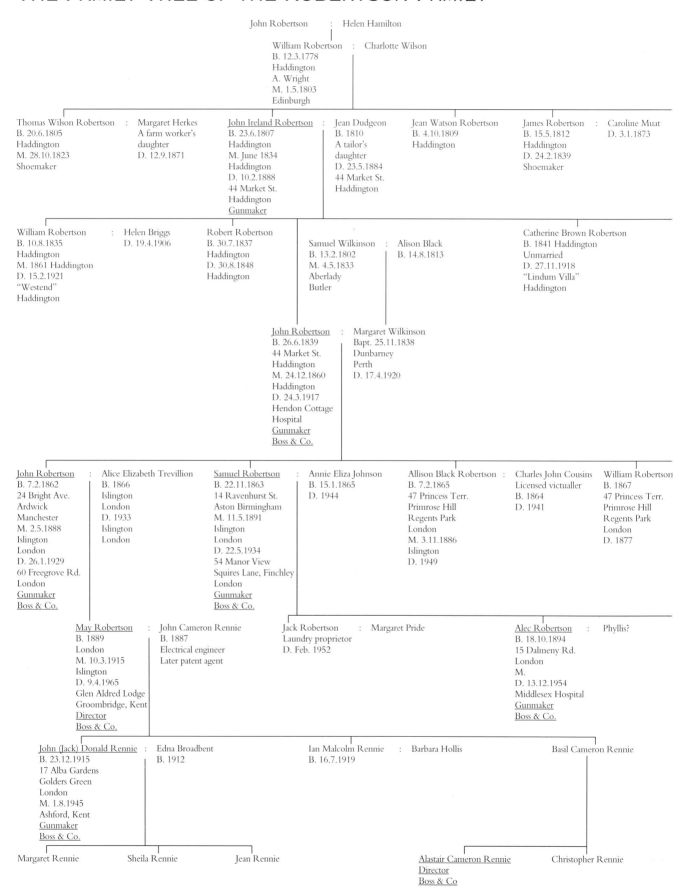

N.B. Individuals underlined denotes a direct connection with the Boss gunmaking business

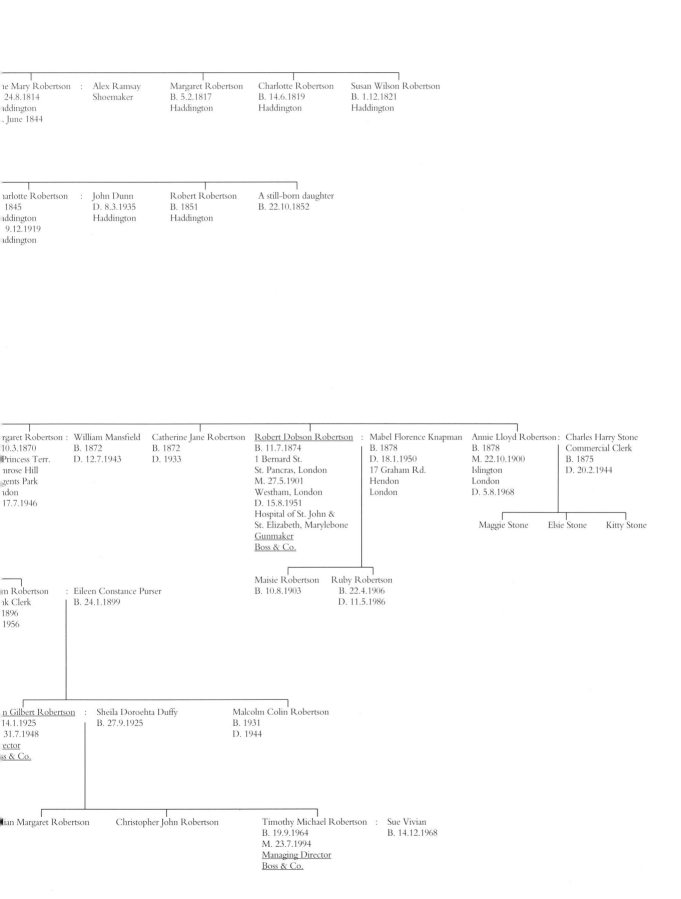

ne Mary Robertson : Alex Ramsay   Margaret Robertson   Charlotte Robertson   Susan Wilson Robertson
24.8.1814   Shoemaker   B. 5.2.1817   B. 14.6.1819   B. 1.12.1821
addington   Haddington   Haddington   Haddington
. June 1844

arlotte Robertson : John Dunn   Robert Robertson   A still-born daughter
1845   D. 8.3.1935   B. 1851   B. 22.10.1852
addington   Haddington   Haddington
9.12.1919
addington

rgaret Robertson : William Mansfield Catherine Jane Robertson   Robert Dobson Robertson : Mabel Florence Knapman   Annie Lloyd Robertson : Charles Harry Stone
10.3.1870   B. 1872   B. 1872   B. 11.7.1874   B. 1878   B. 1878   Commercial Clerk
Princess Terr.   D. 12.7.1943   D. 1933   1 Bernard St.   D. 18.1.1950   M. 22.10.1900   B. 1875
nrose Hill   St. Pancras, London   17 Graham Rd.   Islington   D. 20.2.1944
gents Park   M. 27.5.1901   Hendon   London
ndon   Westham, London   London   D. 5.8.1968
17.7.1946   D. 15.8.1951
                                                                  Hospital of St. John &
                                                                  St. Elizabeth, Marylebone
                                                                  <u>Gunmaker</u>   Maggie Stone   Elsie Stone   Kitty Stone
                                                                  Boss & Co.

                                                                  Maisie Robertson   Ruby Robertson
n Robertson   : Eileen Constance Purser   B. 10.8.1903   B. 22.4.1906
k Clerk   B. 24.1.1899   D. 11.5.1986
1896
1956

n Gilbert Robertson : Sheila Doroehta Duffy   Malcolm Colin Robertson
14.1.1925   B. 27.9.1925   B. 1931
31.7.1948   D. 1944
ector
s & Co.

ian Margaret Robertson   Christopher John Robertson   Timothy Michael Robertson : Sue Vivian
                                                        B. 19.9.1964   B. 14.12.1968
                                                        M. 23.7.1994
                                                        <u>Managing Director</u>
                                                        Boss & Co.

APPENDIX 2

THE BUSINESS ADDRESSES OF BOSS & CO.

The following sources of information have been used:

TRADE DIRECTORIES. Trade directories were published by the Post Office and by private firms. Some were published annually, some bienially. Due to communication problems, in the early period, trade directory information is often tardy or out of date. They must be used as a rough guide.

RATE BOOKS. They were kept by the Parish as a record of rate payments. Being financial, they are very accurate in recording occupiers of premises! The only problem is that since much property was rented, the tenant was often not the ratepayer and hence does not appear in the rate book. In addition many early rate books are missing.

MISCELLANEOUS SOURCES. Eg. Births, Deaths and Marriages, Wills, adverts, etc.

DATE	SHOP ADDRESS
Circa 1816–*circa* 1827	3 Bridge Road, Lambeth, London.
Circa 1827–*circa* 1833	33 Edgware Rd, Marylebone, London.
Circa 1833–*circa* 1835	1 Grosvenor Street, London.
Circa 1835–*circa* 1837	14 Clifford Street, London.

DATE	SHOP ADDRESS
1837–March 1839	76 St James's Street, London.
March 1839–July 1908	73 St James's Street, London.
July 1908–1930	13 Dover Street, London.
1930–July 1960	41 Albemarle Street, London.
July 1960–March 1982	13/14 Cork Street, London.
March 1982–present	13 Dover Street, London.

DATE	FACTORY ADDRESS
Pre 1891	73 St James's Street, London.
1891–99	4 Dansey Yard, Wardour Street, London and 73 St James's Street, London.
1899–1913	1 & 2 Ham Yard, Great Windmill Street, London and 73 St James's Street, London to 1908.
1913–39	6, 8 & 10 Lexington Street, Golden Square, London.
1939–53	34 Osnaburgh Street, Euston Road, London.
1953–73	Horse Shoe Alley, Southwark, London.
1973–present	8 Holyrood Street, Southwark, London.

APPENDIX 3A

BARREL WORDING

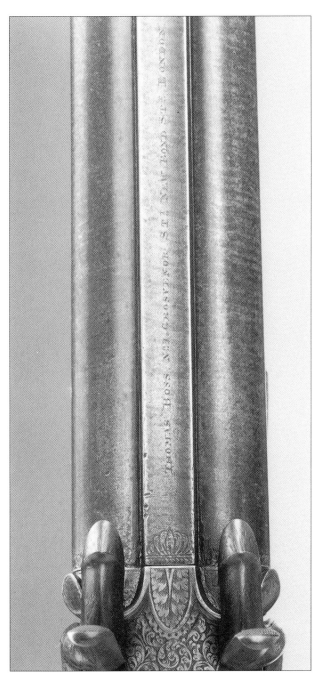 

1. Thomas Boss, No. 1 Grosvenor Street, New Bond Street, London. The style used from *circa* 1833 to *circa* 1835.

2. Thomas Boss, 73 St James' Street, London. The style used from 1839 to *circa* 1857.

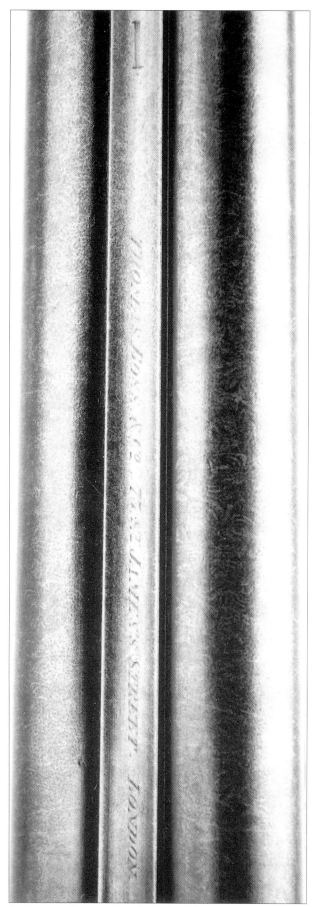

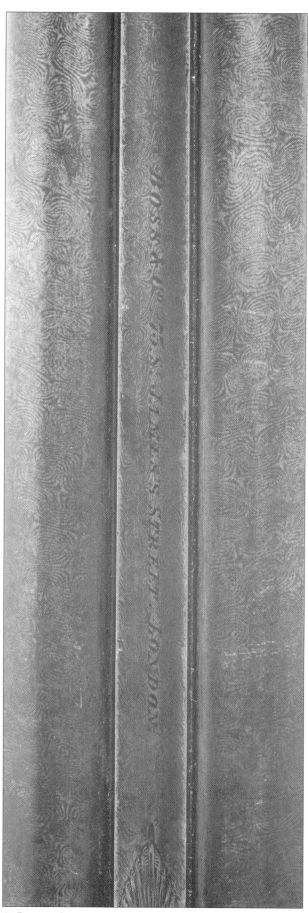

3. Thomas Boss & Co., 73 St James' Street, London. The style used from *circa* 1857 to *circa* 1862.

4. Boss & Co., 73 St James' Street, London. The style used from *circa* 1862 to 1908.

5. Boss & Co., 13 Dover Street, Piccadilly, London. The style used from 1908 to 1930 and 1982 to the present.

6. Boss & Co., 41 Albemarle Street, London. The style used from 1930 to 1960.

APPENDIX 3B

TRADE LABELS

1. William Boss label 1814 to 1817.

2. Thomas Boss
label – early 73
St James's Street
pattern, 1839 to
circa 1850.

3. Thomas Boss
label – later 73
St James's Street
pattern, *circa*
1850 to *circa*
1862.

4. Boss & Co.,
label *circa* 1862 to
1908.

5. Boss & Co.,
label, 13 Dover
Street, 1908 to
1930.

6. Boss & Co., label, 41 Albemarle Street, 1930–60.

7. Boss & Co., label, 13/14 Cork Street, 1960–82.

8. Boss & Co., label, 13 Dover Street, 1982–present.

APPENDIX 4A

BOSS & CO. – CHRONOLOGICAL DIARY OF MAJOR EVENTS UNDER THE BOSS AND PADDISON FAMILIES

DATE	EVENT
Circa 1757	William Boss born Narborough, Leicestershire.
17 Aug. 1773	William Boss begins his apprenticeship under Thomas Ketland, Birmingham.
1780	William Boss finished his apprenticeship.
1780–1784	William Boss moves to London and works with Joseph Manton.
1784	William Boss marries Catherine Seymour, Bethnal Green, London.
25 Feb. 1787	First son William born, Shoreditch, London.
1788	Second son Fisher born, Blackfriars, London.
1790	Third son Thomas born, Blackfriars, London.
1804	Thomas Boss begins his apprenticeship under his father.
Feb. 1808	Catherine Boss, their mother dies, Kennington Lane, London.
June 1809	William Boss (senior) dies, Kennington Lane, London.
1812	Thomas Boss completes his apprenticeship and continues to work with Joseph Manton.
1814	William Boss (junior) commences his gunmaking business at 9 Crown Street, Westminster, London.
Circa 1816	Thomas Boss commences business as a truss and gun manufacturer, 3 Bridge Road, Lambeth, London.
1817	William Boss's (junior) business ceases at 9 Crown Street, Westminster, London.
1825	Edward Fields Paddison born Louth, Lincolnshire.
Circa 1827	Thomas Boss moves to 33 Edgware Road, Marylebone, London.
Circa 1833	Thomas Boss moves to 1 Grosvenor Street, London.
Circa 1835	Thomas Boss moves to 14 Clifford Street, London.

DATE	EVENT
1837	Thomas Boss moves to 76 St James's Street, London.
10 Sept. 1837	Thomas Boss marries Emma Fields from Louth at St George's Parish Church, Bloomsbury, London.
21 Feb. 1838	Edward Paddison begins his apprenticeship under his uncle Thomas Boss.
March 1839	Thomas Boss moves to 73 St James's, Street, London.
28 Jan. 1842	James Paddison born Louth, Lincolnshire.
1845	Edward Fields Paddison completes his apprenticeship.
July 1849	Thomas Boss contracts cholera.
1856	James Paddison begins his apprenticeship under his uncle Thomas Boss.
17 Aug. 1857	Thomas Boss dies at 3 St George's Road, Kemp Town, Brighton.
24 Aug. 1857	Thomas Boss buried in the Brompton Cemetery, London.
1857	Stephen Grant taken into partnership with Emma Boss. Firm becomes known as Thomas Boss & Co.
Circa 1862	The firm adopts the simpler style of heading Boss & Co.
1863	James Paddison completes his apprenticeship.
1866	Stephen Grant leaves Boss to set up on his own at 67 A, St James's Street, London.
1868	James Paddison marries Ellen Grist.
19 Aug. 1870	Edward Paddison signs marriage agreement with his future wife Martha Bowen.
20 Aug. 1870	Edward Paddison marries Martha Bowen. They live at 177 Hampstead Road, London.
29 July 1872	Emma Boss dies at 73, St James's Street. Buried in the Brompton Cemetery along with her husband.
1872	Edward and James Paddison form a partnership to run the firm.

DATE	EVENT	DATE	EVENT
23 Dec. 1873	James Paddison dies at 59 Clapham Road, London.	1886	Second marriage of Edward Paddison to Emelia Allen. They live at 19 Portland Terrace, London.
31 Dec. 1873	James Paddison buried at the Brompton Cemetery, London.	1 Jan 1891	Edward Paddison sells half share in Boss business to John Robertson.
1873	Edward Paddison becomes the sole proprietor of Boss & Co.	3 Apr. 1891	Emelia Paddison dies.
Circa 1880	Boss & Co. is renamed E.F.P. Boss & Co. in reference to Edward Fields Paddison.	2 Sept. 1891	Edward Paddison dies at 19 Portland Terrace, London.
1 Aug. 1884	Martha Paddison dies at 177 Hampstead Road, London.	7 Sept. 1891	Edward Paddison buried at the City of Westminster Cemetery, East Finchley, London.

BOSS & CO. – CHRONOLOGICAL DIARY OF MAJOR EVENTS UNDER THE ROBERTSON FAMILY

DATE	EVENT
12 Mar. 1778	William Robertson born at Haddington, near Edinburgh. A wheelwright by trade.
1 May. 1803	William Robertson marries Charlotte Wilson from Edinburgh.
23 June 1807	John Ireland Robertson, second son born to them at Haddington.
Circa 1830	John Ireland Robertson commences business as a gunmaker at no. 1 Hardgate Haddington.
June 1834	John Ireland Robertson marries Jean Dudgeon, Haddington.
26 June 1839	John Robertson, third son born to them at Haddington.
1852	John Robertson begins his apprenticeship to his father
Circa 1854	The Robertson gunmaking business moves to 44 Market Street, Haddington.
1858	John Robertson completes his apprenticeship, leaves Haddington and travels South to work for Joseph Whitworth, Manchester.
24 Dec. 1860	John Robertson marries Margaret Wilkinson in the Parish Church, Haddington.
7 Feb. 1862	First son, John Robertson (Jnr) born 24 Bright Avenue, Ardwick, Manchester.
1862	John Robertson begins work with Westley-Richards Birmingham.
22 Nov. 1863	Second son, Samuel Robertson born 14 Ravenhurst Street, Birmingham.
1864	John Robertson moves to London and begins work with James Purdey.
1873	John Robertson commences business working for the Trade at 101 Great Titchfield Street, London.
11 July 1874	Third son, Robert Dobson Robertson born 1 Bernard Street, Regent's Park, London.

DATE	EVENT
1876	John Robertson (Jnr) begins his apprenticeship.
1877	Sam Robertson begins his apprenticeship.
1882	Robertson's business moves to 4 George Yard, Wardour Street, London.
15 June 1882	John Robertson's first patent taken out.
1883	John Robertson (Jnr) completes his apprenticeship.
1884	Sam Robertson completes his apprenticeship.
11 July 1888	Robert Robertson begins his apprenticeship on his 14th birthday.
10 Feb. 1888	John Ireland Robertson (John Robertson's father) dies at 44 Market Street, Haddington.
2 May 1888	John Robertson (Jnr) marries Alice Trevillion, Islington, London.
1889	May Robertson born to John and Alice Robertson London.
1 Jan 1891	John Robertson becomes a partner in Boss & Co.
11 May 1891	Sam Robertson marries Annie Johnson, Islington, London.
31 Dec. 1893	Partnership between Walter Fields Paddison and John Robertson dissolved.
18 Oct. 1894	Alec Robertson born to Sam and Annie Robertson, 15 Dalmeny Road, London.
26 Nov. 1894	John Robertson single trigger provisional patent no. 22894.
1895	Bob Robertson completes his apprenticeship.
4 Feb. 1897	John Robertson ejector provisional patent no. 2988.
1899	Factory moves to 1 and 2 Ham Yard, Great Windmill Street, London.
27. May 1901	Bob Robertson marries Mabel Knapman, West Ham, London.
1903	Regent Shooting Ground, Finchley Road set up.

DATE	EVENT
26 March 1903	John Robertson owns the Boss business outright.
15 Dec. 1906	John Robertson takes Purdey's to court for alleged patent infringement of the single trigger.
1908	Regent Shooting School moves to Shire Hall Lane, Hendon.
1 July 1908	Boss & Co. move to 13 Dover Street, Piccadilly, London.
10 Feb. 1909	John Robertson's over-and-under gun and ejector patents nos. 3307/8.
1910	Alec Robertson begins his apprenticeship.
1913	The factory moves to 6, 8 and 10 Lexington Street, Golden Square, Soho, London.
10 March 1915	May Robertson marries John Cameron Rennie, Islington, London.
26 Aug. 1915	John Robertson's grenade thrower, patent no. 12298.
23 Dec. 1915	John (Jack) Donald Rennie born to May and John Rennie, 17 Alba Gardens, Golders Green, London.
1917	Alec Robertson completes his apprenticeship.
24 March 1917	John Robertson dies aged 77, at the Hendon Cottage Hospital, London.
28 March 1917	John Robertson cremated at the Golders Green Crematorium, London.
1922	Fred Oliver joins the firm.
1 March 1923	John, Sam and Bob Robertson draw up Articles of Partnership.
1926	John Robertson (Jnr) plays a major role in establishing the Long Sufferers' Association and becomes its first chairman.
1926	Arthur Sanderson becomes shop manager.

DATE	EVENT
26 Jan. 1929	John Robertson dies aged 67 at 60 Freegrove Road, Holloway, London.
26 Aug. 1929	Regent Shooting Ground moves to Rowley Green, Barnet By Pass.
May 1930	Boss & Co. move to 41 Albemarle Street, Piccadilly, London.
19 June 1930	Boss & Co. granted limited liability status.
1930	Jack Rennie begins his apprenticeship.
22 May 1934	Sam Robertson dies aged 70 at 54 Manor View, Finchley, London.
1938	Bob Robertson celebrates 50 years of gunmaking.
1939	The factory moves to 34 Osnaburgh Street, Euston Road, London.
10 May 1941	The factory in Osnaburgh Street is bomb damaged.
1942	An additional factory is opened at 143 1/2 Euston Road, London.
1951	Boss & Co. exhibit at the Festival of Britain.
15 Aug. 1951	Bob Robertson dies aged 77 at 17 Graham Road, Hendon, London.
13 Dec. 1954	Alec Robertson dies aged 60 at the Middlesex Hospital, London.
1958	The last factory outing to the Ship Hotel, Brighton.
15 July 1960	Boss & Co. move to 13/14 Cork Street, London.
Mid 1960's	O/U production ceases.
1973	The factory moves to 8 Holyrood Street, Southwark, London.
26 Mar. 1982	Boss & Co. return to 13 Dover Street, Piccadilly, London.
1990	Tim Robertson enters the firm as managing director.

APPENDIX 5A

BREAKDOWN OF BOSS GUN PRODUCTION (MUZZLE-LOADERS)

This list is based upon a study of Boss's records dating from gun no. 571 built in 1844. Records do not exist before this period. It can not be a comprehensive list on account of this. Nevertheless it does give a good picture of the type of guns and number of guns produced by Thomas Boss during the period 1844 to the early 1870s. The last muzzle-loader built was a double-barrel 12-bore percussion gun no. 3078 produced in 1872 for an eccentric Sir John Blois. Muzzle-loading gun production tailed off very quickly in the 1860s with the advent of the breech-loader.

TYPE OF GUN	TOTAL NUMBERS BUILT
Double-Barrel Shotguns	1,097
Single-Barrel Shotguns	13
Double-Barrel Tubelock Shotguns	22
Double-Barrel Rifles	31
Single-Barrel Rifles	11
Pea-Rifles (Small Bore Rifles)	4
Boys' Guns	1
Pistols	16
Duelling Pistols	4
Wildfowling Guns (9 Bore and Over)	7
Pepperbox Revolvers	4

NOTE: A fair number of these muzzle-loaders passed through Boss's hands again in the 1870s and 1880s when they were converted to centre fire breech-loaders.

BREAKDOWN OF GUN PRODUCTION (BREECH-LOADERS 1858–90)

Edward Paddison was conservative in the type of guns he produced and slow to accept the rapidly changing innovations in gun design of the late 19th century. The breakdown of gun production at Boss until his death in 1891 shows his reluctance to accept the pace of change in breech-loading development. Less too conservative a picture is inferred, it must be remembered that pinfires reigned supreme 1860 to 1870, centre-fire hammer guns 1870 to 1885 and hammerless guns 1885 to the close of period in this appendix.

The first pinfire produced was a double-barrel 14-bore gun no. 1600 ordered on 9th June 1858 by G. B. Bruce, 1st Regiment Life Guards. The first centre-firegun was a double-barrel 12-bore gun no. 2413 ordered on 16th June 1866 by Wroth Lethbridge. The first snap action (unfortunately the records do not mention what type of snap action) was a double-barrel 12-bore gun no. 2563 ordered on 18th September 1867 by Col. Lord Seaton. The last pinfire built was a double-barrel 12-bore gun no. 2945 ordered on 29th September 1871 by the Earl of Jersey. The first hammerless gun was a double-barrel 12-bore gun no. 3571 ordered on 17th February 1880 by E. W. Herbert (the records do not state what type of hammerless action this was). The first ejector gun was a double-barrel 12-bore hammerless side lever no. 3920 ordered on 3rd June 1887 by Dr G. Johnson, 11 Savile Row, London. This was a Perkes patent ejector.

NOTE: Very few breech-loading pistols were made. I doubt if they were actually made by Boss. Some Tranter and such like revolvers were sold bearing the Boss name and trade label. They were factory made by their respective makers and engraved with the retailer's name, in this instance Boss.

TYPES OF CLOSING ACTION

As stated earlier, although Paddison was conservative, the caveat must be borne in mind that this appendix stops at 1890. Underlevers were in use in the 1860s to the mid 1870s and snap actions thereafter. Where Boss were unusual is in their preponderance of under-levers and their preference for the side snap as opposed to the top snap.

TYPE OF ACTION	TOTAL NUMBERS BUILT
Lever over guard (inert double grip screw under-lever)	1490
Under snap (thumbhole under snap – most to the Purdey pattern)	117
Top snap	69
Side snap	283

TYPE OF GUN	TOTAL NUMBERS BUILT
Pinfire shotguns	735
Pinfire rifles	31
Centre-fire hammer guns	962
Centre-fire hammer ejector guns	8
Centre-fire hammer rifles	75
Hammerless guns	141
Wildfowling guns (9-bore and over)	7

APPENDIX 5C

BREAKDOWN OF GUN PRODUCTION (ROBERTSON ERA 1891–1950)

When John Robertson became a partner in Boss in 1891, the fortunes of Boss turned around. A great many more guns were produced. After WWI, the American market accounted for around fifty per cent of sales. American sporting gun demand differed from its British counterpart. The Americans preferred the conventional double trigger and were more enthusiastic for the O/U. In addition, not so many pairs of guns were ordered by Americans. Orders for trios were common from British customers.

The last hammer gun built was no. 4962, a 12-bore top snap gun for pigeon shooting ordered by W. R. Elliston. It had extra full choke barrels no. 4963. This gun was completed on 11th June 1902. The first single-trigger guns were nos. 4305, 4306 and 4308, all double-barrel 12-bore top lever hammerless ejectors, ordered by H. H. Islam on 2nd April 1894. The first O/U gun was no. 5773, a double-barrel 12-bore with 28″ barrels constructed in 1909.

After the invention of the single-trigger and O/U gun, Boss gun production settled down to a fairly conventional pattern. By far the majority of guns were built with top levers, although a few still retained the side lever. As had happened in the 19th century, whenever customers ordered new barrels or extra barrels, an individual number was allocated to the barrels.

TYPE OF GUN	TOTAL NUMBERS BUILT
Hammer guns	28
Hammer ejectors	14
Hammerless guns (total)	3,886
Single triggers within the total of hammerless guns	2,348
O/Us within the total of hammerless guns	396

It is interesting to note the very high percentage of single-trigger guns built. O/Us were far more expensive than the conventional side-by-side and this helps to explain their lower number.

APPENDIX 5D

AVERAGE GUN PRODUCTION

DECADE	APPROXIMATE NUMBER OF GUNS PRODUCED PER ANNUM
Early 1840s	50 guns
Later 1840s	70 guns
1850–60	75 guns
1860–70	95 guns
1870–80	80 guns
1880–90	55 guns
1890–1900	70 guns
1900–10	100 guns
1910–20	90 guns (hardly any guns were produced 1915–18)
1920–30	120 guns
1930–40	80 guns
1940–50	20 guns (hardly any guns were produced 1939–1945)

THE DATING OF BOSS GUNS

The first record of a Boss gun in the possession of Boss & Co. begins with gun no. 571 built in 1844. However the ledger that this gun appears in does not give dates, it only gives gun type and owner's name.

The first ledger that gives full details of guns built commences in 1850. This begins with gun no. 993 ordered on 5 February: 1850. This is an order ledger and gives full details of the guns, barrel length, stock size, weight, owner, date ordered, date completed, etc. Selected pages from the order ledgers pertaining to the guns described are illustrated throughout the book.

In the period before 1850 educated guesswork must be used. The period 1845 to 1850 does not present too many problems. By studying Boss's letters to customers during this period, it is possible to marry up the customer and gun number in the earlier ledger with the date on the letter. Thus a fairly accurate record can be deduced. Pre-1845 guesswork must be used. I assume that in this early period when he had just entered 73 St James's Street, his output was lower since he was building up his business.

It must be stressed that even using the accurate ledgers from 1850 onwards, complete accuracy is impossible. When a gun was ordered from Boss, the order was recorded in the order ledgers. At this point the gun was given no serial number. In the process of completion, the gun received a number and this number was usually then entered in the order ledger. The gun's completion date was rarely recorded in the order ledger. Sometimes the gun number itself was not noted down. In making up the following table on "The Dating of Boss Guns", I have had to use order dates. Since there is always a variable gap between date of order and date of completion, the table can not be absolutely accurate. It should be accurate to within three or four months. Additionally, Boss's records are not strictly numerical since some guns were completed quicker than others and often previously unused serial numbers can appear at later dates.

The order ledgers can be of variable detail depending upon the person responsible for recording and compiling the information. In some periods virtually every detail is recorded down to who made the stock, who screwed the gun together, etc. In other periods detail is sparse – perhaps simply "A New Breech-loader" and the name of the future owner but little else. For a small fee Boss & Co. will supply copies of the order ledgers for owners' guns built after no. 993.

YEAR	GUN NUMBERS	POINTS OF INTEREST
PRE 1839	–280	(Any dating attempt would be unwise).
1839	Nos. 280–320	
1840	Nos. 320–370	
1841	Nos. 370–420	
1842	Nos. 420–480	
1843	Nos. 480–540	
1844	Nos. 540–610	Boss's records begin with gun no. 571. Nos. 574/5 double pistols. No. 577 double pistol. No. 581 tube lock. No. 593 tube lock.
1845	Nos. 610–680	No. 663 later converted to centre-fire. No. 667 for Boss's own use. Nos. 680 and 681 later converted to centre-fire 1870. Nos. 610/1 tube locks. No. 623 tube lock. Nos. 633/4 tube locks. No. 640 tube lock.
1846	Nos. 680–750	No. 721 for Boss's own use. No. 740 later converted to centre-fire. Nos. 705/6 converted to centre-fire 1871. Nos. 712/3 double pistols. No. 694 tube lock. Nos. 688/9 tube locks. Nos. 733/4 tube locks. No. 746 tube lock.
1847	Nos. 750–820	Nos. 815 and 816 duelling pistols. No. 776 built to match no. 726.
1848	Nos. 820–890	No. 830 extra barrels for no. 716. Nos. 870, 873, 890, 9-bore guns. No 874 converted to centre-fire 1872. No. 827 built to match no. 763.
1849	Nos. 890–970	No. 921 converted to centre-fire 1872. No. 944 converted to centre-fire 1870.

YEAR	*GUN NUMBERS*	*POINTS OF INTEREST*
1850	Nos. 970–1055	Nos. 990/1 tube locks converted to pinfire 1870. Nos. 1026/7 converted to pinfire 1870. Nos. 987/8 pocket pistols. Nos. 997/8 tube locks.
1851	Nos.1055–1130	No. 1117 extra shotgun barrels for rifle no. 956. No. 1114 converted to centre-fire 1869. No. 1120 18-bore gun later converted to a .500 express rifle. Nos. 1061/2 tube locks. No. 1111 built to match no. 934. No. 1056 double pistol. Nos. 1059/60 tube locks. No. 1125 9-bore.
1852	Nos.1130–1200	No. 1155 rifle later converted to breech loader and re-numbered 3153. No. 1165 converted to centre-fire 1887 and re-numbered 3955. No. 1201 boys' gun. Nos. 1190/1 converted to centre-fire 1868. No. 1147 built to match no. 985. No. 1161 built to match no. 1113. No. 1153 built to match no. 1070. No. 1180 built to match no. 1093. No. 1194 built to match no. 1010.
1853	Nos.1200–1300	No. 1234 boy's rifle. Nos. 1232/3 pair of 40-bore pistols. Nos. 1266/ 7 converted to centre-fire 1880. Nos. 1276/7 duelling pistols. No. 1273 built to match no. 1252. No. 1284 built to match no. 1109. No. 1291 built to match no. 1136. Nos. 1136/1291 converted to centre-fire 1869. No. 1216 converted to centre-fire 1871. No. 1248 built to match no. 900. No. 1250 built to match no. 884.
1854	Nos.1300–1390	No. 1338 8-bore. Nos. 1301/2 converted to centre-fire 1883. No. 1342 built to match no. 1198. No. 1357 built to match no. 995. No. 1389 9-bore. No. 1388 cancelled – false address given! No. 1359 built to match no. 1043. Nos. 1303/4 over and under pocket pistols. Nos. 1305/6 single pistols. No. 1307 5-barrel pepperbox revolver. No. 1308 6-barrel pepperbox revolver.
1855	Nos.1390–1450	No. 1406 9-bore. No. 1428 built to match no. 1204. No. 1436 built to match no. 1209.
1856	Nos.1450–1530	No. 1463 built to match no. 1388. No. 1496 converted to centre-fire 1884. No. 1466 built to match no. 1243. No. 1490 built to match no. 1444. No. 1479 built to match no. 1376. No. 1503 built to match no. 1124. No. 1446 converted to centre-fire. No. 1476 converted to pinfire 1870. No. 1519 built to match no. 1417.
1857	Nos.1530–1590	No. 1539 built to match no. 1210. No. 1548 built to match no. 1506. No. 1534 built to match no. 1511.
1858	Nos.1590–1660	No. 1594 built to match no. 730. No. 1614 built to match no. 1252. No. 1617 converted to pinfire 1869. No. 1601 converted to centre-fire 1871. First breech-loader ordered 9th April, 1858, but the records state, "Not to be put in hand at present". No. 1593 plain gun for a keeper. No. 1624 built to match no. 867. No. 1600 first pinfire built. No. 1620 second pinfire built. No. 1646 built to match no. 1567.
1859	Nos.1660–1740	No. 1680 built to match no. 1590. No. 1664 built to match no. 1402. No. 1686 built to match no. 1583. No. 1700 built to match no. 1615. No. 1702 built to match no. 1476. No. 1714 built to match no. 1597. No. 1711 converted to centre-fire 1870. Nos. 1691/2 converted to centre-fire 1870.
1860	Nos.1740–1850	No. 1761 built to match no. 1668. No. 1779 built to match no. 1546. No. 1788 built to match Purdey no. 4360. No. 1744 converted to centre-fire 1872. No. 1825 built to match no. 1559.
1861	Nos.1850–1950	No. 1897 converted to centre-fire. No. 1896 built to match no. 1709. No. 1932 converted to centre-fire 1872. No. 1936 Grant patent breech-loader. No. 1940 converted to centre-fire 1881.
1862	Nos.1950–2020	Nos. 1967/8 Grant patent breech-loaders.
1863	Nos.2020–2120	No. 2028 6 bore. No. 2098 6-bore. No. 2118 converted to centre-fire.
1864	Nos.2120–2240	No. 2124 converted to centre-fire 1872. No. 2180 built to match no. 2005. No. 2205 6 bore. No. 2336 built to match no. 1952.
1865	Nos.2240–2400	No. 2252 Grant patent breech-loader. No. 2279 converted to centre fire 1888. No. 2266 converted to centre-fire. No. 2263 converted to centre-fire. Nos. 2284/5 converted to centre-fire. No. 2294 converted to centre-fire. Nos. 2321/2 converted to centre-fire. No. 2338 converted to centre-fire. No. 2340 converted to centre-fire. No. 2346 converted to centre-fire. No. 2364 converted to centre-fire 1884. No. 2361 converted to centre-fire. No. 2362 converted to centre-fire. No. 2371 converted to centre-fire 1885. No. 2392 converted to

YEAR	GUN NUMBERS	POINTS OF INTEREST
		centre-fire. No. 2394 converted to centre-fire 1881. No. 2253 4-bore.
1866	Nos.2400–2500	No. 2401 converted to centre-fire. No. 2417 converted to centre-fire 1883. No. 2420 built to match no. 2387. No. 2439 Grant patent breech loader. No. 2461 second centre-fire. No. 2465 built to match no. 2377. Nos. 2480/1 to Lancaster's patent. No. 2417 converted to centre-fire 1883. No. 2496 converted to centre-fire. No. 2498 converted to centre-fire 1885. No. 2499 converted to centre-fire 1885. No. 2500 converted to centre-fire.
1867	Nos.2500–2580	Nos. 2517/8 converted to centre-fire 1883. No. 2523 built to match no. 2189. No. 2575 muzzle loading pigeon gun. No. 2563 first snap action. No. 2536 converted to centre-fire 1878. No. 2555 converted to centre-fire. Nos. 2517/8 converted to centre-fire 1883. No. 2502 built to match no. 2245.
1868	Nos.2580–2680	Nos. 2583/4 pair of breech-loading pistols using Snider cartridges. No. 2616 built to match no. 2532. No. 2661 built to match no. 2260. No. 2622 built to match no. 2617. No. 2673 pigeon gun. No. 2678 pigeon gun.
1869	Nos.2680–2780	No. 2693 muzzle-loading pigeon gun. No. 2705 built to match no. 2160. No. 2778 built to match no. 2211.
1870	Nos.2780–2880	No. 2784 pigeon gun. No. 2783 9-bore muzzle-loader. No. 2860 8-bore. No. 2824 built to match no. 2604. No. 2834 built to match no. 2592. No. 2844 built to match no. 2755. No. 2847 built to match no. 2739. No. 2814 4-bore. No. 2864 built to match no. 2720. Nos. 2873/4 built to match no. 2788. No. 2880 built to match no. 2837.
1871	Nos.2880–2950	No. 2904 built to match no. 2807. No. 2886 built to match no. 2673. No. 2887 8 bore. No. 2945 last pin fire. Nos. 3008/9/10 trio. No. 2935 built to match no. 2643.
1872	Nos.2950–3060	No. 3022 built to match no. 2983. No. 3002 built to match no. 2909. No. 3018 built to match no. 2697. No. 3028 built to match no. 2570. No. 3078 last muzzle-loader built. No. 3056 built to match no. 3012. No. 3034 built to match no. 2827.
1873	Nos.3060–3140	No. 3102 built to match no. 3027. No. 3120 built to match no. 2828. No. 3128 built to match no. 2596.
1874	Nos.3140–3220	No. 3142 built to match no. 3045. No. 3146 built to match no. 2193. No. 3174 built to match no. 2964. No. 3218 built to match no. 2387. No. 3208 built to match no. 2902.
1875	Nos.3220–3300	No. 3269 built to match no. 2980. No. 3274 built to match no. 3122. No. 3244 built to match no. 2229.
1876	Nos.3300–3370	No. 3314 built to match no. 3246. No. 3328 built to match no. 3127.
1877	Nos.3370–3450	No. 3370 built to match no. 3092. Nos. 3376/7/8 trio. No. 3382 built to match no. 2051. No. 3417 built to match no. 3166.
1878	Nos.3450–3520	No. 3492 built to match no. 2672. Nos. 3489/90 built to match no. 3439. No. 3474 built to match no. 2909. No. 3478 built to match no. 2248. No. 3484 built to match no. 3296. No. 3502 built to match no. 3061. No. 3500 built to match no. 2733. No. 3520 8 bore. Nos. 3505/6 built to match nos. 3435/6.
1879	Nos.3520–3570	No. 3540 built to match no. 2348. No. 3532 built to match no. 2261. No. 3536 built to match no. 3279. No. 3540 built to match no. 2882. No. 3546 built to match no. 3310. No. 3556 built to match no. 3240. No. 3562 built to match no. 3441. No. 3566 8 bore.
1880	Nos.3570–3600	No. 3571 first hammerless gun. No. 3582 8-bore. No. 3586 built to match no. 2906. No. 3585 built to match no. 3562.
1881	Nos.3600–3660	No. 3622 built to match no. 3353. No. 3608 built to match no. 3534. No. 3630 built to match no. 3540. No. 3640 built to match no. 2591. No. 3656 built to match no. 3231. No. 3652 built to complete a trio with nos. 3223/4.
1882	Nos.3660–3730	No. 3674 built to match no. 3449. Nos. 3668/9/10 trio. No. 3680 pigeon gun. No. 3690 built to match no. 3050. No. 3692 built to match no. 3188. No. 3708 built to match no. 3438. No. 3715 8-bore.
1883	Nos.3730–3770	No. 3748 built to match no. 2059. No. 3770 built to match no. 3329.1884 Nos.3770–3813 No. 3772 built to match no. 2495. No. 3798 built to match no. 3682. No. 3802 built to match no. 3614.

YEAR	GUN NUMBERS	POINTS OF INTEREST
1885	Nos.3813–3850	No. 3758 Boss Prize in the "Ascot Optional Handicap" 13th June 1885. Live pigeon match. No. 3828 built to match no. 3779. No. 3836 built to match no. 3766. No. 3844 built to match no. 2817. No. 3848 built to match no. 3529.
1886	Nos.3850–3900	No. 3860 built to match no. 3491. No. 3897 pigeon gun. No. 3900 pigeon gun.
1887	Nos.3900–3950	No. 3906 pigeon gun. No. 3920 first ejector gun. No. 3885 pigeon gun.
1888	Nos.3950–4010	No. 3968 built to complete a trio with nos. 3597/8. Nos. 3963/4 to complete a trio with no. 3260. No. 3976 built to match no. 3935. No. 3982 hammer ejector. No. 3984 hammer ejector. No. 3995 pigeon gun. No. 3972 built to match no. 3844.
1889	Nos.4010–4070	Nos. 4015/6 hammer ejectors. No. 4022 built to match no. 3648. Nos. 4033/4 hammer ejectors. No. 4050 built to match no. 3946. No. 4059 pigeon gun. No. 4056 pigeon gun.
1890	Nos.4070–4120	Nos. 4089/90 hammer ejectors. No. 4124 pigeon gun. No. 4102 built to match no. 3653. No. 4113 built to match no. 3714.
1891	Nos.4120–4175	No. 4137 built to match no. 3823. Nos. 4146/7/8 trio hammer ejectors. No. 4126 hammer ejector. No. 4124 12-bore paradox.
1892	Nos.4175–4242	No. 4185 hammer ejector. No. 4190 pigeon gun. Nos. 4183/4 hammer ejectors. No. 4194 built to match no. 4129. No. 4206 12-bore ball and shotgun. No. 4205 24-bore hammer ejector. Nos. 4207/8 hammer ejectors. Nos. 4237/8 built to match nos. 4051/2. No. 4234 built to match no. 4086. No. 4182 hammer ejector.
1893	Nos.4242–4310	No. 4249 pigeon gun.
1894	Nos.4310–4360	No. 4316 to complete a trio with nos. 4043/4. Nos. 4318/19/20 trio. No. 4325 hammer ejector. No. 4326 pigeon gun. Nos. 4305, 4306, 4308 first single triggers. No. 4341 built to match no. 3184. No. 4350 hammer ejector built to match no. 4185. No. 4317 built to match no. 4315. No. 4356 to complete a trio with nos. 4301/2.
1895	Nos.4360–4410	Nos. 4361/2/3 trio. No. 4378 pigeon gun. Nos. 4295/6/7 trio. No. 4380 hammer ejector.
1896	Nos.4410–4470	No. 4451 to complete a trio with nos. 4251/2. No. 4410 built to match no. 4177. No. 4422 built to match no. 4402. No. 4430 built to match no. 4202. No. 4433 built to match no. 4156. No. 4454 built to match no. 4434. No. 4458 built to match no. 4358.
1897	Nos.4470–4590	No. 4484 to complete a trio with nos. 4149/50. Nos. 4471/2/3 trio. No. 4500 built to match no. 4399. Nos. 4490/1/2 trio. Nos. 4551/2/3 trio. Nos. 4554/5/6 trio. No. 4566 pigeon gun. No. 4564 built to match no. 4010. Nos. 4570/1/2 trio. No. 4486 built to match no. 4192. No. 4574 built to match no. 3587. No. 4495 pigeon gun. Nos. 4501–4550 Winchester Rifles.
1898	Nos.4590–4680	Nos. 4591/2/3 trio. No. 4648 built to match no. 4637. Nos. 4667/8/9 trio. No. 4661 built to match no. 4073. No. 4595 to complete a trio with nos. 4481/2. No. 4605 three-barrel gun. No. 4594 pigeon gun. No. 4670 pigeon gun. No. 4633 pigeon gun. Nos. 4635/6 first selective single trigger. No. 4647 pigeon gun.
1899	Nos.4680–4750	No. 4708 to complete a trio with nos. 4465/6. Nos. 4717/8/9 trio. No. 4726 to complete a trio with nos. 4411/2. No. 4690 three-barrel gun. No. 4733 to complete a trio with nos. 4475/6. No. 4731 built to match no. 3975. No. 4734 built to match no. 4273. Nos. 4739 /40/41 trio. No. 4737 pigeon gun.
1900	Nos.4750–4840	No. 4767 to complete a trio with nos. 4459/60. No. 4795 built to match no. 4196. Nos. 4809/10/11 trio. No. 4816 built to match no. 4742. No. 4815 built to match no. 4736. No. 4840 built to match no. 4759. Nos. 4837/8/9 trio.
1901–1905	Nos. 4840–5360	Nos. 4857/8/9 trio. No. 4879 pigeon gun. No. 4902 pigeon gun. No. 4864 built to match no. 4803. No. 4931 pigeon gun. No. 4926 built to match no. 4448. No. 4908 to complete a trio with nos. 4671/2. No. 4921 pigeon gun. No. 4943 to complete a quartet with nos. 4857/8/9. No. 4939 built to match no. 4337. No. 4940 built to match no. 4856. No. 4962 last hammer gun. No. 4961 single trigger try gun. No. 4854 to complete a trio with nos. 4347/8. No. 4889 pigeon gun. No. 4926 built to match no. 4448. No. 4955 built to match no.

YEAR	*GUN NUMBERS*	*POINTS OF INTEREST*
		4785. No. 4951 to complete a trio with nos. 4655/6. No. 4978 pigeon gun. Nos. 5001/2 pigeon guns. Nos. 4975/6/7 trio. No. 5004 pigeon gun. No. 5007 pigeon gun. No. 4925 pigeon gun. Nos 4964/5/6 trio. No. 5015 pigeon gun. No. 4986 built to match no. 4833. Nos. 5053/4/5 trio. No. 5084 built to match no. 4911. Nos. 5086/7/8 trio. No. 5085 built to match no. 3966. Nos. 4932/5089 pigeon guns. No. 5103 pigeon gun. No. 5108 built to match no. 4899. No. 5107 to complete a trio with nos. 3893/4. No. 5112 built to match no. 4632. Nos. 5113/4/5/6 quartet. No. 5138 pigeon gun. No. 5119 pigeon gun. No. 5139 pigeon gun. No. 5155 to complete a trio with nos. 5045/6. No. 5168 pigeon gun. Nos. 5159/60/61 trio. No. 5144 pigeon gun. Nos. 5169/70/71 trio. No. 5175 built to match no. 4912. Nos. 5141/2/3 trio. No. 5177 pigeon gun. No. 5192 to complete a trio with nos. 4683/4. No. 5191 built to match no. 5110. Nos. 5159/60/61 trio. No. 5176 pigeon gun. No. 5211 built to match no. 5172. No. 5212 pigeon gun. No. 5162 pigeon gun. No. 5227 pigeon gun. No. 5228 built to match no. 4585. No. 5198 pigeon gun. No. 5199 pigeon gun. No. 5165 built to match no. 4606. Nos. 5237/8/9 trio. Nos. 5241/2/3 trio. No. 5140 pigeon gun. No. 5289 to complete a trio with nos. 5053 /5. No. 5283 built to match no. 4855. No. 5284 to complete a trio with nos. 4157/8. No. 5300 built to match no. 4639. Nos. 5303/4/5 trio. No. 5315 pigeon gun. No. 5306 to complete a trio with nos. 4625/6. No. 5317 built to match no. 5262. No. 5162 pigeon gun. No. 5349 to complete a trio with nos. 4755/6. No. 5350 built to match no. 4781. No. 5301 pigeon gun. No. 5356 built to match no. 4927.
1906–1910	Nos. 5360–5930	No. 5439 built to match no. 5288. Nos. 5377/8/9 trio. No. 5376 to complete a trio with nos. 5231/2. Nos. 5365/6 to complete a quartet with nos. 4381/2. No. 5385 12-bore try gun. Nos. 5401/2 to complete a quartet with nos. 4721/2. No. 5415 built to match no. 4828. No. 5416 pigeon gun. No. 5422 to complete a trio with nos. 5275/6. No. 5440 built to match no. 4849. No. 5472 pigeon gun. No. 5450 pigeon gun. No. 5462 pigeon gun. No. 5449 built to match no. 4288. No. 5454 pigeon gun. No. 5494 pigeon gun. No. 5509 built to match no. 4916. Nos. 5531/2/3 trio. No. 5535 to complete a trio with nos. 4731/2. Nos. 5564/5/6 trio. No. 5550 built to match no. 4836. No. 5559 pigeon gun. No. 5552 pigeon gun. No. 5563 built to match no. 5071. No. 5571 to complete a trio with nos. 4709/ 10. No. 5577 10-bore pigeon gun. No. 5575 built to match no. 4874. No. 5578 built to match Purdey No. 18704. No. 5579/80/81 trio. No. 5510 to complete a trio nos. 5431/2. No. 5515 to complete trio with nos. 5343/4. No. 5596 built to match no. 4835. No. 5603 Robertson's own 20-bore boxlock. Nos. 5609/10/11 trio. No. 5658 to complete a trio with nos. 4611/2. No. 5637 20-bore try gun. No. 5770 Robertson's own .300 rifle. No. 5656 to complete a trio with nos. 5495/6. Nos. 5645/6/5676 trio. No. 5687 built to match no. 5120. No. 5703 to complete a trio with nos. 4693/4. No. 5682 to complete a trio with nos. 5125/6. Nos. 5704 to complete a trio with nos. 4327/8. No. 5717 built to match no. 5572. No. 5763 /4 to complete a quartet with nos. 4631/2. Nos. 5849/50/5759 trio. No. 5700 pigeon gun. No. 5745 pigeon try gun. No. 5756 built to match no. 4896. No. 5765 built to match Atkin no. 1985. No. 5755 built to match no. 5426. No. 5695 built to match no. 5261. Nos. 5718/5731/2 trio. No. 5795 to complete a quartet with nos. 4683 /4/5192. No. 5773 first O/U. No. 5735 built to match no. 4761. No. 5760 to complete a trio with nos. 5459/60. Nos. 5801/2/3 trio. Nos. 5798/9/5800 trio. No. 5807 built to match no. 5394. No. 5746 pigeon gun. No. 5834 to complete a trio with nos. 5467/8. No. 5829 built to match no. 5298. No. 5838 built to match no. 4850. No. 5830 pigeon gun. No. 5804 built to match no. 5688. No. 5835 try gun. No. 5907 Robertson's own 28-bore boxlock. No. 5905 Robertson's own .410. No. 5858 to complete a trio with nos. 5051/2. No. 5849/50 /51 trio. No. 5853 to complete a trio with nos. 4967/8. Nos. 5865 /6/7 trio. Nos. 5879/80/81 trio. No. 5929 O/U try gun.

YEAR	*GUN NUMBERS*	*POINTS OF INTEREST*
1911–1915	Nos. 5930–6500	No. 5956 built to match no. 5554. Nos. 5957/8/9 trio. No. 5940 to complete a trio with nos. 5781/2. No. 5987 built to match no. 5874. No. 5937 built to match no. 5109. No. 5981 pigeon gun. Nos. 5949 /50/51 trio. Nos. 6001/2/3 trio. Nos. 6014 to complete a trio with nos. 4957/8. No. 6017 pigeon gun. Nos. 6051/2/3 trio. Nos. 6041/2/3 trio. No. 6023 built to match no. 4782. Nos. 6067/8/9 trio. No. 5975 pigeon gun. No. 6076 built to match no. 4884. No. 6021 built to match no. 5934. No. 6062 built to match no. 5902. No. 6155 to complete a trio with nos. 5361/2. Nos. 6141/2/3 trio. No. 6017 pigeon gun. No. 6150 to complete a trio with nos. 5353/4. Nos. 6121 /2/3 trio. No. 6138 built to match no. 5032. No. 6149 to complete a trio with nos. 5129/30. Nos. 6451/2/3 trio. No. 6156 to complete a trio with nos. 5173/4. No. 6204 built to match no. 5786. Nos. 6207 /8/9 trio. Nos. 6201/2/3 trio. Nos. 5961/2/3 trio. No. 6214 built to match no. 6061. Nos. 6211/2/3 trio. No. 6240 pigeon gun. No. 6244 to complete a trio with nos. 5235/6. No. 6255 built to match no. 5681. No. 6262 built to match no. 5165. Nos. 6275/6/7 trio. No. 6279 built to match no. 5974. Nos. 6379/80/81 trio. No. 6332 to complete a trio with nos. 6093/4. Nos. 6357/8/9 trio. Nos. 6325/6/7 trio. Nos. 6329/30/31 trio. No. 6347 built to match no. 5476. No. 6348 built to match no. 5475. No. 6346 built to match no. 6116. No. 6355 pigeon gun. Nos. 6361/2/3 trio. No. 6356 built to match no. 5821. No. 5360 to complete a trio with nos. 5335/6. No. 6391/2/3 trio. Nos. 6395/6/7 trio. No. 6020 pigeon gun. Nos. 6405/6 to complete a quartet with nos. 4765 /6. No. 6404 built to match no. 5556. Nos. 6451/2/3 trio. No. 6386 to complete a quartet with nos. 5335/6/6360. Nos. 6475/6/7 trio. No. 6439 built to match no. 5992. No. 6445 to complete a quartet with nos. 4481/2/4595. No. 6309 built to match no. 6218 No. 6454 to complete a trio with nos. 4621/2. Nos. 6483/4 to complete a quartet with nos. 6297/8. No. 6485 built to match no. 6436. No. 6478 to complete a trio with nos. 5874/5987. No. 6461 to complete a trio with nos. 5967/8. No. 6528 to complete a trio with nos. 4701/2. No. 6478 built to match no. 6419. No. 6497 built to match no. 6090. No. 6480 built to match no. 6354. No. 6565 built to match no. 5938. No. 6566 pigeon gun. No. 6582 built to match no. 5067.
1916–1920	Nos. 6500–6800	Nos. 6537/8/6547 trio. No. 6527 to complete a trio with nos. 5545 /6. Nos. 6515/6/6540 trio. No. 6548 to complete a trio with nos. 6487/8. Nos. 6557/8/9 trio. Nos. 6429/30/6683 trio. Nos. 6633/4 to complete a quartet with nos. 5311/2. No. 6604 pigeon gun. No. 6529 built to match no. 6478. No. 6659 built to match no. 6627. No. 6675 pigeon gun. Nos. 6691/2/3 trio. No. 6720 built to match no. 4481. No. 6727 to complete a trio with nos. 6639/40. No. 6734 built to match no. 4890. No. 6762 pigeon gun. No. 6751 to complete a trio with nos. 6389/90. No. 6722 built to match no. 6019. No. 6797 to complete a trio with nos. 6595/6.
1921–1925	Nos. 6800–7300	No. 6824 to complete a trio with nos. 5845/6. No. 6807 to complete a trio with nos. 6116/6346. Nos. 6901/2/6910 trio. Nos. 6919/20/21 trio. No. 6823 built to match no. 6614. No. 6899 built to match no. 6342. No. 6940 built to match no. 6694. No. 6939 to complete a trio with nos. 5383/4. No. 6931 built to match no. 6668. No. 6973 built to match no. 6271. No. 6830 built to match no. 6517. No. 7121 built to match no. 5743. No. 7023 to complete a trio with nos. 5899/ 5900. No. 6980 built to match no. 6793. No. 6783 to complete a trio with nos. 6817/8. No. 7061 built to match no. 5592. No. 6997 built to match no. 6951. No. 7062 to complete a trio with nos. 6481/2. No. 7112 20-bore try gun. No. 7120 built to match no. 6971. Nos. 7067/8/7077 trio. No. 7132 built to match no. 6315. No. 7098 to complete a trio with nos. 6985/6. No. 6990 built to match no. 6789 No. 7096 built to match no. 6773. No. 7240 built to match no. 6712. No. 7211 built to match no. 4864. Nos. 7207/8/7227/8 quartet. No. 7171 built to match no. 6794. No. 7277 pigeon gun. Nos. 7265/6/7 trio. No. 7284 built to match no. 4863.

YEAR	*GUN NUMBERS*	*POINTS OF INTEREST*
		No. 7298 built to match no. 6923. No. 7270 to complete a trio with nos. 5943/4. No. 7287 built to match no. 5525. No. 7080 built to match no. 6777. No. 7268 to complete a trio with nos. 7139 /40. No. 7256 to complete a trio with nos. 7261/2.
1926–1930	Nos. 7300–7900	No. /304 to complete a trio with nos. 6640/7047. Nos. 7301/2/3 trio. No. 7333 pigeon gun. No. 7214 single-barrel trap gun. No. 7334 pigeon gun. No. 7369 to complete a trio with nos. 4856/4940. Nos. 7365/6/7 trio. No. 7372 built to match no. 5593. No. 7444 built to match no. 4471. No. 7428 built to match no. 5828. No. 7431 built to match no. 4560. No. 7433 built to match no. 6892. No. 7434 built to match no. 4794. No. 7446 built to match no. 7399. No. 7459 built to match no. 6932. No. 7467 built to match no. 6979. No. 7490 built to match no. 6861. No. 7557 built to match no. 6877. No. 7509 to complete a trio with nos. 6631/2. Nos. 7505/6/7/8 quartet. No. 7515 built to match no. 7145. No. 7522 to complete a trio with nos. 7449/50. No. 7594 pigeon gun. Nos. 7563/7745 to complete a quartet with nos. 6723/4. No. 7578 pigeon gun. No. 7095 built to match no. 7035. No. 7601 built to match no. 7248. No. 7617 built to match no. 5290. No. 7663 built to match no. 4721. No. 7611 built to match no. 7522. No. 7755 combined 20-bore and .256 rifle. No. 7730 built to match no. 6618. No. 7740 built to match no. 7523. No. 7756 built to match no. 6830. No. 7774 built to match no. 6616. No. 7773 built to match no. 6603. No. 7770 built to match no. 7380. No. 7826 to complete a trio with nos. 6449 /50. No. 7824 built to match no. 5293. No. 7777 built to match no. 5826. No. 7848 built to match no. 7788. No. 7860 built to match no. 5722. Nos. 7779/80/7855 trio. No. 7655 built to match no. 7319.
1931–1935	Nos. 7900–8350	No. 7913 built to match no. 6913. No. 7923 built to match no. 7769. No. 7967 built to match no. 7609. No. 7908 built to match no. 7883. No. 8032 built to match no. 7789. No. 8055 built to match no. 7639. No. 8056 to complete a trio with nos. 7788/7748. Nos. 8107/8 to complete a quartet with nos. 7105/6. No. 8117 built to match no. 8035. No. 8141 to complete a trio with nos. 6199/6200. No. 8142 built to match no. 4793. No. 8125 built to match no. 8081. No. 8132 built to match no. 7616. No. 8134 built to match no. 7636. No. 8139 built to match no. 7996. No. 8178 built to match no. 7178. No. 8186 built to match no. 5085. No. 8216 built to match no. 6681. No. 8201 to complete a trio with nos. 4336/ 4387. No. 8202 built to match no. 6891. No. 8040 built to match no. 7841. No. 8240 to complete a trio with nos. 7377/8. No. 8277 built to match no. 7882. No. 8322 256 O/U rifle. Nos. 8314/5/6 trio. No. 8338 built to match no. 8279. Nos. 8333/4/5 trio.
1936–1940	Nos. 8350–8670	No. 8386 built to match no. 7461. No. 8393 to complete a trio with nos. 7191/2. No. 8389 built to match no. 7795. No. 8429 Abercrombie & Fitch try gun. No. 8369 built to match no. 8158. No. 8413 built to match no. 8011. No. 8411 to complete a trio with nos. 8075/6. No. 8266 built to match no. 7019. No. 8476 built to match no. 7919. No. 8418 built to match no. 8082. No. 8475 built match no. 7318. No. 8440 built to match no. 6852. No. 8536 built to match no. 7888. No. 8346 to complete a trio with nos. 8103/4. No. 8494 built to match no. 7137. No. 8499 built to match no. 8059. No. 8554 built to match no. 8338. No. 7907 built to match no. 7623. No. 8593 built to match no. 6924. No. 8633 pigeon gun. No. 8620 built to match no. 7587. No. 8630 built to match no. 8602. No. 8645 built to match no. 8554. No. 8690 built to match no. 8596. No. 8695 built to match no. 8393. No. 8696 built to match no. 8502. No. 7589 built to match no. 6259.
1941–1945	Nos. 8670–8700	
1946–1950	Nos. 8700–8890	No. 8677 built to match no. 8172. No. 8830 built to match no. 4812.

After 1950 – Please apply to Boss & Co.

GUNMAKERS EMPLOYED BY BOSS SINCE 1890

Boss possess some wage books that detail their employees from 1890 onwards. Sample years are recorded below with the specialisation of the men when known. It is interesting to note the long service given by many of the gunmakers and how many of their sons followed in their father's footsteps.

December 1890   *73 St James's Street*
J. Ranger
J. Burns
Harry Parry
G. Knight
W. Davis
S. Bevan
S. Kelly
William Adams
C. Allen
W. Pither
E. Westley

January 1912   *13 Dover Street – Shop*
John Robertson   – owner
Bob Henderson   – factory manager
H. Paice
Bob Robertson   – assistant to John Robertson/ shooting coach
Arthur F. Clement   – shop manager
A. Temple
S. Clinton
F. Peart
E. Peart
A. F. Embleton   – manager of the firm

January 1912   *1 & 2 Ham Yard – Factory*
C. Johnson
W. Pither   – foreman
J. Vyse   – finisher
R. Adams   – finisher
H. Parry
J. Ranger
R. Adams
H. Reeves
Crabbe

Cullum
Charlie Padgett
Ernest Sanderson
Southgate
C. Perkins   – stocker
W. Johnson   – stocker
Hughes
Adam Speaight   – machinist
A. Urie
Limby
Mayo
Ince
Smith
J. Urie
Tailing   – apprentice
Vyse (Jnr)   – apprentice
Sherry   – apprentice
Alec Robertson   – apprentice
Shepherd   – apprentice
John Robertson (Jnr)
Sam Robertson

February 1919   *13 Dover Street – Shop*
Arthur Clement   – shop manager
Louis Western   – secretary
H. Paice
Arthur Sanderson   – administrative assistant
Sandall
A. Walters
Smart
J. Felix
J. Dean
John Robertson (Jnr)   – general manager
Bob Robertson   – shooting instructor

February 1919   *6, 8 & 10 Lexington Street – Factory*
Sam Robertson   – factory manager
Green   – foreman
C. Johnson
R. Adams   – finisher
L. Adams
E. Westley

W. Johnson	– stocker
Adam Speaight	– machinist
H. Parry	
W. Baker	– finisher
Charlie Padgett	
Ernest Sanderson	
Hunter	
J. Ranger	
J. Vyse	– finisher
Alf Grant	– machinist
Jim Iredale	– single trigger and ejectors
Charlie Austin	– action filer
Edwin Pither	– actioner
Truss	– apprentice
Barrett	– apprentice

April 1937   *41 Albemarle Street – Shop*

Alec Robertson	– general manager
Louis Western	– secretary
Arthur Sanderson	– shop manager
Jack Sumner	– engraver
Walters	
Felix	
Fred Oliver	– book-keeper
Griffin	
Leycote	
Bill Harris	
Bob Robertson	– shooting instructor

April 1937   *6, 8 & 10 Lexington Street – Factory*

R. Adams	– finisher
W. Johnson	
C. Henderson	– forend stocker
H. Parry	
Adam Speaight	– machinist
Alf Grant	– machinist
S. Hook	– extractor maker
T. Longstaff	
Bill Wakefield	– barrel-maker

Ernie Nobbs	– barrel-maker
Jack Rennie	– barrel-maker
G. Bates	
A. Henderson	
E. Sanderson	
Bob Henderson	– factory manager
Jim Iredale	– single trigger and ejectors
Charlie Padgett	
Albert Grant	
H. Dewen	
Charlie Austin	– action filer
Bill Wise	– bolt and lever work
Edwin Pither	– actioner
Sydney Gall	– finisher
J. Vyse	– finisher
W. Baker	– finisher
Doug Bayliss	– stocker
Bellamy	

October 1957   *41 Albemarle Street – Shop*

Bob Henderson	– factory manager
Arthur Sanderson	– shop manager
Bill Harris	
Fred Oliver	– secretary

October 1957   *Horse Shoe Alley – Factory*

Bill Wise	– foreman
Jim Iredale	– single trigger and ejectors
Charlie Austin	– action filer
Edwin Pither	– action filer
Dave Cox	– action filer
Doug Bayliss	– stocker
Ernie Noble	– barrel maker
Alf Grant	– machinist
Adam Speaight	– machinist
Sydney Gall	– machinist
Roy Henderson	– forend stocker
Bill Allan	– stocker
Harry Clark	– finisher
Jack Rennie	– barrel-maker

APPENDIX 8

THE PATENTS OF BOSS & CO.

Until John Robertson took over Boss & Co. in 1891, only one patent bears the firm's address, that of Stephen Grant in 1861. Neither Thomas Boss nor Edward Paddison applied for any patents. In total contrast John Robertson applied for twenty- five patents, nineteen of which bear Boss & Co.'s address.

A patent gave an inventor a monopoly to profit from his invention for a certain length of time. This depended upon two conditions:

1. The inventor had to pay prescribed fees to enforce his patent.
2. First of all a Provisional Patent was applied for. This was a general description kept secret by the Patent Office. The Provisional Patent had to be backed up by a Complete Specification. This Complete Specification had to be filed within six months. In the Complete Specification the inventor had to describe in complete detail his patent.

If the fees were not paid or the Complete Specification not filed, then the patent became void. This explains why although John Robertson could list twenty-four Provisional Patents, only seventeen were published as Complete Specifications. For reasons known to himself he did not proceed with seven of his Provisional Patents.

STEPHEN GRANT'S PATENT NO. 1538,
15 JUNE 1861 (shown above)
Grant took out this patent whilst he was in partnership with Mrs Boss. Instead of the gun opening close to the breech as

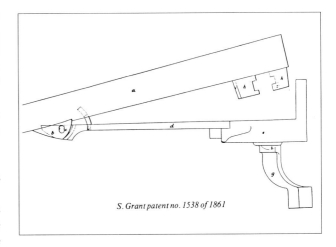

S. Grant patent no. 1538 of 1861

was normal, in Grant's patent the barrels pivot at the extreme end of the forend.

PROVISIONAL PATENT NO. 2833
15TH JUNE 1882 (shown right)
This was the first patent of John Robertson. Robertson at this time was working for the trade at 4 George Yard, Wardour Street, Soho, London. This patent covers two mechanisms. Firsty a new cocking mechanism is described. Fitted to the front lump of the barrels is a cam. When the barrels drop down, the lump rises and this draws forward two pins (I) that project into the slot of the action bar. These pins are the forward ends of two cocking rods (G) and when they move forward, they pull on the bottom of the tumblers (E) thereby rotating them to full cock.

THE JOHN ROBERTSON PATENTS
The Patents marked ★ were not proceeded with as complete specifications.

PROVISIONAL PATENT NO. & DATE		PATENTEE	IMPROVEMENT
No. 2833	15th June 1882	John Robertson	Safety Catches and Cocking Mechanism
No. 23	1st January 1883	Henry Holland John Robertson	Cocking Mechanism
No. 5834	21st April 1887	Henry Holland John Robertson	Extractor Mechanism (Ejectors)
No. 9372	1st July 1887	Henry Holland John Robertson	★

PROVISIONAL PATENT NO. & DATE		PATENTEE	IMPROVEMENT
No. 11623	26th August 1887	Henry Holland John Robertson	Extractor Mechanism (Ejectors)
No. 16691	16th November 1888	Henry Holland John Robertson	Extractor Mechanism (Ejectors)
No. 20122	25th October 1893	John Robertson	★
No. 20873	3rd November 1893	John Robertson	Single Trigger
No. 5897	21st March 1894	John Robertson	Single Trigger
No. 22894	26 November 1894	John Robertson	Single Trigger
No. 624	10 January 1895	John Robertson	★
No. 18135	28 September 1895	John Robertson William Adams	Safety Mechanism
No. 114	2nd January 1896	John Robertson	★
No. 2988	4th February 1897	John Robertson William Adams	Ejector Mechanism
No. 3112	5th February 1897	John Robertson	★
No. 10949	13th May 1898	John Robertson	Selective Single Trigger
No. 8718	11th May 1900	John Robertson	★
No. 241	5th January 1903	John Robertson	Improvements to Revolving Turret
No. 11278	30th May 1905	John Robertson	Improvements to Single Trigger Safety
No. 11400	31st May 1905	John Robertson	Improvement to Trigger Pull
No. 11400B	31st May 1905	John Robertson	Improved Safety Mechanism
No. 3307	10th February 1909	John Robertson	Over and Under Gun
No. 3308	10th February 1909	John Robertson	Over and Under Ejector
No. 563	13th January 1915	John Robertson	★
No. 12298	26th August 1915	John Robertson	Grenade Thrower

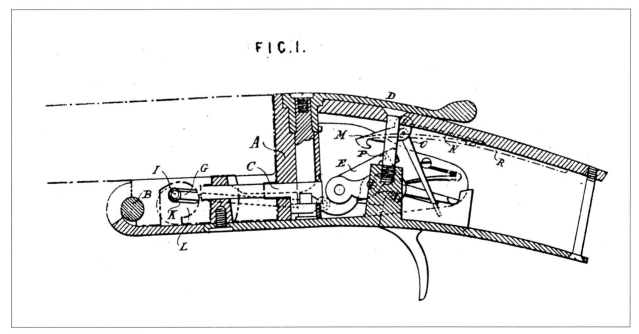

The second part of the patent concerned safety catches. A safety hook (M) would catch the tumbler (E) should a lock sear fail. To clear this safety hook for normal use, a link (O) connected the safety hook and the trigger blade. When the trigger blade lifted, the link pushed the safety hook upwards and the tumbler could fall unimpeded. In addition to the normal bar action side lock shown in the diagram, the patent also illustrates how the safety lock could be applied to the Anson and Deeley boxlock.

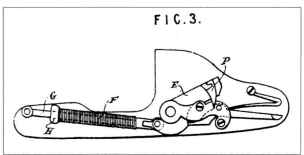

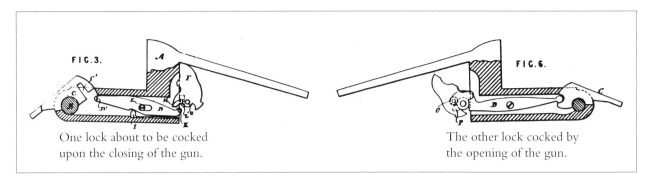

One lock about to be cocked
upon the closing of the gun.

The other lock cocked by
the opening of the gun.

PROVISIONAL PATENT NO. 23
1ST JANUARY 1883 – COCKING MECHANISM
(shown above)

This was a combined patent between Henry Holland and John Robertson. This patent was a new system for cocking hammerless guns. In most guns the locks were cocked simultaneously when the gun was opened. In this patent one lock was cocked when the gun opened and the other cocked when the gun closed.

PROVISIONAL PATENT NO. 5834
21ST APRIL 1887 – EJECTOR (shown below)

Again this was a combined patent between Henry Holland and John Robertson. Robertson was still working for the Trade at 4 Dansey Yard, Wardour Street, Soho, London. (4 George Yard had been renamed 4 Dansey Yard in 1886.) This patent was an ejector mechanism contained within the forend. When the gun was opened both cartridges were withdrawn as usual a short distance by the extractor mechanism and afterwards if one or other of the cartridges had been previously fired the case was ejected by the action of a coiled spring contained within the forend.

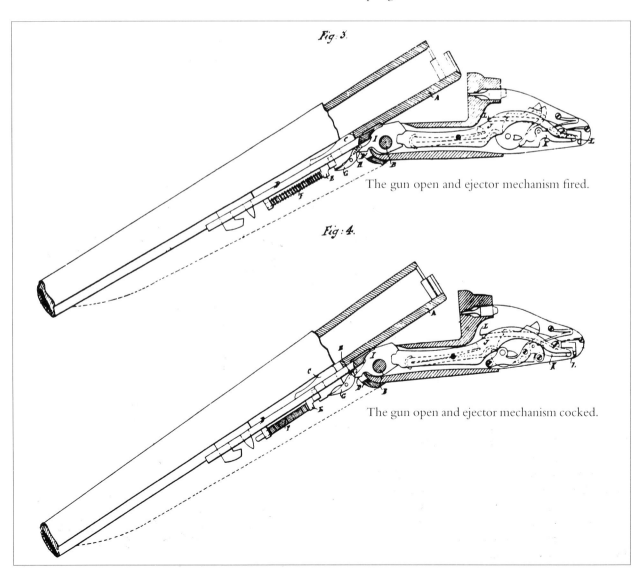

The gun open and ejector mechanism fired.

The gun open and ejector mechanism cocked.

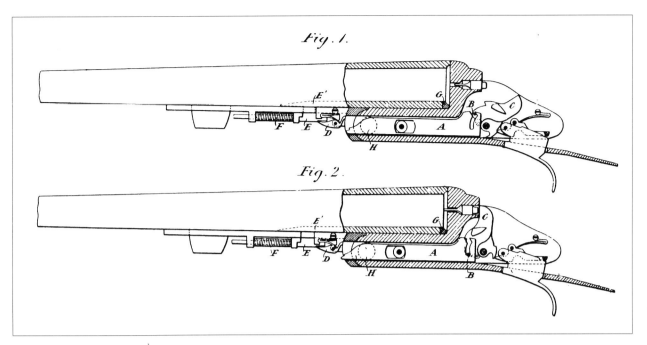

Fig. 1.

Fig. 2.

PROVISIONAL PATENT NO. 11623
26TH AUGUST 1887 – EJECTOR (shown above)
Another combination by Henry Holland and John Robertson pre- dating his time at Boss. This improved upon the tripping mechanism for the ejector on the previous patent No. 5834. In this patent a moving slide of thin metal (A in the diagram) tripped the ejector.

PROVISIONAL PATENT NO. 16691
16TH NOVEMBER 1888 – EJECTOR (shown below)
This patent was the final combination of Holland and Robertson. It was a further improvement upon the tripping mechanism for the ejector of previous patent No. 5834. In this improvement, when the gun was fired, the ejector sear was only partially tripped and fully tripped upon the further opening of the gun and the cocking of the hammer.

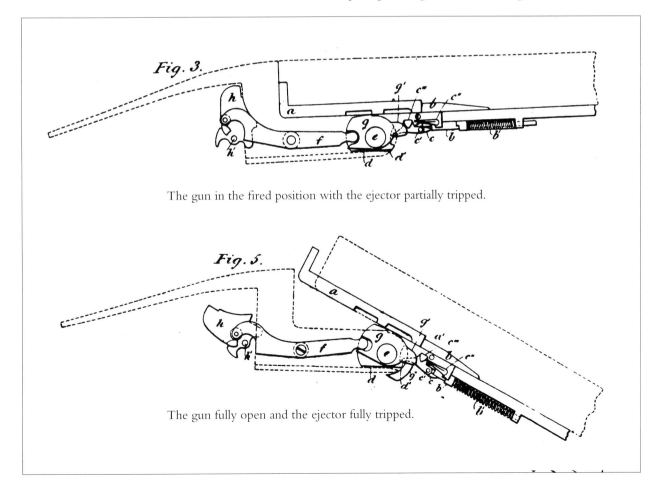

Fig. 3.

The gun in the fired position with the ejector partially tripped.

Fig. 5.

The gun fully open and the ejector fully tripped.

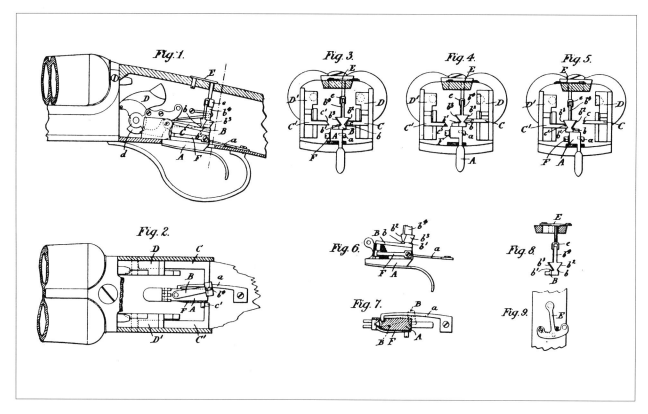

PROVISIONAL PATENT NO. 20873
3RD NOVEMBER 1893 – SINGLE TRIGGER
(shown above)

Not only was this the first single-trigger mechanism patented by John Robertson, it was also his first patent whilst proprietor of Boss & Co. It was not the three-pull system that he would later perfect and use in "The Boss Single Trigger". This patent was a two-pull single trigger somewhat delicate in operation. It was not very satisfactory, the two pull often leading to a double discharge since the second involuntary pull had not been properly investigated. A spring powered pivoted arm (B) would first fire the right barrel (Figure 4). Upon the trigger blade dropping, the inclined surface on the sear (C) would meet the inclined surface on the pivot (b2) and throw the pivot (B) ready to fire the next barrel (Figure 5). A lever fitted to this pivoted arm outside the stock (E) could over-ride the mechanism and select which barrel desired to be fired.

PROVISIONAL PATENT NO. 5897
21ST MARCH 1894 – SINGLE TRIGGER
(shown below)

This was another early attempt at a single trigger upon the two-pull system, again unsatisfactory in that it often led to an unintentional double discharge. It was very complicated and involved many small parts and springs that must have affected its reliability and safety. Figures 9 and 10 show the sears (A) of the lock plates. Small spring operated pivots (B) were fitted to the end of the sears. Using Figure 2 showing the firing of the right barrel, a tumbler (D) operated by a powerful spring (E) would overcome the small spring operated pivot on the sear and bring it into position over the trigger blade to enable the right hand lock to be fired. Upon pressing the trigger, a cam (h) on the lock plate would force out the pivot (B) which would then in turn rotate the tumbler (D) into position for firing the next barrel (Figure 7).

Again a selective system could be employed with this device. In this patent Robertson showed a great many variations upon this system. This system was ingenious and well

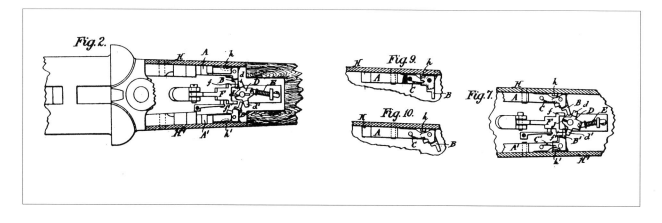

thought out but due to its complication it must have been very difficult to construct. For every day use a simpler system was necessary.

PROVISIONAL PATENT NO. 22894
26 NOVEMBER 1894 – SINGLE TRIGGER
This patent is the famous Boss three-pull single trigger that

has done so much to make Boss known as the speciality maker of single-trigger guns. It was a masterpiece of inventive ingenuity by John Robertson far surpassing his previous two attempts. Although the patent bears a single name, "John Robertson", it is known that his foreman, William Adams, contributed a great deal to the design. Like all good inventions it is in essence relatively simple using few moving parts and combining safety with simplicity.

AMENDED SPECIFICATION.

Reprinted as amended in accordance with the decision of the Supervising Examiner acting for the Comptroller-General, dated the 24th day of February 1908.

(The Amendments are shown in erased and italic type).

Nº **22,894***   **A.D. 1894**

Date of Application, 26th Nov., 1894
Complete Specification Left, 19th Sept., 1895—Accepted, 19th Oct., 1895

PROVISIONAL SPECIFICATION

"Improvements in Drop-down Guns".

I, JOHN ROBERTSON, trading as Boss & Co., of 73 St. James Street, Pall Mall, in the County of Middlesex, Gunmaker, do hereby declare the nature of this invention to be as follows:—

In the Specification of my prior Patent No. 20873 dated 3rd. November, 1893,
5 and also in that of my pending application for Patent No. 5897, dated 21st. March, 1894, I have described means whereby the two barrels of a double-barreled drop-down gun can be fired in succession by the action of a single trigger, this effect being produced by causing the first pull of the trigger which fires one barrel to shift or move a part in the action so as to bring it into the necessary
10 position for acting on the sear of the other barrel when the trigger is again pulled.
In practice I find that in the act of making the first pull on the trigger an involuntary action of the firing finger frequently occurs and which results in relaxing the pressure slightly on the trigger and then immediately pulling the
15 trigger hard again. The effect of this is to allow the trigger to descend sufficiently so that when the subsequent hard pull comes the shifting part (which has already moved so that it engages the second sear) will act on the second sear, and both barrels are thus discharged practically simultaneously, the second one of course unintentionally.
20 The object of the present invention is to prevent this occuring, and the means I employ while capable of application to the constructions described in the specifications of my prior patents above referred to, can also be applied to guns of any other construction, and may be varied to suit different constructions.

The introduction to patent No. 22894 the Boss single trigger.

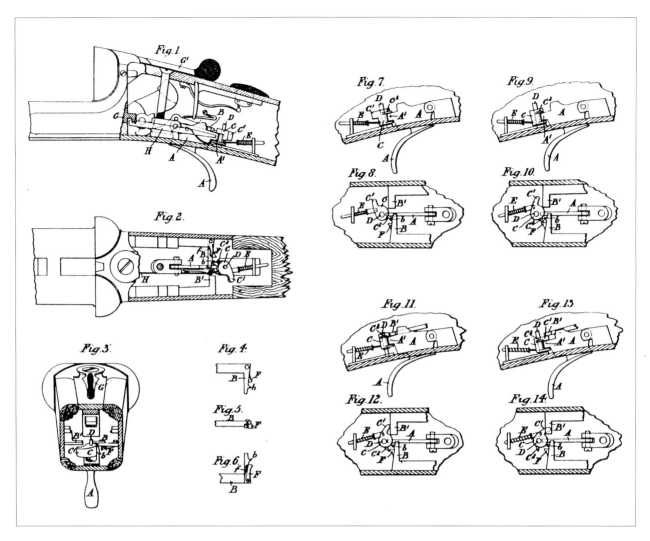

This patent is one of the most detailed gun patents I have ever investigated. The description runs to twelve pages and there are one hundred and one drawings. As an example, illustrated above are the first fourteen drawings.

The mode of carrying out the invention was varied extensively, with several different variations on the three pull system described in detail. The central core of the patent is the revolving turret that went into production in 1895 and has been used on Boss single triggers ever since then.

The mechanism is carried on a trigger plate (see diagram right). Revolving around a vertical spindle (S) is a turret or tumbler (T). Inside the turret is a watchmaker's coiled spring to provide the force to turn the turret (not illustrated in the diagram). The early single trigger did not use such a spring. They used a single external spring. On top of the spindle (S) there is a lug to prevent the turret riding up this spindle except when the turret is in one particular position when it must move up. The turret has two grooves cut into it. Into these grooves are cogs (a,b,c,d) all of them slightly differing shapes.

The gun ready to fire is shown in position A. When the trigger is pressed is assumes the position shown by the dotted lines. The sear of the right lock (R) is raised and this fires the right barrel. The turret can not revolve since the raised trigger blade engages cog a. This is the end of the first

pull. The recoil of the gun means that the shooter now inadvertently releases his grip on the trigger and the trigger reverts to its original position. The turret is now free to turn and it revolves until it is stopped by cog b coming into contact with the lower part of the trigger blade (position B).

The involuntary pull (or second pull) now takes place. The trigger blade slips out of cog b and the turret revolves once more until cog c catches the upper part of the trigger blade (position C). This is the end of the second pull. Again the shooter inadvertently releases his grip on the trigger. The trigger reverts to its original position and the turret revolves until cog d comes into contact with the lower part of the trigger blade (position D).

The left-hand barrel can now be fired. The sear of the left-hand lock (L) fits into a groove in the turret. Thanks to the lug on top of the spindle (S), the turret can not ride up. Throughout the cycle so far, the left-hand sear has been locked and can not be fired. However when the turret assumes position D, a slot in the middle of the turret is directly opposite the lug on the spindle, meaning that the turret can now ride up the spindle. When the trigger is pressed for the third time, the entire turret is lifted up the spindle and the left-hand sear (L) is raised causing the left barrel to be discharged. After the trigger has been released, the turret remains as in position D.

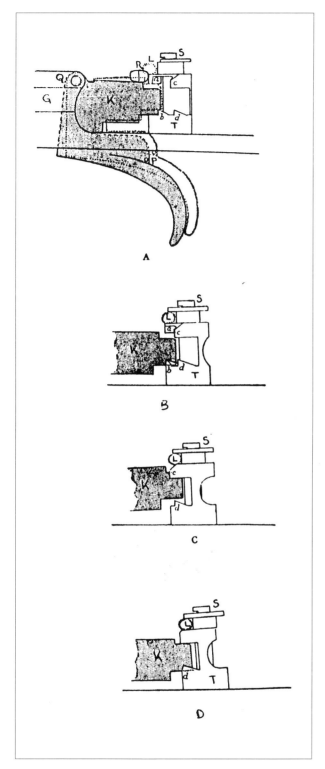

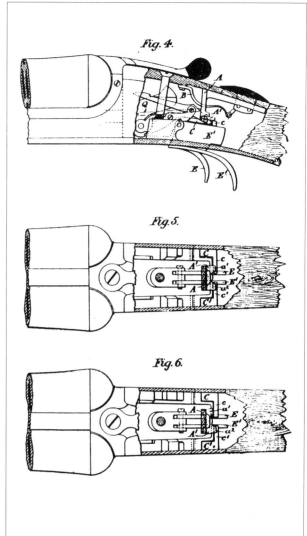

When the gun is opened, a lever (G) is pushed back, engages the outer edge of the turret and re-cocks the turret. When the locks are cocked, the right-hand sear (R) drops and locks the turret and the left-hand sear (L) engages in the upper groove of the turret.

Throughout the action of the turret is carefully regulated and can only rotate in well-defined movements, thereby rendering it impossible for the left-hand barrel to involuntarily jar off.

PROVISIONAL PATENT NO. 18135
28th SEPTEMBER 1895 – SAFETY MECHANISM
(shown above)

This was a combined patent by John Robertson and his foreman at Boss & Co, William Adams of 4 Havelock Terrace, Battersea, London. This was a safety mechanism to bolt either one sear or both sears. In addition a further modification could bolt the triggers.

When the safety lever (A) was pushed backwards into the locked position, both sears (C1 and C) were locked by projecting arms a1 and a2. Figure 6 illustrates how only one barrel could be made safe. After the right-hand barrel has been discharged and the safety bolt pulled backwards to the safety position, the sear (C) of the fired barrel will be in the raised position and this will block the projecting arm (a1) causing the rocking part (A1) at the bottom of the safety lever (A) to swivel and block sear (C1) of the right-hand barrel. This mechanism could be modified to fit the single trigger.

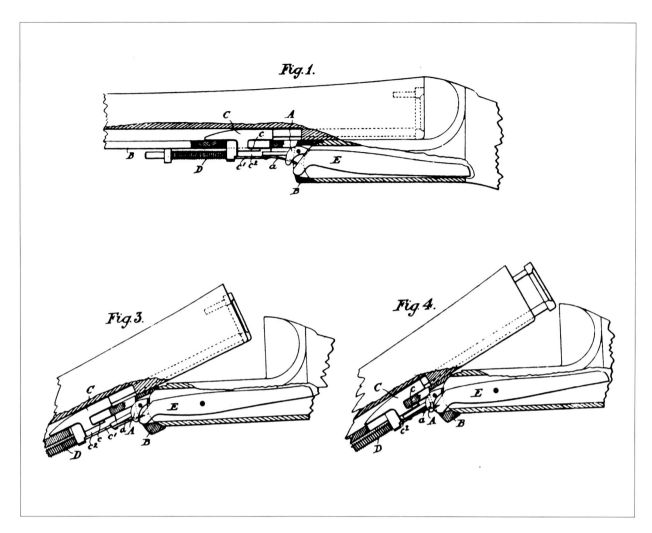

PROVISIONAL PATENT NO. 2988
4 FEBRUARY 1897 – EJECTOR MECHANISM
(shown above)

This patent refers to the famous Boss ejector mechanism reknowned for its simplicity and its ability to extract unfired cartridges considerably further than in other guns. Once again it was a combined patent between John Robertson and William Adams.

A slide (C) is operated by a coiled spring (D). A hole or gutter (c2) is cut in this slide. See figure 1. When the gun is opened unfired, the spring forces the slide against the extractor. The slide can travel backwards to the knuckle due to the gutter (c2) being able to accommodate the arm of the tipper (A). This motion is gradual and does not produce and rapid ejection. With the gun fully open, the spring pushes the extractor to the full limit of its travel, thereby pushing the unfired cartridges to an extent greater than in any other ejector system. This makes unloading far easier particularly in cold weather. See figure 4. In addition the force of this spring, by pushing the extractors hard against the action face, assists with the opening of the gun.

When the gun is fired, the cocking lever (E) lifts and strikes the top of the tipper (A), rotating it downwards until it rests against the slide at position c1 (see figure 3). When the gun is opened, the cocking lever strikes the tipper rotating it slightly upwards until its front point comes opposite the gutter (c2) in the slide. There is now nothing to contain the ejector spring and it flicks the slide and extractors rearwards to produce ejection. The ejectors are then cocked upon the closing of the gun.

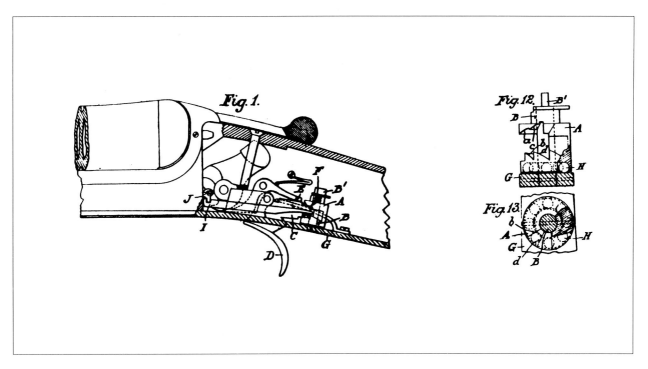

PROVISIONAL PATENT NO. 10949 13TH MAY 1898 – SELECTIVE SINGLE TRIGGER (shown below)

John Robertson's single trigger patent No. 22894 of 26th November 1894 did not offer a selective device whereby the shooter could choose which barrel to fire first. This patent, some five years later, rectified this.

The revolving turret system still remained in use. Over the trigger blade (B) there is a horizontal shaped piece (A) that can pivot on its axis (b). This piece has two arms (a and a1), one arm of which can be brought under the sear (C or C1) of the barrel to be fired. Figure 5 shows the right hand barrel about to be fired. A lever on the right hand lock (d1 in figure 2) operates the piece to select the barrel to be fired.

PROVISIONAL PATENT NO. 241 5TH JANUARY 1903 – IMPROVEMENTS TO THE REVOLVING TURRET (shown above)

John Robertson was concerned that the spring in the revolving turret might break and render the gun inoperable. In this patent he dispensed with the spring all together and outlined various methods of doing this. One of the methods is shown above. the trigger blade operated a series of inclined planes (a,b,c,d) that turned the turret. To reduce friction, ball bearings (H) were employed.

The spring free system never found favour. It was too complicated and could be unreliable. Boss overcame the potential spring failure problem by gold–plating the spring to prevent corrosion, the method that is used today making the spring out of gold.

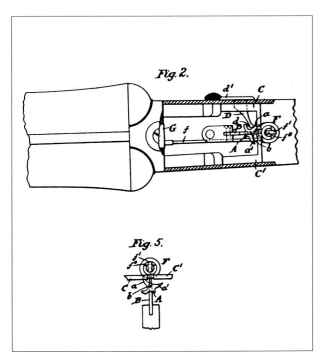

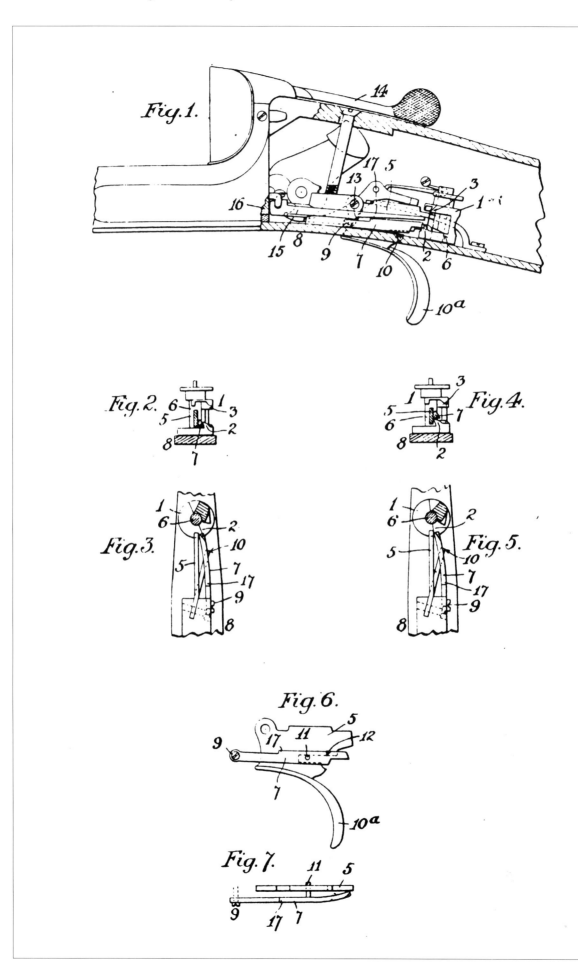

Fig.1.

Fig.2.

Fig.4.

Fig.3.

Fig.5.

Fig.6.

Fig.7.

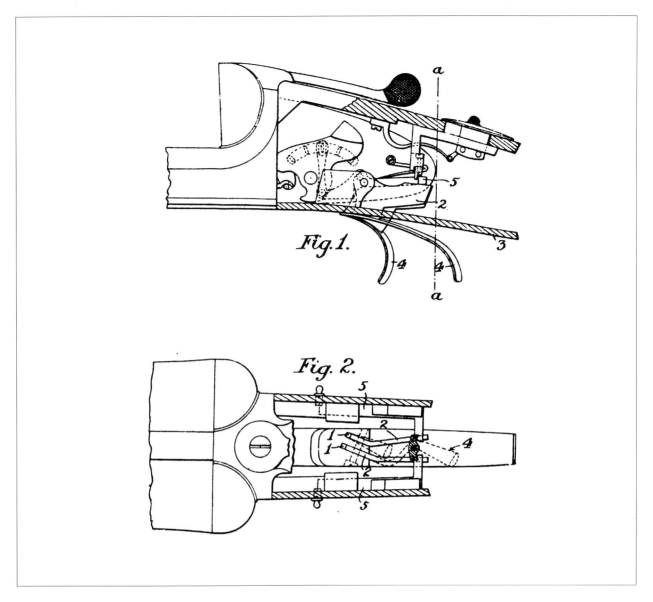

Fig.1.

Fig. 2.

PROVISIONAL PATENT NO. 11278
30TH MAY 1905 – IMPRVEMENTS TO SINGLE
TRIGGER SAFETY *(shown left)*

The single-trigger mechanism relied upon the full lift of the trigger on the first pull to bring into operation a series of carefully controlled events. If for some reason, a lock sear was not properly engaged, the slightest movement of the trigger could discharge the gun. Since the full lift of the trigger would not have taken place, the revolving turret could revolve faster than anticipated and the second pull (the involuntary pull) could cause the second barrel to be discharged.

A safety part (7) is arranged to the left of the trigger blade (5). A small pin (11) connects the safety part to the trigger blade. It is not a rigid fixture, there is a certain amount of play therein. When the trigger blade rises, the safety part will remain in position until this play has been taken up, then it will rise too. Figure 2 shows how even if the trigger blade (5) rises slightly, the safety part (7) will remain in position and lock the revolving turret (1).

PROVISIONAL PATENT NO. 11400 31ST MAY
1905 – IMPROVEMENT TO TRIGGER PULL
(shown above)

In most guns by the nature of a shooter's grip on the wrist, when the trigger is pulled, the trigger is not pulled directly back, it is pulled backwards and sideways at the same time. John Robertson feared that the sideways pull could in some instances cause the trigger blade to bind against the side of the slot in the trigger plate and thus affect the discharge of the gun.

In this invention he did not have the slots (1) in the trigger plate (3) parallel to it he cut them obliquely. The trigger blades (2) were bent so that they were still at right angles to the sears (5). The triggers (4) followed the line of the oblique slots and as such would now be pulled directly backwards by the shooter. The improvement could also be applied to the single trigger.

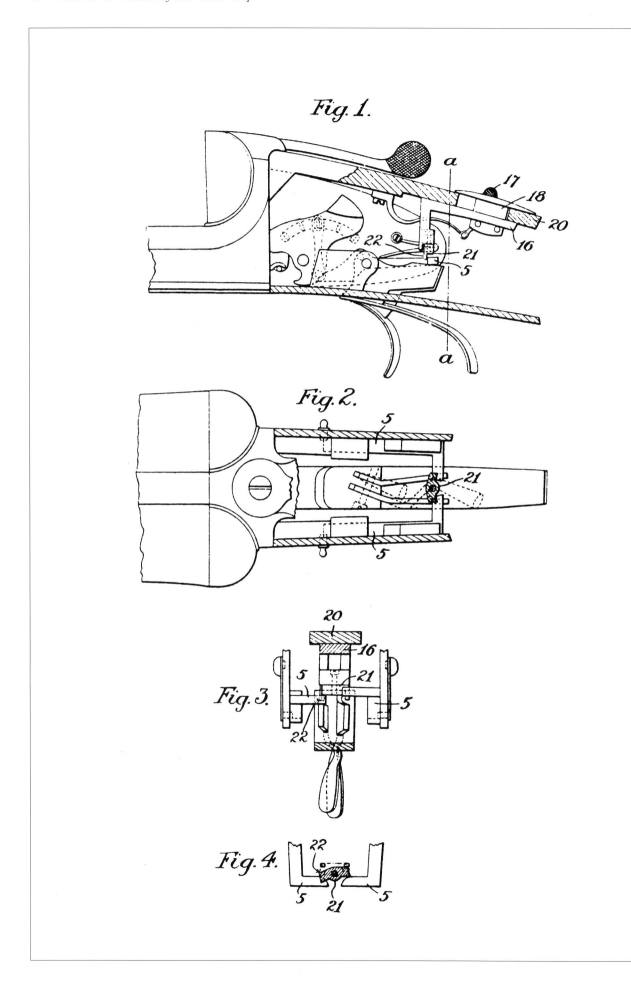

Fig. 1.

Fig. 2.

Fig. 3.

Fig. 4.

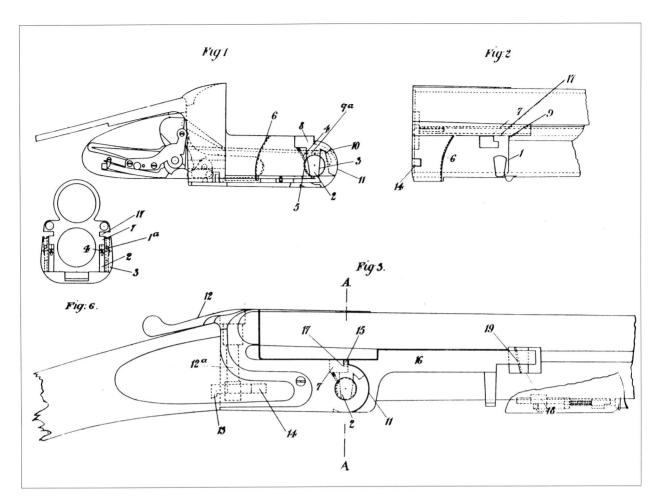

PROVISIONAL PATENT NO. 11400 B 31ST MAY 1905 – IMPROVED SAFETY MECHANISM *(shown left)*

This was an improvement to the safety mechanism of John Robertson and William Adams patent no. 18135 of 28th September 1895.

This safety mechanism no. 18135 locked either both the sears or the sear of the unfired barrel. A rocking part (21) attached to the safety lever (16) locked both sears. As in figure 4, when the right-hand barrel was fired and the safety lever pulled back, the raised sear (5) rotated the rocking part and caused it to lock the sear of the left-hand barrel.

This patent no. 11400 B improved upon the previous patent by having projecting lips (22) on the bottom of the rocking part to ensure that the rocking part caught the sear of the fired barrel and caused it to rotate.

PROVISIONAL PATENT NO. 3307 10TH FEBRUARY 1909 – OVER-AND-UNDER GUN *(shown above)*

This patent refers to the famous over-and-under Boss gun that has won so much acclaim over the years. The great advantage of this over-and-under system is that it makes for a very light gun and with the depth of action being about the same as that of an ordinary gun, it makes for a very attractive gun. Bob Henderson, the factory manager played a major part in its development. He never fully received public recognition for the part he played and his name does not appear in the patent specification.

Stud pieces (1) are placed on either side of the lower barrel and fit into corresponding slots (2) in the breech that revolve (3). Eccentric surfaces on the lumps (6) and breeches (6) mate with each other to take the strain away from the studs. The barrels are locked by the bolt (14).

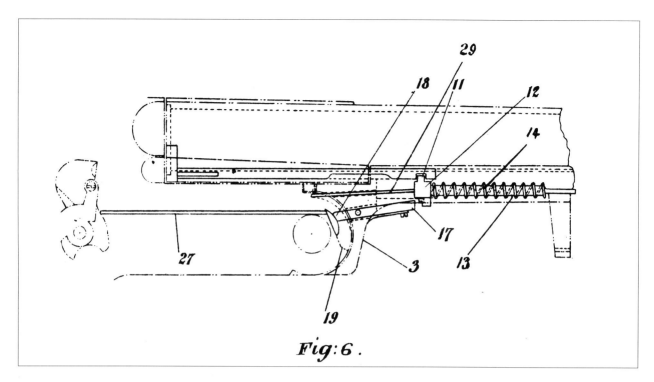

Fig:6.

PROVISIONAL PATENT NO. 3308
10TH FEBRUARY 1909 – OVER-AND-UNDER
EJECTOR (shown above and below)
A special ejector had to be designed for the over-and-under gun. The ejectors, contained within the forend, are separately fastened one on each side of the barrel, flush with the top end of the forend. This ejector was contained in the forend and was neat, compact and light.

Figure 6 shows the gun after it has been fired. In order to eject the spent cartridge, the breech is opened and barrels dropped until the point 18 of the ejector sear (17) comes into contact with point 19 on the knuckle. The sear will then be tripped from the head of the ejector rod (12) causing the spring (14) to rapidly force forward the extractors and eject the cartridges. Upon the barrels dropping the gun will be recocked and as part of this process, an arm (27) will be forced

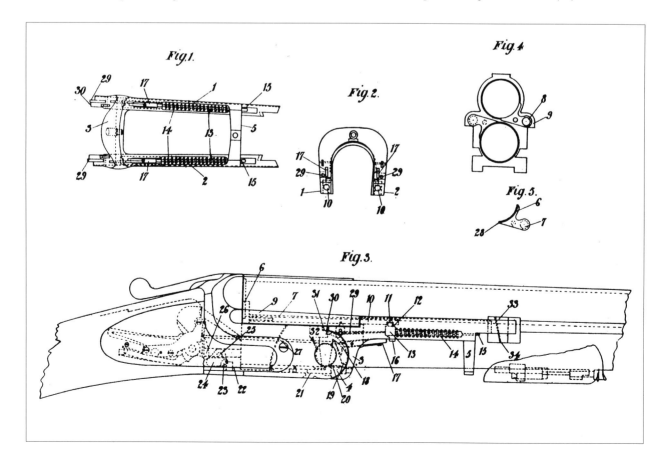

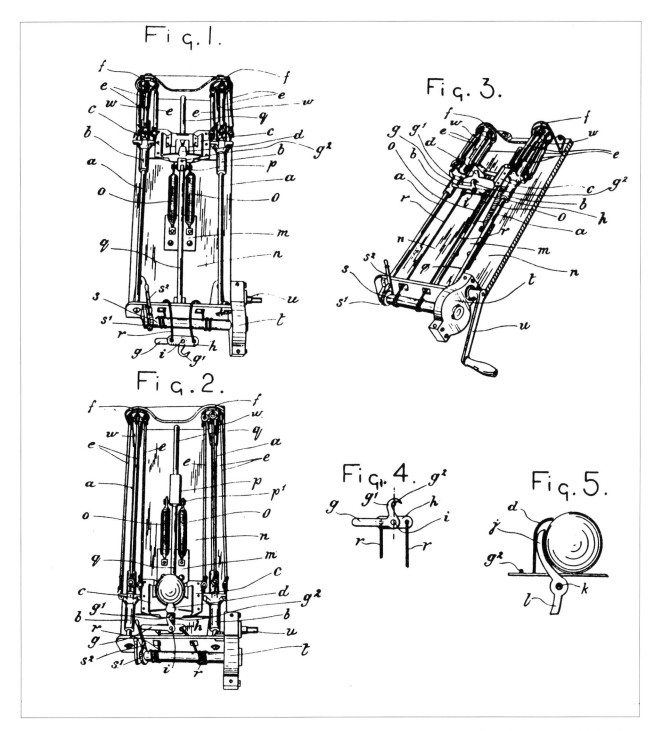

Fig.1.

Fig.3.

Fig.2.

Fig.4.

Fig.5.

forward to depress the end of the sear (17) so that upon opening the gun with an unfired cartridge, the head of the ejector rod (12) will not catch this sear an ordinary extraction will take place. When the gun is fired, arm 27 will slide backwards and the ejector sear (17) will rise to retain the ejector rod and spring ready for ejection.

PROVISIONAL PATENT NO. 12298
26TH AUGUST 1915 – GRENADE THROWER
(shown above)
The object behind this grenade thrower was to construct a device that could throw grenades a pre-determined distance far further than by hand. Two sleeves (b) ran along bars (a).

The sleeves were connected by a bridge-piece (c) that held the bomb. The motive power was provided by lengths of rubber (e). Calibrations were provided on the bars so that when the ratchet handle (u) pulled back the bridge-piece, the desired range could be determined. The bomb was lit, the trigger (g) pulled, and the bridge-piece flew forward. To give the bomb increased impotus immediately prior to the commencement of its flight, a lever (l) resting against the bomb, hit a trip block (p).

SELECT
BIBLIOGRAPHY
AND PHOTOGRAPHIC
ACKNOWLEDGEMENTS

Instructions to Young Sportsmen, etc – Col. Peter Hawker, London. 1833

The Shotgun and Sporting Rifle – J. H. Walsh ("Stonehenge") London. 1859

Modern Breech Loaders – W. W. Greener, London. 1869

The Badminton Library "Shooting" – Lord Walsingham and Sir R. Payne-Gallwey, London. 1887

The Gun and Its Development – W. W. Greener, London. 1888

Experts on Guns and Shooting – G. T. Teasdale-Buckell, London. 1900

The Modern Shotgun – Major Gerald Burrard, London. 1931

The Mantons, Gunmakers – W. Keith Neal and D. H. L. Back, London. 1967

Game Guns and Rifles – Richard Akehurst, London. 1969

Forsyth and Co., Patent Gunmakers – W. Keith Neal and D. H. L. Back, London. 1969

Hart's Army List

The British Shotgun – I. M. Crudgington and D. J. Baker, London. 1979

British Gunmakers, Their Trade Cards Cases and Equipment – W. Keith Neal and D. H. L. Back, London. 1980

A Dictionary of London Gunmakers 1350–1850 – H. L. Blackmore

Purdey's – The Guns and The Family – Richard Beaumont, London. 1984

The Shooting Field With Holland & Holland, London. 1990

The Field.

Land & Water.

The County Gentleman.

Rod & Gun.

The Shooting Times.

Arms and Explosives.

The Haddingtonshire Courier.

Bell's Life in London.

Photographic Acknowledgements

I am grateful to the following people and organisations for making their guns and historical material available for examination and photography.

Archie Walker *Plate* 1.

Royal Museums of Scotland P4, 5, 220.

Boss & Co. 9, 10, 11, 12, 18, 21, 25, 26, 28, 37, 41, 42, 47, 50, 52, 54, 55, 57, 60, 61, 64, 65, 66, 73, 74, 75, 78, 79, 81, 82, 83, 85, 86, 90, 91, 92, 93, 94, 96, 97, 99, 110, 111, 117, 118, 125, 126, 130, 132, 136, 137, 138, 139, 142, 143, 145, 146, 153, 154, 156, 157, 160, 161, 162, 169, 170, 173, 175, 176, 180, 181, 182, 183, 184, 185, 186, 190, 191, 193, 194, 196, 198, 199, 200, 201, 202, 203, 204, 205, 219, 223, 224. *Plates* 3, 17, 18, 24, 31, 34, 39, 40, 41, 42, 43, 44, 45, 46, 47, 48, 49, 50, 51, 52, 75, 76, 81, 82, 83, 84, 85, 86, 87, 88, 89, 90, 91, 92.

Mike Clarkson P46, 48, 77, 80, 89, 105, 106, 130. *Plates* 6, 7, 9, 19, 25, 27.

Sir Ilay Campbell P45.

Weller & Dufty P50.

Jonathon Lawrence *Plates* 10, 32, 61.

J. R. Collins P53.

The Guildhall Library P65.

I. M. Hall *Plate* 26.

Eric Swann P80.

E. A. Andrews *Plate* 30.

A. J. Welham P98. *Plate* 33.

Alan Stewart P134, 135, 136, 195. *Plates* 63, 64.

The Robertson Family P107, 112, 113, 129, 146, 155.

Peter Sanderson P159, 163, 165.

British Library P164.

Ken Hunt P184.

G. Allan Brown (Courtesy Cada Gun Journal) *Plate* 56.

Brian Thompson P195. *Plate* 62.

John Poole *Plates* 57, 58.

R. Garcia-Rodow *Plates* 77, 78, 79.

E. Rosner P39, 40, 87, 217. *Plate* 2.

R. M. Lees *Plates* 75, 76.

D. O. Higley *Plates* 59, 60.

Hon D. Elliott *Plates* 6, 7.

Elsie Brough P146.

Kitty Hancock P129, 143.

Colonel J. B. Awford P126.
Marco Scipioni *Plates* 65, 66, 67, 68, 69.
Angus McKenzie *Plate* 70.
Martin Wood P127. *Plate* 71, 72.
Sotheby's *Plate* 73, 74.
Ben Pon *Plate* 80.
J. A. R. Green P141, 152, 171.

I am also grateful to the following photographers for their work in photographing the guns.
Photo Express, Edinburgh P20, 23, 40, 77, 85, 89, 117, 118. *Plates* 6, 7, 25, 38.
Stewart Menelaws, Edinburgh, P41, 42, 43, 44, 45, 46, 48, 56, 59, 80, 81, 82, 84, 87, 88, 91, 92, 98, 99, 100, 134, 135, 136, 195, 217, 218, 219. *Plates* 3, 4, 5, 8, 9, 16, 17, 18, 19, 20, 21, 22, 24, 27, 28, 29, 31, 33, 34, 35, 36, 63, 64.
David Grant, Birmingham *Plates* 11, 12, 13, 14, 15.
Bob Stevens *Plates* 10, 32, 61.
David Baker P80.
Jonathon Green P39, 40. *Plates* 2, 39, 40, 41, 42, 53, 54, 55, 73, 74, 75, 76, 81, 82, 83, 84, 85, 86, 87, 88, 90, 91, 92.
Ivan McKeown P195. *Plate* 62.
Prudence Cuming Associates *Plates* 77, 78, 79 .
Jason Shenai P177.
Quentin Harriot *Plate* 45.
George Taylor *Plates* 43, 52.

INDEX